久保帯人

Mom, Dad, are you guys watching? I finally did it. The *Bleach* anime is on TV Tokyo, with scenes that move and dialogue that you can hear. I'm so happy, I could cry. Anyway, I'm originally from Hiroshima, but TV Tokyo doesn't have a local affiliate there.

Mom, Dad, can you see it there?
-Tite Kubo

It'll be shown in Hiroshima, too, don't worry. -Editorial Department

BLEACH is author Tite Kubo's second title. Kubo made his debut with *ZOMBIE POWDER*, a four-volume series for *WEEKLY SHONEN JUMP*. To date, *BLEACH* has been translated into numerous languages and has also inspired an animated TV series that began airing in Japan in 2004. Beginning its serialization in 2001, *BLEACH* is still a mainstay in the pages of *WEEKLY SHONEN JUMP*. In 2005, *BLEACH* was awarded the prestigious Shogakukan Manga Award in the *shonen* (boys) category.

BLEACH
Vol. 14: WHITE TOWER ROCKS
The SHONEN JUMP Manga Edition

STORY AND ART BY
TITE KUBO

English Adaptation/Lance Caselman
Translation/Joe Yamazaki
Touch-Up Art & Lettering/Andy Ristaino
Design/Sean Lee
Editor/ Yuki Takagaki

Managing Editor/Frances E. Wall
Editorial Director/Elizabeth Kawasaki
VP & Editor in Chief/Yumi Hoashi
Sr. Director of Acquisitions/Rika Inouye
Sr. VP of Marketing/Liza Coppola
Exec. VP of Sales & Marketing/John Easum
Publisher/Hyoe Narita

Printed in the U.S.A.

Published by VIZ Media, LLC
P.O. Box 77010
San Francisco, CA 94107

JUMP Manga Edition
7 6 5 4 3 2
August 2006
ugust 2006

Creak, creak, tower of purgatory
Piercing the world like light
Sway, sway, tower of spine
Will it be us or the sky that falls?

BLEACH14 WHITE TOWER ROCKS

STARS AND

Rukia Kuchiki

Byakuya Kuchiki

Ichigo Kurosaki

plot

Soul Reaper Rukia Kuchiki has been taken back to the Soul Society and condemned to death for giving Ichigo her powers. Ichigo and his friends infiltrate the Seireitei, the stronghold of the Soul Reapers, in a desperate bid to save her. Now, following an epic battle with Captain Kenpachi Zaraki, Ichigo lies gravely wounded just a few steps from Rukia's cell. Ganju and Hanatarô get to her first but discover that Rukia is the Soul Reaper who killed Ganju's older brother! But before Ganju can have his revenge, Rukia's brother, Byakuya Kuchiki, appears…

BLEACH ALL

涅マユリ

Mayuri Kurotsuchi

石田雨竜

Uryû Ishida

Orihime Inoue

井上織姫

STORIES

BLEACH14

WHITE TOWER ROCKS

Contents

116. White Tower Rocks

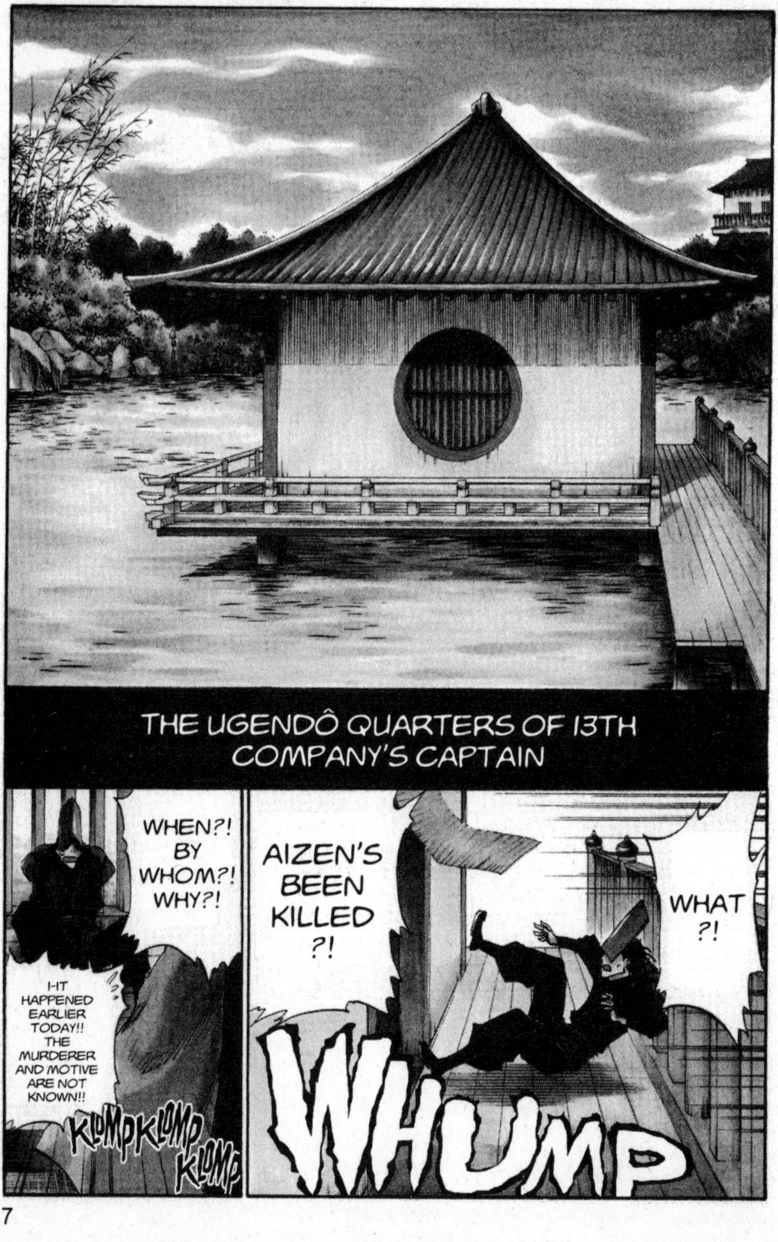

THE UGENDÔ QUARTERS OF 13TH COMPANY'S CAPTAIN
WHAT ?!
AIZEN'S BEEN KILLED ?!
WHUMP
WHEN?! BY WHOM?! WHY?!
I-IT HAPPENED EARLIER TODAY!! THE MURDERER AND MOTIVE ARE NOT KNOWN!!
KLOMPKLOMP KLOMP

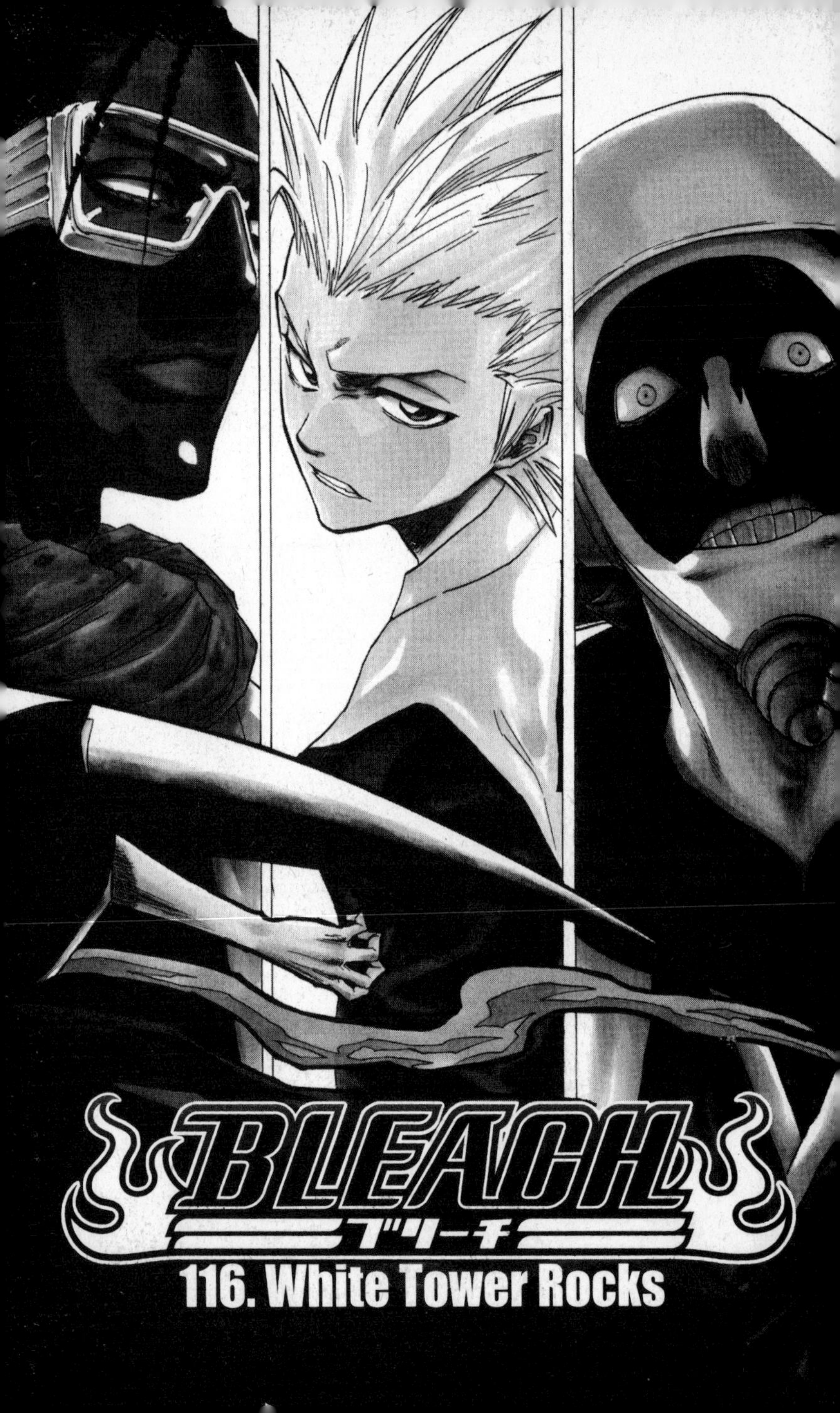
BLEACH
ブリーチ
116. White Tower Rocks

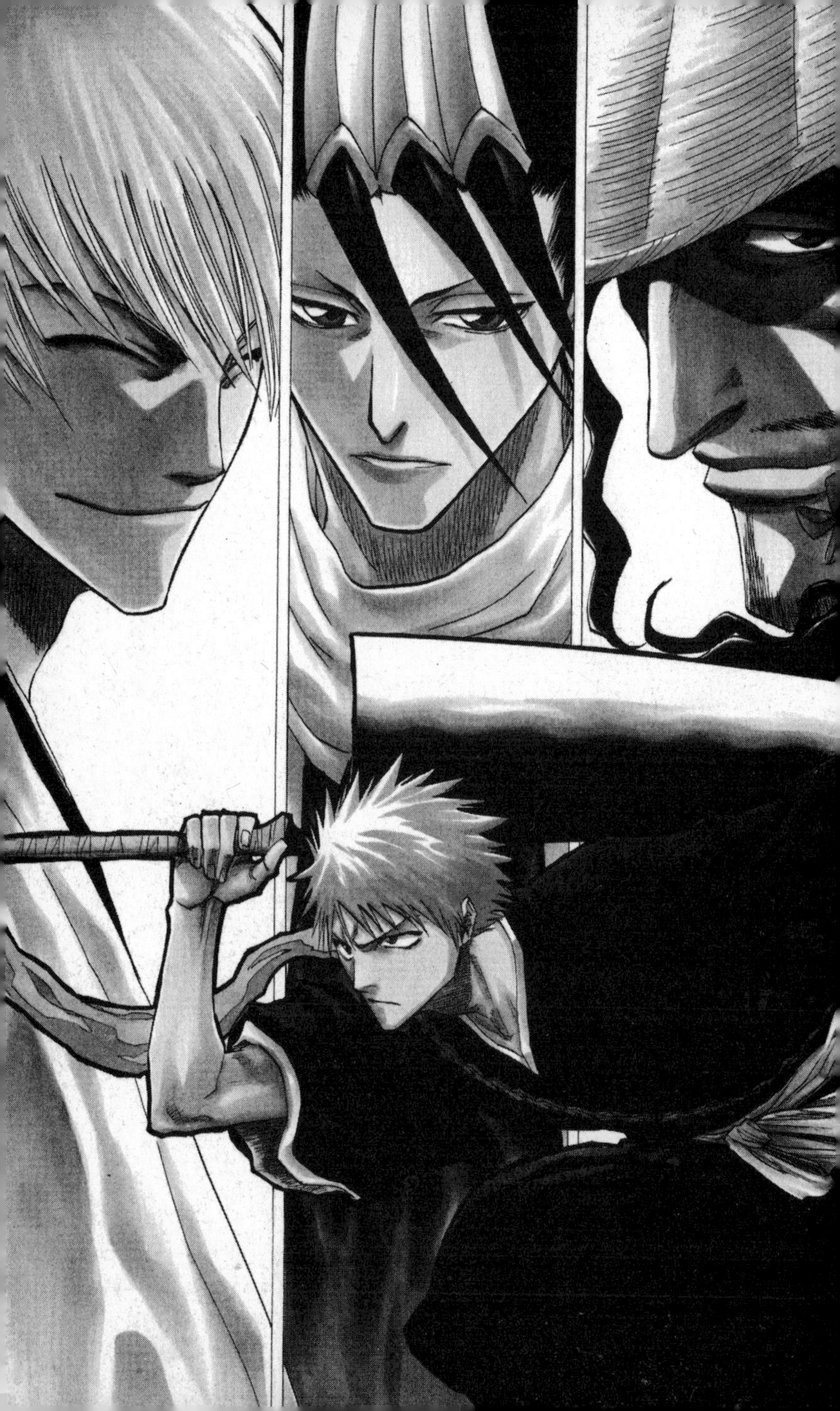

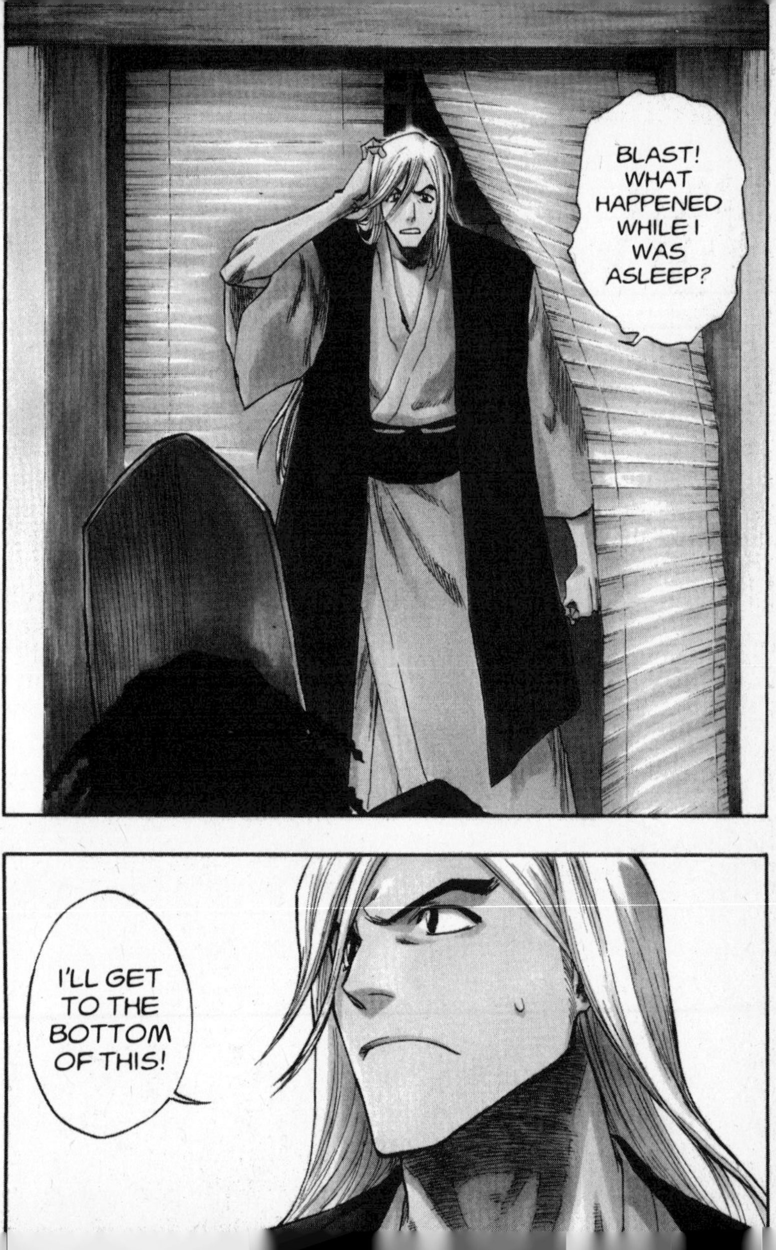
BLAST! WHAT HAPPENED WHILE I WAS ASLEEP?
I'LL GET TO THE BOTTOM OF THIS!

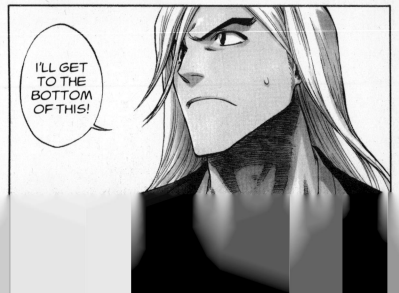

READ THIS WAY

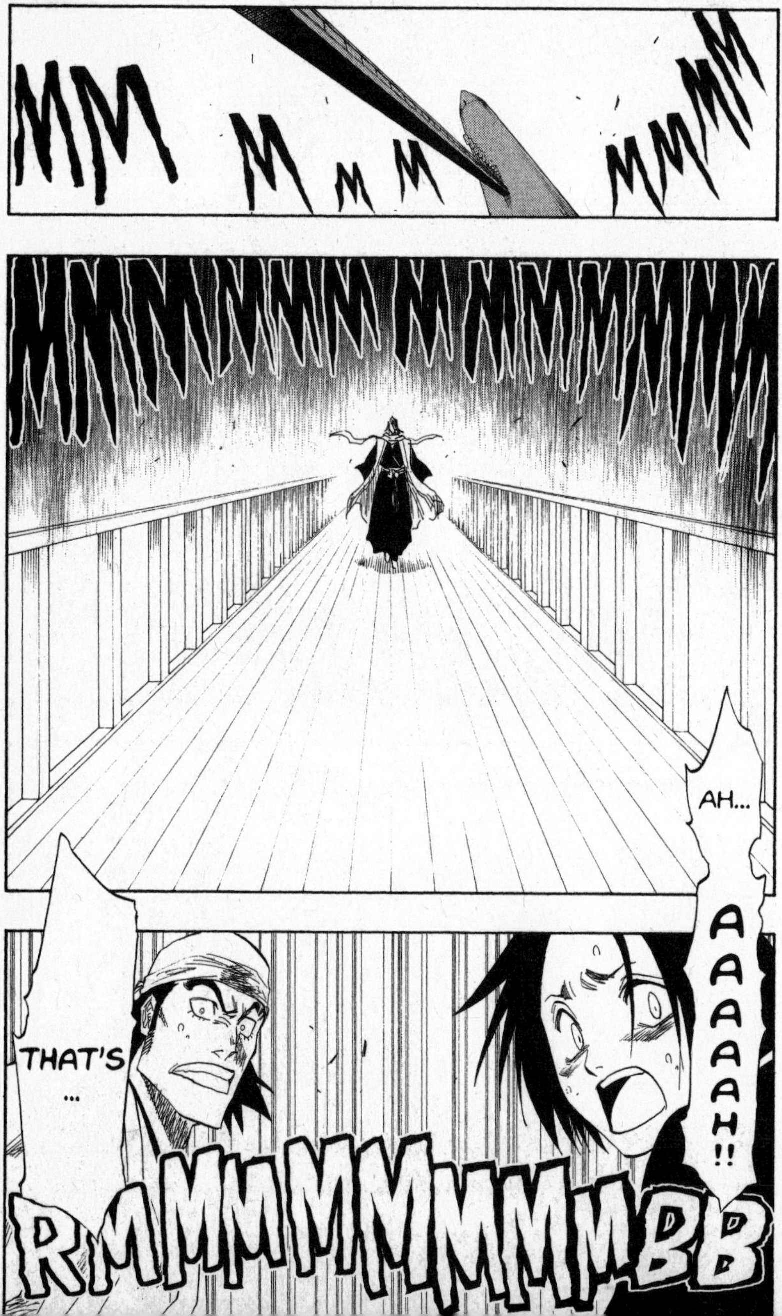
MMMMMMMMM
MMMMMMMMMMMMMMM
AH...
AAAAAAH!!
THAT'S ...
RMMMMMMMMMBB

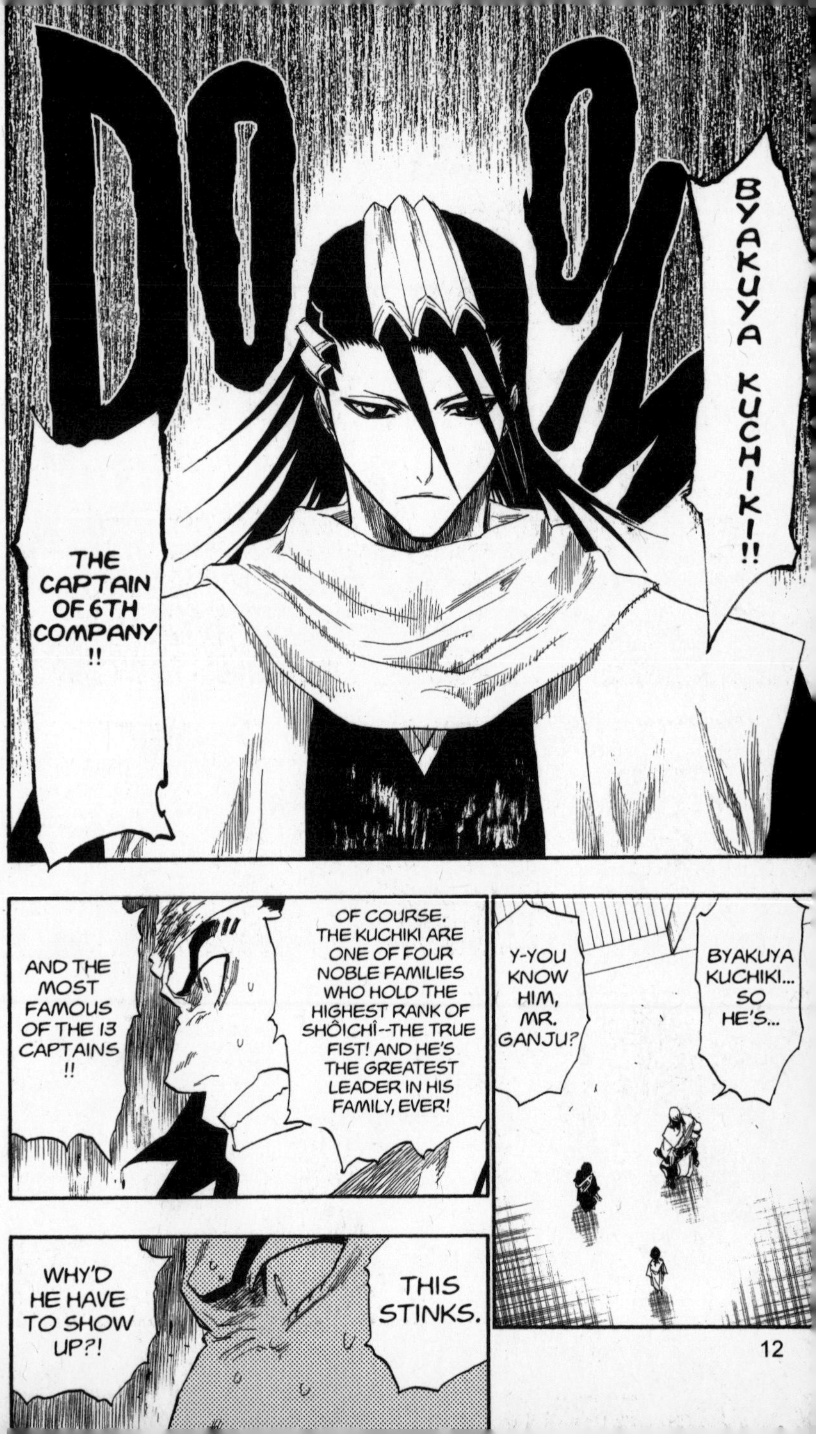

DOOM
BYAKUYA KUCHIKI!!
THE CAPTAIN OF 6TH COMPANY !!
BYAKUYA KUCHIKI... SO HE'S...
Y-YOU KNOW HIM, MR. GANJU?
OF COURSE. THE KUCHIKI ARE ONE OF FOUR NOBLE FAMILIES WHO HOLD THE HIGHEST RANK OF SHÔICHÎ--THE TRUE FIST! AND HE'S THE GREATEST LEADER IN HIS FAMILY, EVER!
AND THE MOST FAMOUS OF THE 13 CAPTAINS !!
THIS STINKS.
WHY'D HE HAVE TO SHOW UP?!

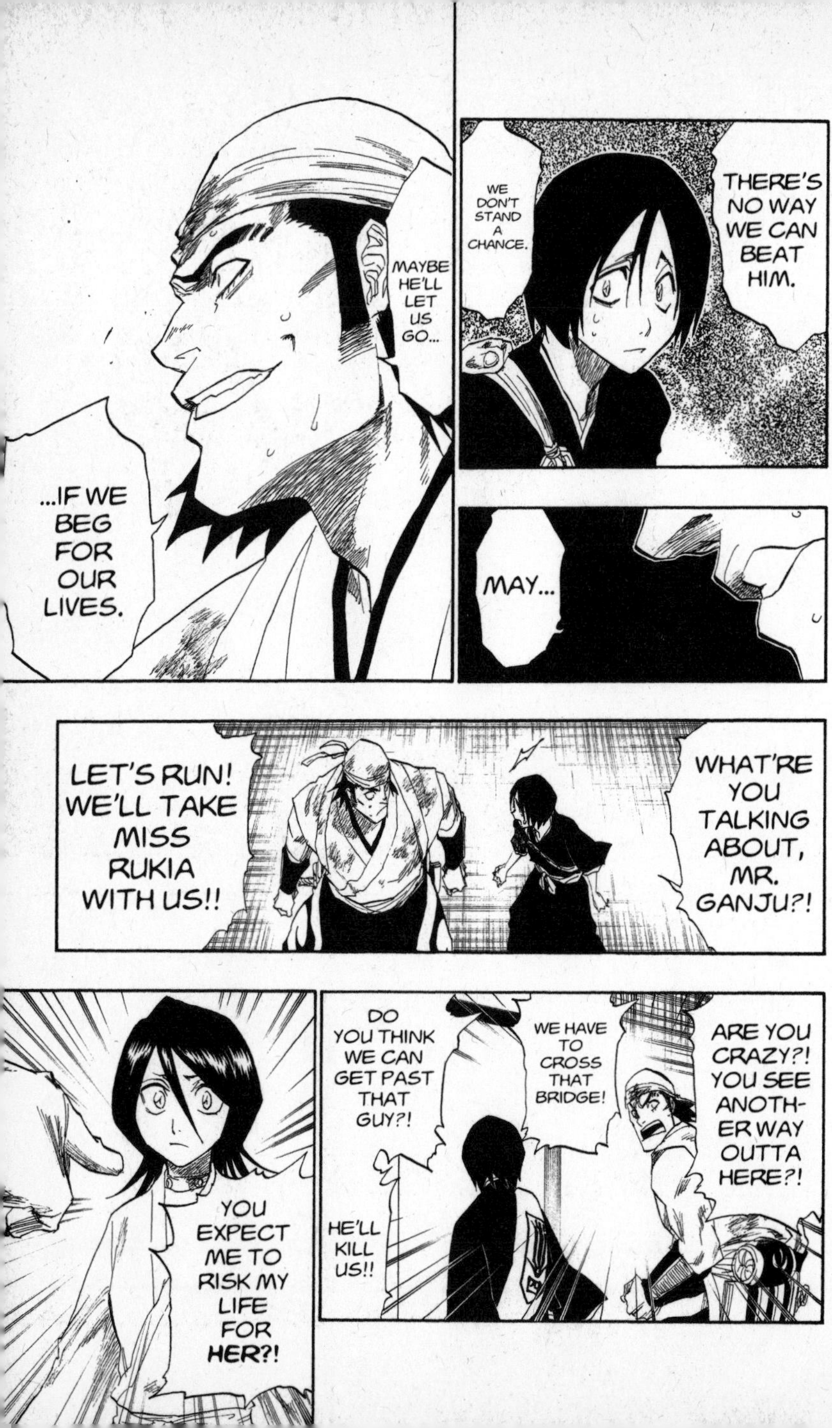
THERE'S NO WAY WE CAN BEAT HIM.
WE DON'T STAND A CHANCE.
MAY...
MAYBE HE'LL LET US GO...
...IF WE BEG FOR OUR LIVES.
WHAT'RE YOU TALKING ABOUT, MR. GANJU?!
LET'S RUN! WE'LL TAKE MISS RUKIA WITH US!!
ARE YOU CRAZY?! YOU SEE ANOTH-ER WAY OUTTA HERE?!
WE HAVE TO CROSS THAT BRIDGE!
DO YOU THINK WE CAN GET PAST THAT GUY?!
HE'LL KILL US!!
YOU EXPECT ME TO RISK MY LIFE FOR HER?!

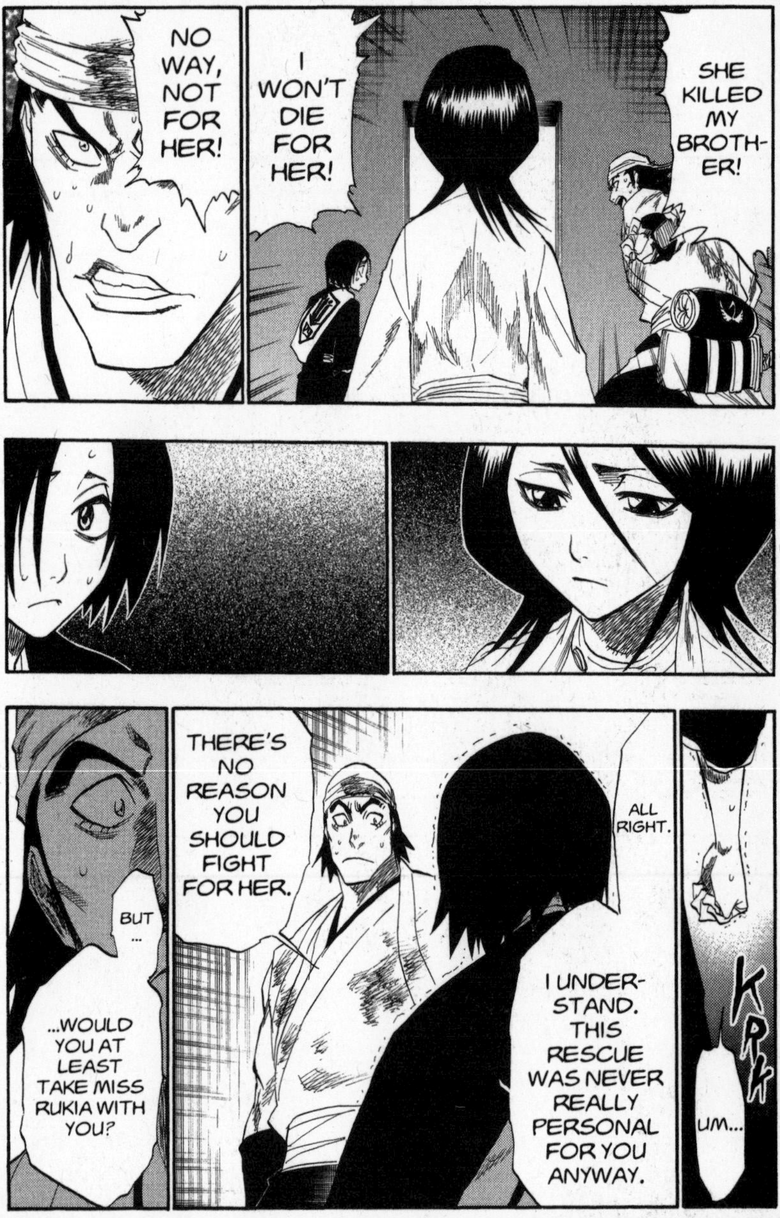
SHE KILLED MY BROTH-ER!
I WON'T DIE FOR HER!
NO WAY, NOT FOR HER!
KRK
UM...
ALL RIGHT.
THERE'S NO REASON YOU SHOULD FIGHT FOR HER.
I UNDER-STAND. THIS RESCUE WAS NEVER REALLY PERSONAL FOR YOU ANYWAY.
BUT ...
...WOULD YOU AT LEAST TAKE MISS RUKIA WITH YOU?

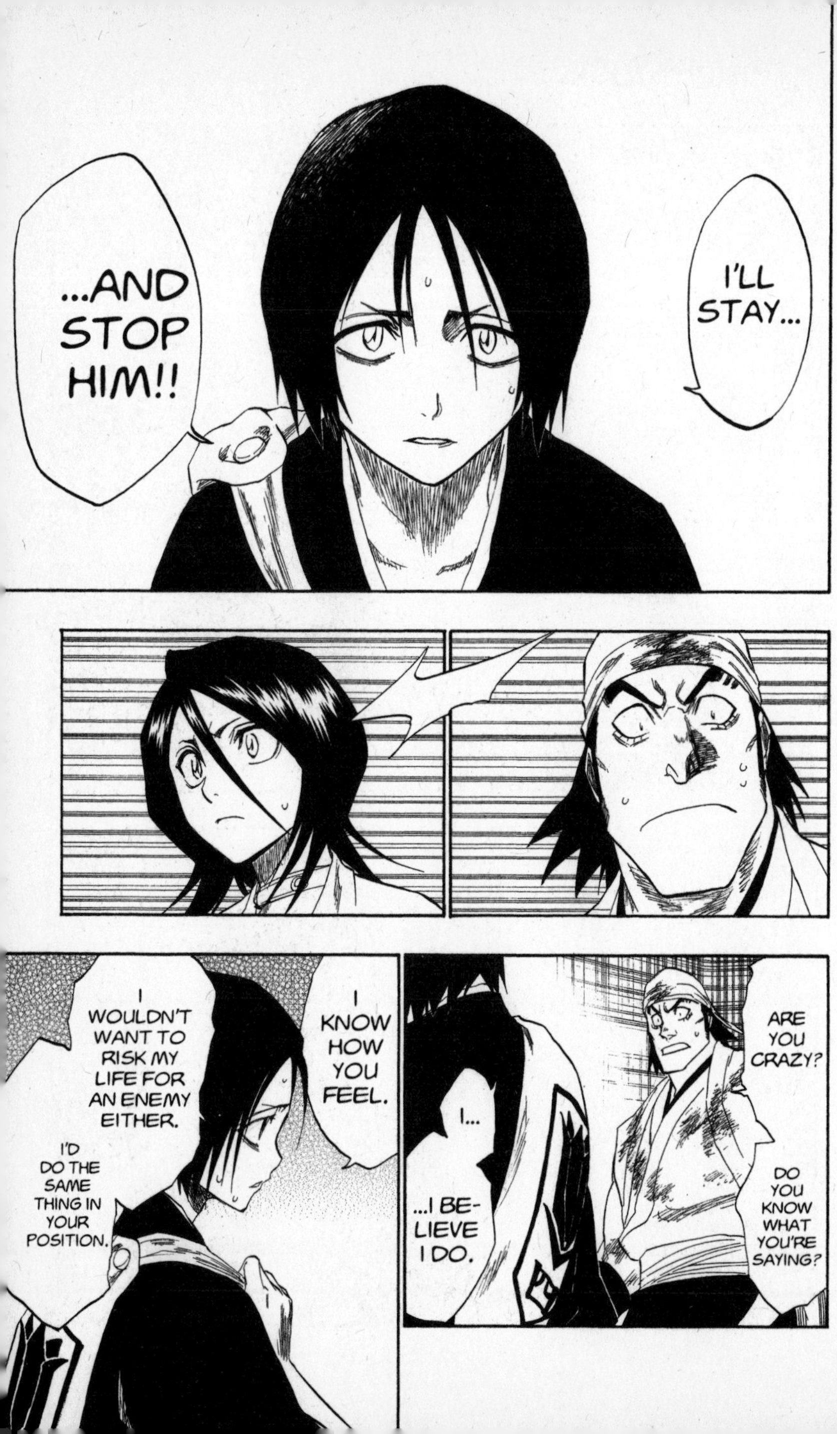
I'LL STAY...
...AND STOP HIM!!
ARE YOU CRAZY?
DO YOU KNOW WHAT YOU'RE SAYING?
I...
...I BE-LIEVE I DO.
I KNOW HOW YOU FEEL.
I WOULDN'T WANT TO RISK MY LIFE FOR AN ENEMY EITHER.
I'D DO THE SAME THING IN YOUR POSITION.

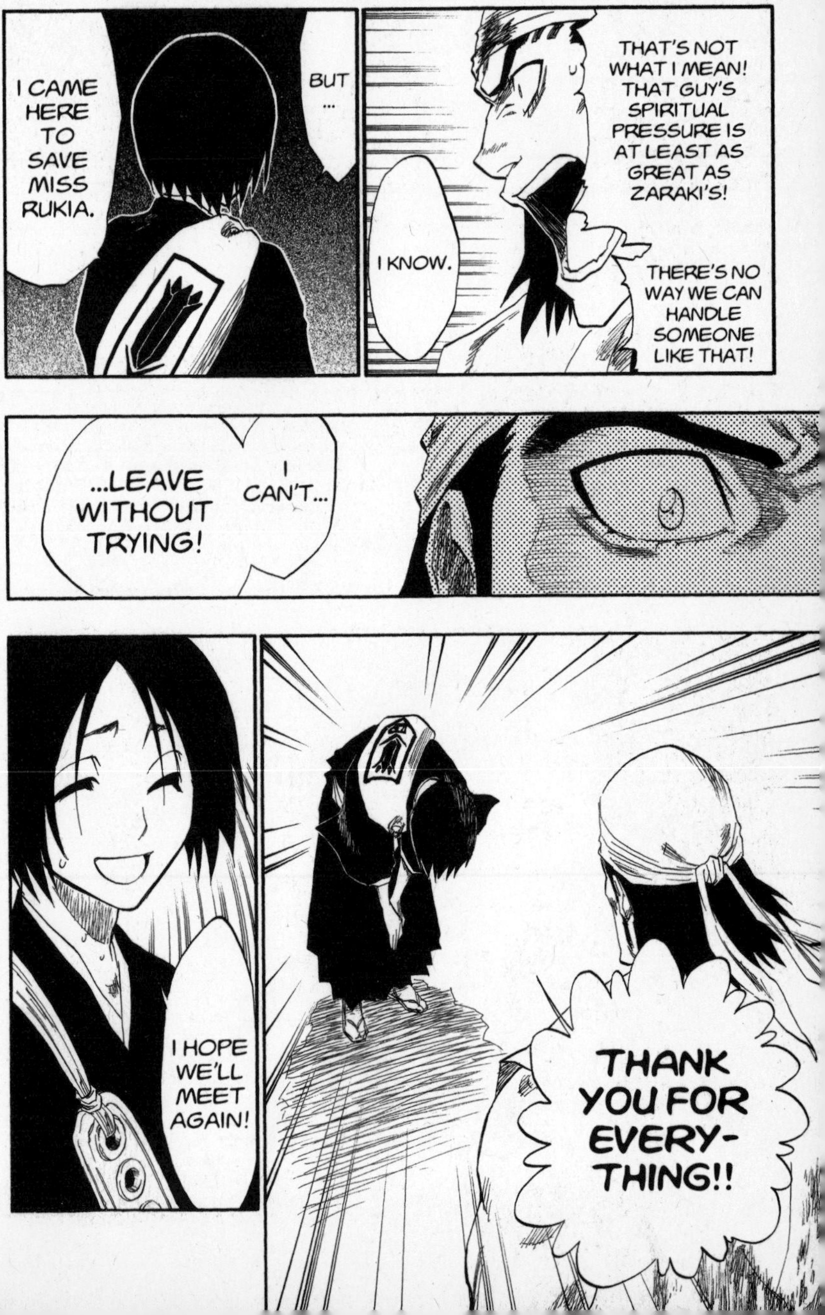
THAT'S NOT WHAT I MEAN! THAT GUY'S SPIRITUAL PRESSURE IS AT LEAST AS GREAT AS ZARAKI'S!
THERE'S NO WAY WE CAN HANDLE SOMEONE LIKE THAT!
I KNOW.
BUT ...
I CAME HERE TO SAVE MISS RUKIA.
I CAN'T...
...LEAVE WITHOUT TRYING!
THANK YOU FOR EVERY-THING!!
I HOPE WE'LL MEET AGAIN!

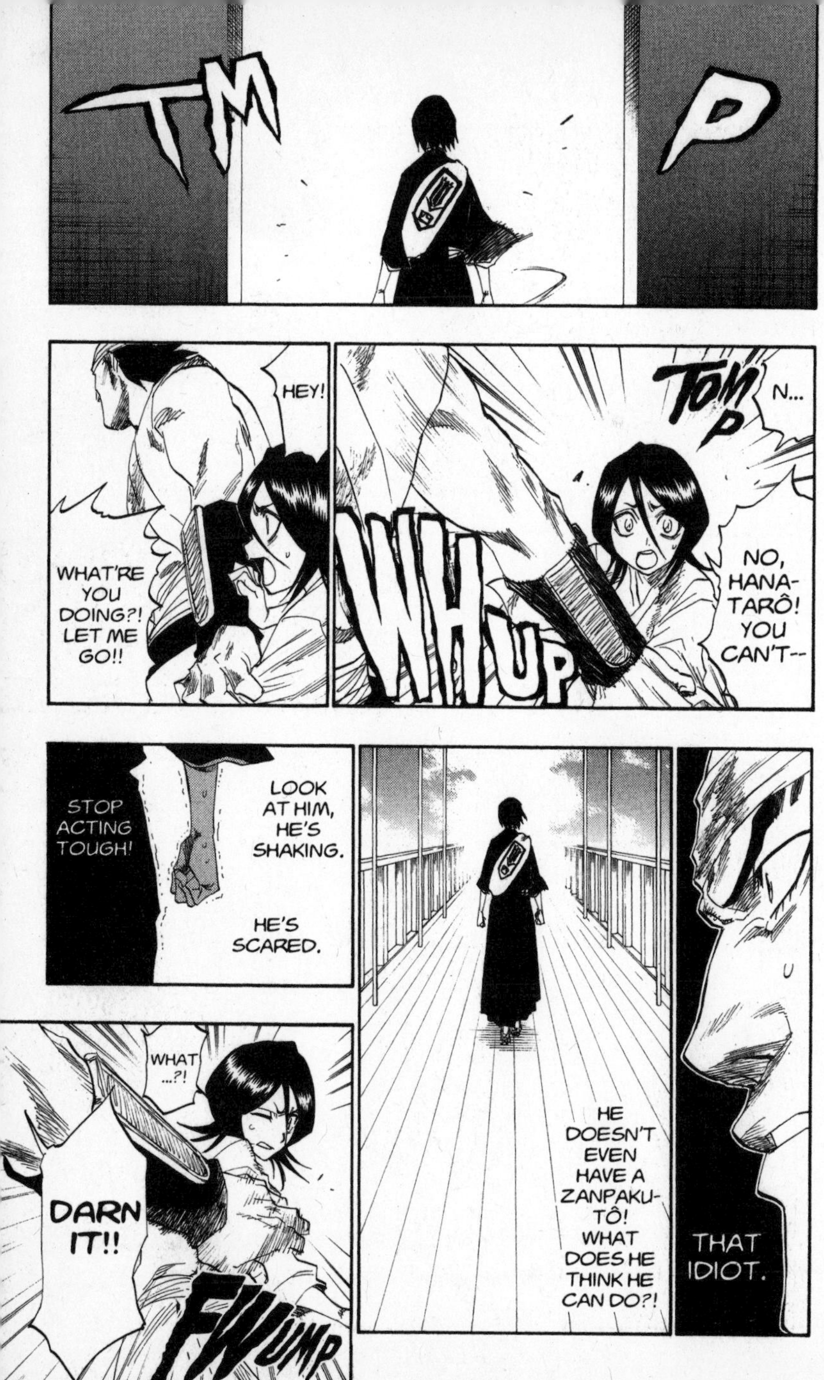

TMP
TOMP
N...
NO, HANA-TARÔ! YOU CAN'T--
WHUP
HEY!
WHAT'RE YOU DOING?! LET ME GO!!
THAT IDIOT.
HE DOESN'T EVEN HAVE A ZANPAKU-TÔ! WHAT DOES HE THINK HE CAN DO?!
LOOK AT HIM, HE'S SHAKING.
HE'S SCARED.
STOP ACTING TOUGH!
WHAT ...?!
DARN IT!!
FWUMP

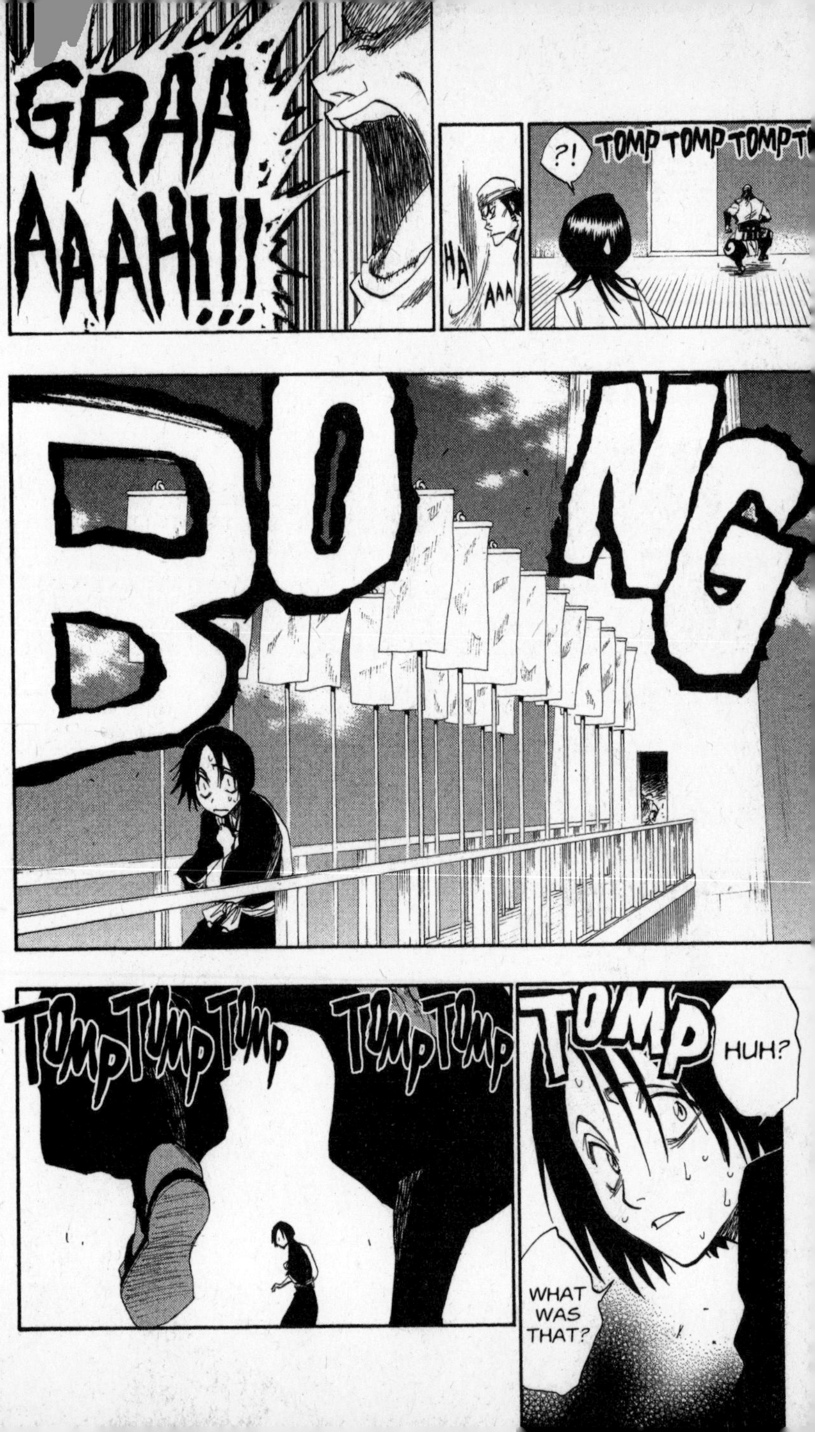
?!
TOMP TOMP TOMP T
HA AAA
GRAA AAAH!!!
DONG
TOMP
HUH?
WHAT WAS THAT?
TOMP TOMP TOMP
TOMP TOMP

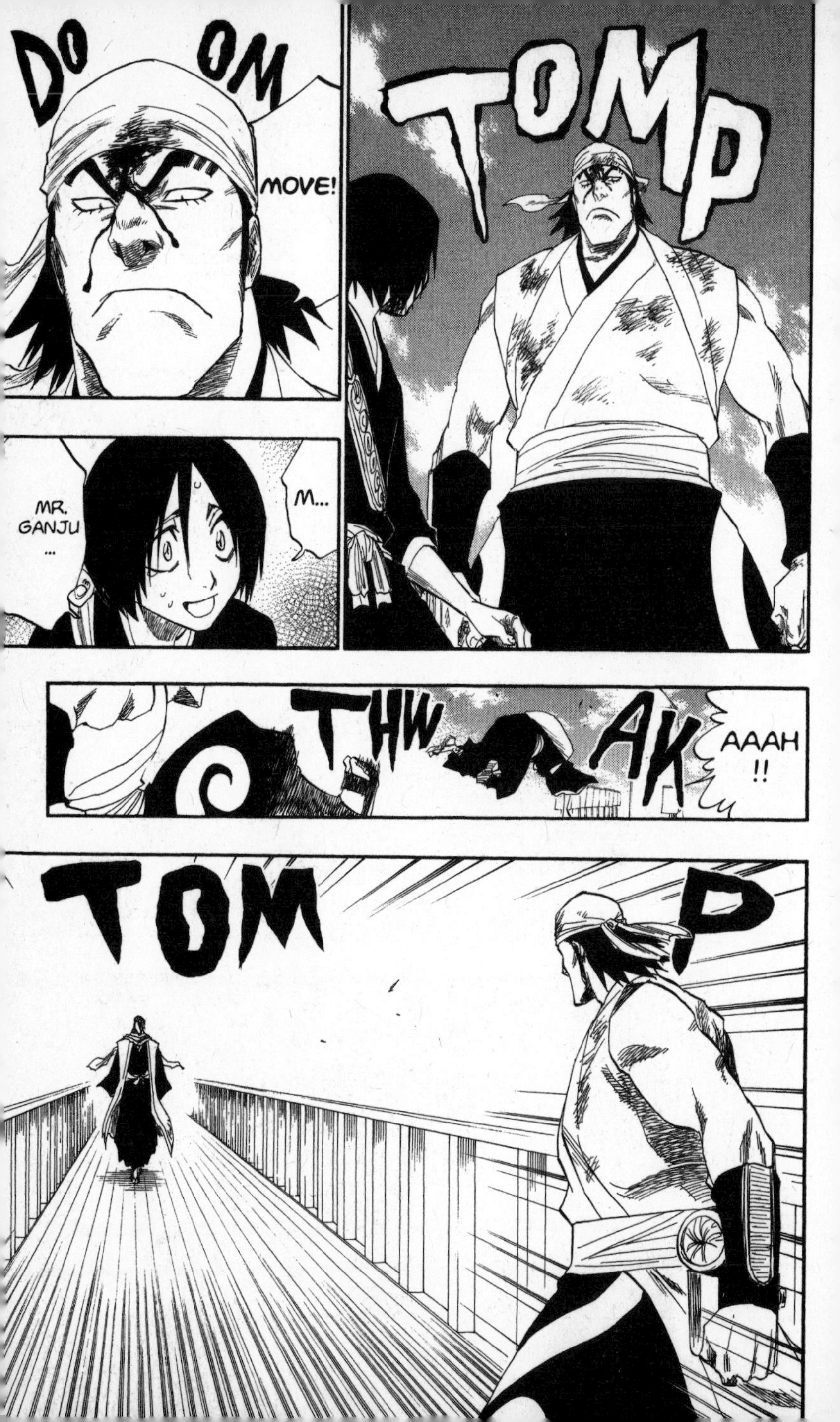
TOMP
DOOM
MOVE!
M...
MR. GANJU ...
THWAK
AAAH !!
TOMP

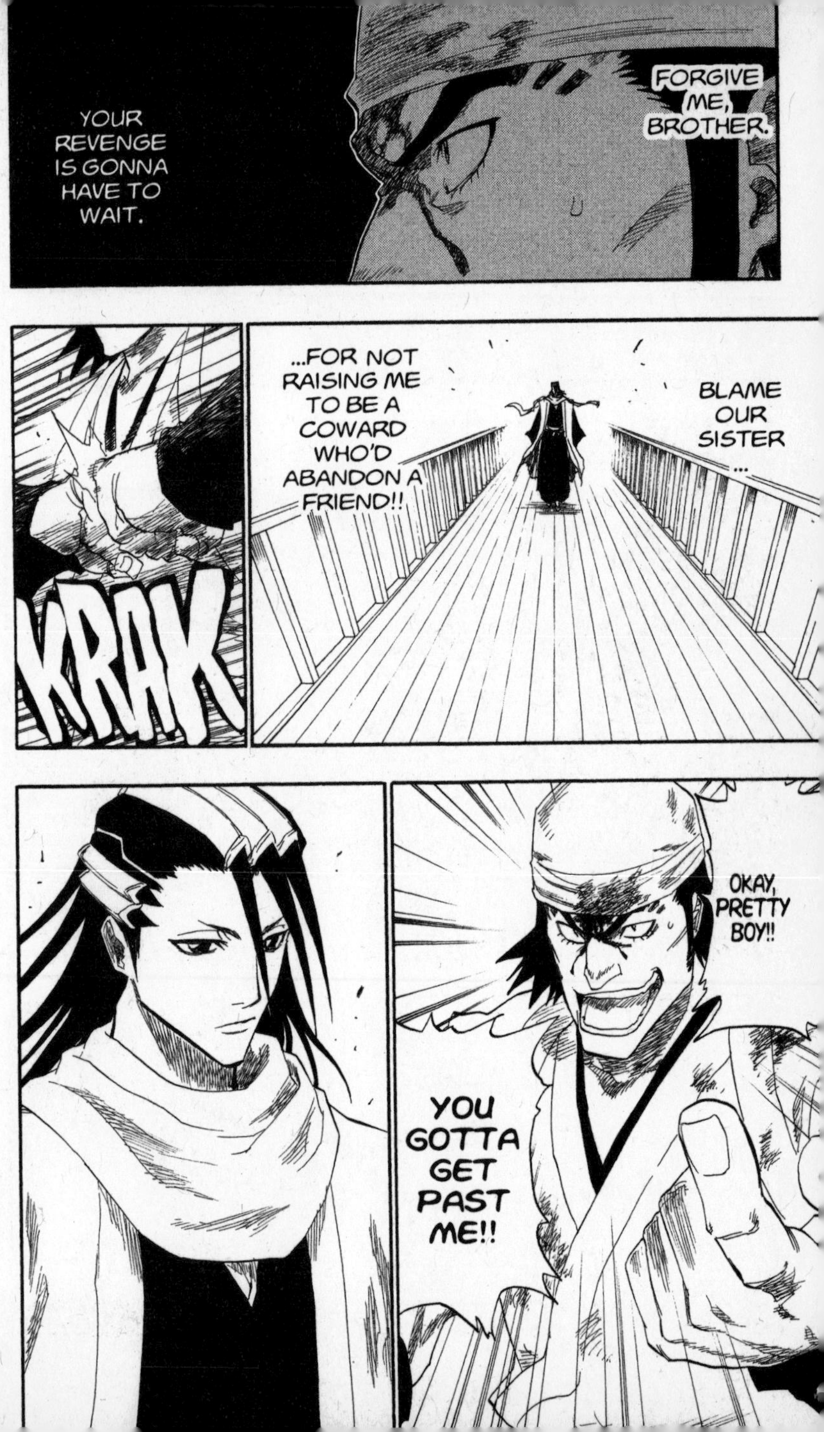
FORGIVE ME, BROTHER.
YOUR REVENGE IS GONNA HAVE TO WAIT.
BLAME OUR SISTER ...
...FOR NOT RAISING ME TO BE A COWARD WHO'D ABANDON A FRIEND!!
KRAK
OKAY, PRETTY BOY!!
YOU GOTTA GET PAST ME!!

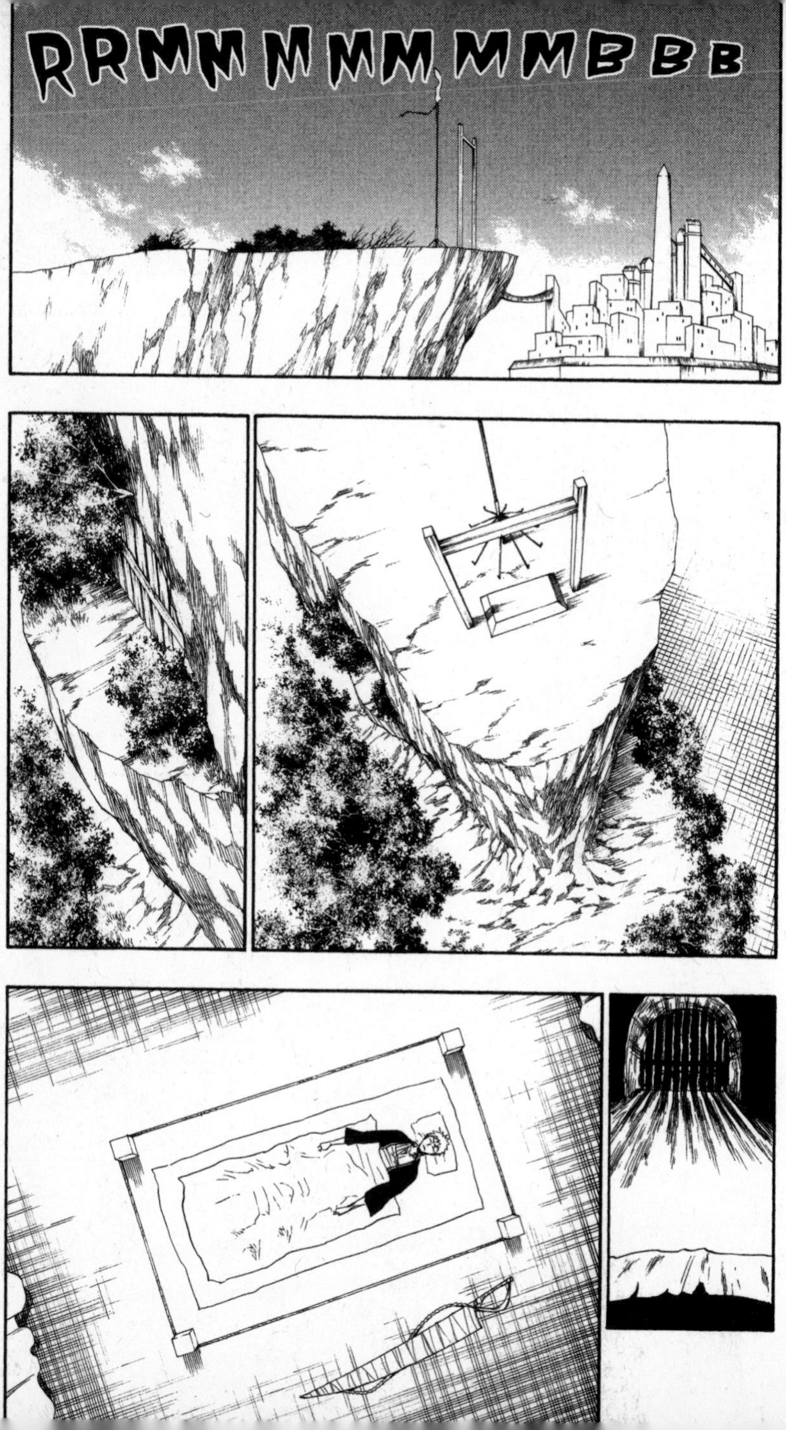
RRMMMMMMMMMBBB

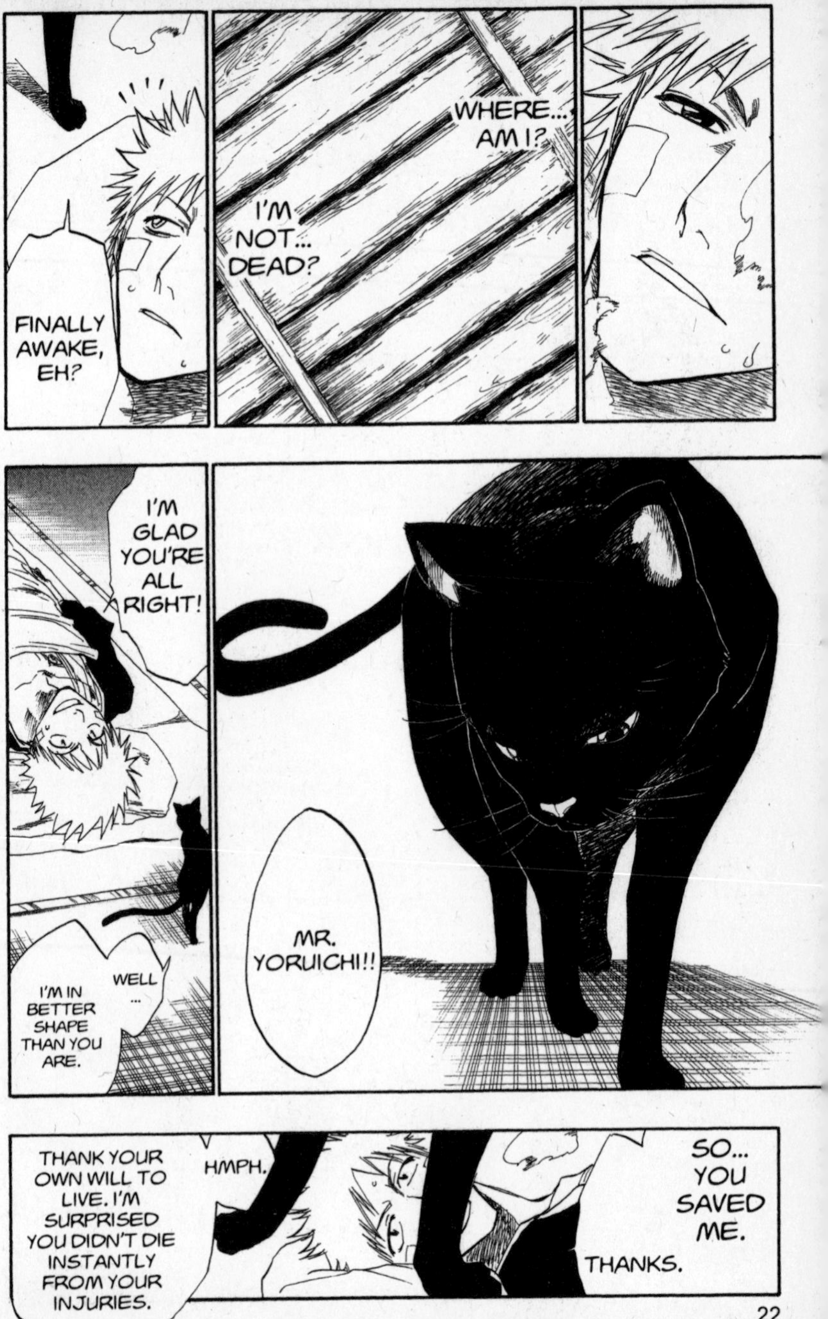
WHERE... AM I?
I'M NOT... DEAD?
FINALLY AWAKE, EH?
MR. YORUICHI!!
I'M GLAD YOU'RE ALL RIGHT!
WELL...
I'M IN BETTER SHAPE THAN YOU ARE.
SO... YOU SAVED ME.
THANKS.
HMPH.
THANK YOUR OWN WILL TO LIVE. I'M SURPRISED YOU DIDN'T DIE INSTANTLY FROM YOUR INJURIES.

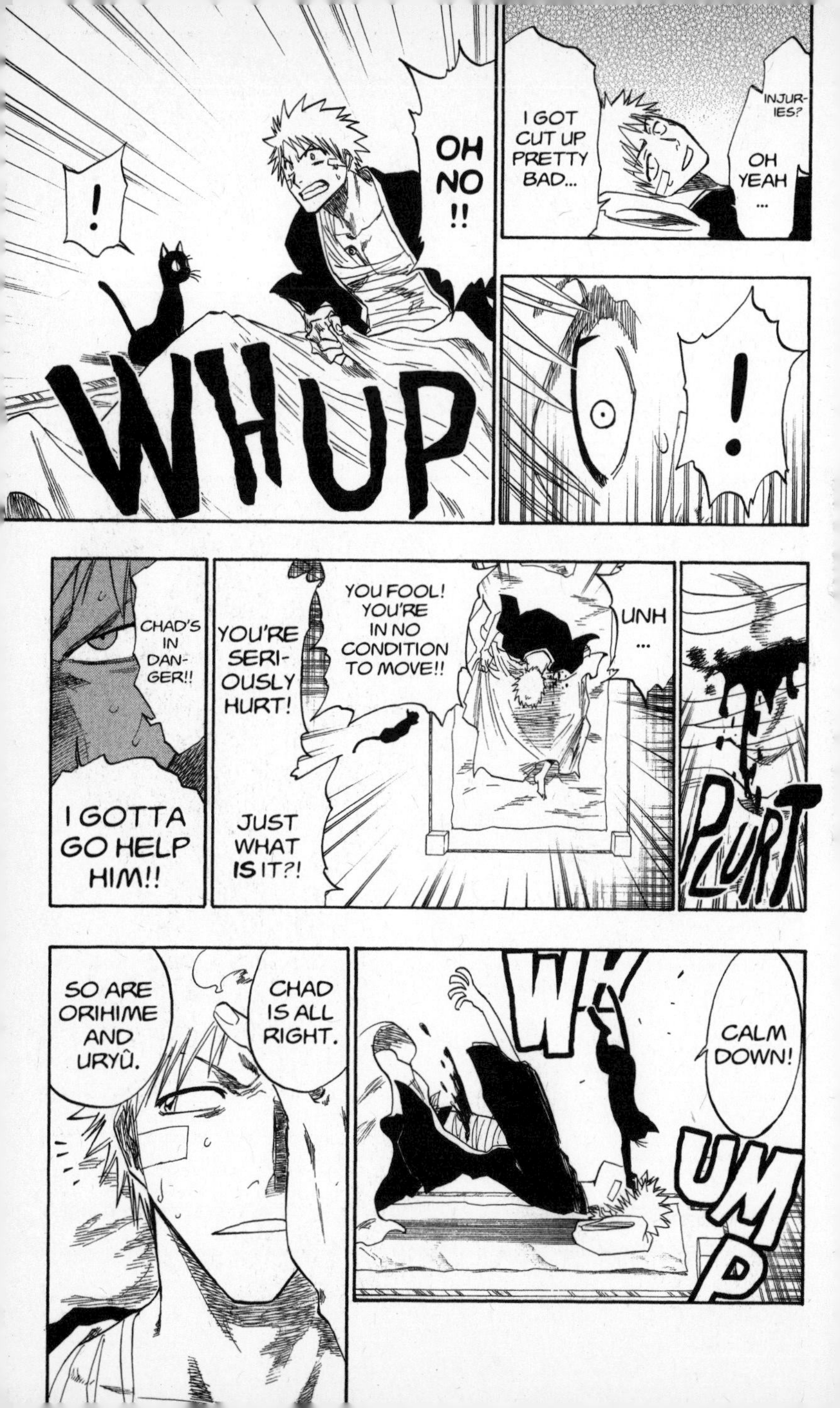
INJURIES? OH YEAH...
I GOT CUT UP PRETTY BAD...
!
OH NO!!
!
WHUP
PLURT
UNH...
YOU FOOL! YOU'RE IN NO CONDITION TO MOVE!!
YOU'RE SERIOUSLY HURT!
JUST WHAT IS IT?!
CHAD'S IN DANGER!!
I GOTTA GO HELP HIM!!
CALM DOWN!
WHUMP
CHAD IS ALL RIGHT.
SO ARE ORIHIME AND URYÛ.

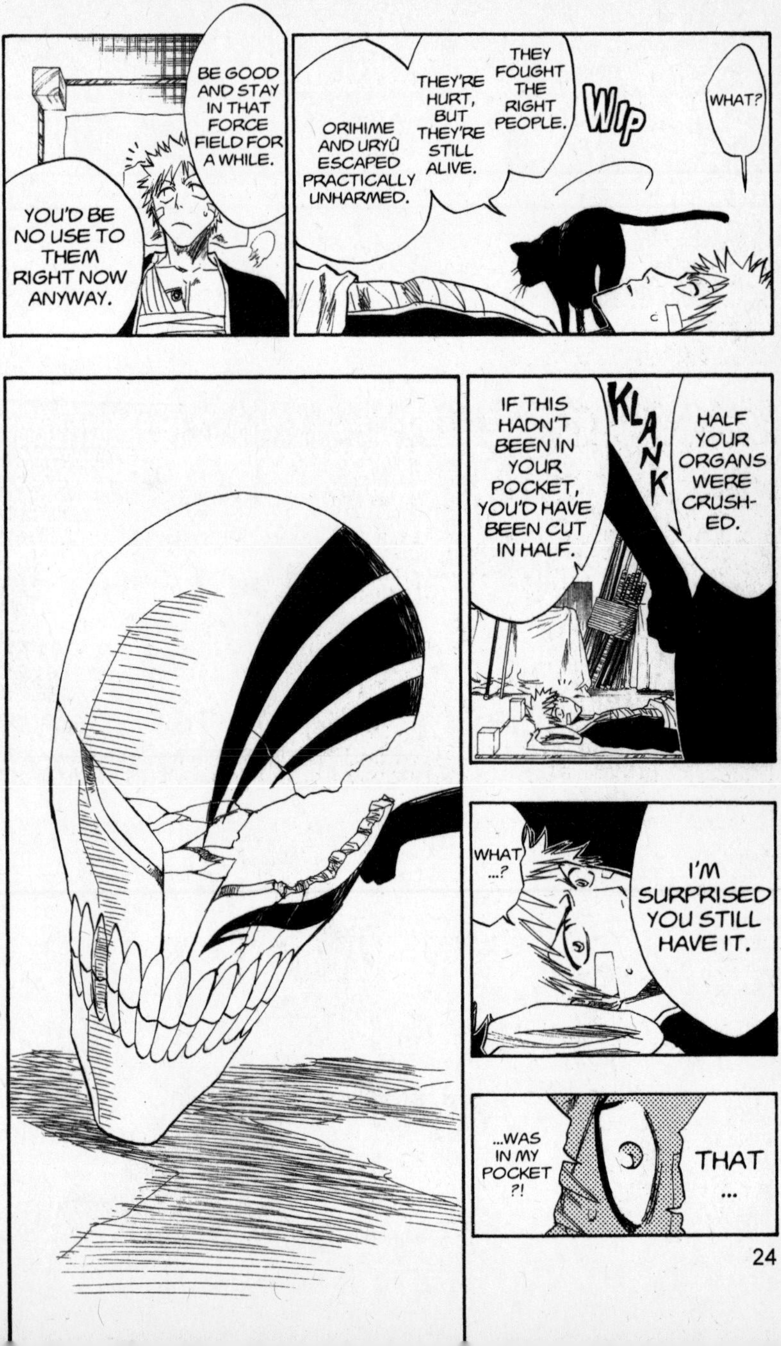
WHAT?
WIP
THEY FOUGHT THE RIGHT PEOPLE.
THEY'RE HURT, BUT THEY'RE STILL ALIVE.
ORIHIME AND URYÛ ESCAPED PRACTICALLY UNHARMED.
BE GOOD AND STAY IN THAT FORCE FIELD FOR A WHILE.
YOU'D BE NO USE TO THEM RIGHT NOW ANYWAY.
HALF YOUR ORGANS WERE CRUSH-ED.
KLANK
IF THIS HADN'T BEEN IN YOUR POCKET, YOU'D HAVE BEEN CUT IN HALF.
I'M SURPRISED YOU STILL HAVE IT.
WHAT ...?
THAT ...
...WAS IN MY POCKET ?!

READ THIS WAY

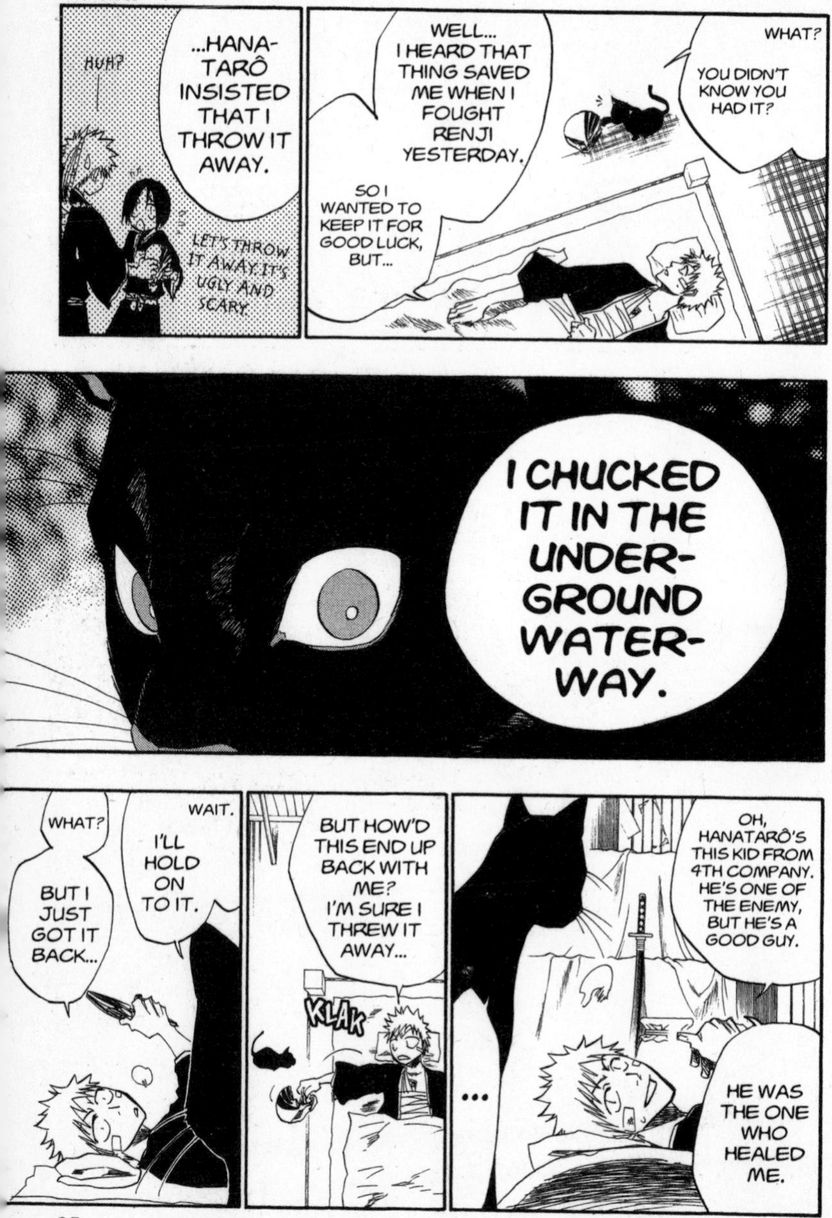

WHAT?
YOU DIDN'T KNOW YOU HAD IT?
WELL... I HEARD THAT THING SAVED ME WHEN I FOUGHT RENJI YESTERDAY.
SO I WANTED TO KEEP IT FOR GOOD LUCK, BUT...
...HANA-TARÔ INSISTED THAT I THROW IT AWAY.
HUH?
LET'S THROW IT AWAY. IT'S UGLY AND SCARY.
I CHUCKED IT IN THE UNDER-GROUND WATER-WAY.
OH, HANATARÔ'S THIS KID FROM 4TH COMPANY. HE'S ONE OF THE ENEMY, BUT HE'S A GOOD GUY.
...
HE WAS THE ONE WHO HEALED ME.
BUT HOW'D THIS END UP BACK WITH ME? I'M SURE I THREW IT AWAY...
KLAK
WAIT.
I'LL HOLD ON TO IT.
WHAT?
BUT I JUST GOT IT BACK...

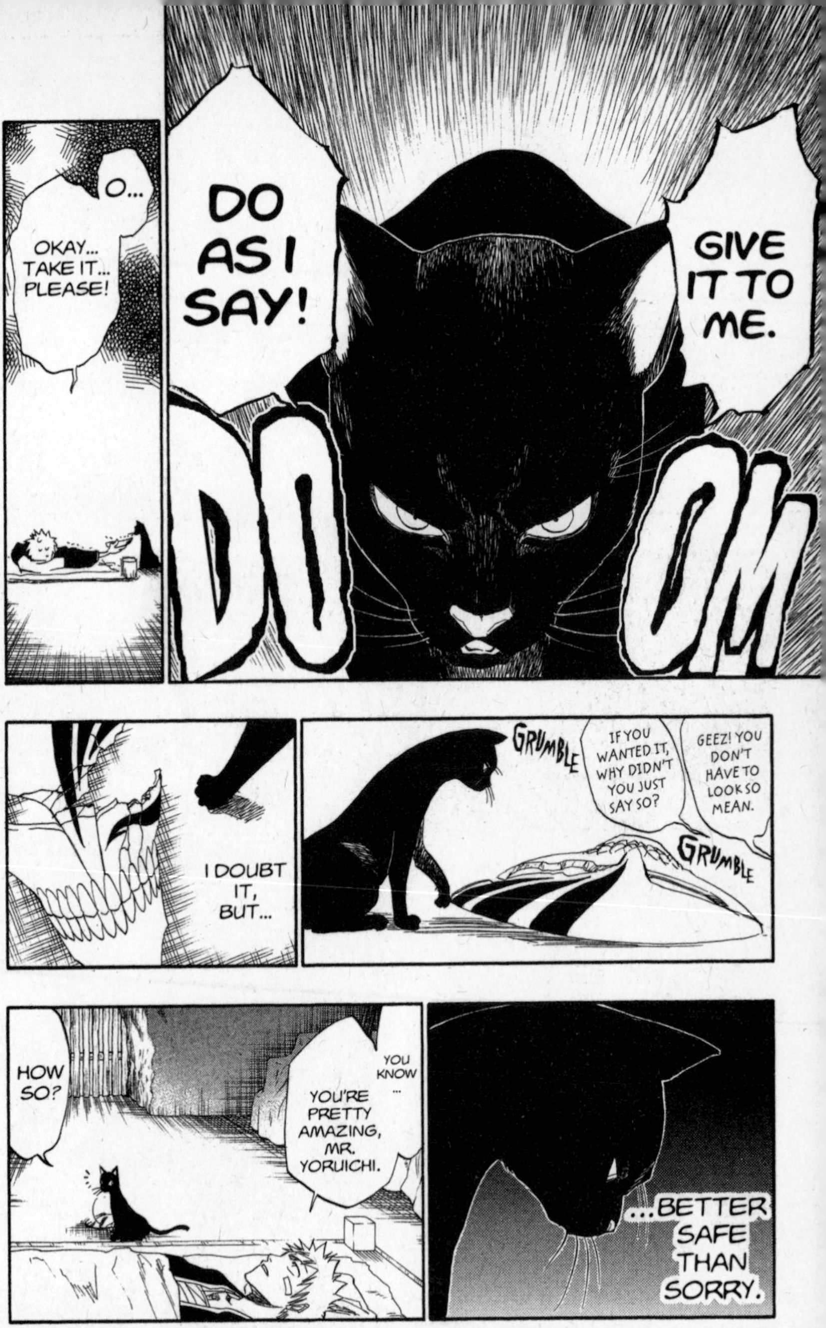
GIVE IT TO ME.
DO AS I SAY!
DOOM
O...
OKAY... TAKE IT... PLEASE!
GEEZ! YOU DON'T HAVE TO LOOK SO MEAN.
IF YOU WANTED IT, WHY DIDN'T YOU JUST SAY SO?
GRUMBLE
GRUMBLE
I DOUBT IT, BUT...
...BETTER SAFE THAN SORRY.
YOU KNOW...
YOU'RE PRETTY AMAZING, MR. YORUICHI.
HOW SO?

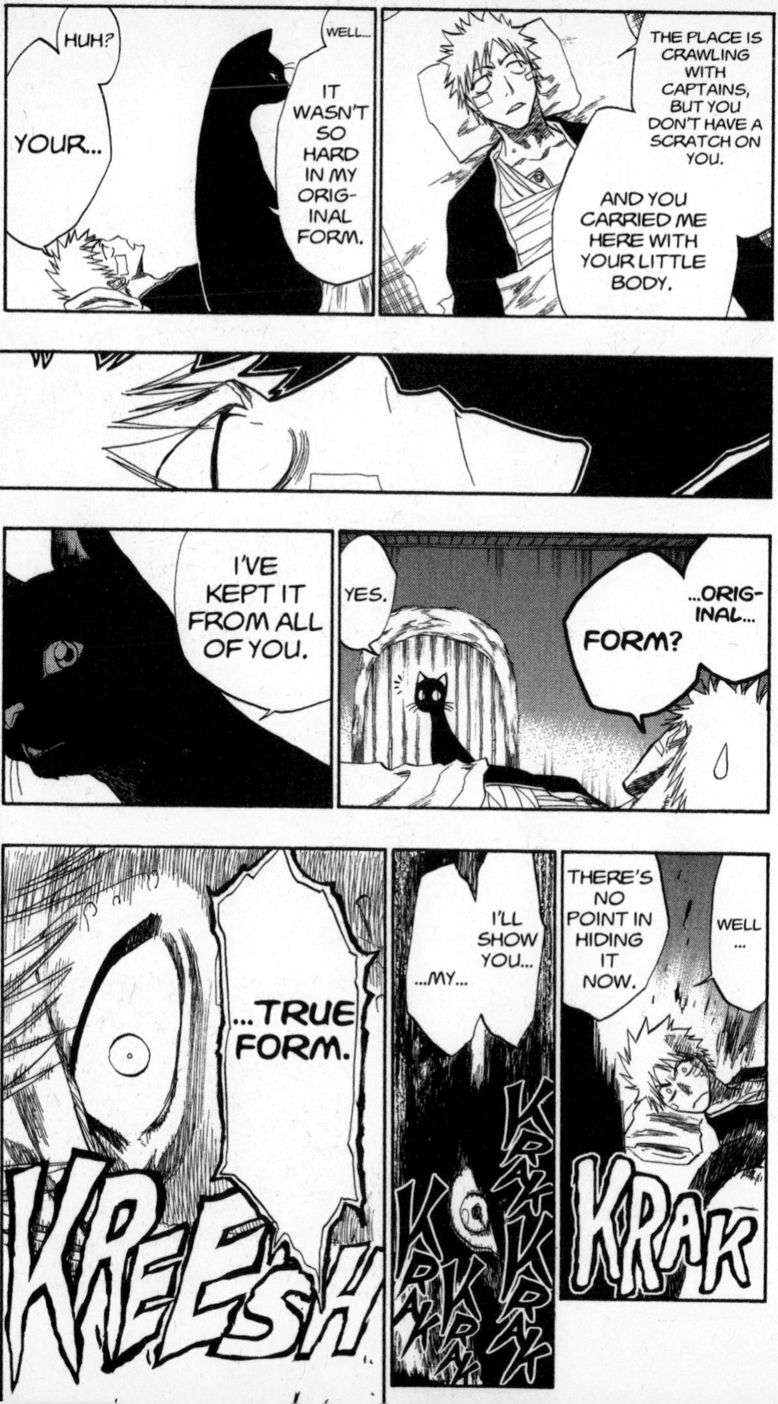
THE PLACE IS CRAWLING WITH CAPTAINS, BUT YOU DON'T HAVE A SCRATCH ON YOU.
AND YOU CARRIED ME HERE WITH YOUR LITTLE BODY.
WELL...
IT WASN'T SO HARD IN MY ORIG-INAL FORM.
HUH?
YOUR...
...ORIG-INAL...
FORM?
YES.
I'VE KEPT IT FROM ALL OF YOU.
WELL...
THERE'S NO POINT IN HIDING IT NOW.
KRAK
I'LL SHOW YOU...
...MY...
KRAK KRAK KRAK
...TRUE FORM.
KREESH

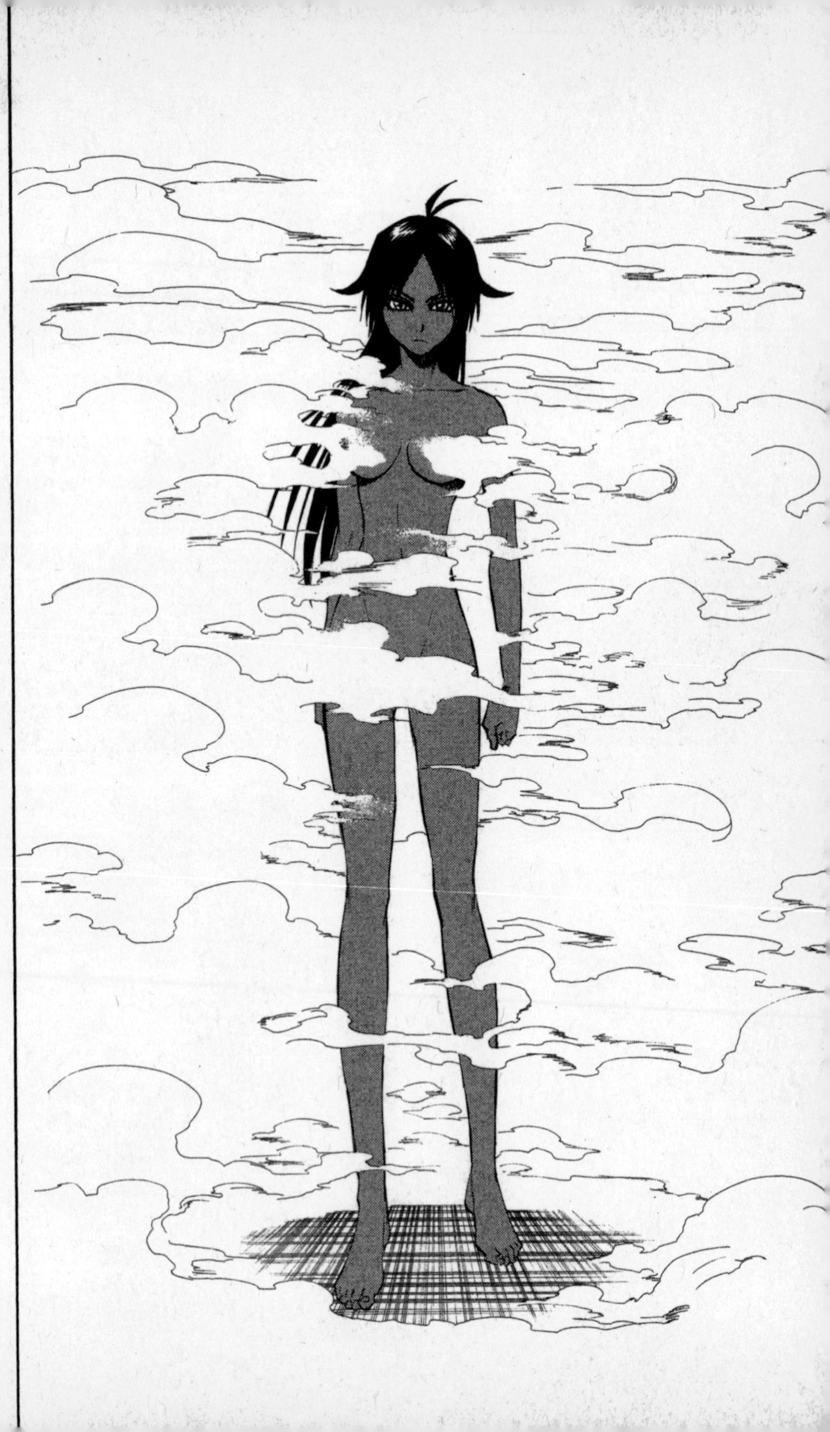

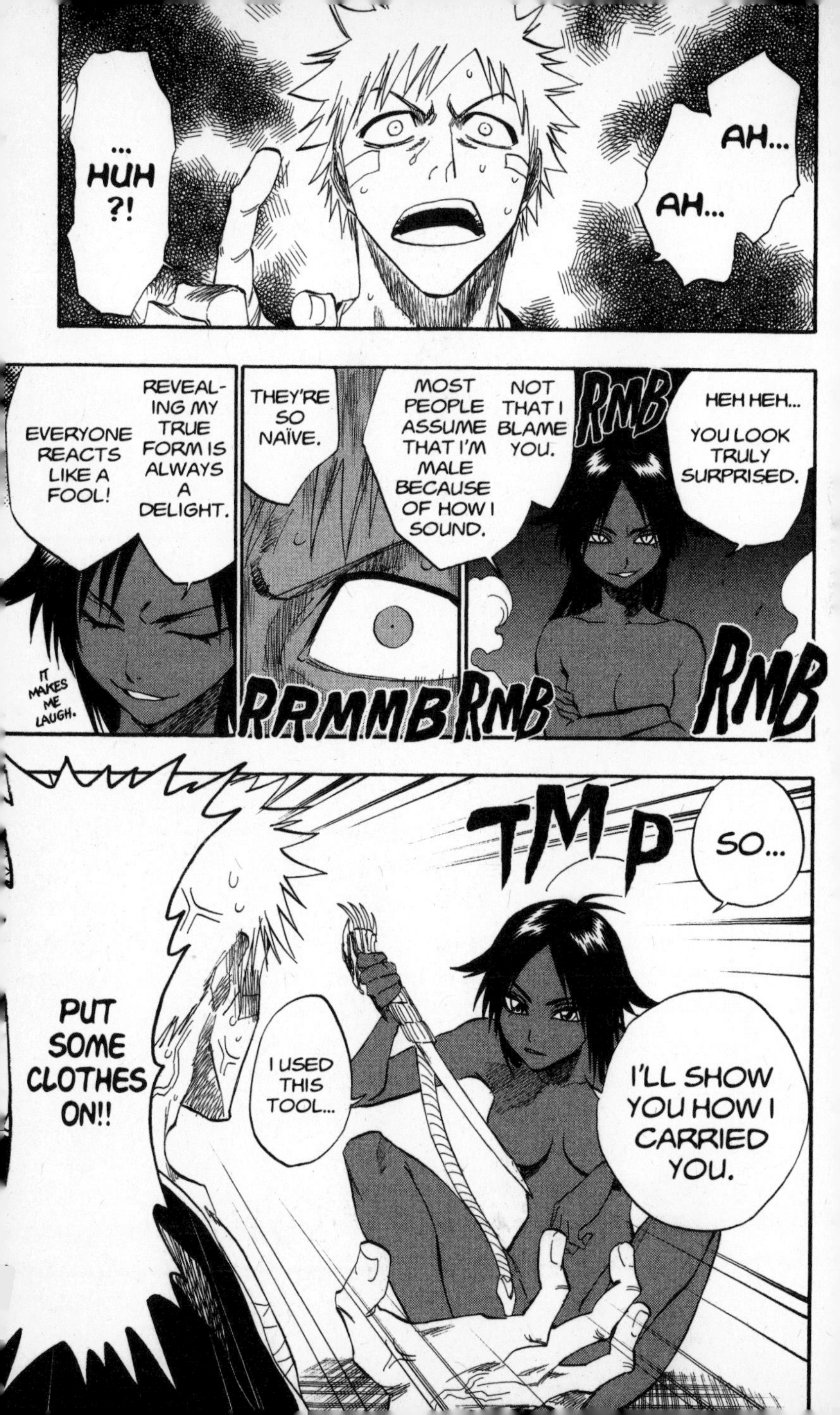
AH... AH...
... HUH ?!
HEH HEH... YOU LOOK TRULY SURPRISED.
RMB
RMB
NOT THAT I BLAME YOU.
MOST PEOPLE ASSUME THAT I'M MALE BECAUSE OF HOW I SOUND.
THEY'RE SO NAÏVE.
RRMMB RMB
REVEAL-ING MY TRUE FORM IS ALWAYS A DELIGHT.
EVERYONE REACTS LIKE A FOOL!
IT MAKES ME LAUGH.
SO...
TMP
I'LL SHOW YOU HOW I CARRIED YOU.
I USED THIS TOOL...
PUT SOME CLOTHES ON!!

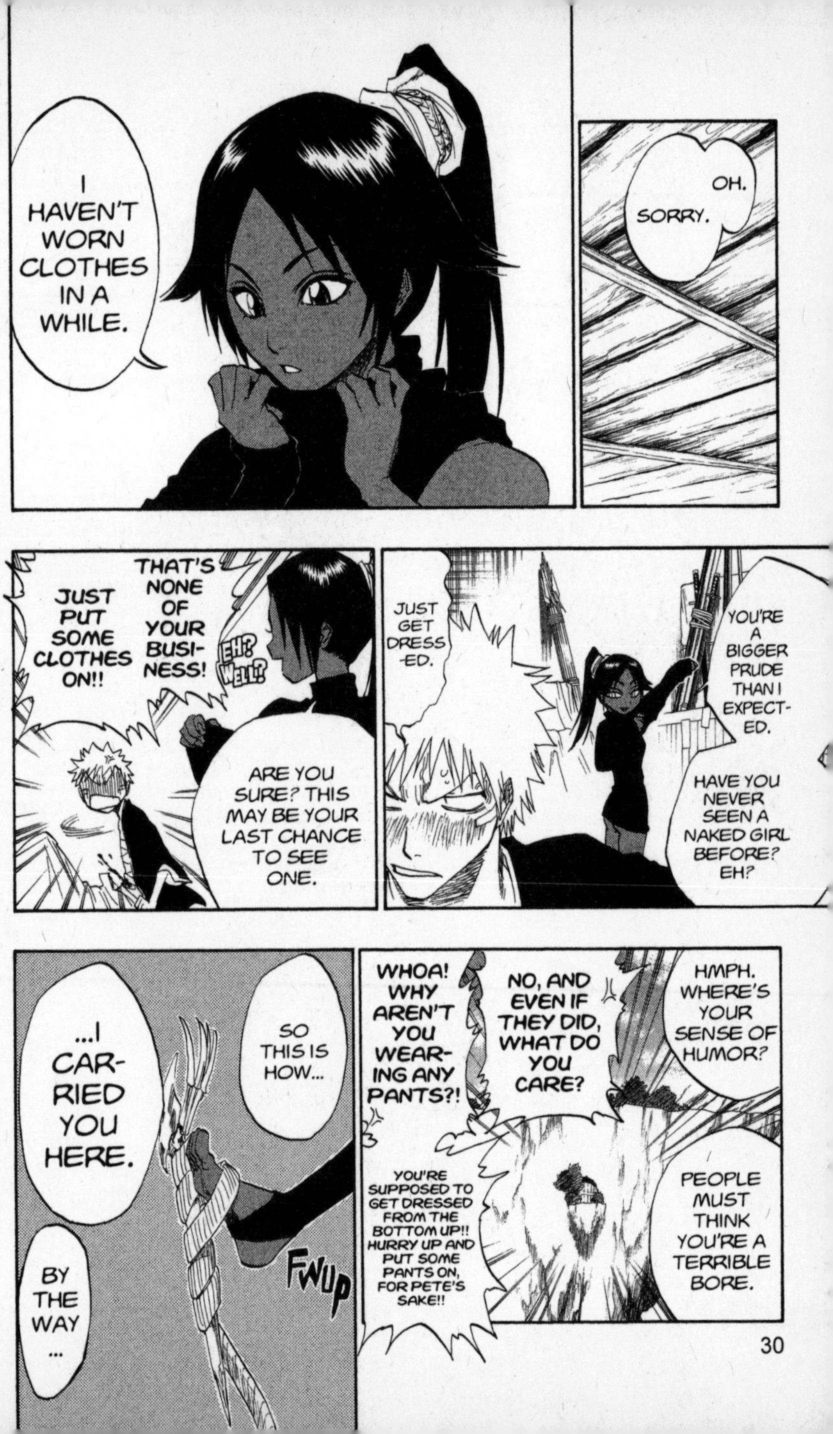
OH. SORRY.
I HAVEN'T WORN CLOTHES IN A WHILE.
YOU'RE A BIGGER PRUDE THAN I EXPECTED.
HAVE YOU NEVER SEEN A NAKED GIRL BEFORE? EH?
JUST GET DRESSED.
ARE YOU SURE? THIS MAY BE YOUR LAST CHANCE TO SEE ONE.
EH? WELL?
THAT'S NONE OF YOUR BUSINESS!
JUST PUT SOME CLOTHES ON!!
HMPH. WHERE'S YOUR SENSE OF HUMOR?
PEOPLE MUST THINK YOU'RE A TERRIBLE BORE.
NO, AND EVEN IF THEY DID, WHAT DO YOU CARE?
WHOA! WHY AREN'T YOU WEARING ANY PANTS?!
YOU'RE SUPPOSED TO GET DRESSED FROM THE BOTTOM UP!! HURRY UP AND PUT SOME PANTS ON, FOR PETE'S SAKE!!
SO THIS IS HOW...
...I CARRIED YOU HERE.
BY THE WAY...
FWUP

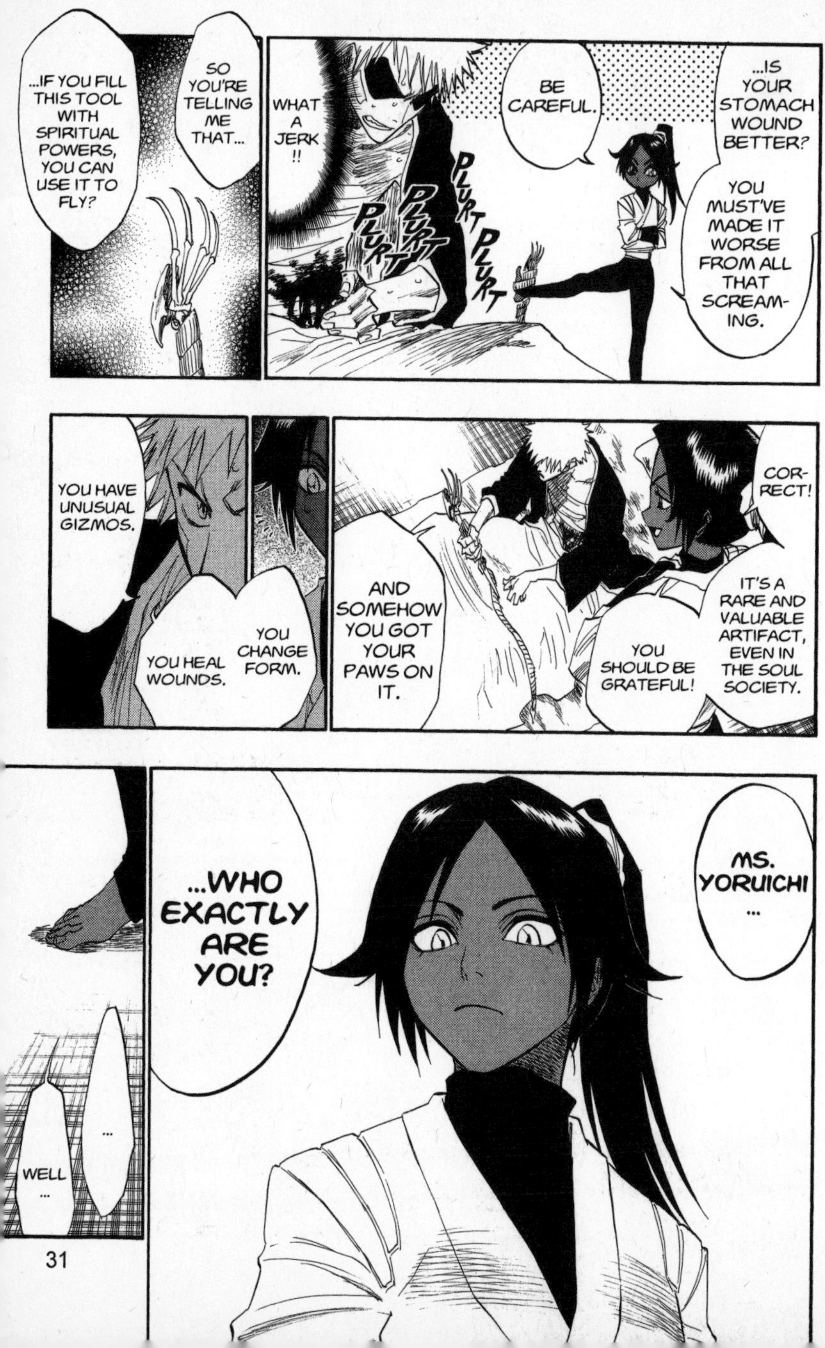
...IS YOUR STOMACH WOUND BETTER?
YOU MUST'VE MADE IT WORSE FROM ALL THAT SCREAM-ING.
BE CAREFUL.
WHAT A JERK!!
PLURT PLURT PLURT PLURT
SO YOU'RE TELLING ME THAT...
...IF YOU FILL THIS TOOL WITH SPIRITUAL POWERS, YOU CAN USE IT TO FLY?
COR-RECT!
IT'S A RARE AND VALUABLE ARTIFACT, EVEN IN THE SOUL SOCIETY.
YOU SHOULD BE GRATEFUL!
AND SOMEHOW YOU GOT YOUR PAWS ON IT.
YOU HAVE UNUSUAL GIZMOS.
YOU CHANGE FORM.
YOU HEAL WOUNDS.
MS. YORUICHI...
...WHO EXACTLY ARE YOU?
...
WELL...

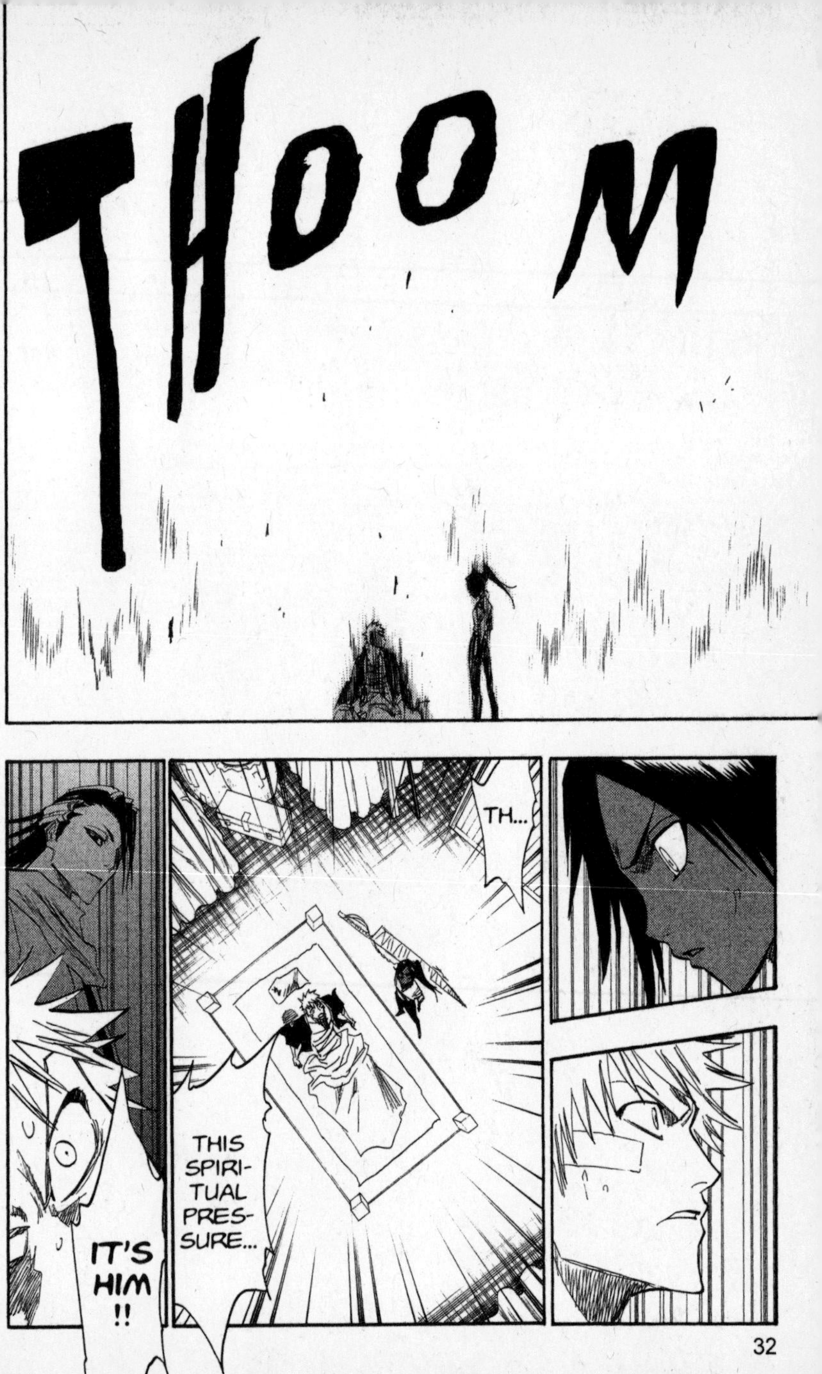
THOOM
TH...
THIS SPIRITUAL PRESSURE...
IT'S HIM!!

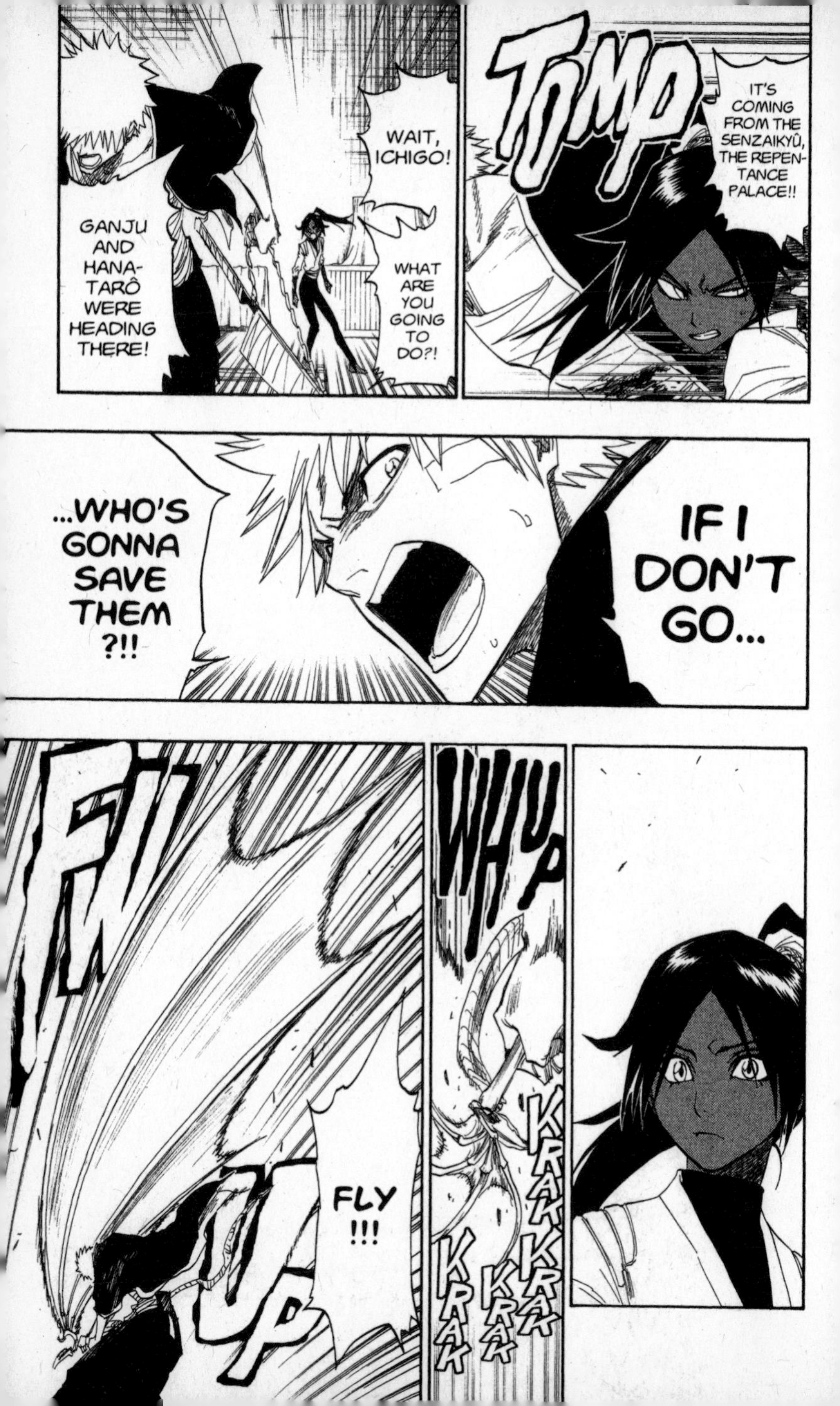
TOMP
IT'S COMING FROM THE SENZAIKYÛ, THE REPENTANCE PALACE!!
WAIT, ICHIGO!
WHAT ARE YOU GOING TO DO?!
GANJU AND HANATARÔ WERE HEADING THERE!
IF I DON'T GO...
...WHO'S GONNA SAVE THEM?!!
WHUP
KRAK KRAK
KRAK KRAK
KRAK
FLY !!!

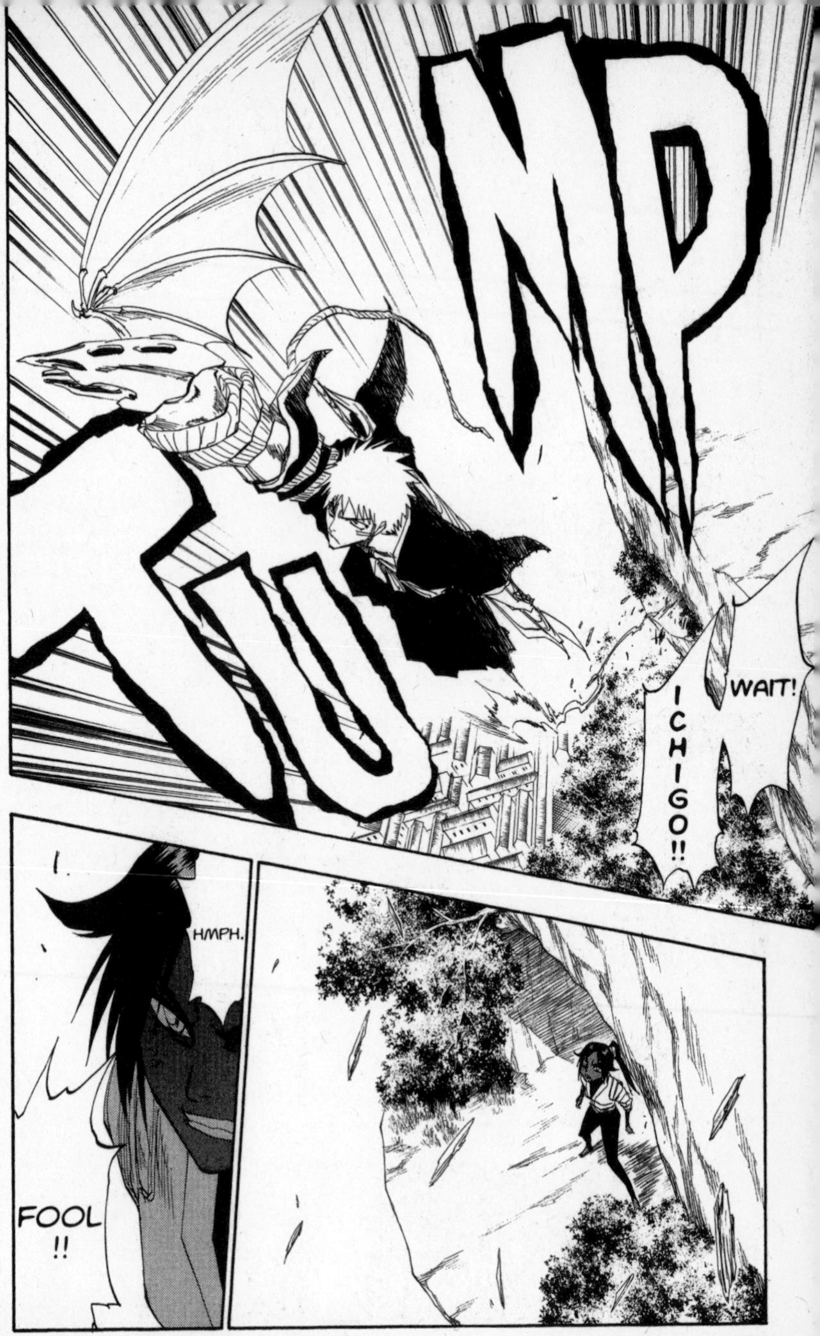
JUMP
WAIT! ICHIGO!!
HMPH.
FOOL!!

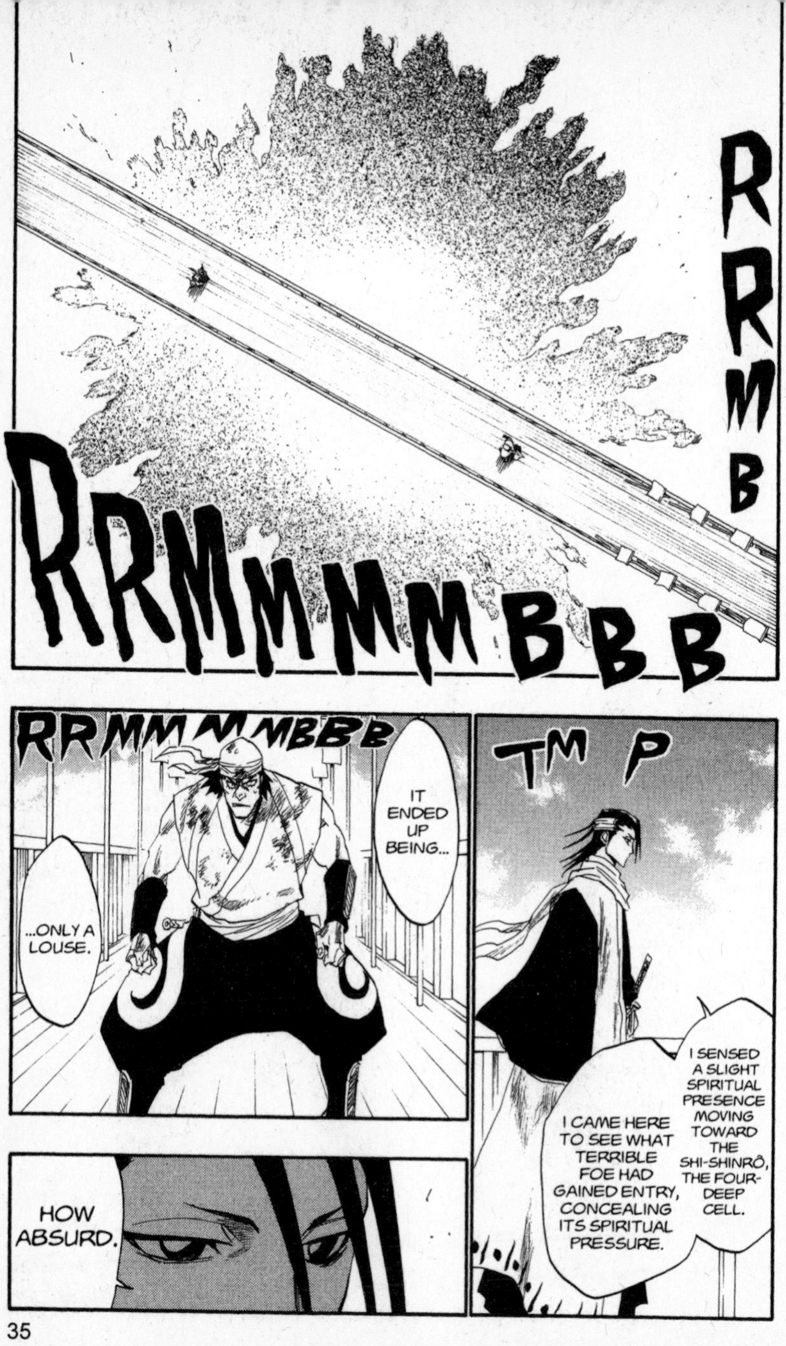
RRMB
RRMMMMBBB
TMP
I SENSED A SLIGHT SPIRITUAL PRESENCE MOVING TOWARD THE SHI-SHINRÔ, THE FOUR-DEEP CELL.
I CAME HERE TO SEE WHAT TERRIBLE FOE HAD GAINED ENTRY, CONCEALING ITS SPIRITUAL PRESSURE.
RRMMMMBBB
IT ENDED UP BEING...
...ONLY A LOUSE.
HOW ABSURD.

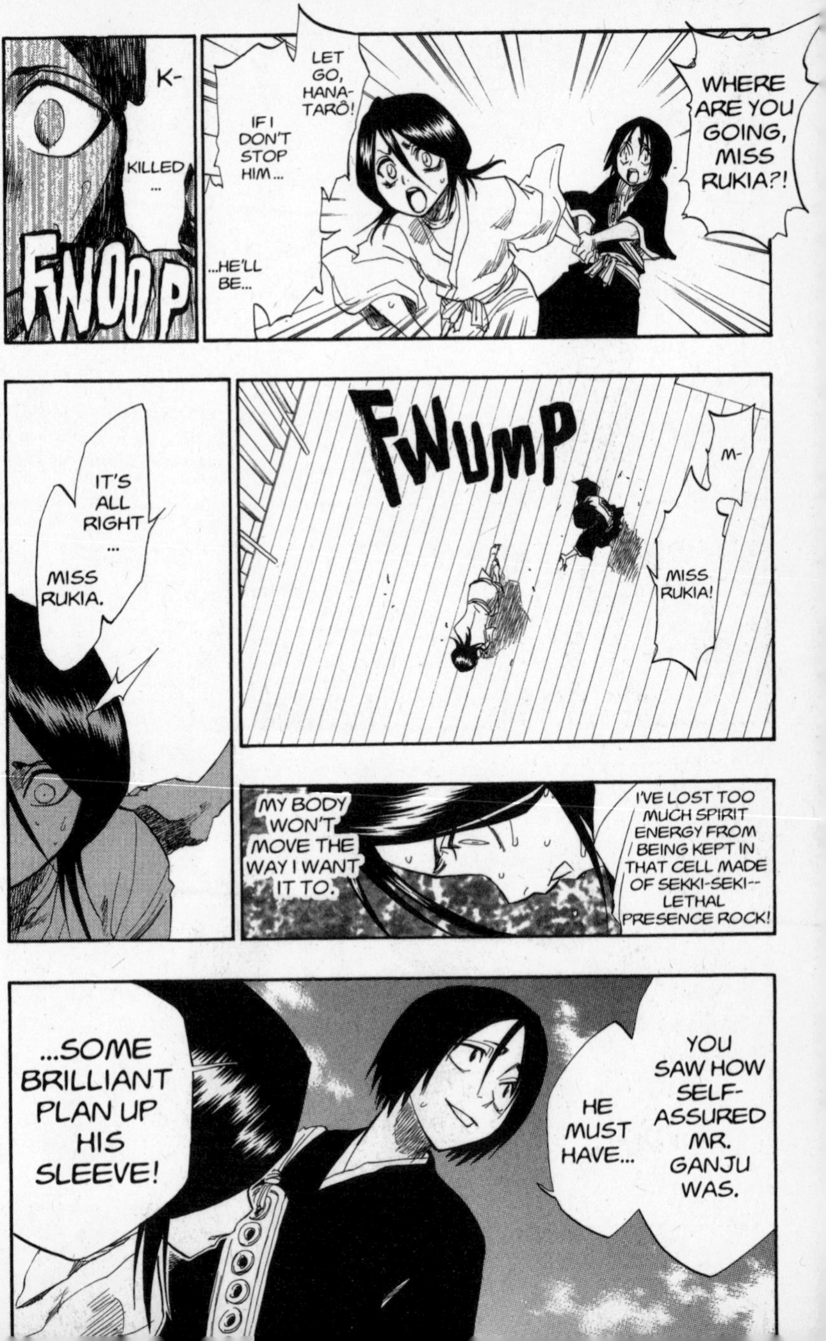
WHERE ARE YOU GOING, MISS RUKIA?!
LET GO, HANATARÔ!
IF I DON'T STOP HIM...
...HE'LL BE...
K-
KILLED...
FWOOP
M-
MISS RUKIA!
FWUMP
I'VE LOST TOO MUCH SPIRIT ENERGY FROM BEING KEPT IN THAT CELL MADE OF SEKKI-SEKI--LETHAL PRESENCE ROCK!
MY BODY WON'T MOVE THE WAY I WANT IT TO.
IT'S ALL RIGHT... MISS RUKIA.
YOU SAW HOW SELF-ASSURED MR. GANJU WAS.
HE MUST HAVE...
...SOME BRILLIANT PLAN UP HIS SLEEVE!

READ THIS WAY

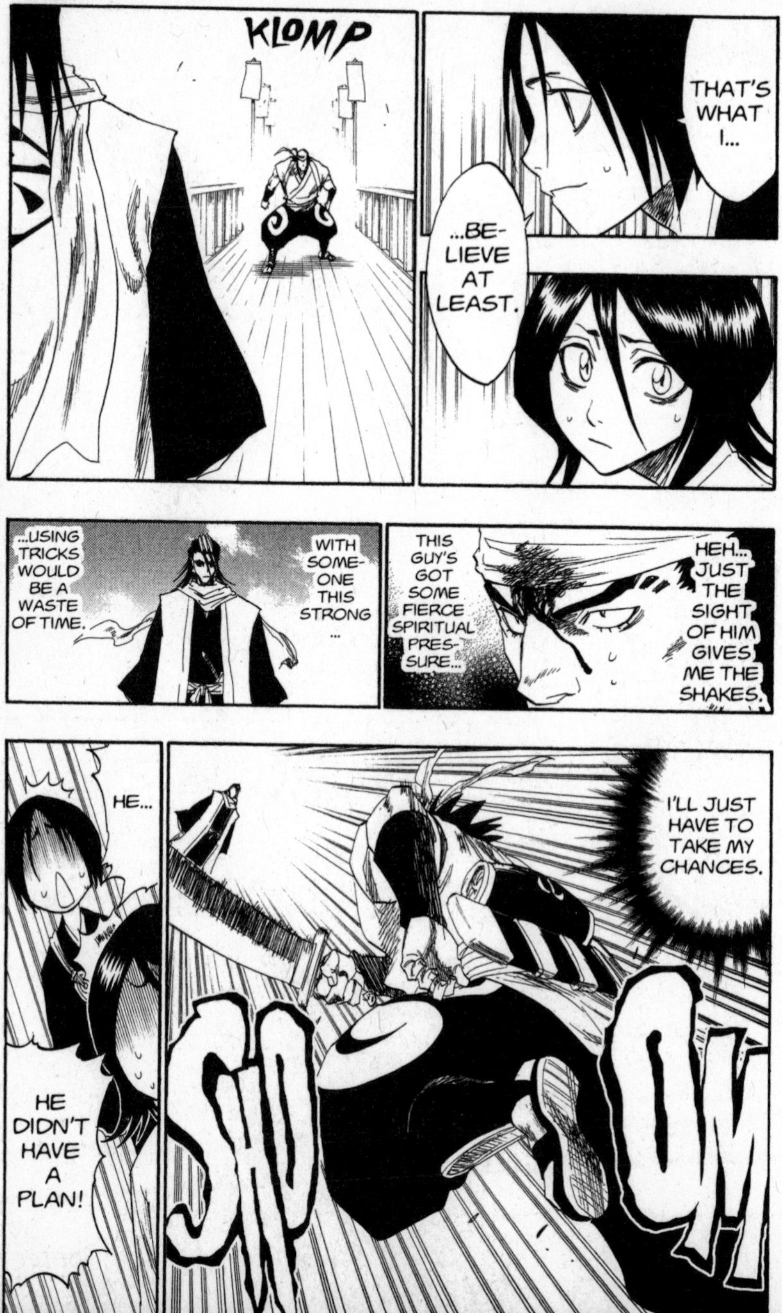
THAT'S WHAT I...
...BE-LIEVE AT LEAST.
KLOMP
HEH... JUST THE SIGHT OF HIM GIVES ME THE SHAKES.
THIS GUY'S GOT SOME FIERCE SPIRITUAL PRES-SURE...
WITH SOME-ONE THIS STRONG ...
...USING TRICKS WOULD BE A WASTE OF TIME.
I'LL JUST HAVE TO TAKE MY CHANCES.
SHOOM
HE...
HE DIDN'T HAVE A PLAN!

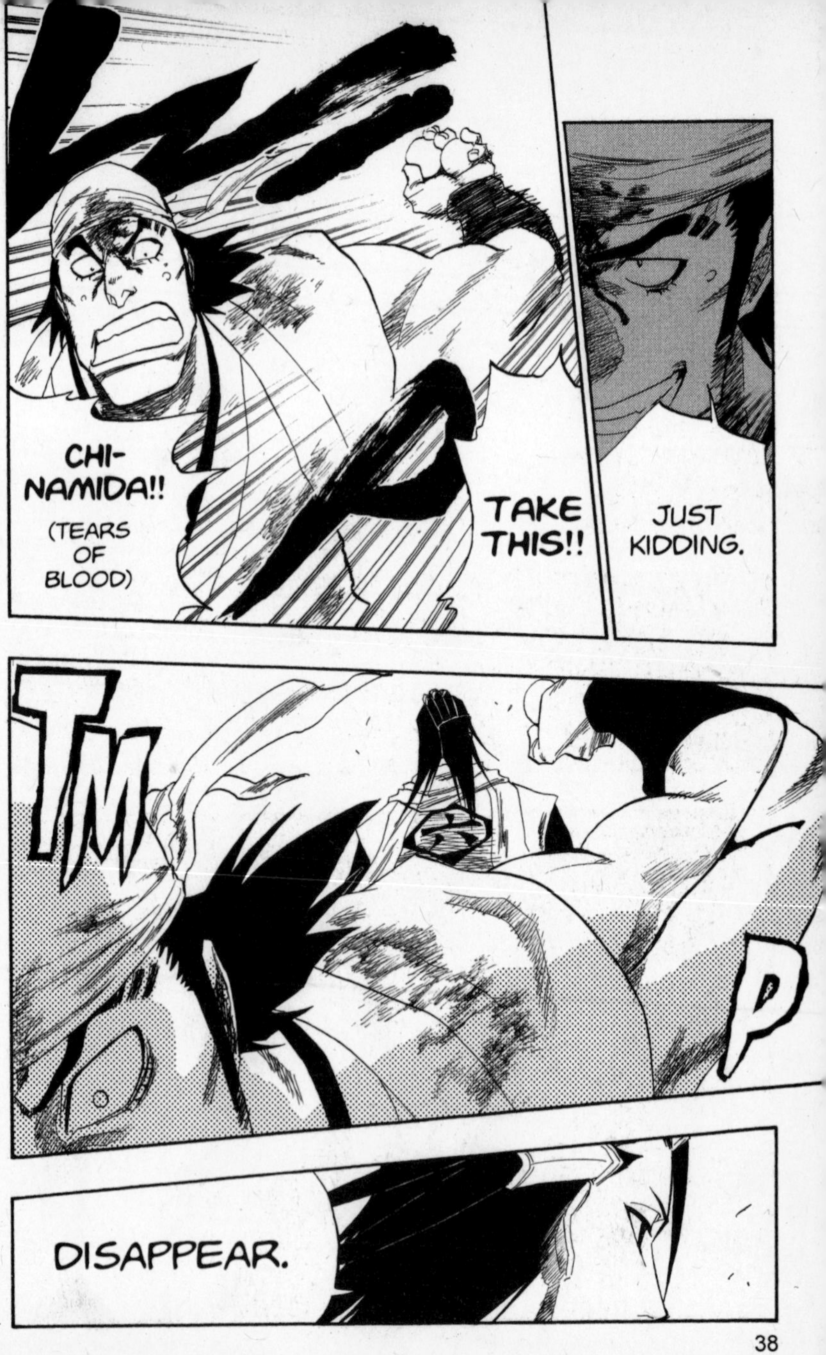
JUST KIDDING.
TAKE THIS!!
CHI-NAMIDA!!
(TEARS OF BLOOD)
TM
P
DISAPPEAR.

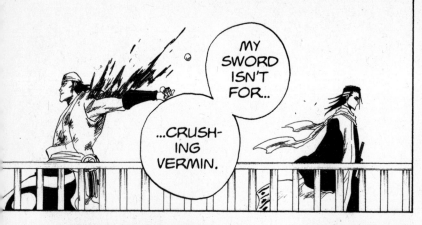

MY SWORD ISN'T FOR...

...CRUSH-ING VERMIN.

GRAAAAAAH!!

N-

NOT SO FAST!

MR. GANJU!!

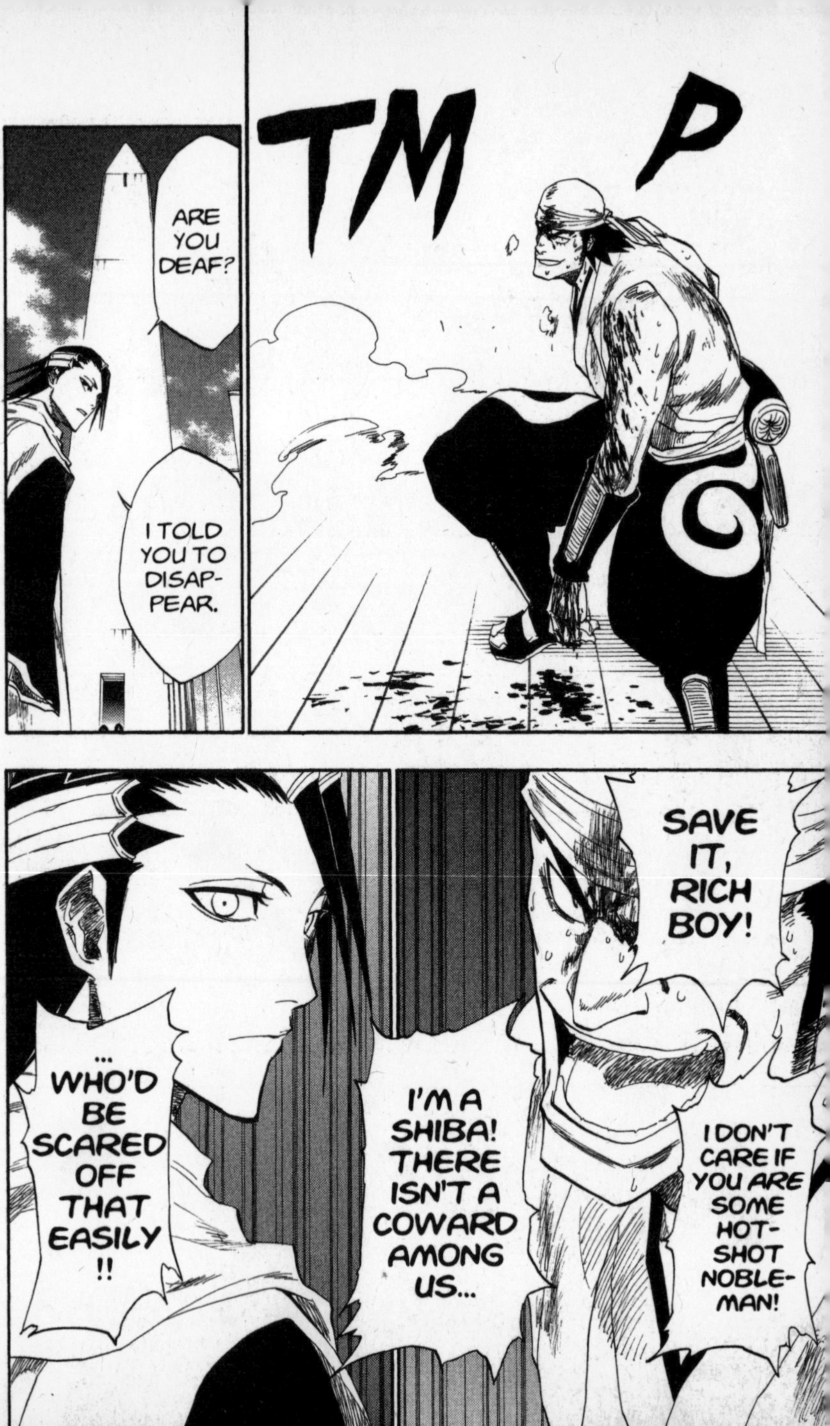
TMP
ARE YOU DEAF?
I TOLD YOU TO DISAP-PEAR.
SAVE IT, RICH BOY!
I DON'T CARE IF YOU ARE SOME HOT-SHOT NOBLE-MAN!
I'M A SHIBA! THERE ISN'T A COWARD AMONG US...
...WHO'D BE SCARED OFF THAT EASILY!!

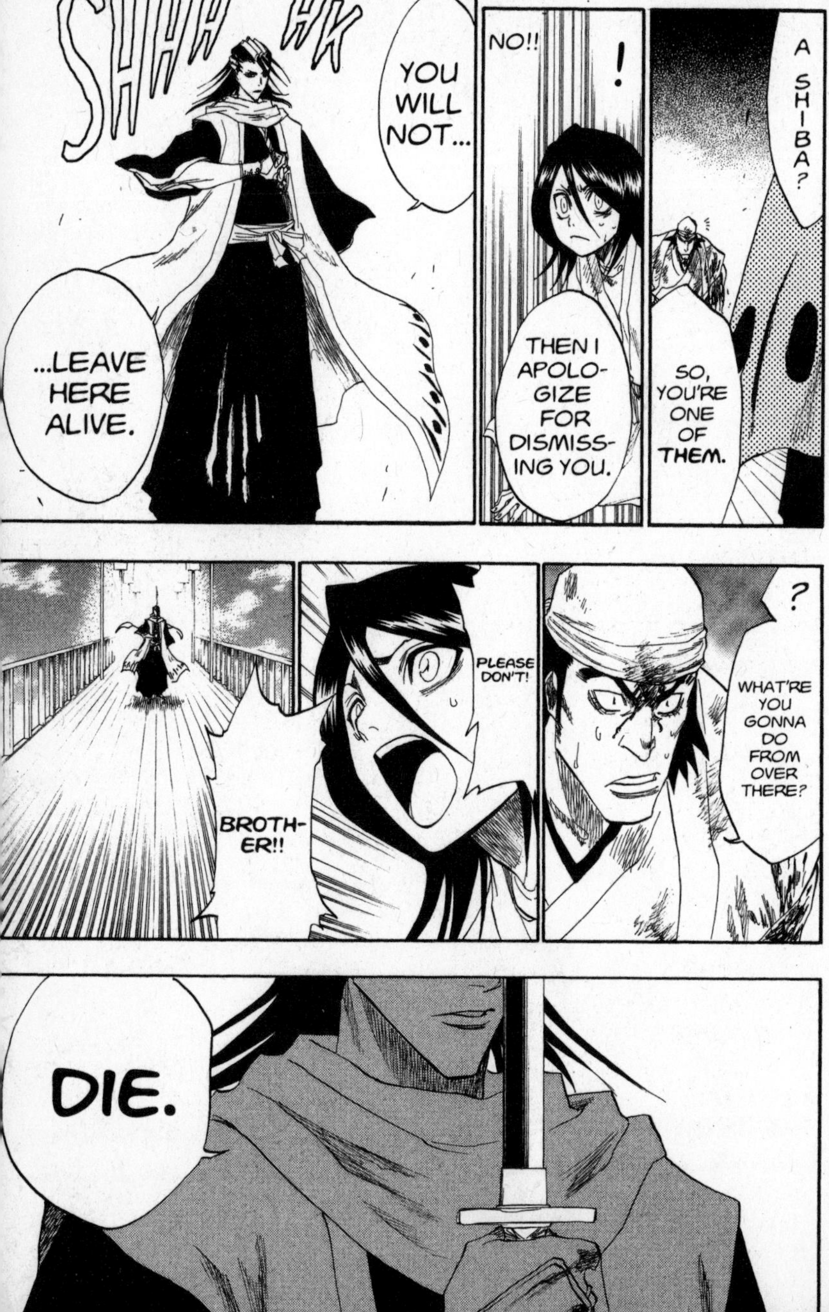
A SHIBA?
SO, YOU'RE ONE OF THEM.
!
NO!!
THEN I APOLOGIZE FOR DISMISSING YOU.
YOU WILL NOT...
SHHHHK
...LEAVE HERE ALIVE.
?
WHAT'RE YOU GONNA DO FROM OVER THERE?
PLEASE DON'T!
BROTHER!!
DIE.

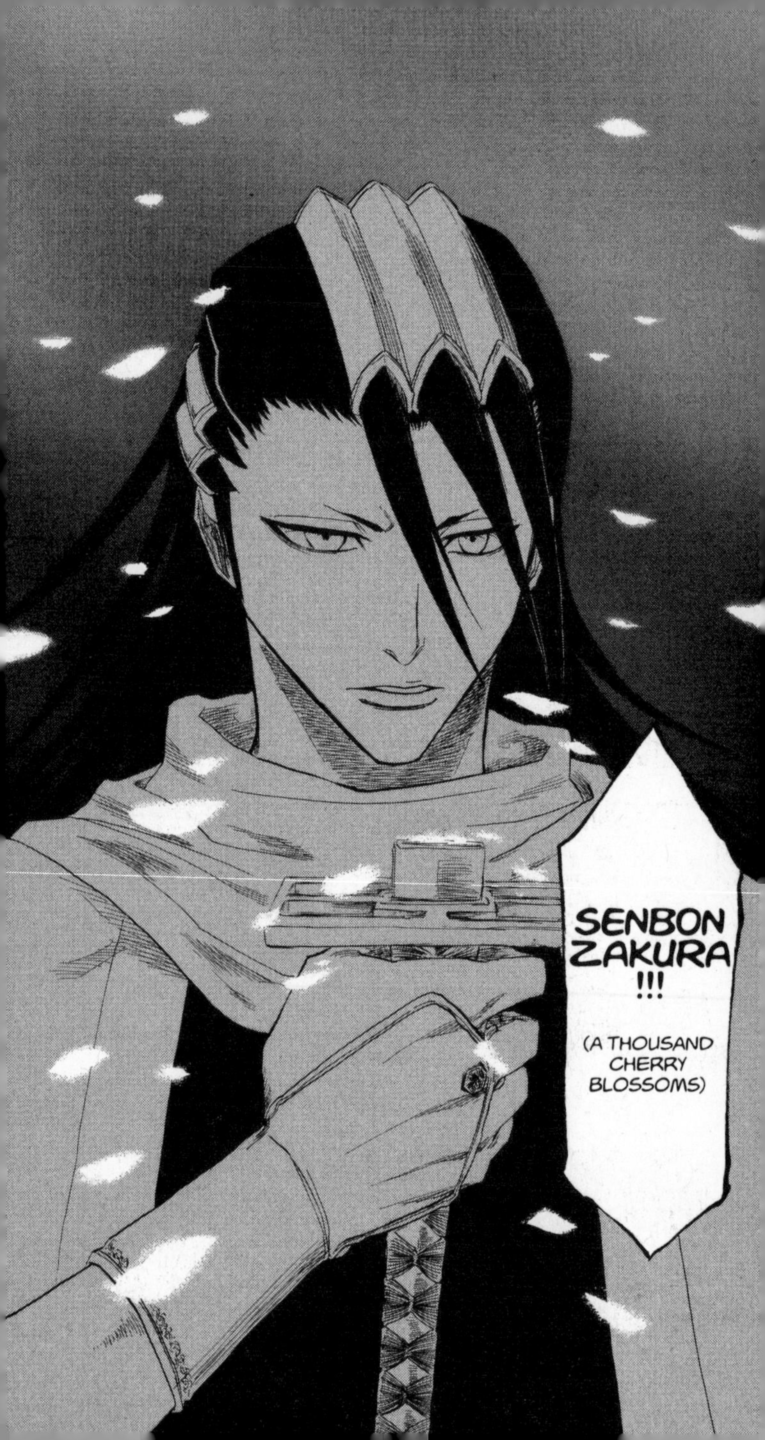
SENBON ZAKURA !!!
(A THOUSAND CHERRY BLOSSOMS)

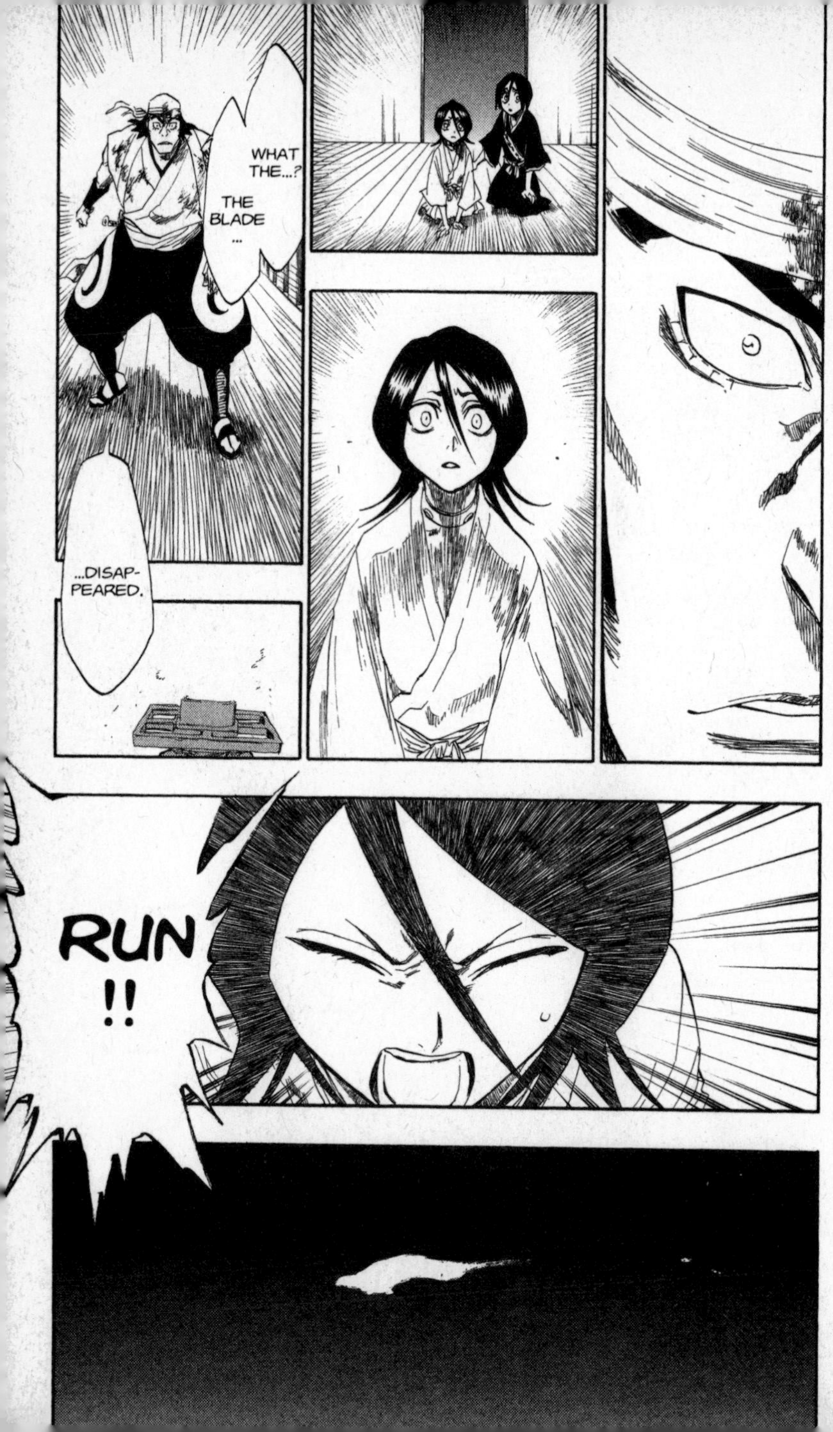
WHAT THE...? THE BLADE ...
...DISAP-PEARED.
RUN !!

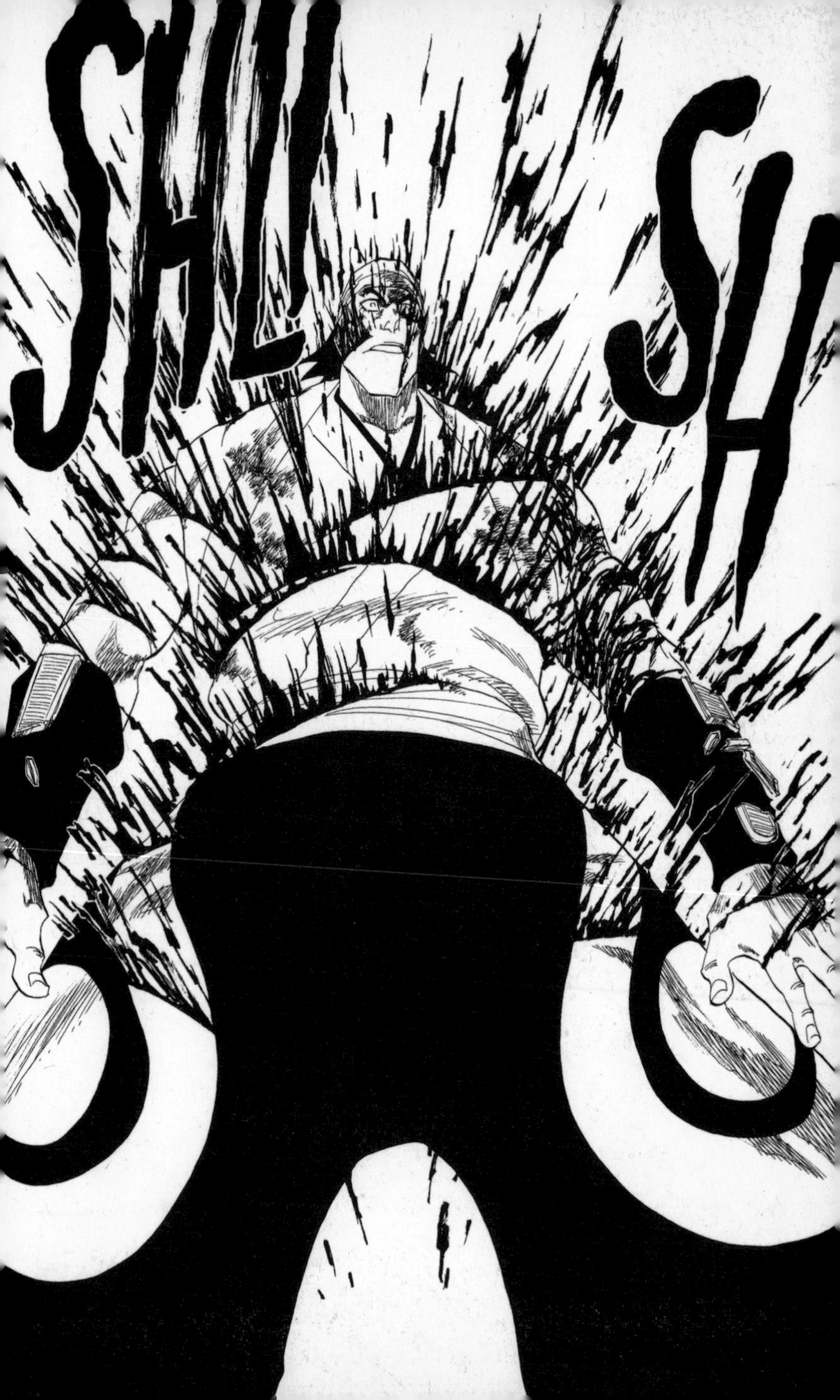
SH
SHU

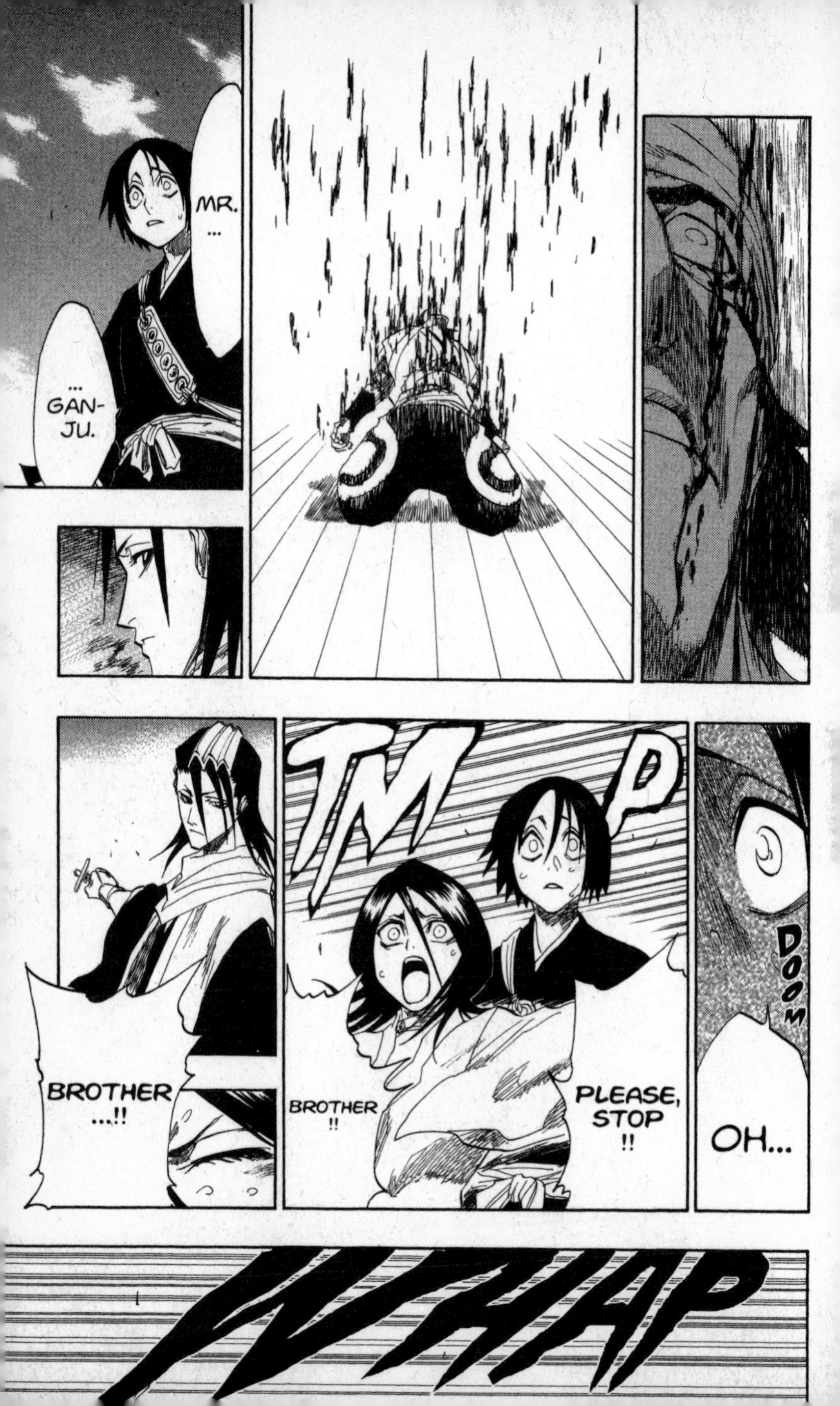
MR. ...
... GAN-JU.
DOOM
OH...
TMP
PLEASE, STOP !!
BROTHER !!
BROTHER ...!!
WHAP

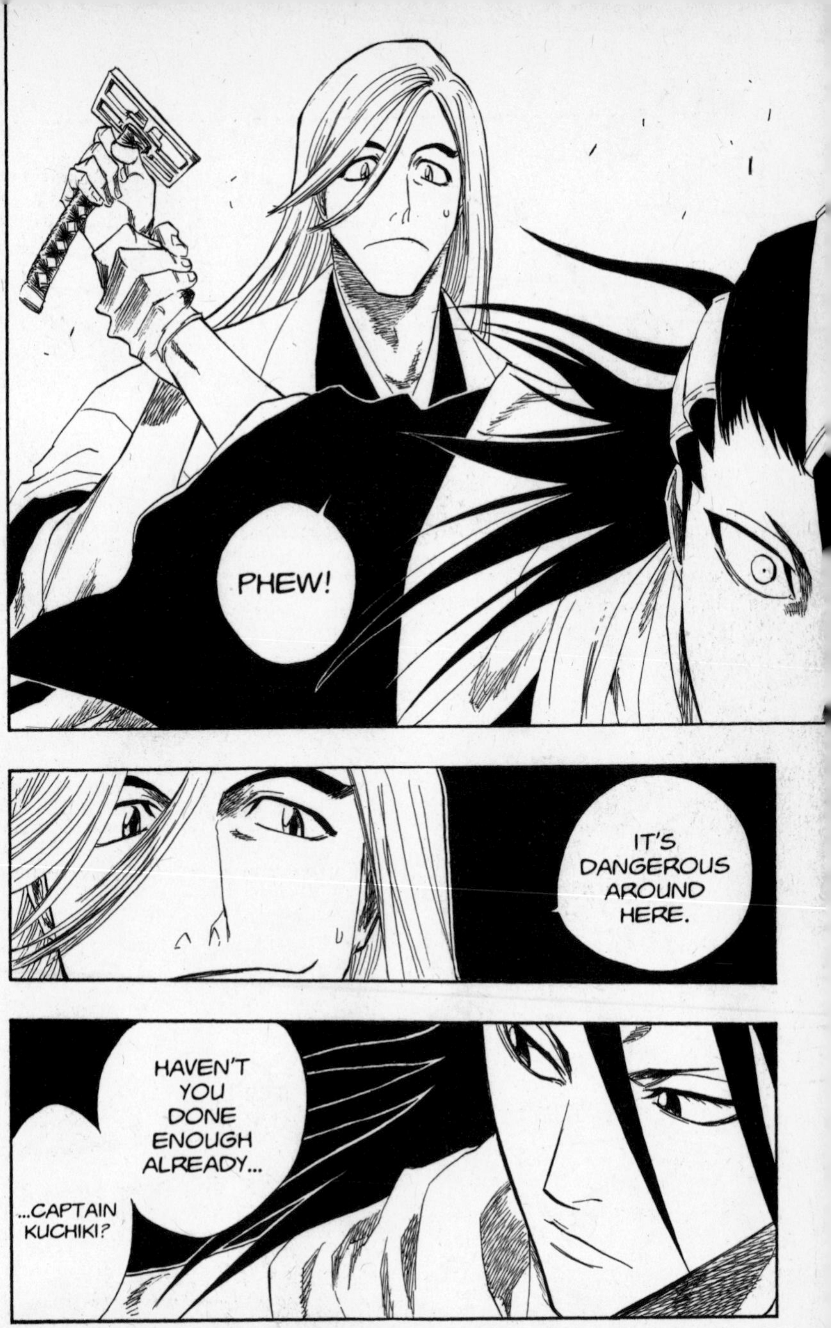
PHEW!
IT'S DANGEROUS AROUND HERE.
HAVEN'T YOU DONE ENOUGH ALREADY...
...CAPTAIN KUCHIKI?

READ THIS WAY

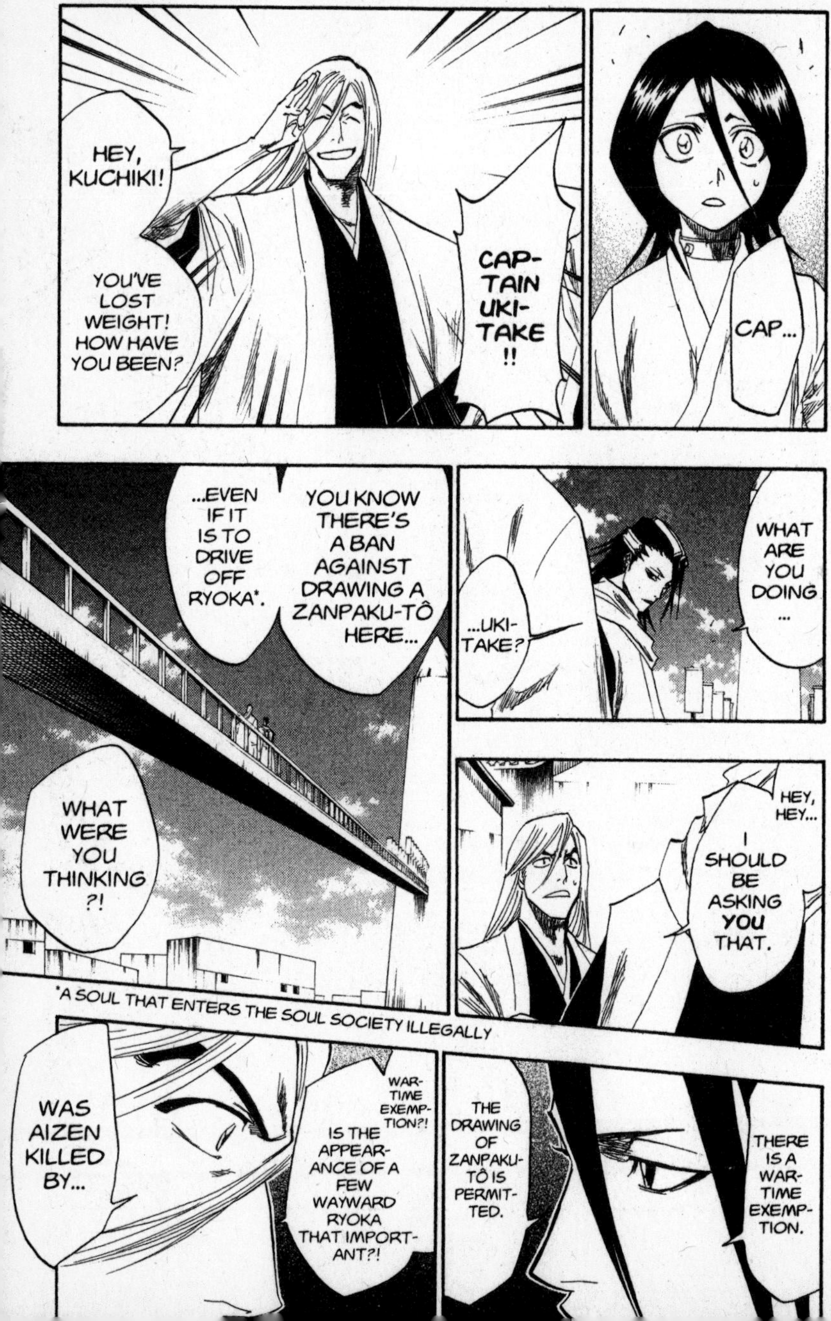
CAP...
CAP-TAIN UKI-TAKE !!
HEY, KUCHIKI!
YOU'VE LOST WEIGHT! HOW HAVE YOU BEEN?
WHAT ARE YOU DOING...
...UKI-TAKE?
HEY, HEY...
I SHOULD BE ASKING YOU THAT.
YOU KNOW THERE'S A BAN AGAINST DRAWING A ZANPAKU-TÔ HERE...
...EVEN IF IT IS TO DRIVE OFF RYOKA*.
WHAT WERE YOU THINKING ?!
*A SOUL THAT ENTERS THE SOUL SOCIETY ILLEGALLY
THERE IS A WAR-TIME EXEMP-TION.
THE DRAWING OF ZANPAKU-TÔ IS PERMIT-TED.
WAR-TIME EXEMP-TION?!
IS THE APPEAR-ANCE OF A FEW WAYWARD RYOKA THAT IMPORT-ANT?!
WAS AIZEN KILLED BY...

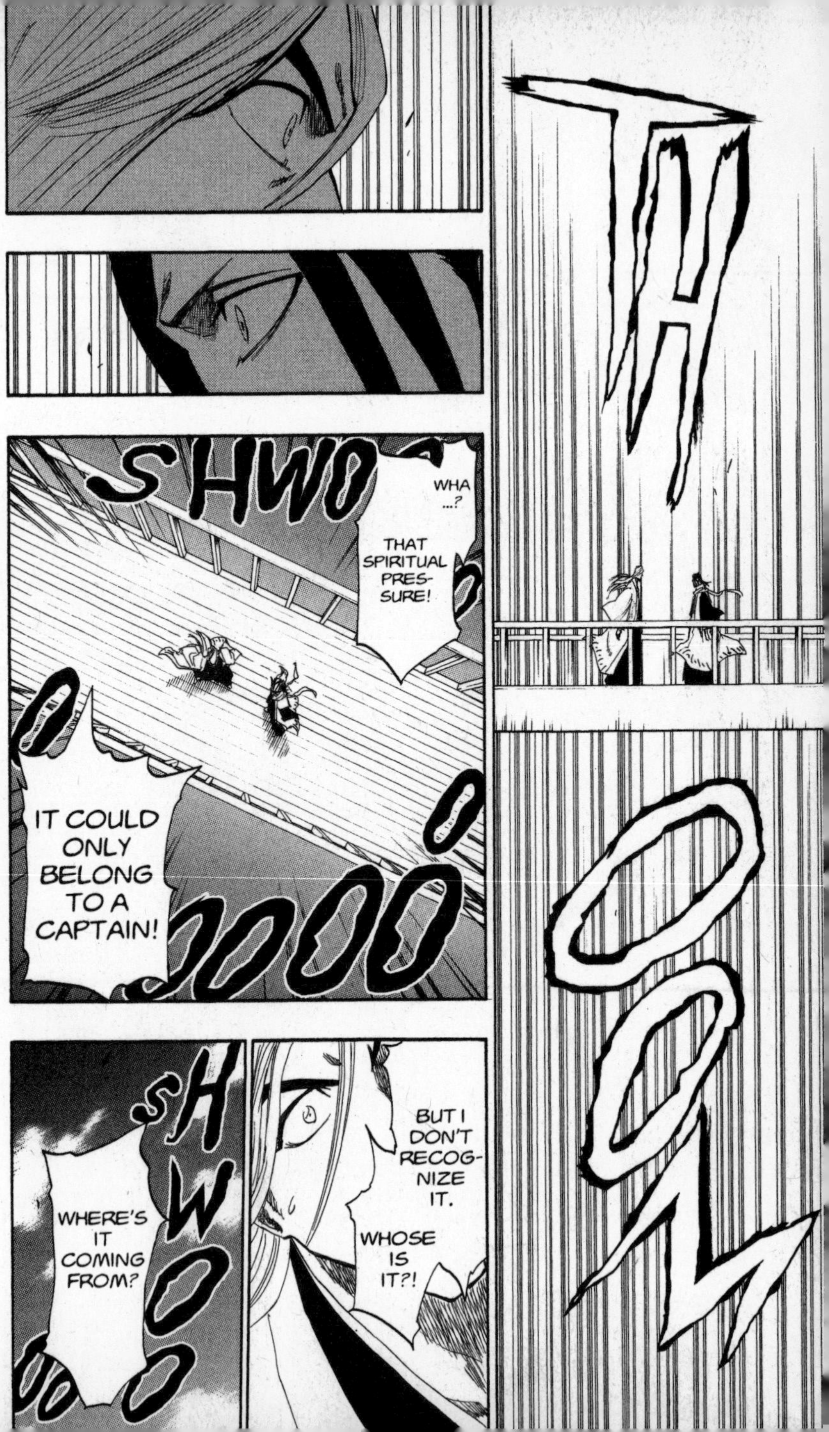
TH
OOM
SHWO
OOOOOO
WHA ...?
THAT SPIRITUAL PRESSURE!
IT COULD ONLY BELONG TO A CAPTAIN!
BUT I DON'T RECOGNIZE IT.
WHOSE IS IT?!
SHWOOOO
WHERE'S IT COMING FROM?

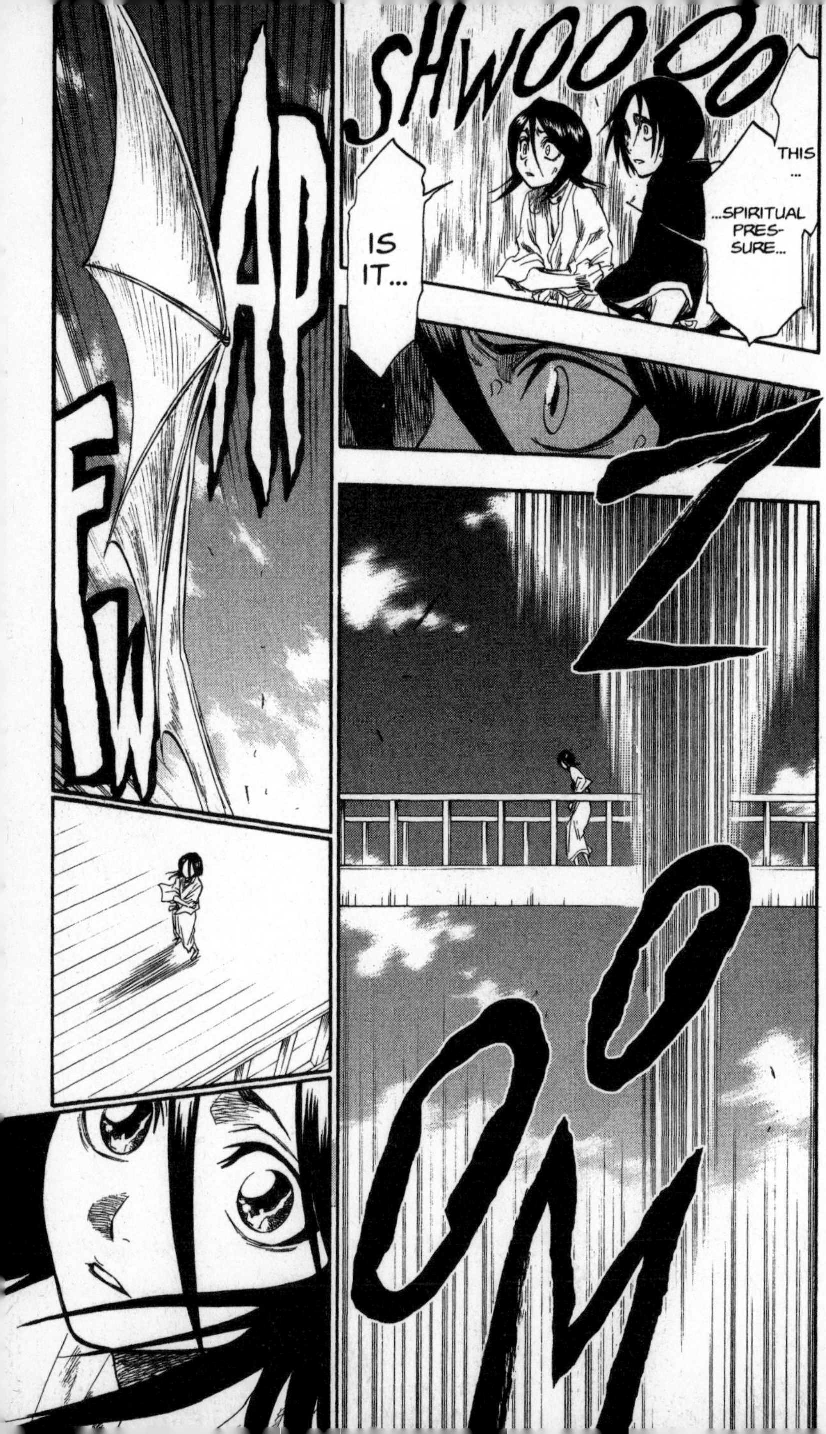
SHWOOOO
THIS ...
...SPIRITUAL PRES-SURE...
IS IT...
ZOOOM
FWAP

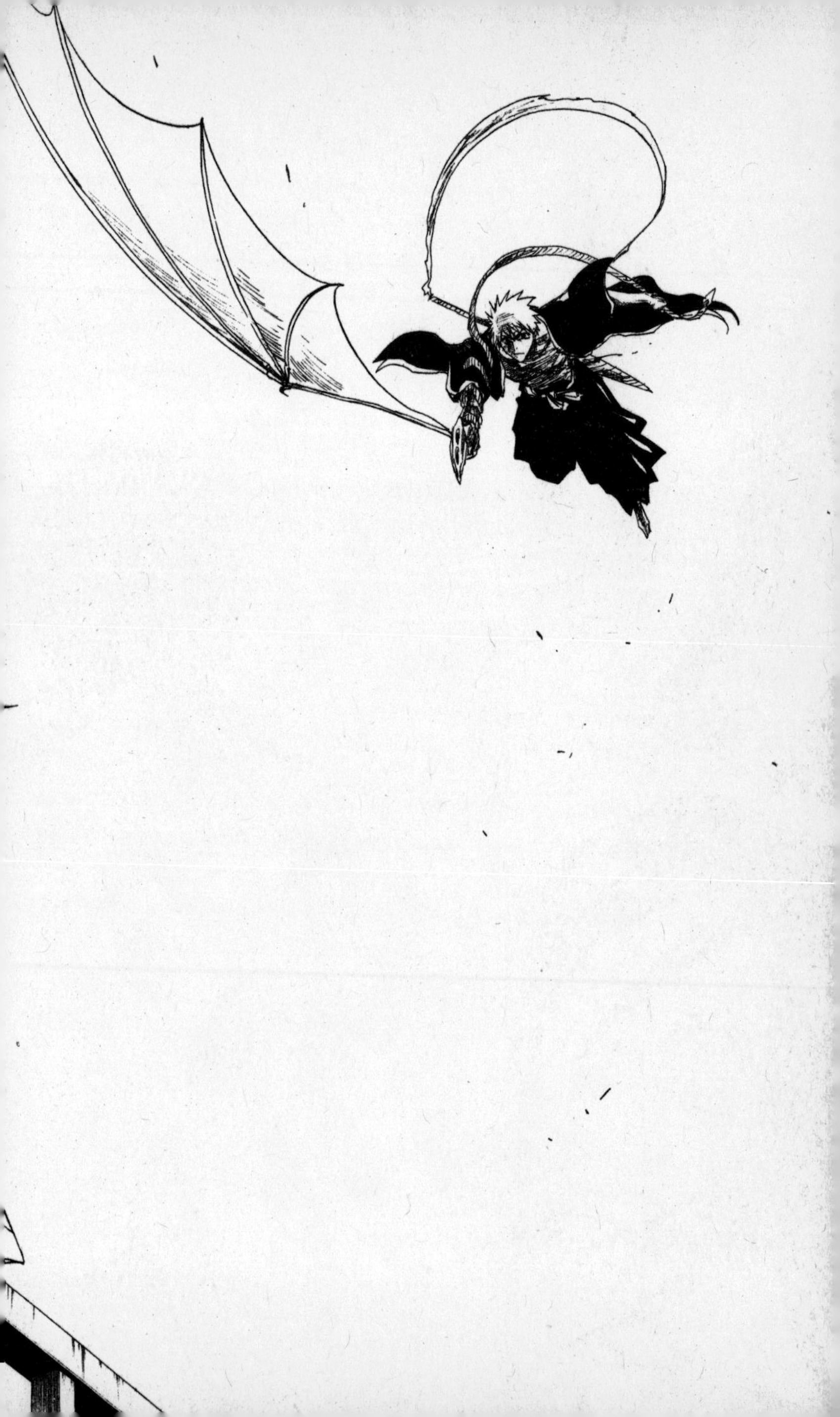

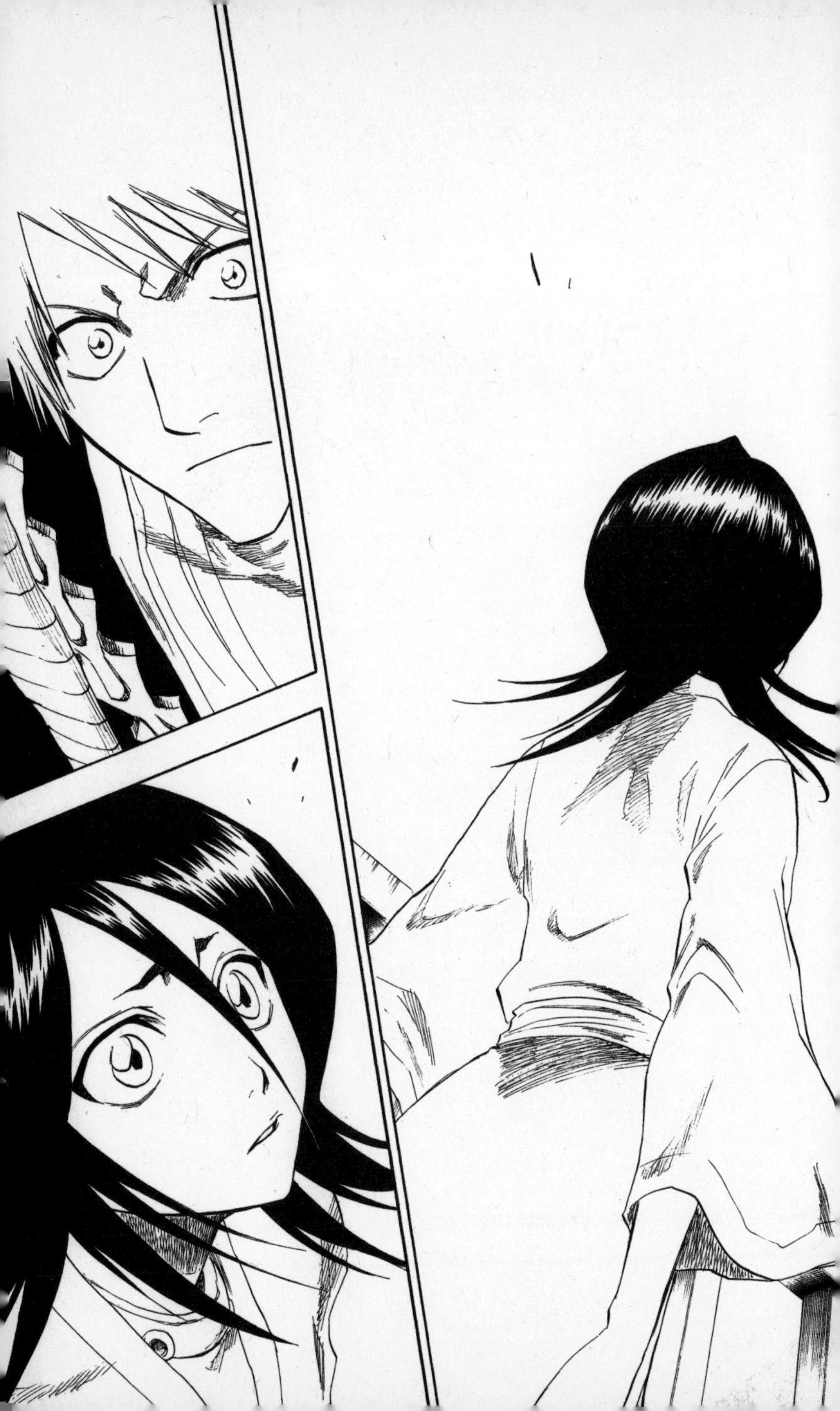

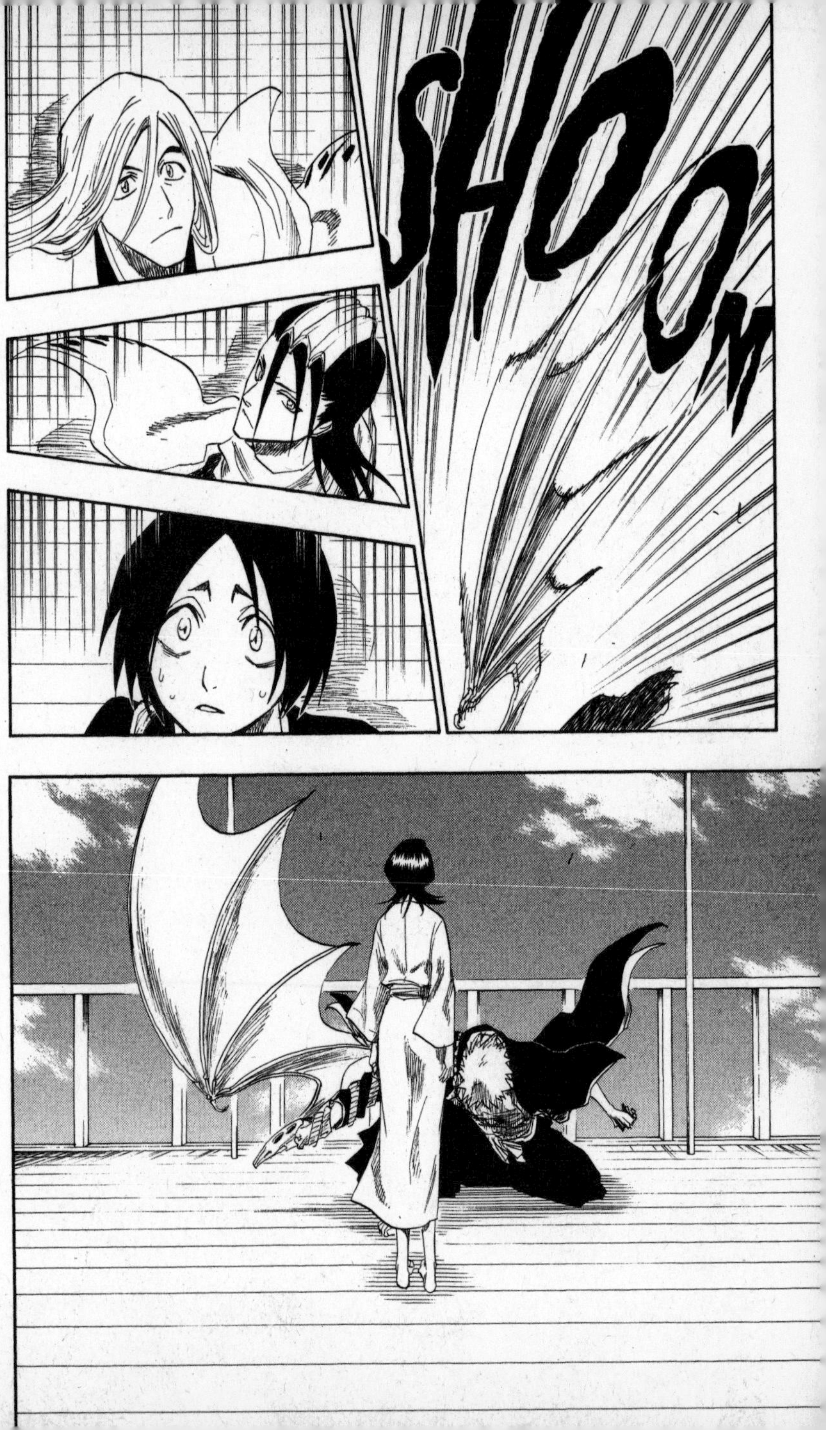
SHOOM

READ THIS WAY

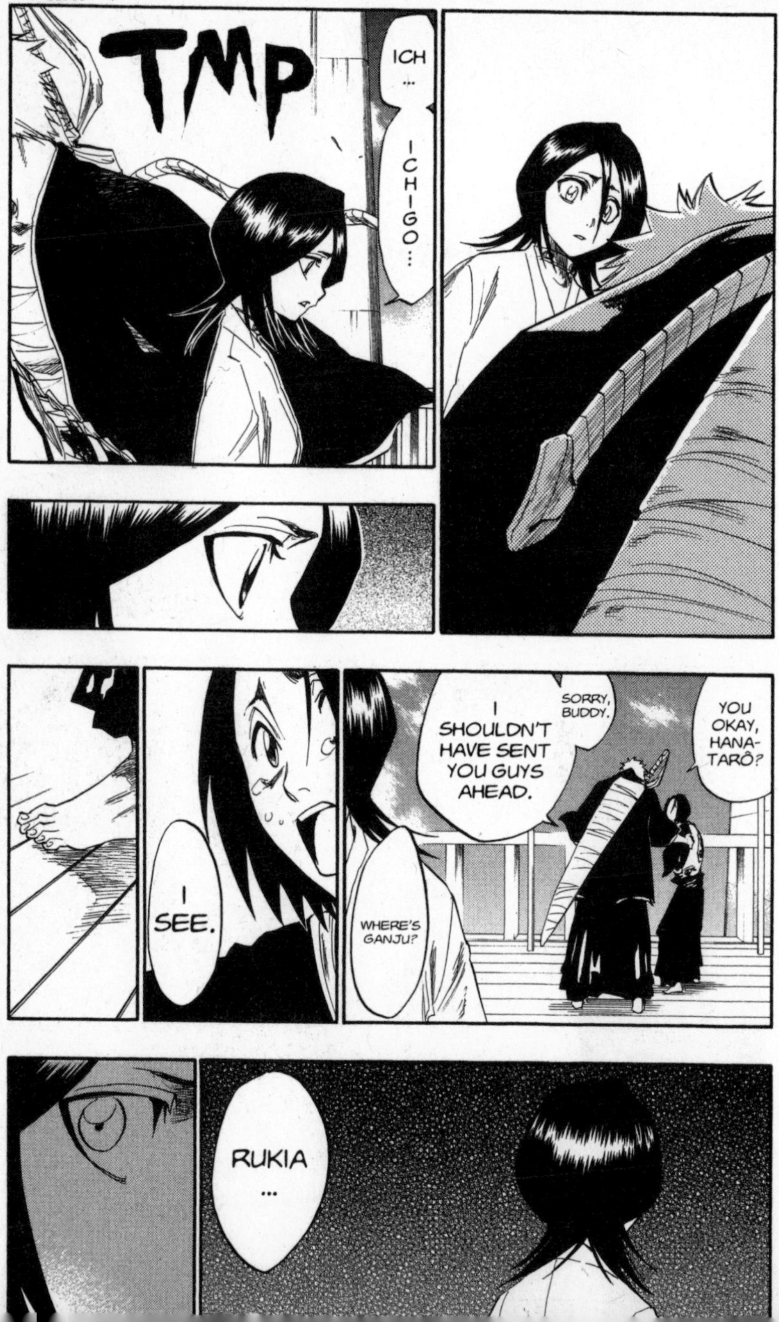
ICH ...
ICHIGO...
TMP
YOU OKAY, HANATARÔ?
SORRY, BUDDY.
I SHOULDN'T HAVE SENT YOU GUYS AHEAD.
WHERE'S GANJU?
I SEE.
RUKIA ...

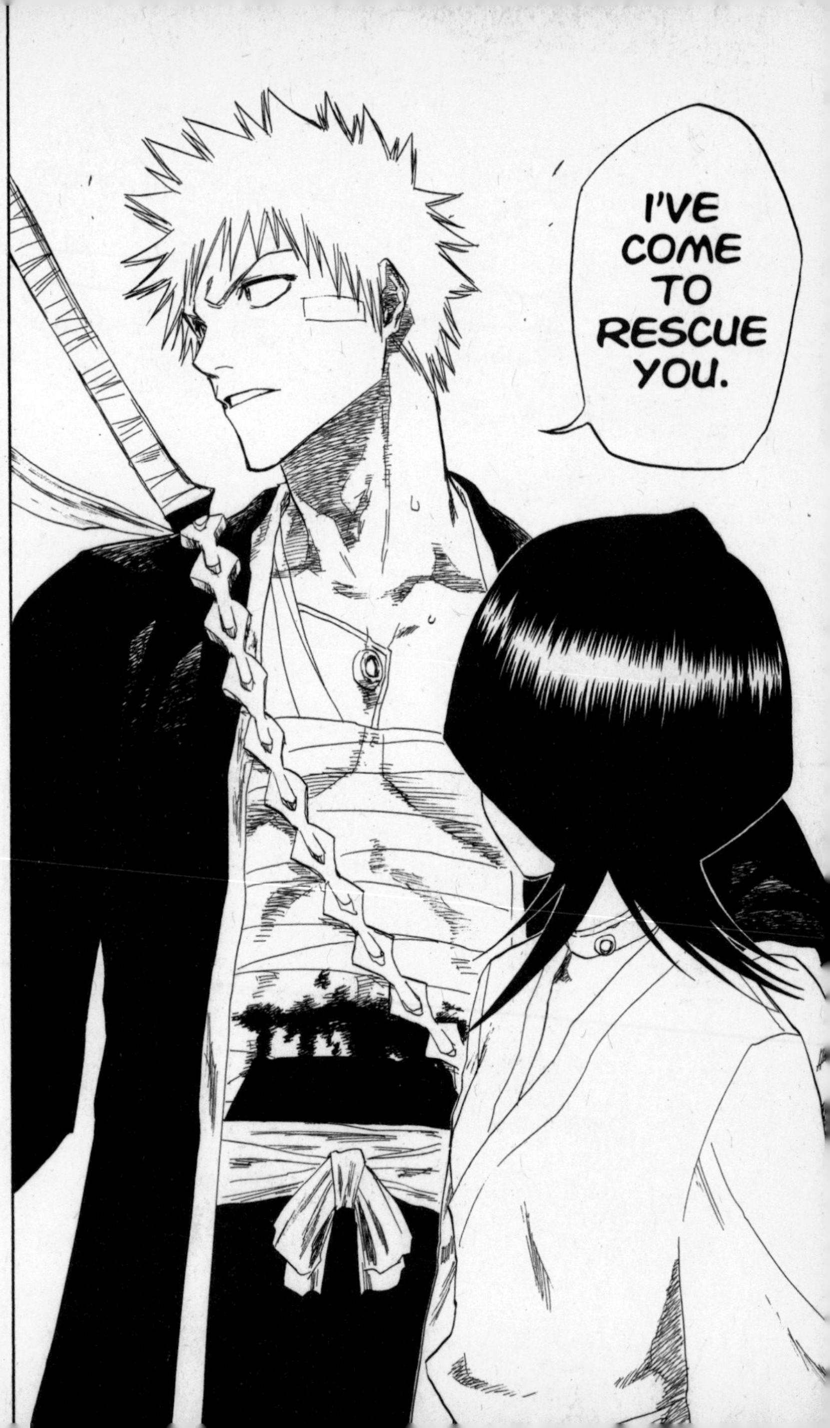
I'VE COME TO RESCUE YOU.

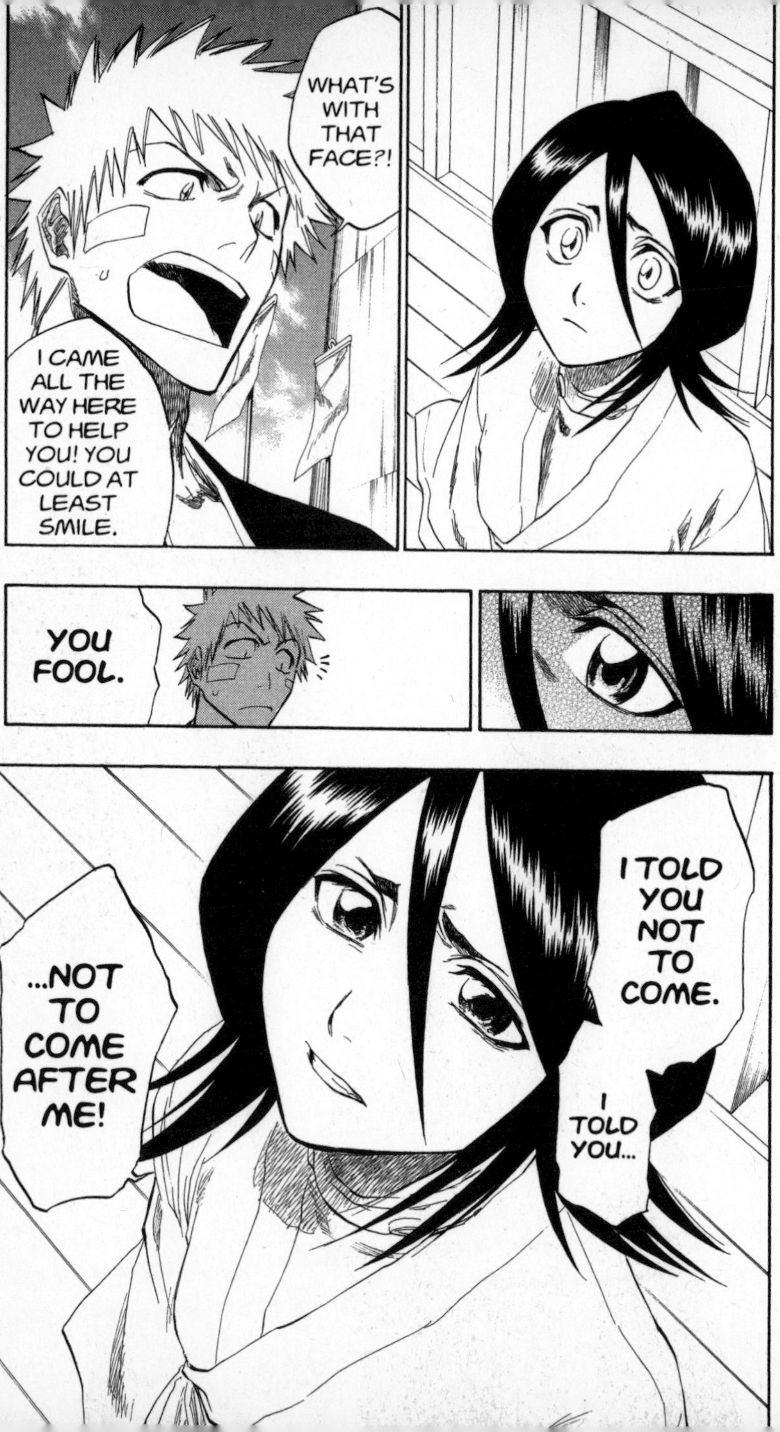
WHAT'S WITH THAT FACE?!
I CAME ALL THE WAY HERE TO HELP YOU! YOU COULD AT LEAST SMILE.
YOU FOOL.
I TOLD YOU NOT TO COME.
I TOLD YOU...
...NOT TO COME AFTER ME!

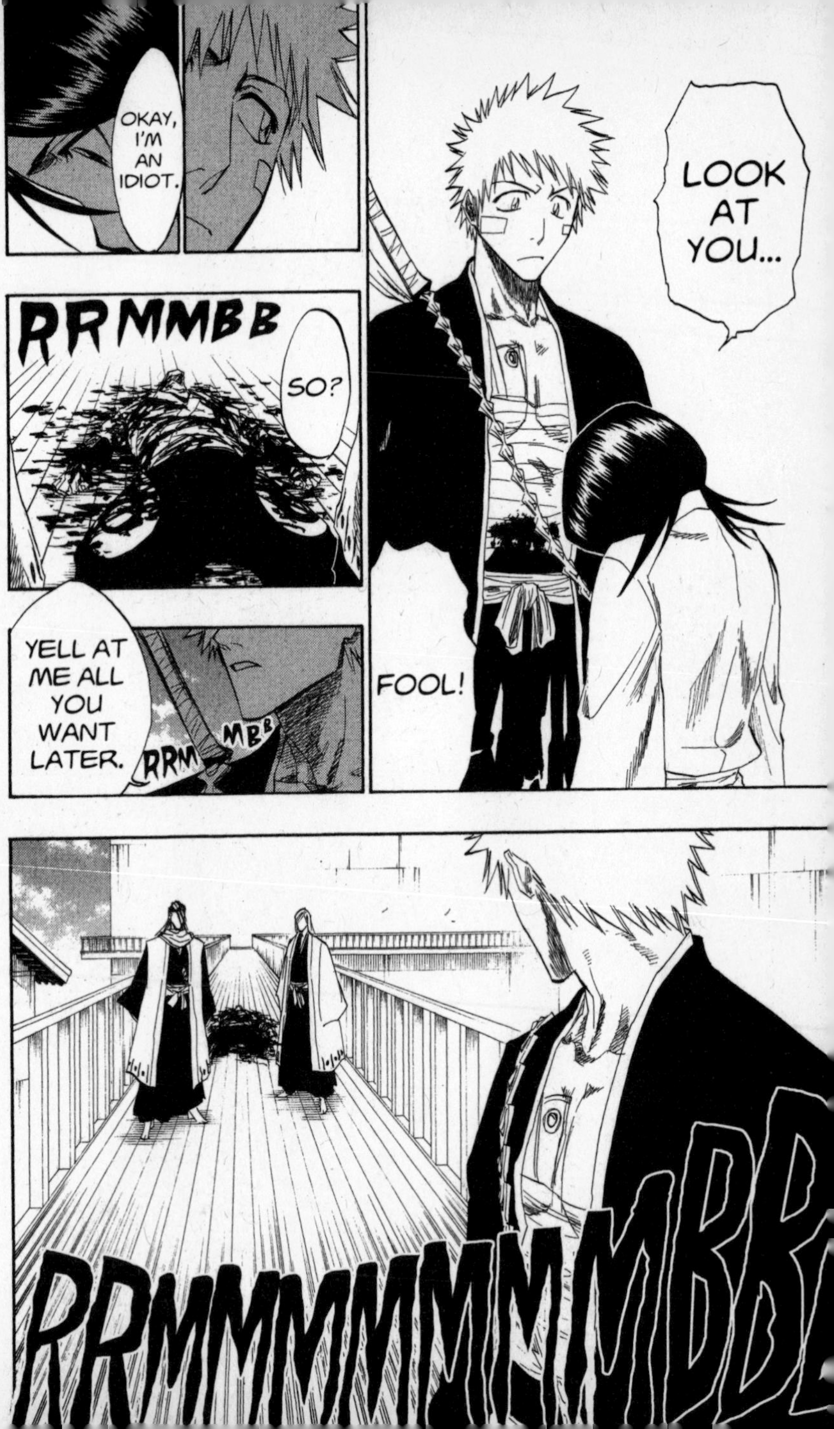
LOOK AT YOU...
FOOL!
OKAY, I'M AN IDIOT.
RRMMBB
SO?
YELL AT ME ALL YOU WANT LATER.
RRMMBB
RRMMMMMMMBB

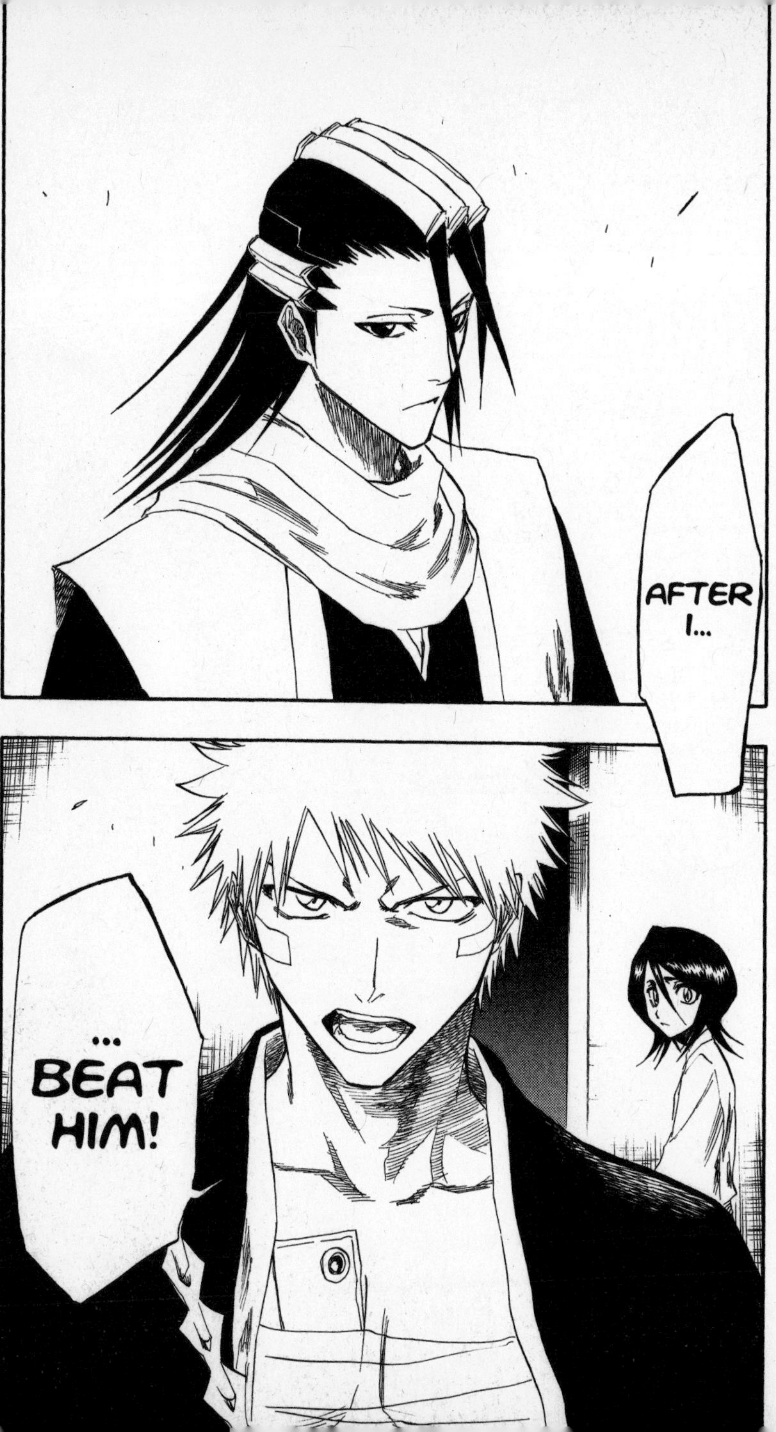
AFTER I...
... BEAT HIM!

"MEANWHILE, IN THE WORLD OF THE LIVING," SERIES 2

♡ MIDORIKO'S SECRET DIARY ♡

5TH GRADE, CLASS 1, #13, MIDORIKO TÔNO, JULY 21. SUNNY. TODAY MY LONG-AWAITED SUMMER VACATION FINALLY BEGINS!

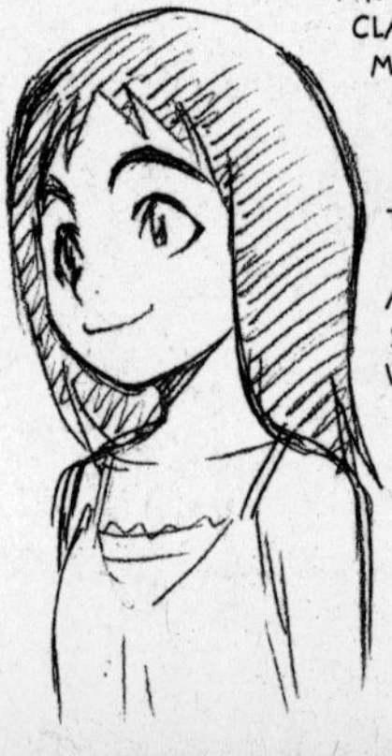

I WAS AT YUZU AND KARIN'S BECK AND CALL DURING FIRST SEMESTER, AS USUAL, BUT NOW THAT I'M FREE OF THEM, I'M GOING TO HAVE LOTS OF FUN! I'M REALLY EXCITED TO KNOW WHAT MEMORIES I'LL MAKE OVER THE SUMMER. ♡ I WISH SUMMER VACATION WOULD NEVER END! ♪

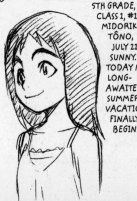

117. Remnant 2 (Deny the Shadow)

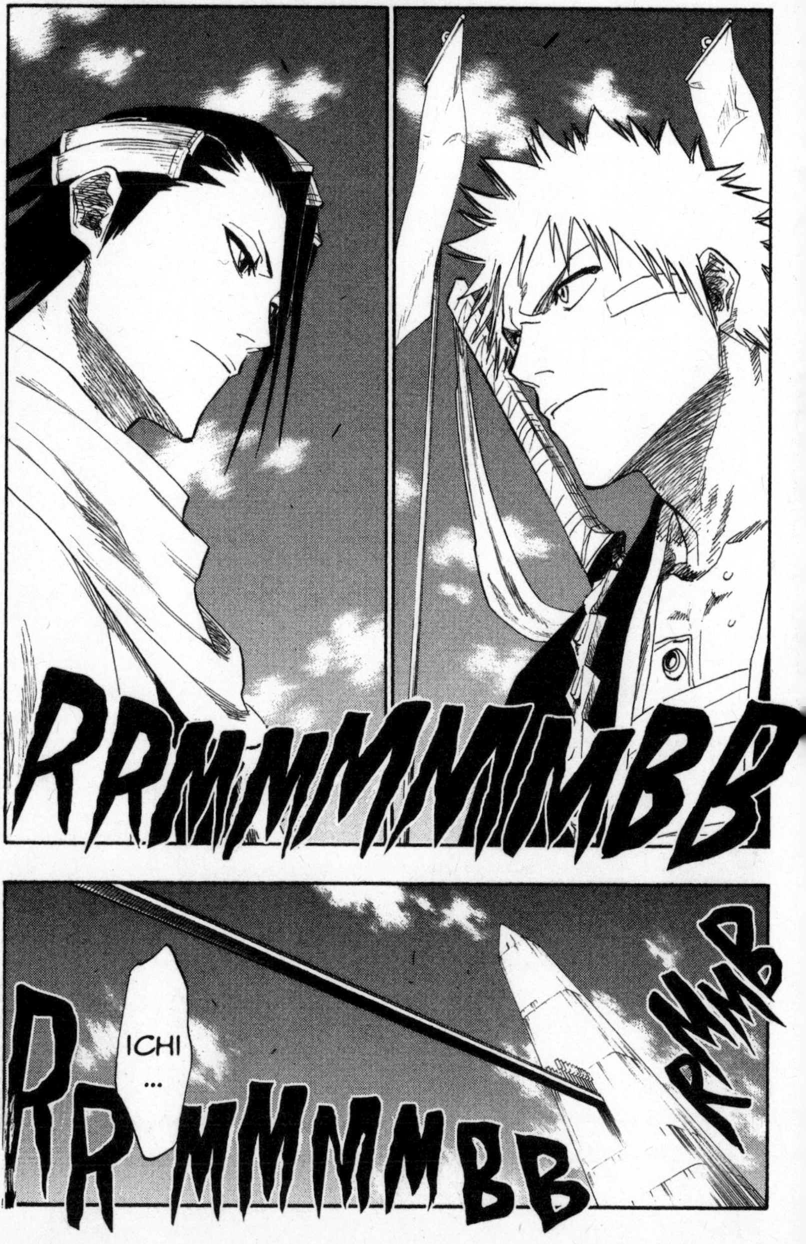
RRMMMMMMBB
RMMB
ICHI ...
RRMMMMMBB

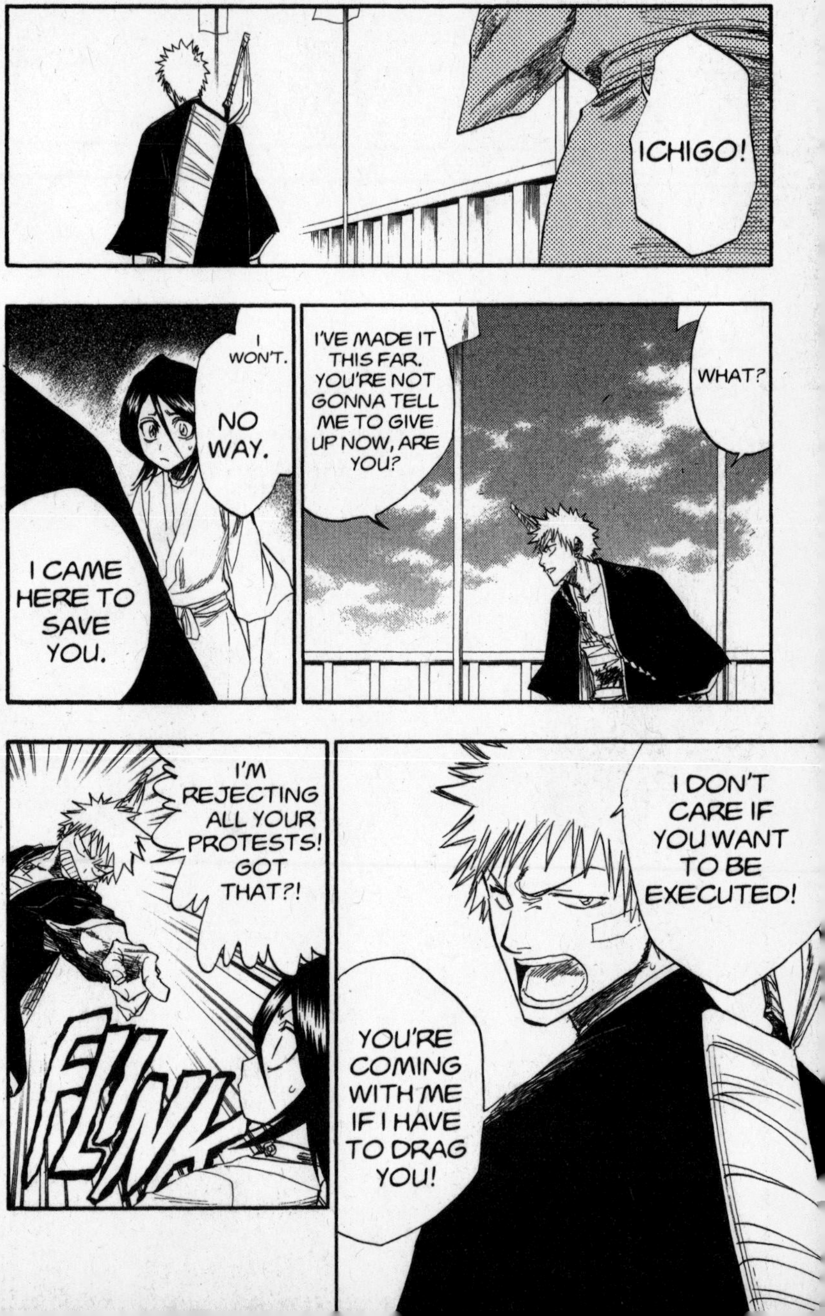
ICHIGO!
WHAT?
I'VE MADE IT THIS FAR. YOU'RE NOT GONNA TELL ME TO GIVE UP NOW, ARE YOU?
I WON'T.
NO WAY.
I CAME HERE TO SAVE YOU.
I DON'T CARE IF YOU WANT TO BE EXECUTED!
YOU'RE COMING WITH ME IF I HAVE TO DRAG YOU!
I'M REJECTING ALL YOUR PROTESTS! GOT THAT?!
FLINK

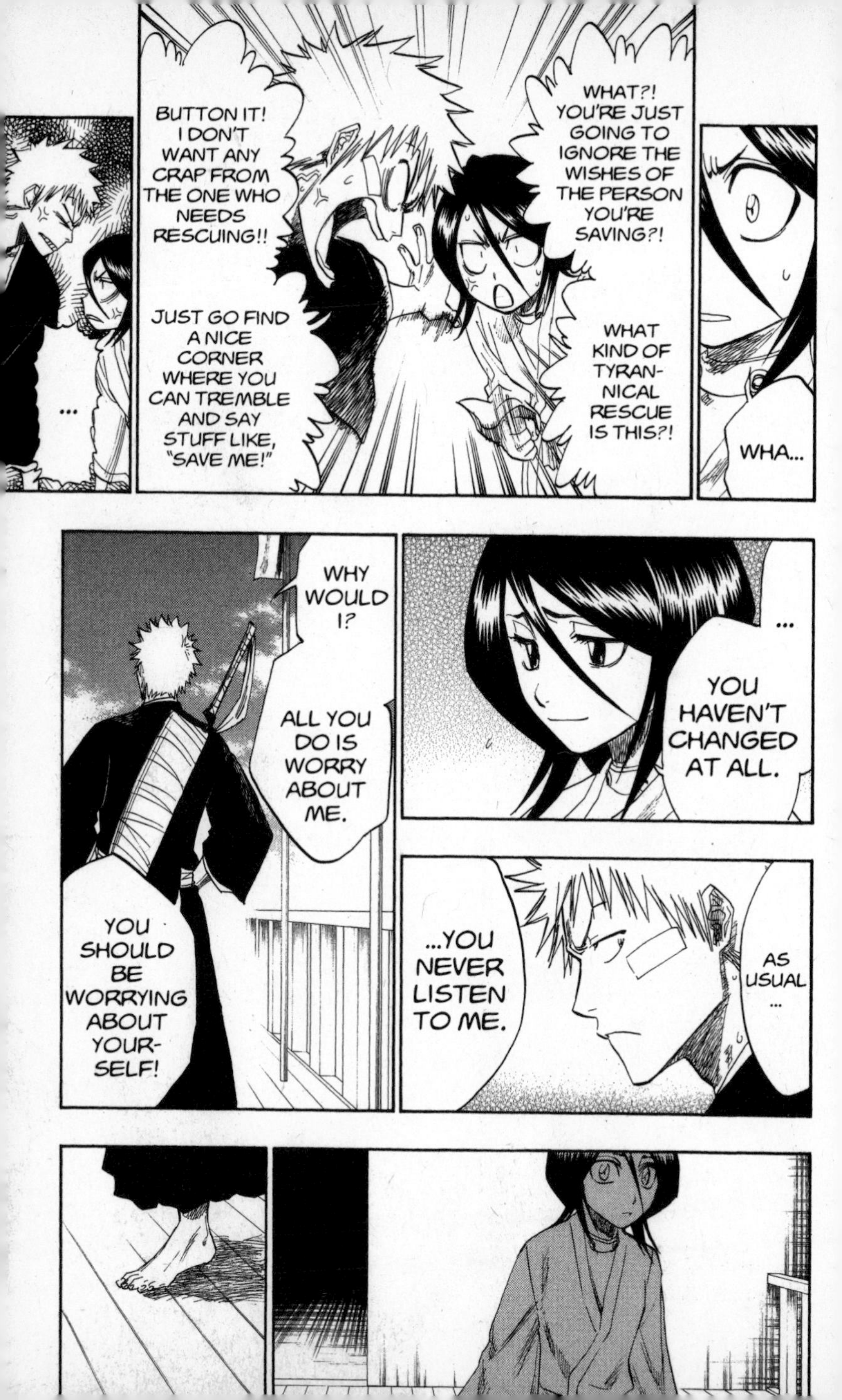
WHA...
WHAT?! YOU'RE JUST GOING TO IGNORE THE WISHES OF THE PERSON YOU'RE SAVING?!
BUTTON IT! I DON'T WANT ANY CRAP FROM THE ONE WHO NEEDS RESCUING!!
WHAT KIND OF TYRAN-NICAL RESCUE IS THIS?!
JUST GO FIND A NICE CORNER WHERE YOU CAN TREMBLE AND SAY STUFF LIKE, "SAVE ME!"
...
...
YOU HAVEN'T CHANGED AT ALL.
AS USUAL...
...YOU NEVER LISTEN TO ME.
WHY WOULD I?
ALL YOU DO IS WORRY ABOUT ME.
YOU SHOULD BE WORRYING ABOUT YOUR-SELF!

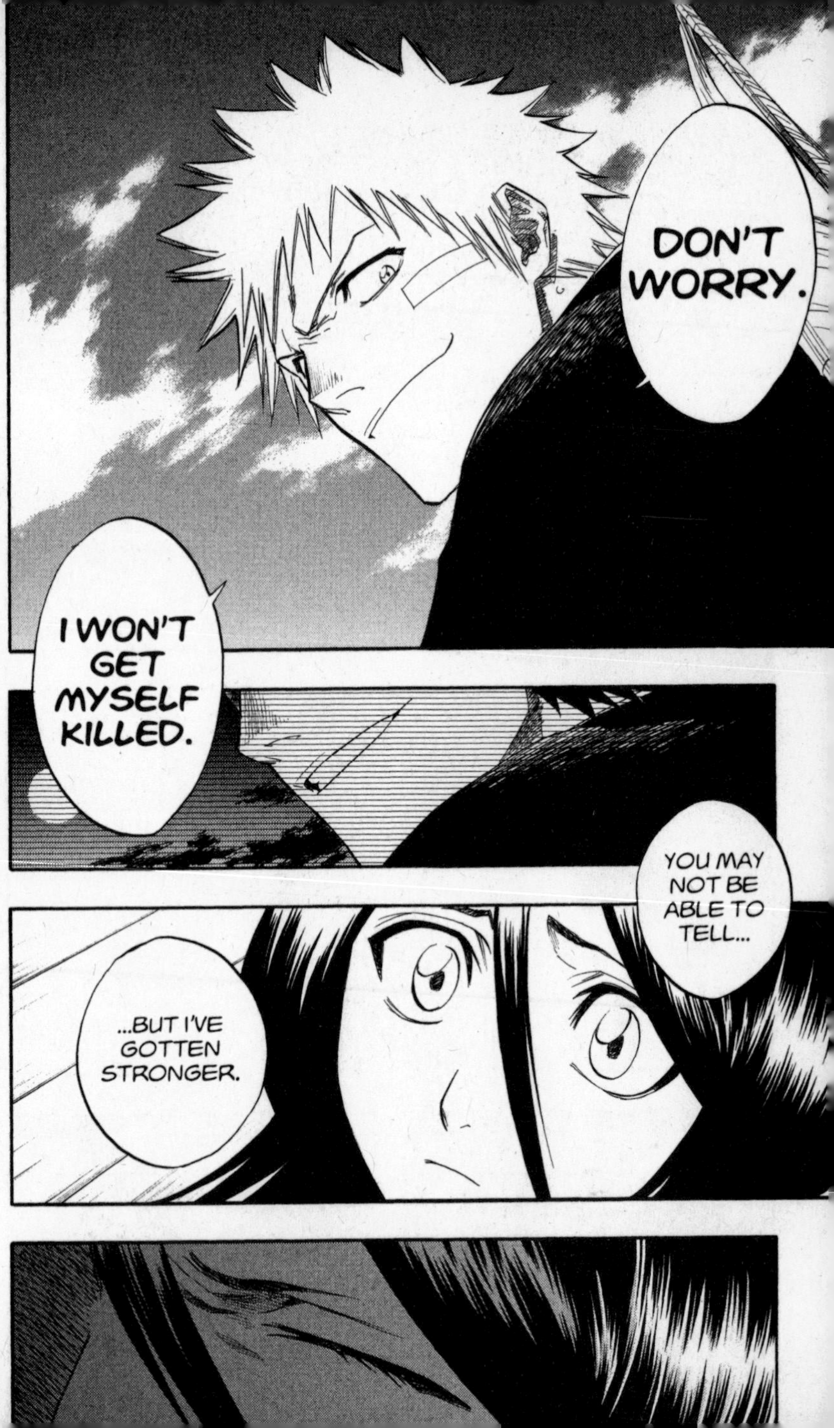
DON'T WORRY.
I WON'T GET MYSELF KILLED.
YOU MAY NOT BE ABLE TO TELL...
...BUT I'VE GOTTEN STRONGER.

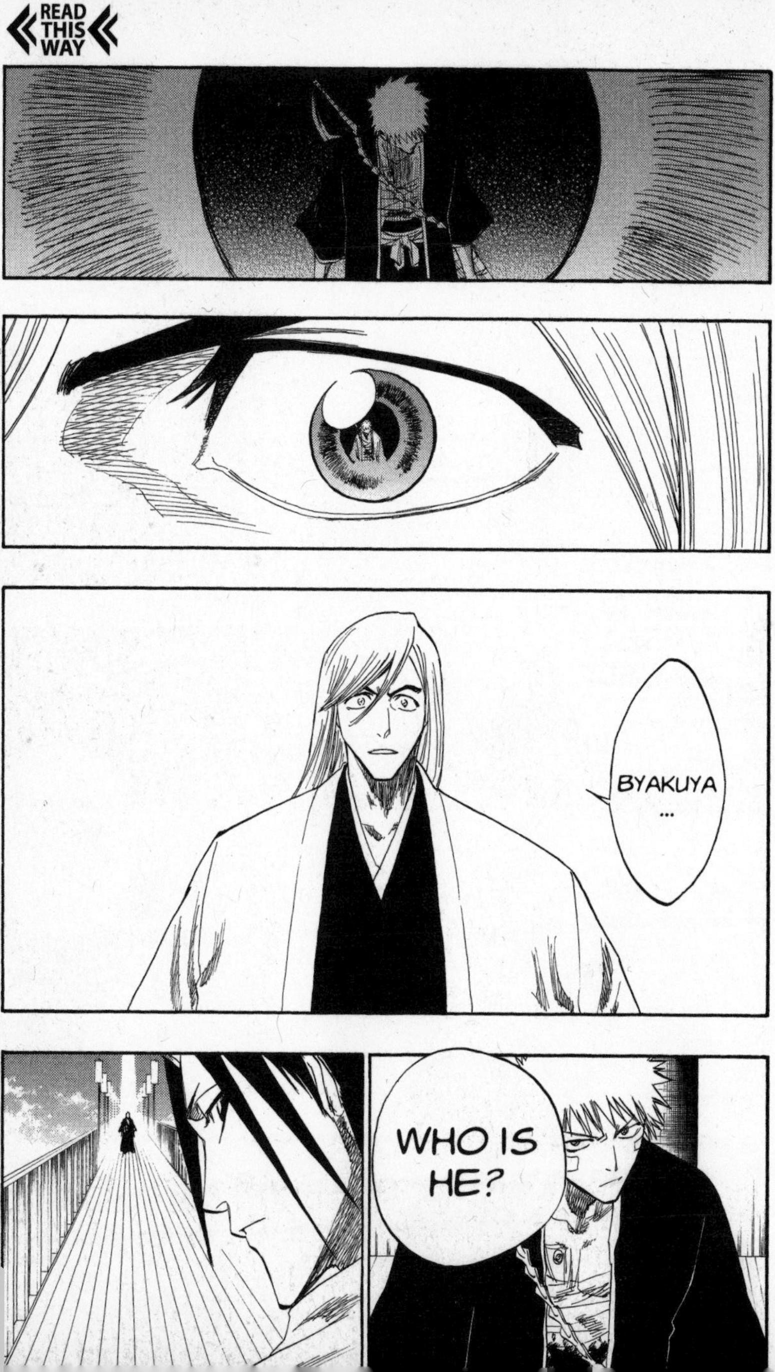
READ THIS WAY
BYAKUYA ...
WHO IS HE?

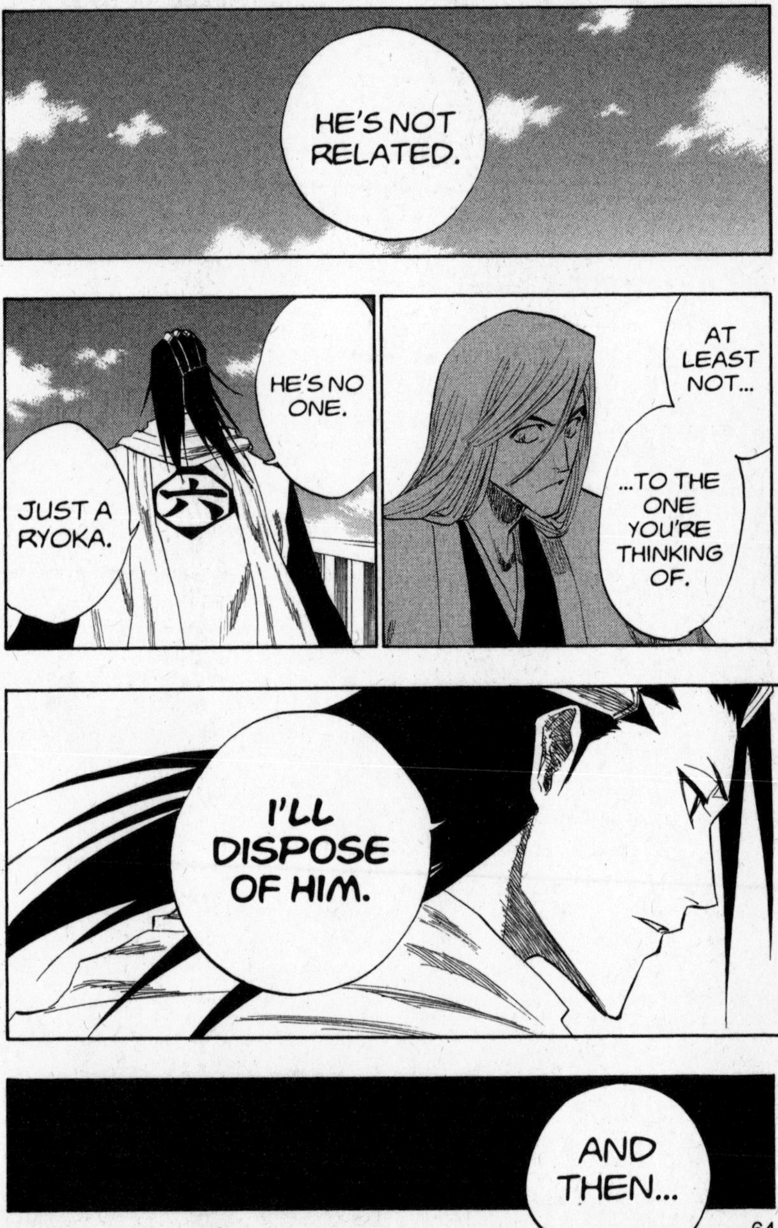
HE'S NOT RELATED.
AT LEAST NOT...
...TO THE ONE YOU'RE THINKING OF.
HE'S NO ONE.
JUST A RYOKA.
I'LL DISPOSE OF HIM.
AND THEN...

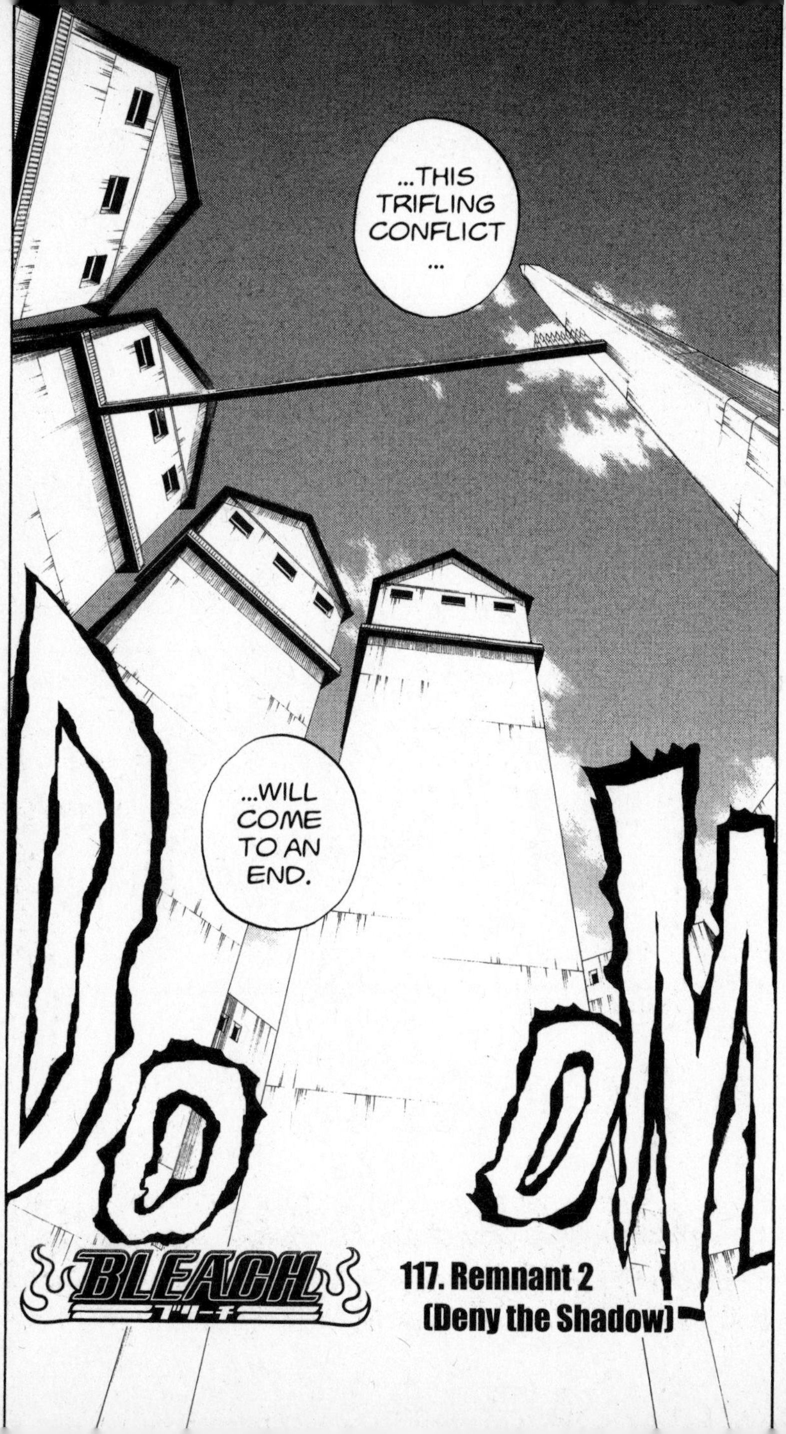
...THIS TRIFLING CONFLICT ...
...WILL COME TO AN END.
DOOM
BLEACH
ブリーチ
117. Remnant 2
(Deny the Shadow)

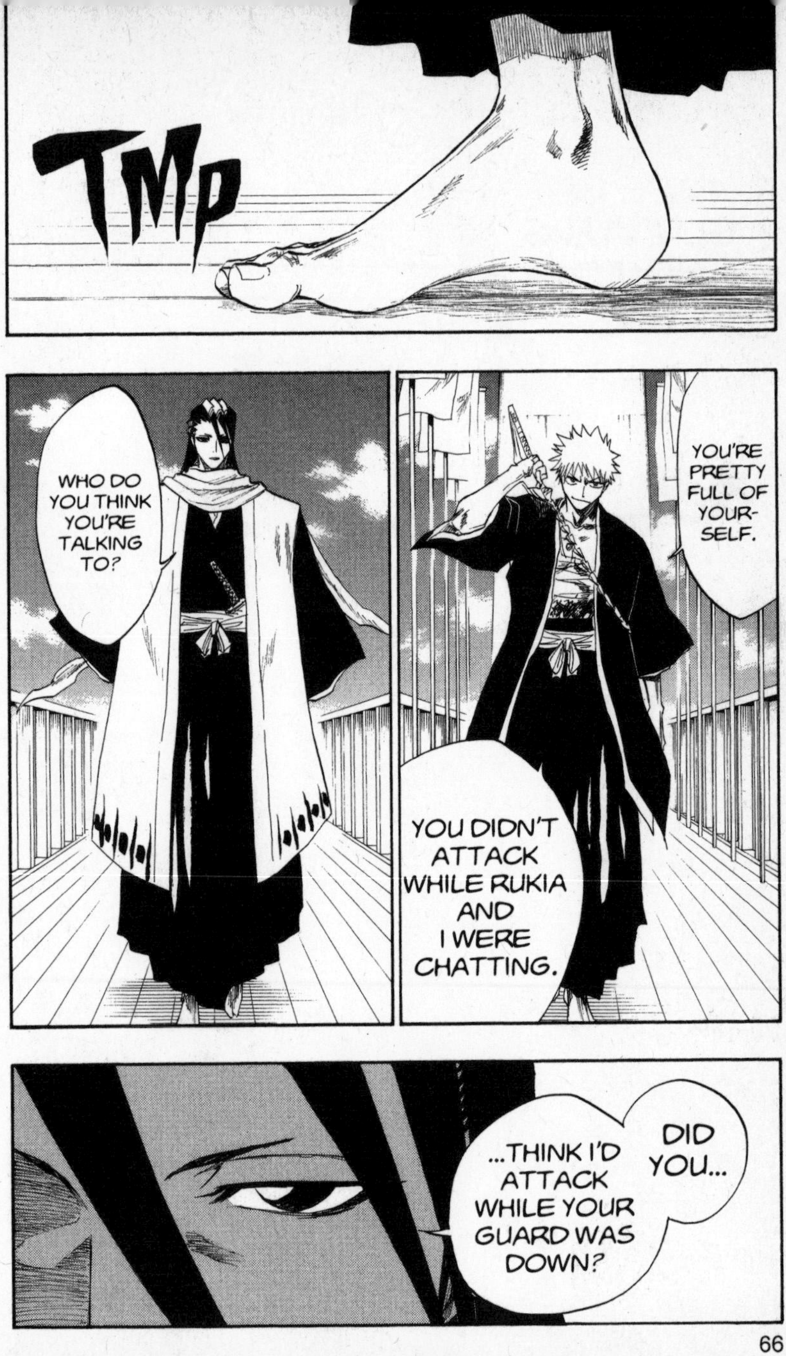
TMP
YOU'RE PRETTY FULL OF YOUR-SELF.
YOU DIDN'T ATTACK WHILE RUKIA AND I WERE CHATTING.
WHO DO YOU THINK YOU'RE TALKING TO?
DID YOU...
...THINK I'D ATTACK WHILE YOUR GUARD WAS DOWN?

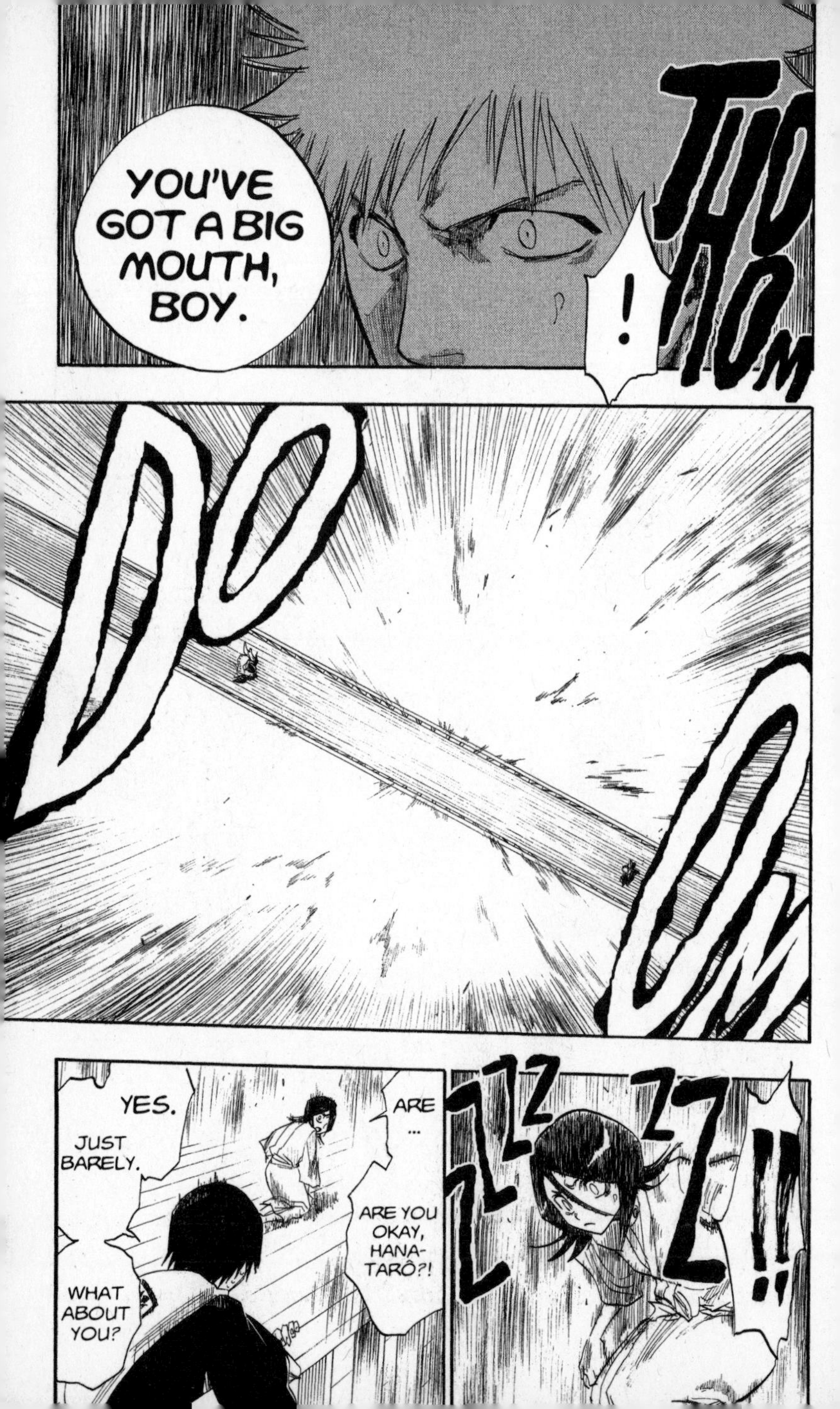
THO
OOM
!
YOU'VE GOT A BIG MOUTH, BOY.
DO
OOM
ZZZZZ!!
ARE ...
ARE YOU OKAY, HANATARÔ?!
YES.
JUST BARELY.
WHAT ABOUT YOU?

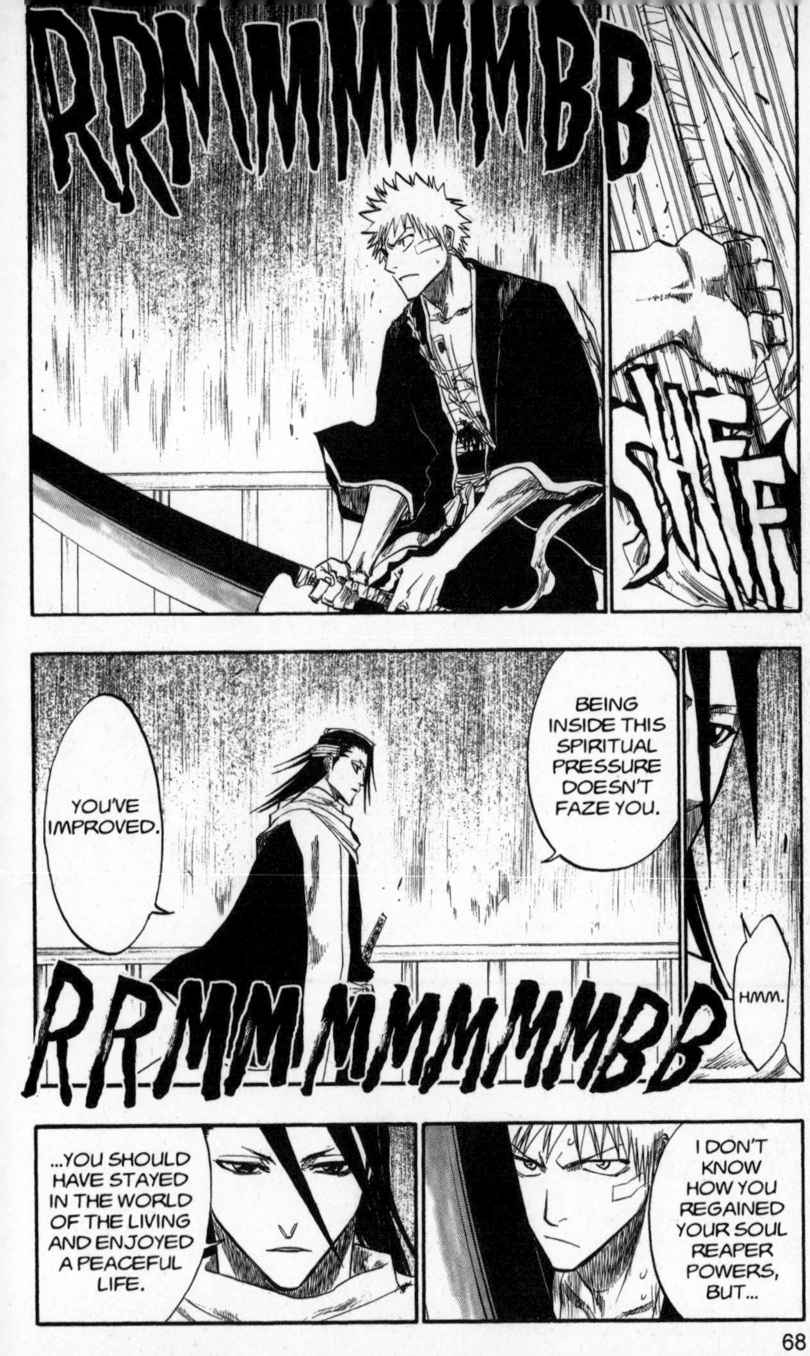
SHF
RRMMMMMBB
HMM.
BEING INSIDE THIS SPIRITUAL PRESSURE DOESN'T FAZE YOU.
YOU'VE IMPROVED.
RRMMMMMMMBB
I DON'T KNOW HOW YOU REGAINED YOUR SOUL REAPER POWERS, BUT...
...YOU SHOULD HAVE STAYED IN THE WORLD OF THE LIVING AND ENJOYED A PEACEFUL LIFE.

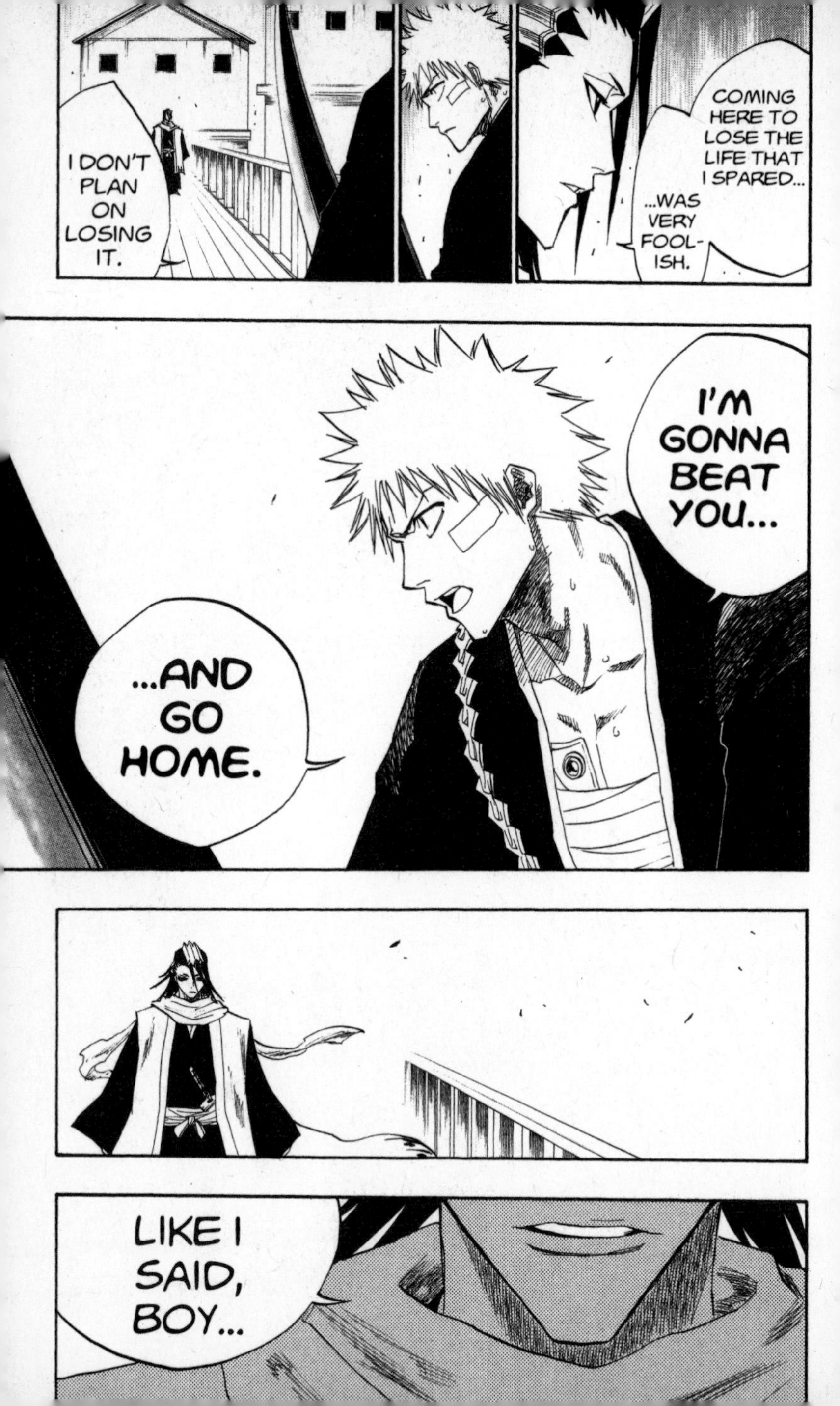
COMING HERE TO LOSE THE LIFE THAT I SPARED...
...WAS VERY FOOL-ISH.
I DON'T PLAN ON LOSING IT.
I'M GONNA BEAT YOU...
...AND GO HOME.
LIKE I SAID, BOY...

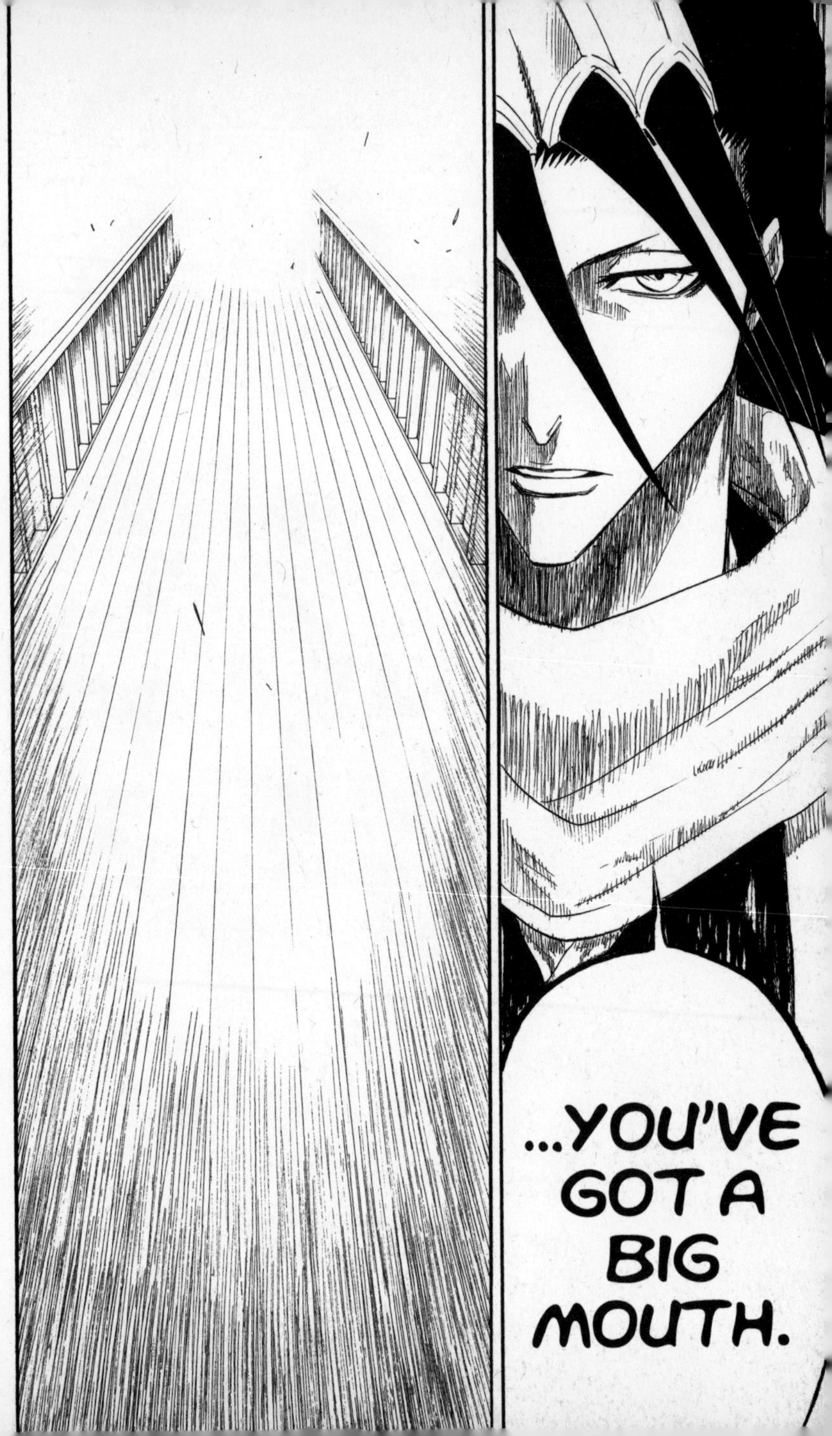
...YOU'VE GOT A BIG MOUTH.

READ THIS WAY

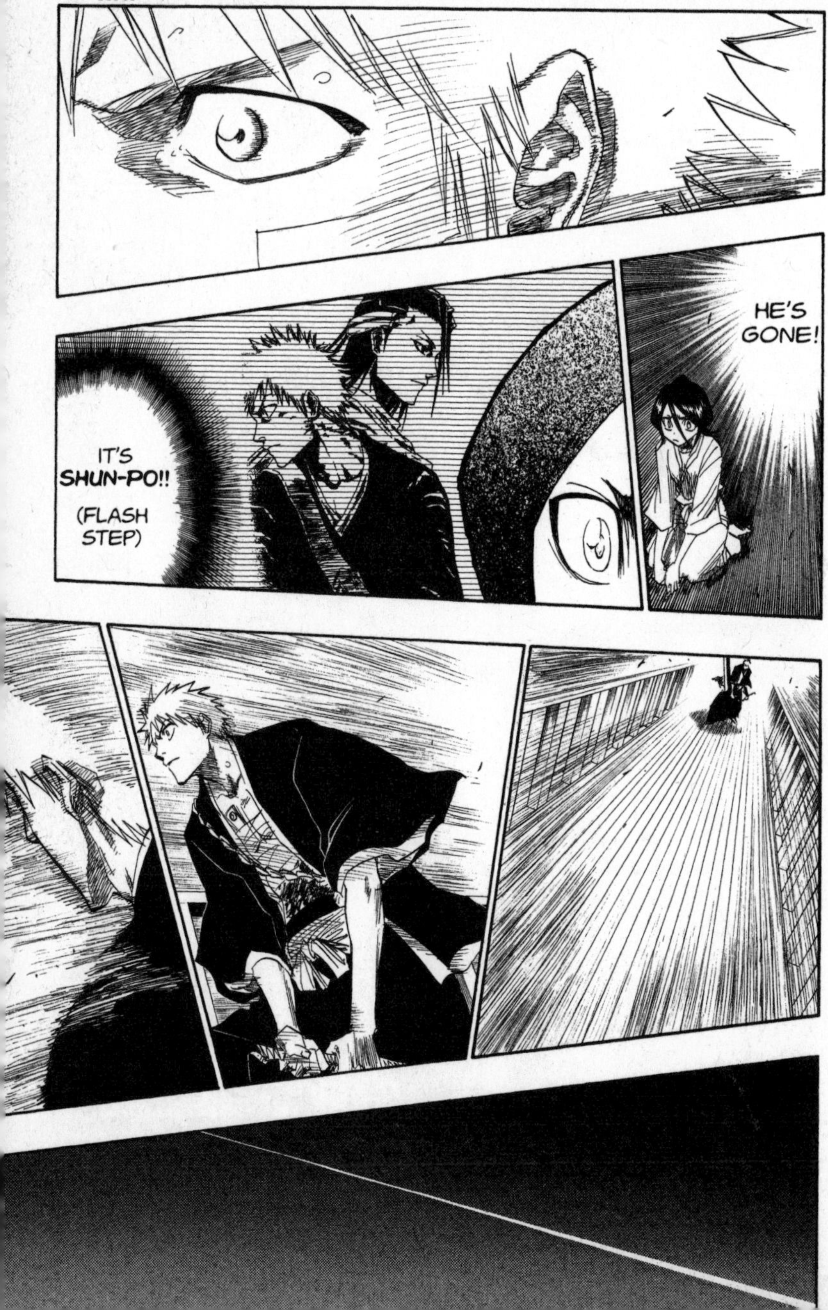
HE'S GONE!
IT'S SHUN-PO!!
(FLASH STEP)

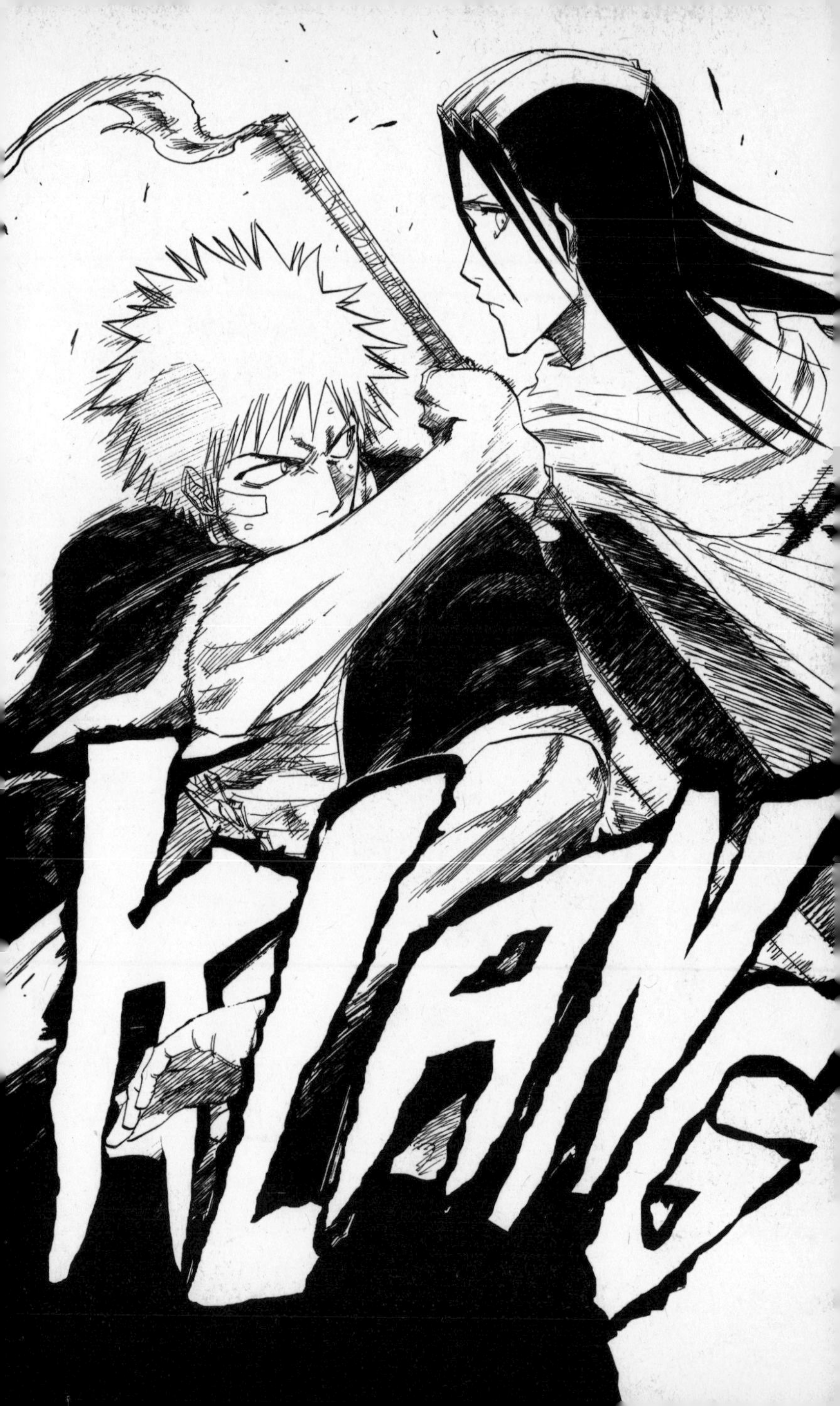
KLANG

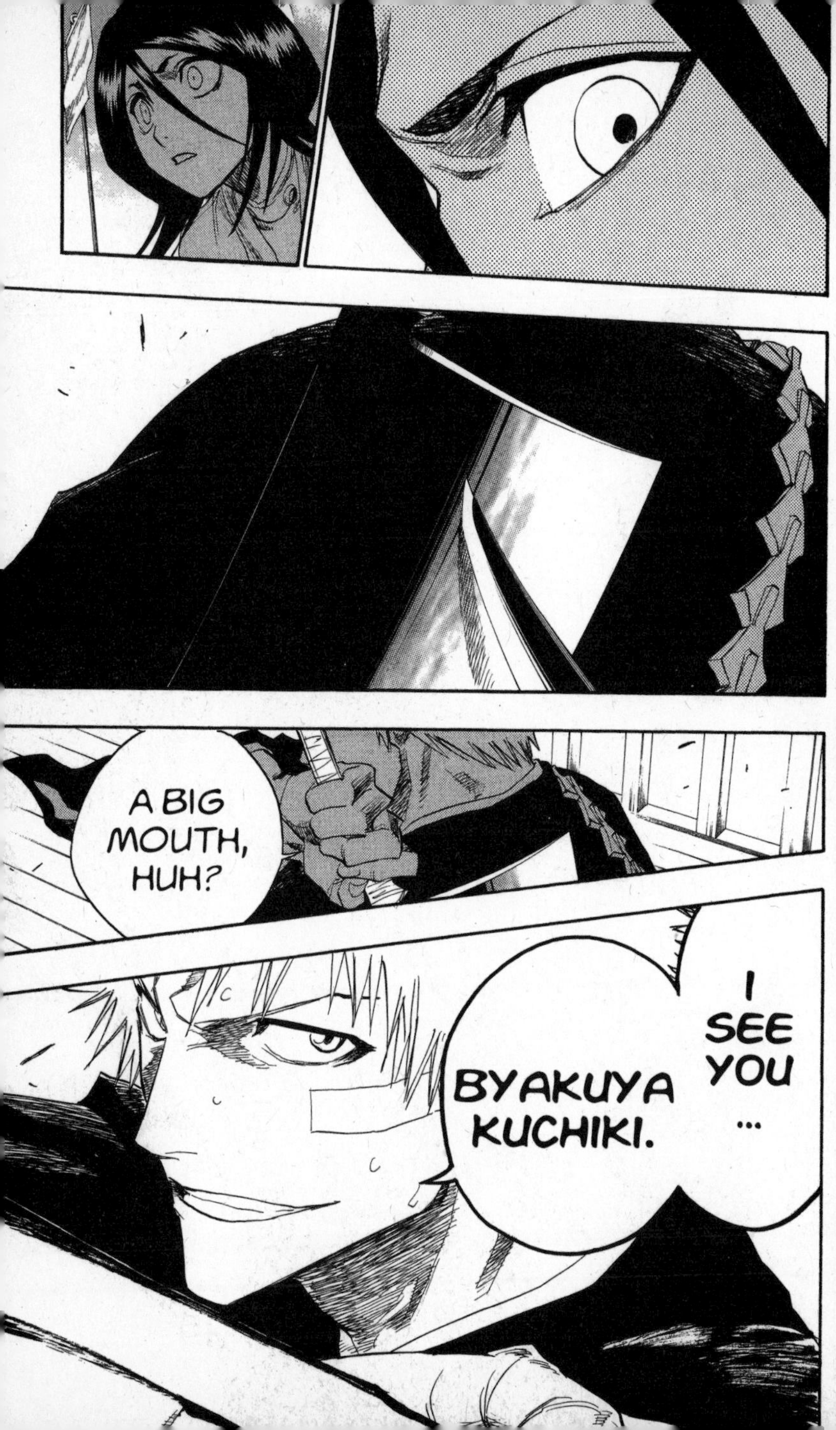
A BIG MOUTH, HUH?
I SEE YOU ...
BYAKUYA KUCHIKI.

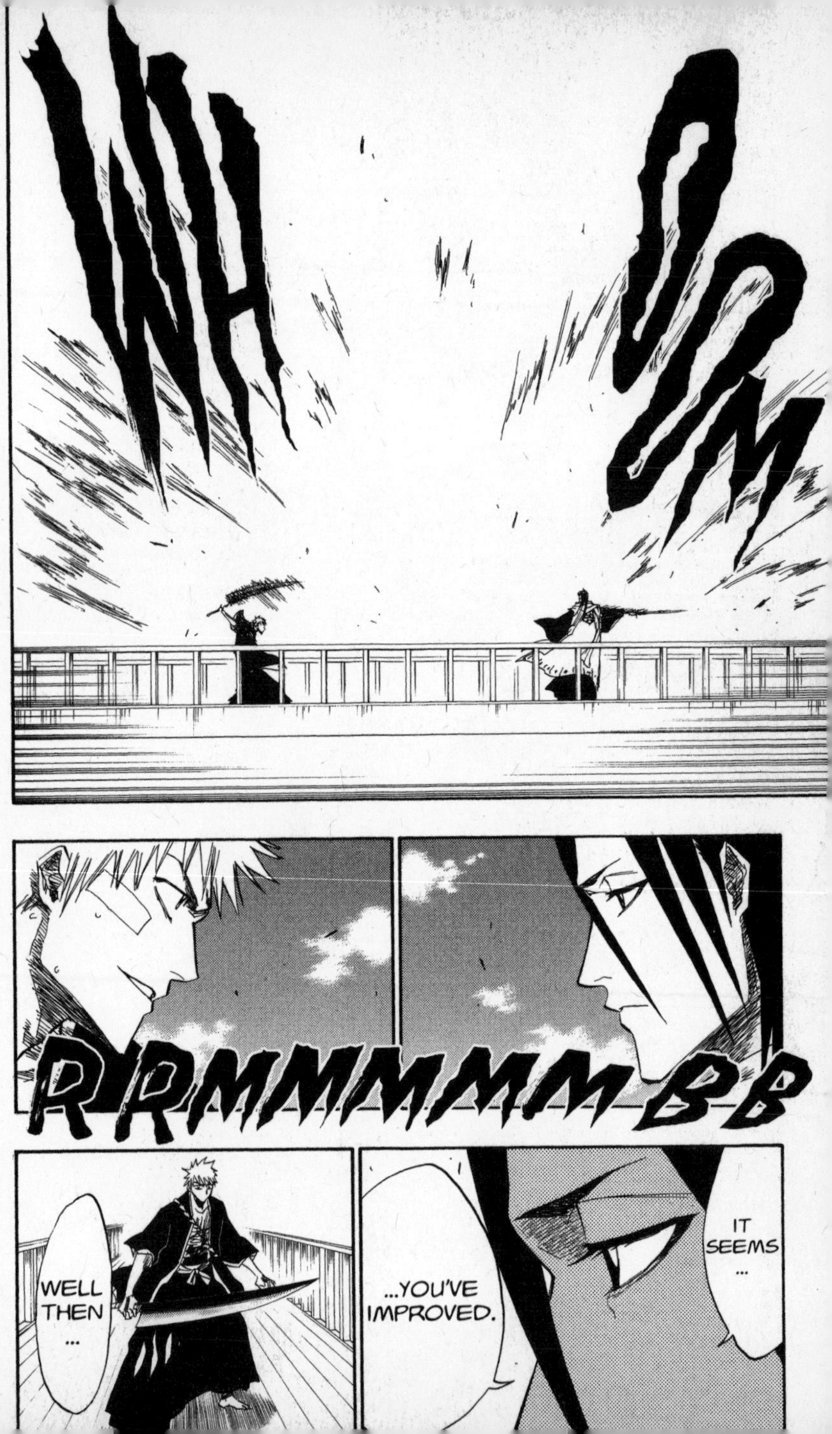
RRMMMMMM BB
IT SEEMS ...
...YOU'VE IMPROVED.
WELL THEN ...

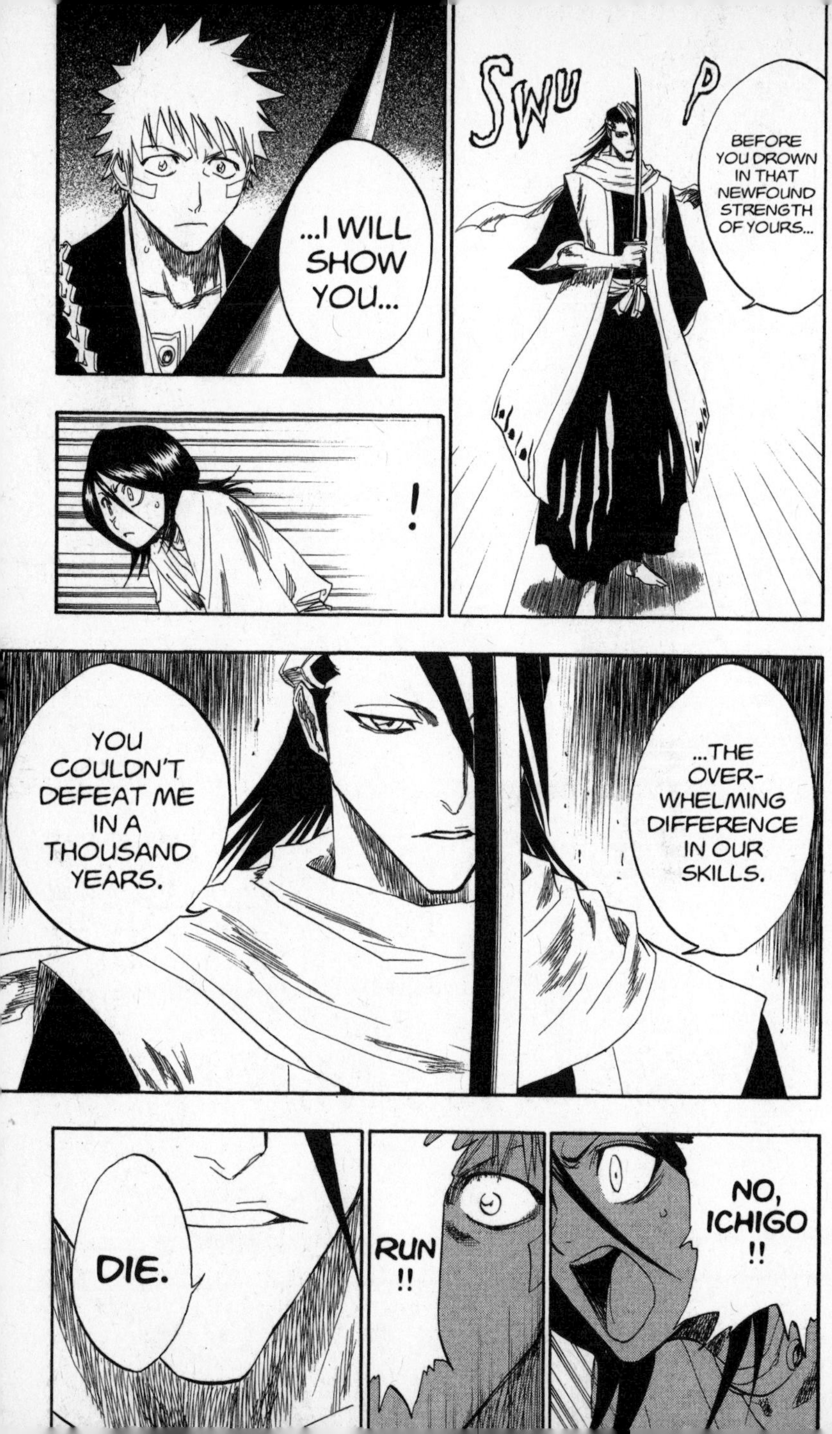
SWUP
BEFORE YOU DROWN IN THAT NEWFOUND STRENGTH OF YOURS...
...I WILL SHOW YOU...
!
...THE OVER-WHELMING DIFFERENCE IN OUR SKILLS.
YOU COULDN'T DEFEAT ME IN A THOUSAND YEARS.
NO, ICHIGO!!
RUN!!
DIE.

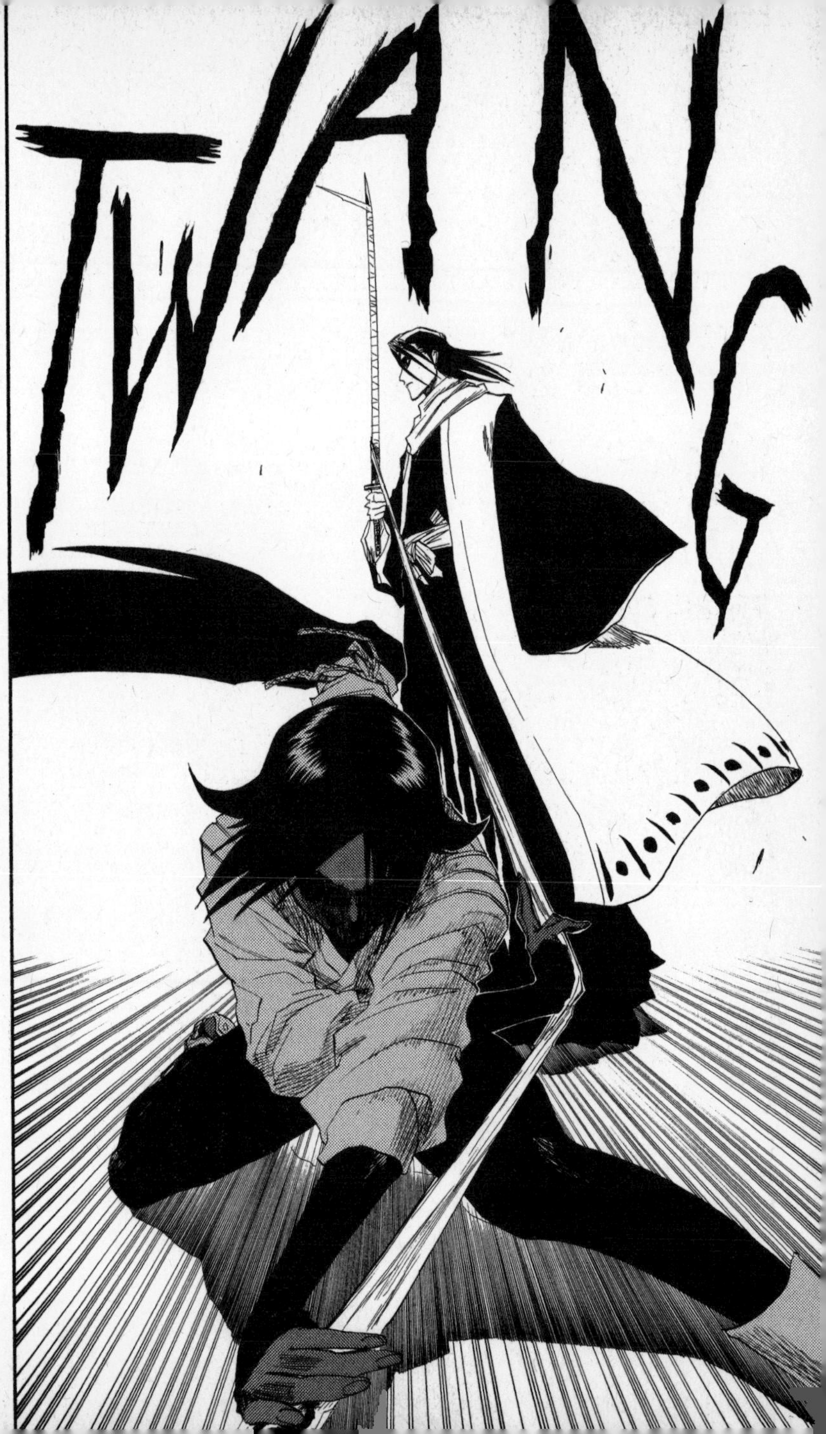
TWANG

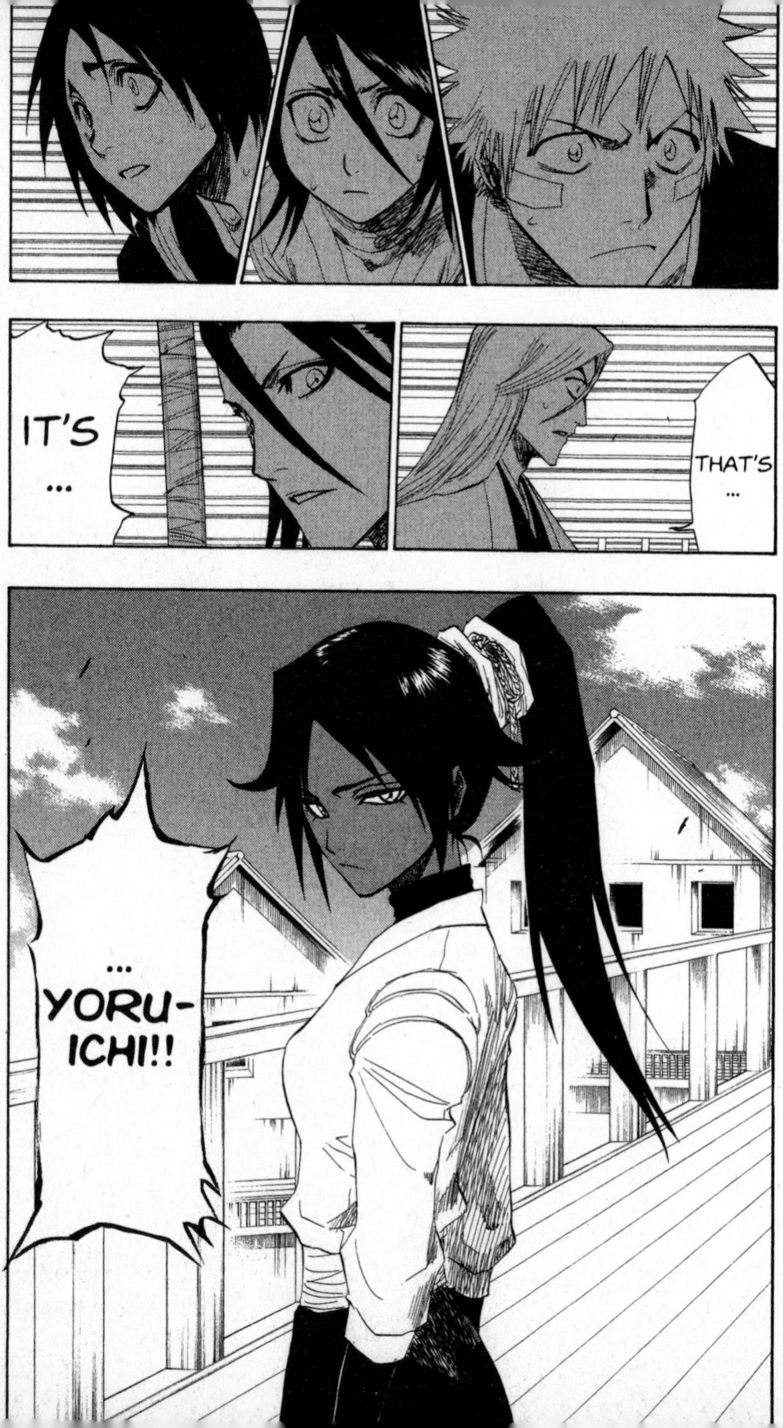
THAT'S ...
IT'S ...
... YORU-ICHI!!

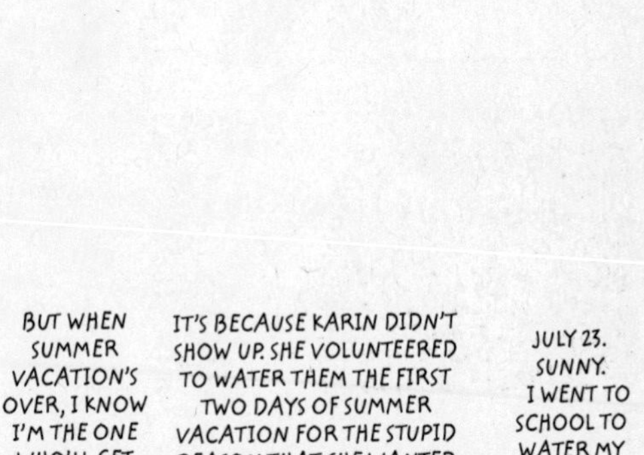
JULY 23. SUNNY. I WENT TO SCHOOL TO WATER MY CLASSMATES' CHRYSANTHE-MUMS. EVERY SINGLE ONE OF THEM WAS DEAD.
IT'S BECAUSE KARIN DIDN'T SHOW UP. SHE VOLUNTEERED TO WATER THEM THE FIRST TWO DAYS OF SUMMER VACATION FOR THE STUPID REASON THAT SHE WANTED TO GET IT OVER WITH.
BUT WHEN SUMMER VACATION'S OVER, I KNOW I'M THE ONE WHO'LL GET THE BLAME.
OH... IF ONLY SUMMER VACATION WOULD NEVER END.

118. Supernal Tag

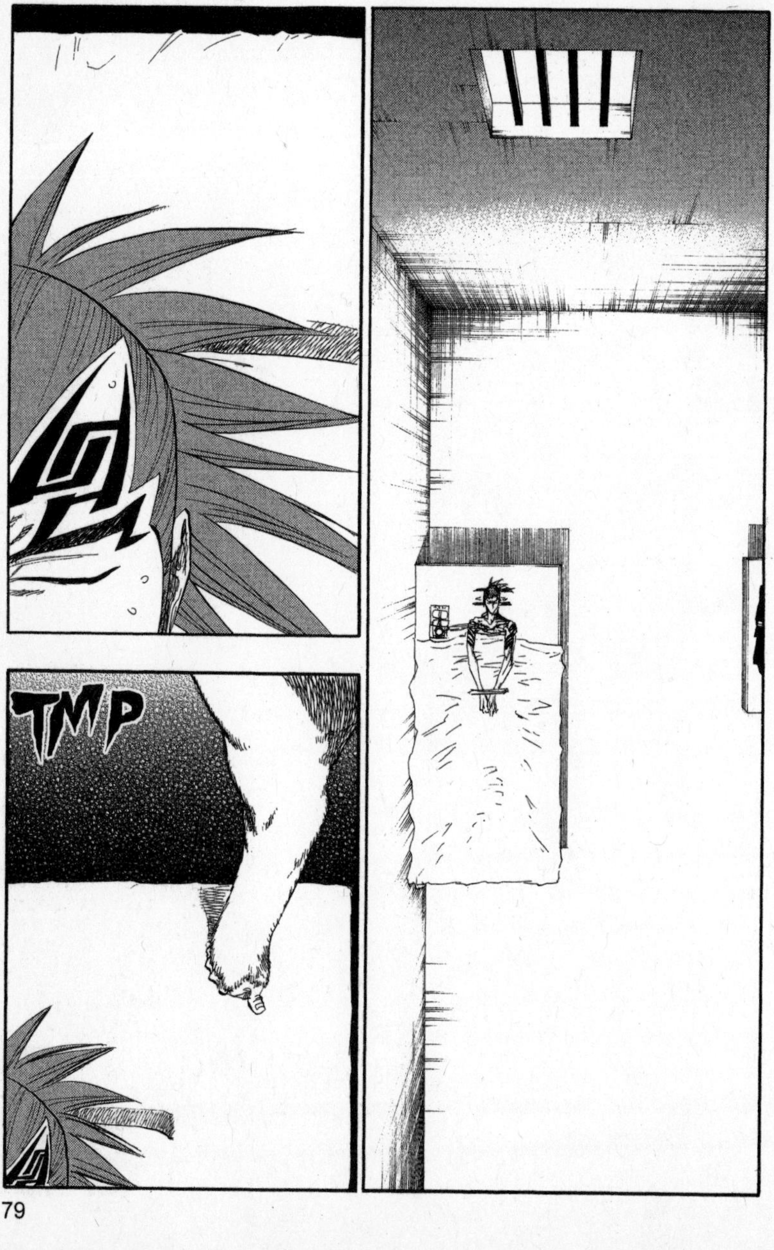
TMP

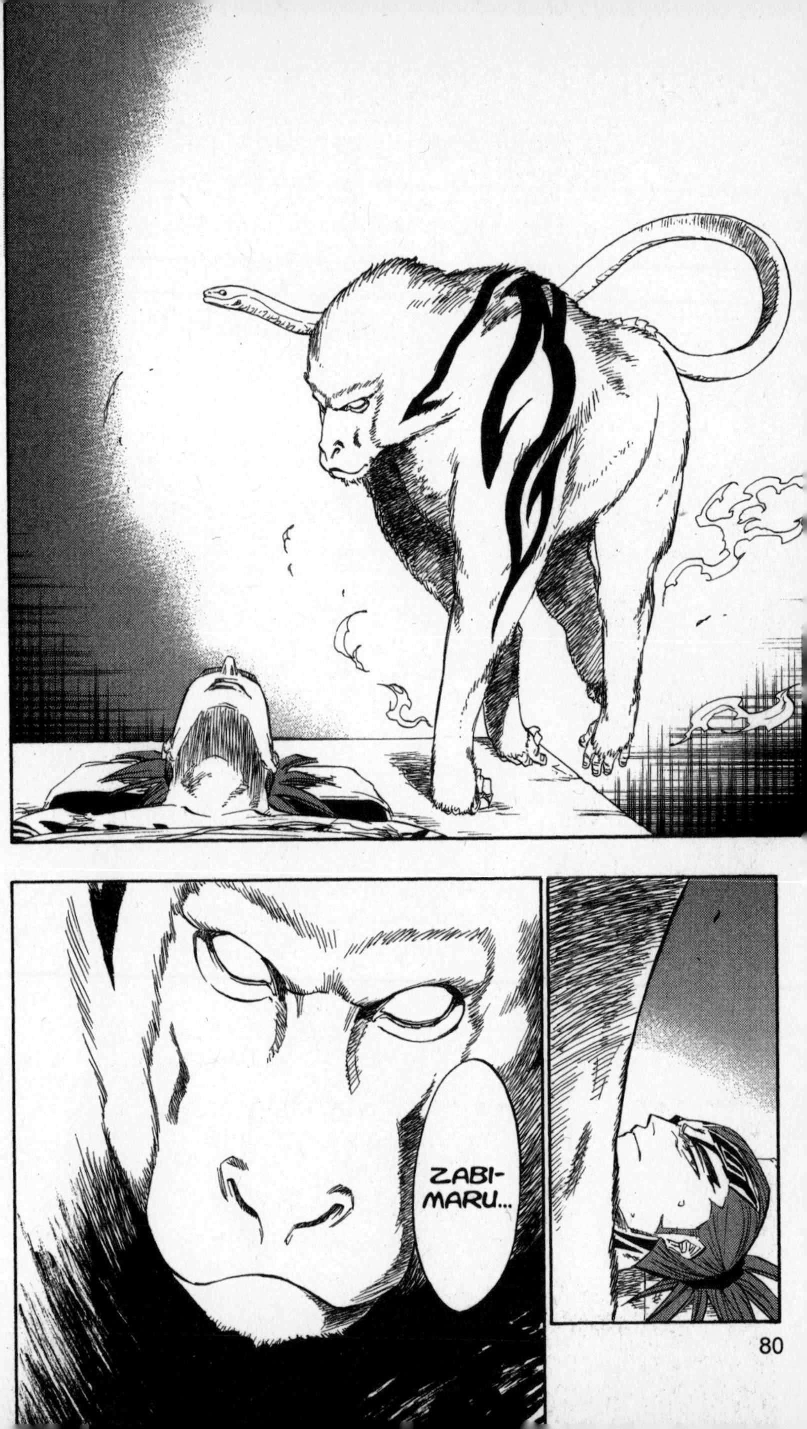
ZABI-
MARU...

READ THIS WAY

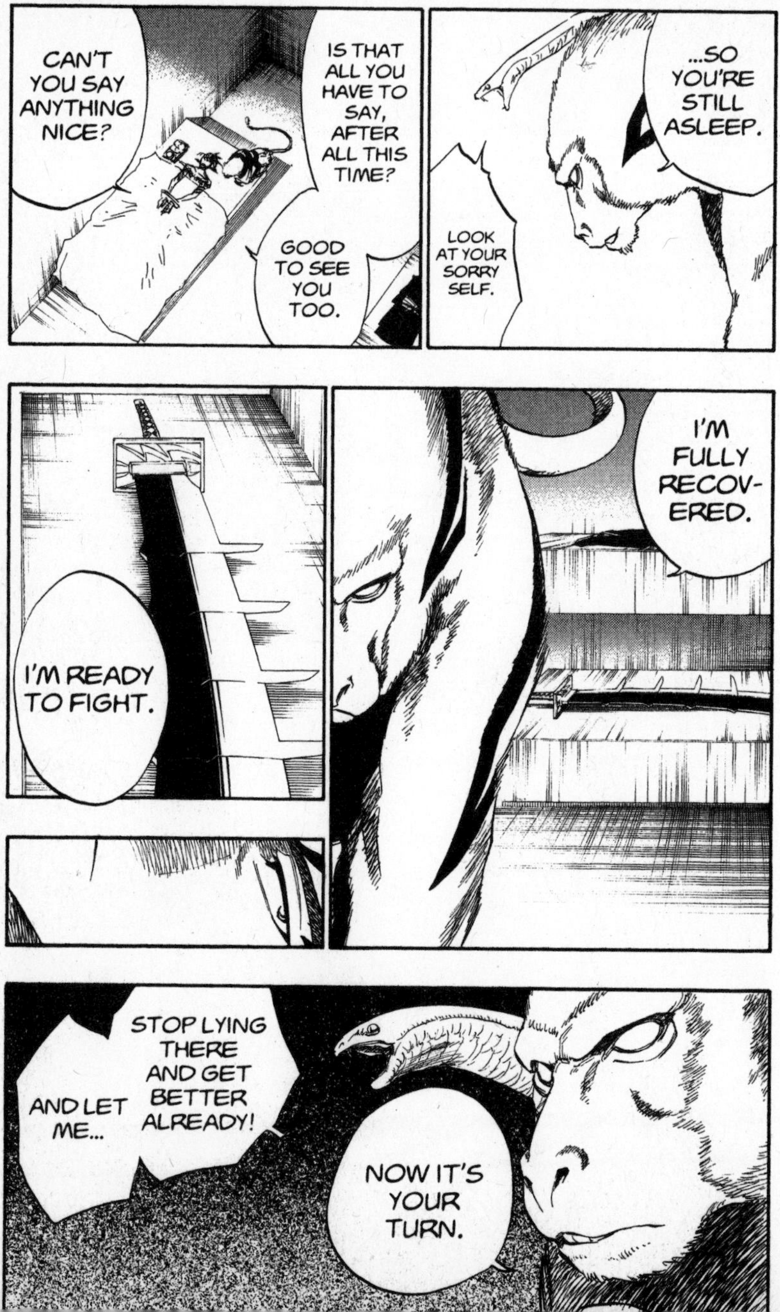

...SO YOU'RE STILL ASLEEP.
LOOK AT YOUR SORRY SELF.
IS THAT ALL YOU HAVE TO SAY, AFTER ALL THIS TIME?
GOOD TO SEE YOU TOO.
CAN'T YOU SAY ANYTHING NICE?
I'M FULLY RECOV-ERED.
I'M READY TO FIGHT.
NOW IT'S YOUR TURN.
STOP LYING THERE AND GET BETTER ALREADY!
AND LET ME...

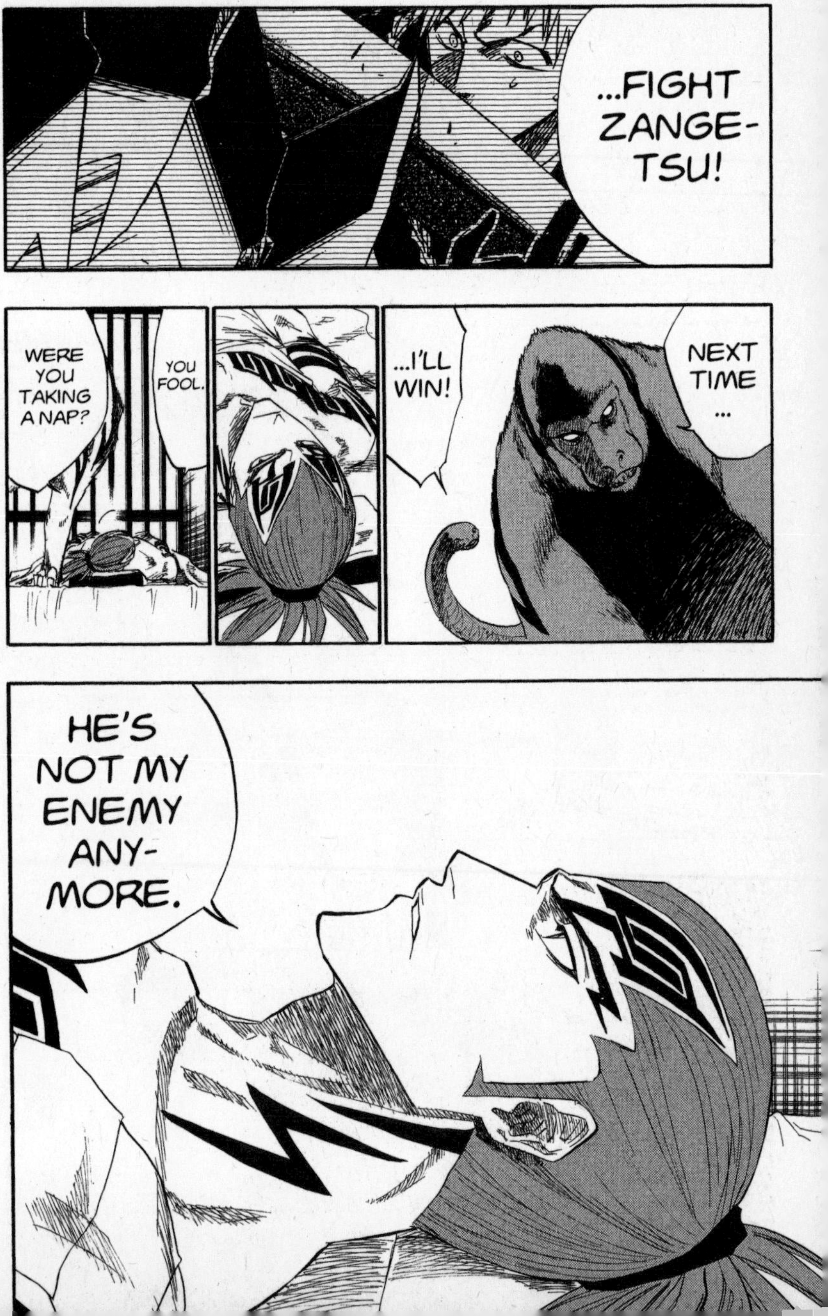
...FIGHT ZANGE-TSU!
NEXT TIME ...
...I'LL WIN!
YOU FOOL.
WERE YOU TAKING A NAP?
HE'S NOT MY ENEMY ANY-MORE.

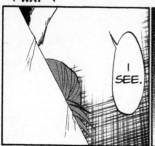

I SEE.

THEN WHO...

...IS YOUR ENEMY?

WHO WILL YOU FIGHT NOW?

118. Supernal Tag

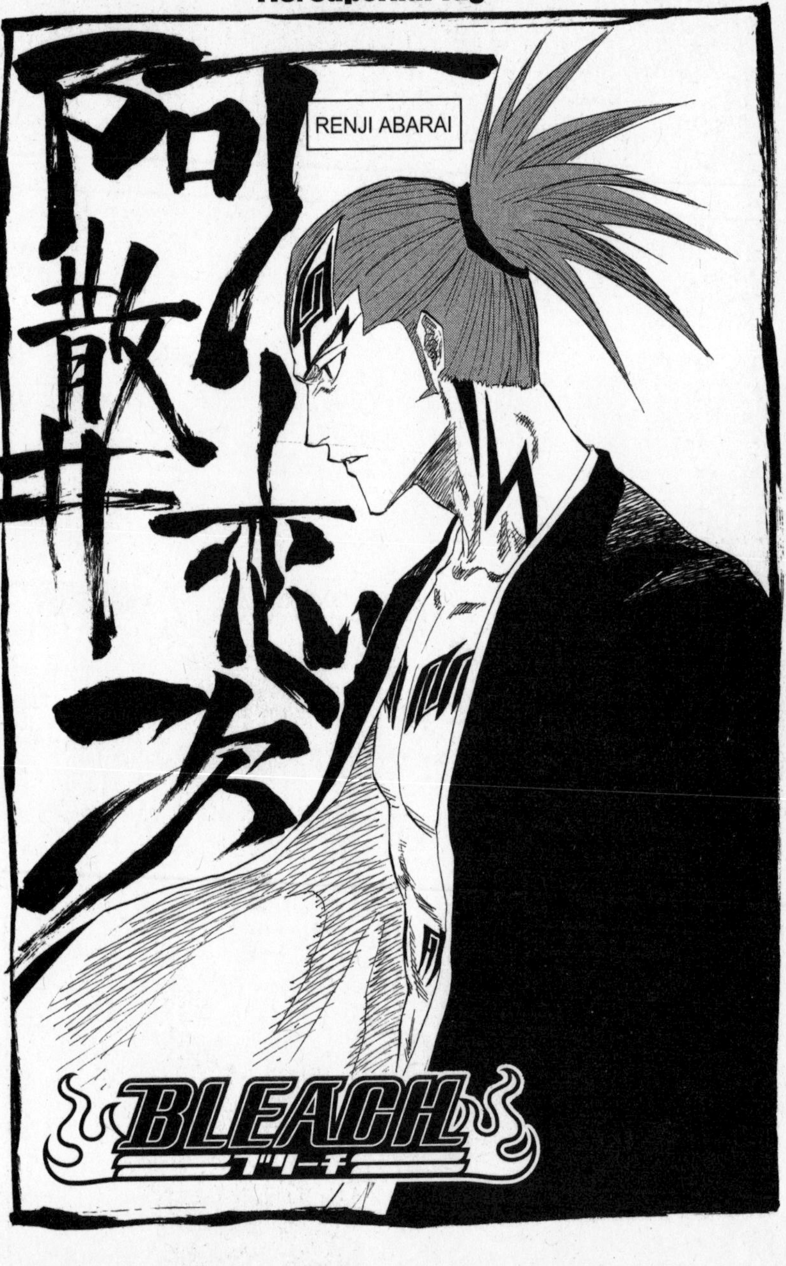

阿散井恋次
RENJI ABARAI
BLEACH
ブリーチ

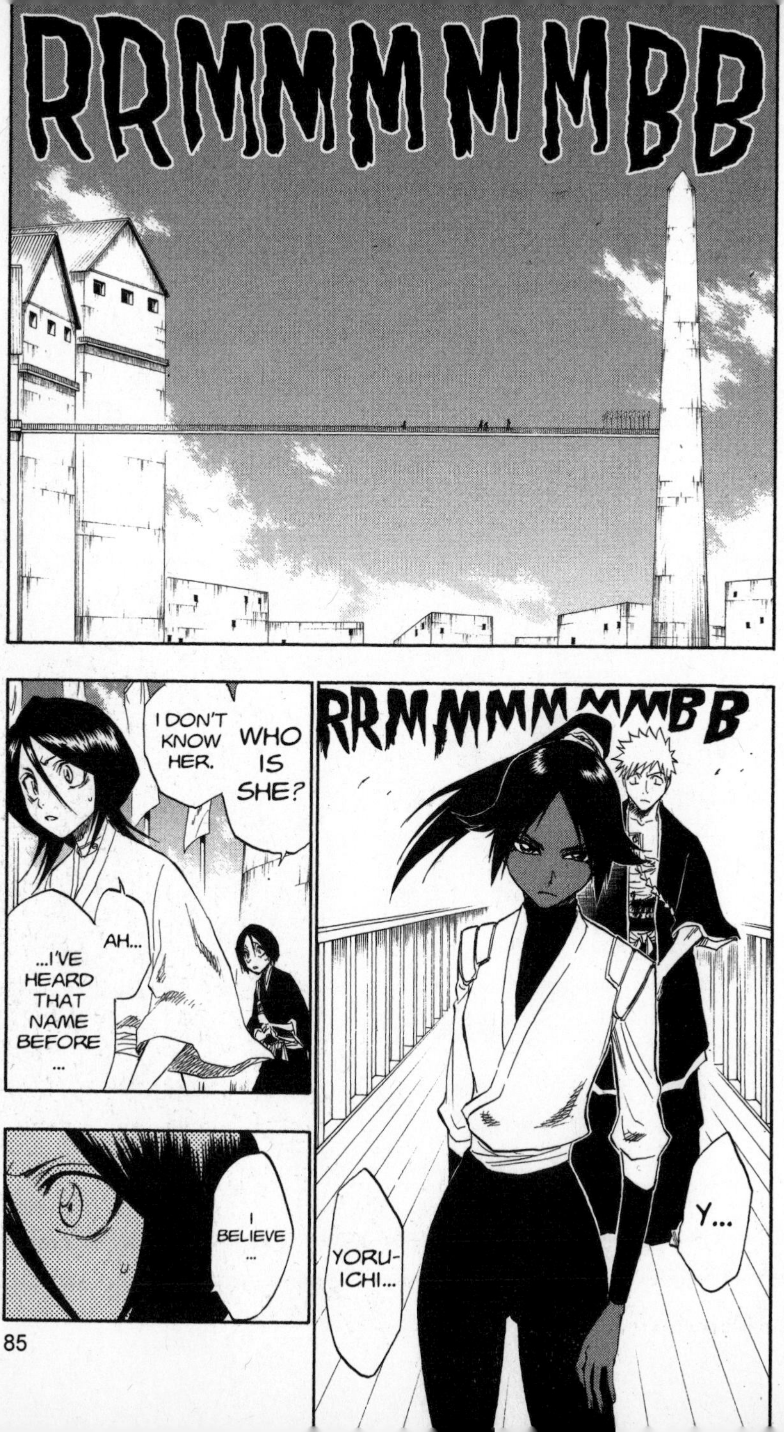
RRMMMMMMBB
RRMMMMMMBB
Y...
YORU-ICHI...
WHO IS SHE?
I DON'T KNOW HER.
AH...
...I'VE HEARD THAT NAME BEFORE...
I BELIEVE...

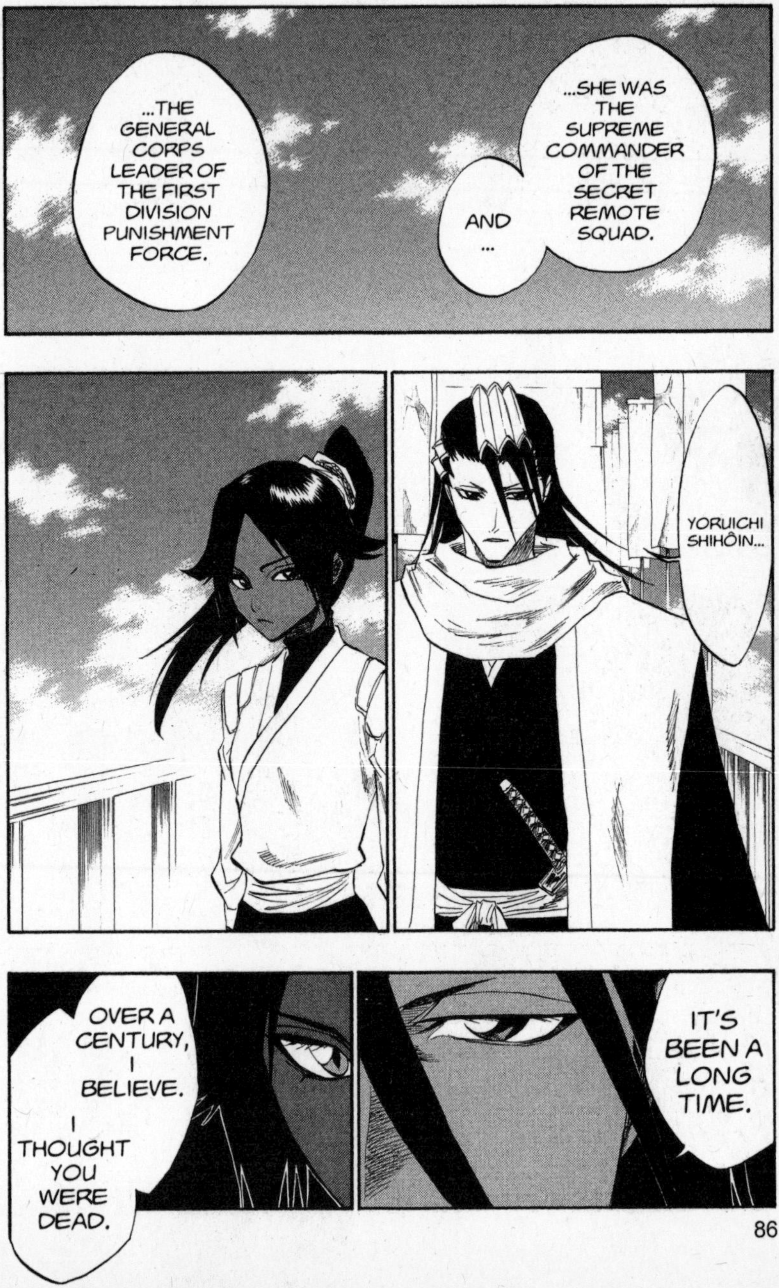
...SHE WAS THE SUPREME COMMANDER OF THE SECRET REMOTE SQUAD.
AND ...
...THE GENERAL CORPS LEADER OF THE FIRST DIVISION PUNISHMENT FORCE.
YORUICHI SHIHÔIN...
IT'S BEEN A LONG TIME.
OVER A CENTURY, I BELIEVE.
I THOUGHT YOU WERE DEAD.

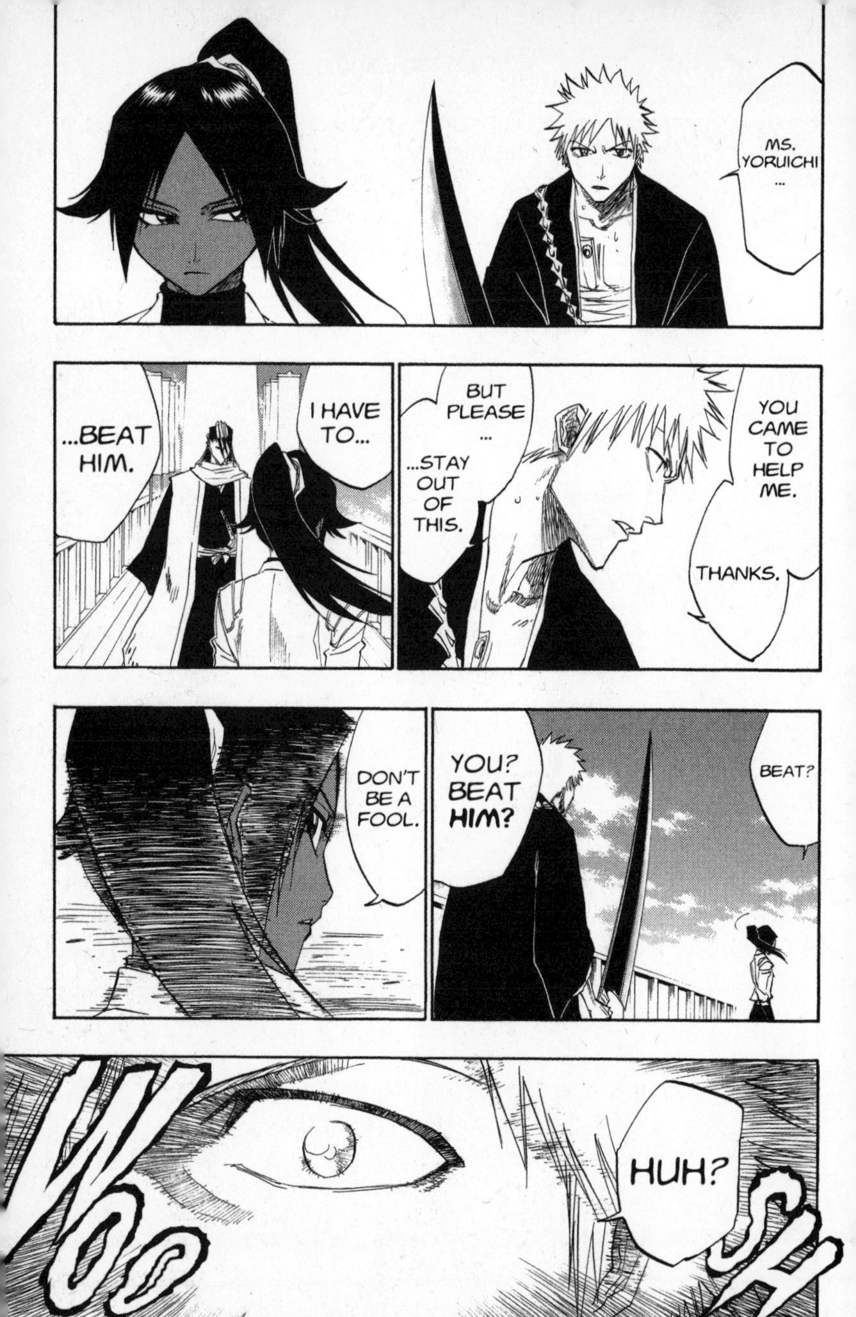

MS. YORUICHI ...
YOU CAME TO HELP ME.
THANKS.
BUT PLEASE ...
...STAY OUT OF THIS.
I HAVE TO...
...BEAT HIM.
BEAT?
YOU? BEAT HIM?
DON'T BE A FOOL.
HUH?
WOO
SH

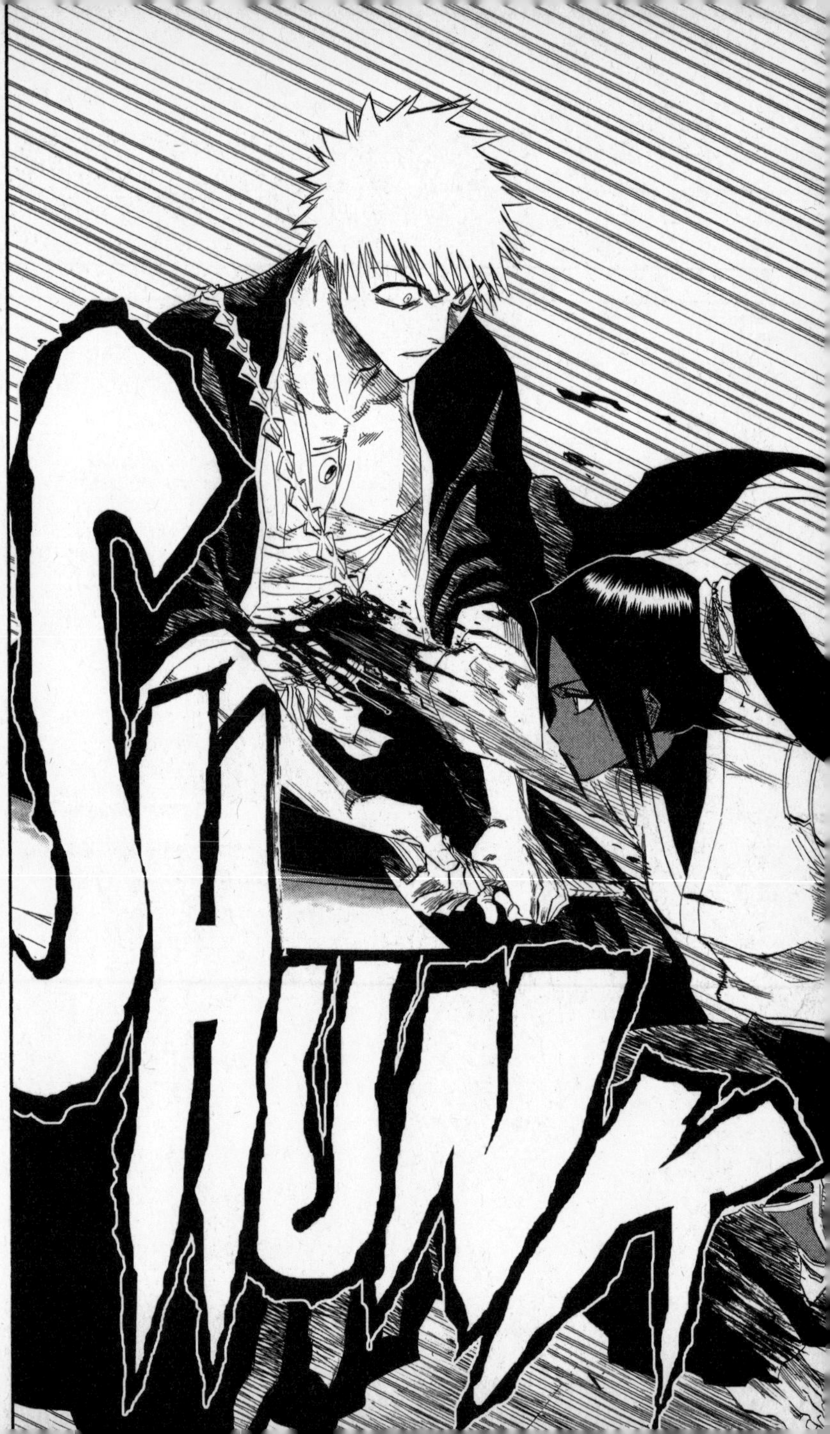
SHUNK

READ THIS WAY

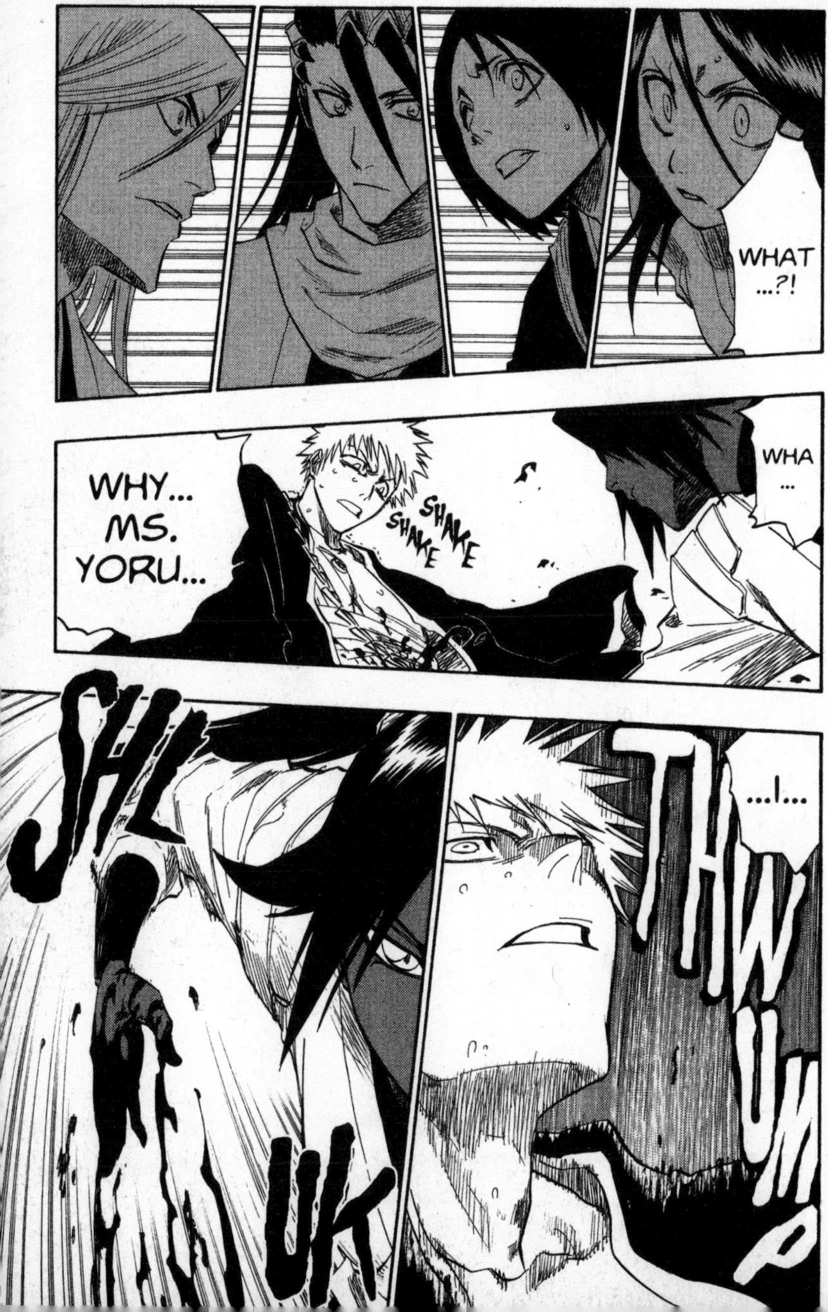
WHAT ...?!
WHA ...
SHAKE SHAKE
WHY... MS. YORU...
...I...
THWUMP
SHLUK

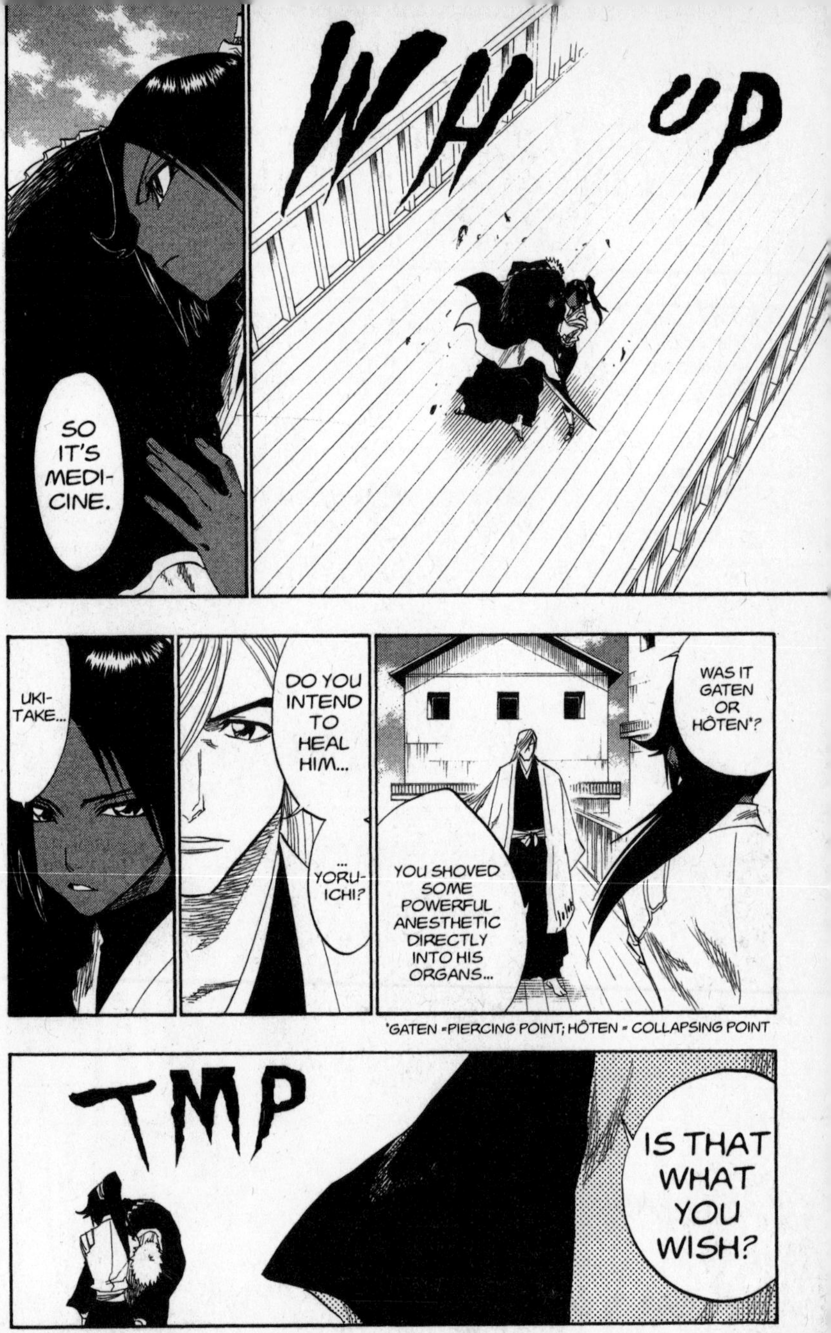
WHUP
SO IT'S MEDICINE.
WAS IT GATEN OR HÔTEN*?
YOU SHOVED SOME POWERFUL ANESTHETIC DIRECTLY INTO HIS ORGANS...
DO YOU INTEND TO HEAL HIM...
...YORUICHI?
UKITAKE...
IS THAT WHAT YOU WISH?
TMP

*GATEN = PIERCING POINT; HÔTEN = COLLAPSING POINT

READ THIS WAY

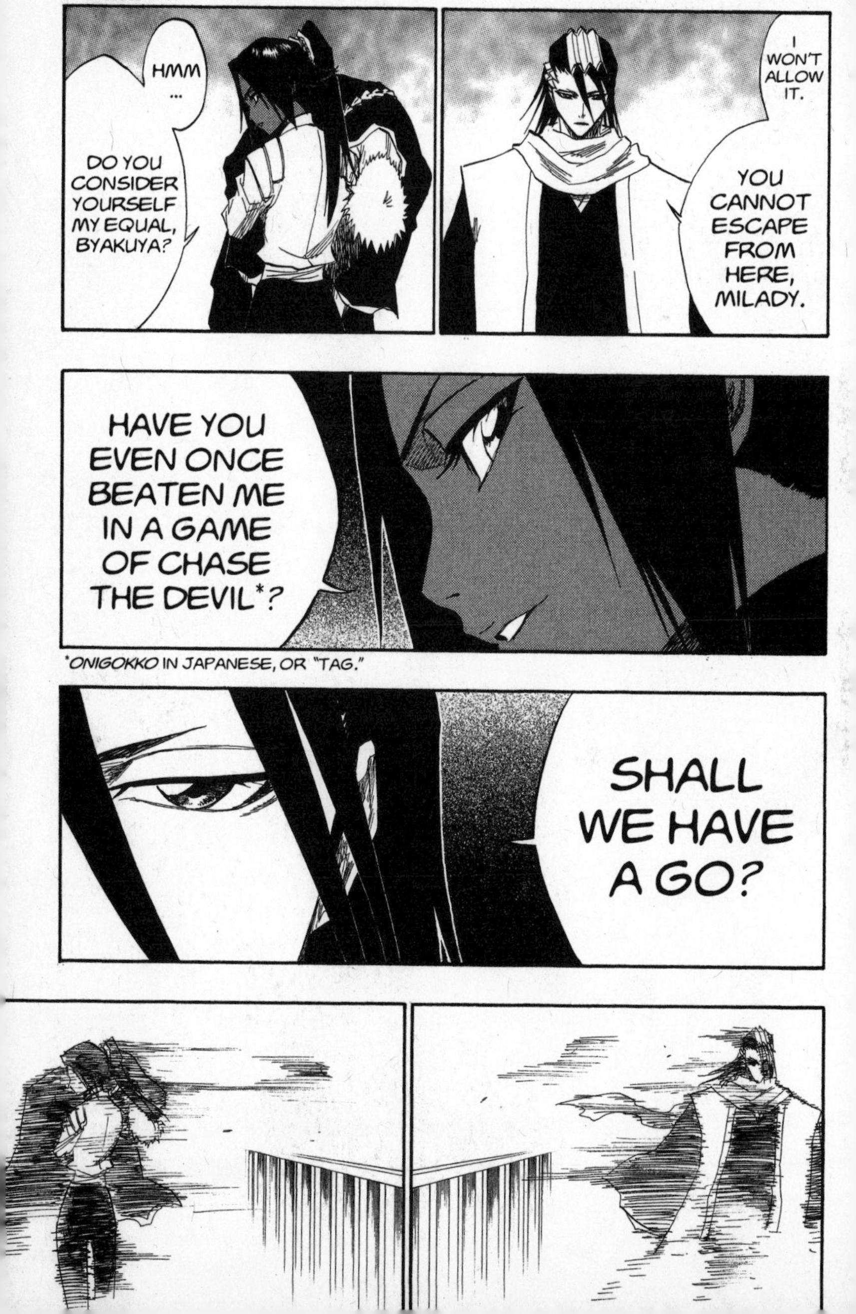
I WON'T ALLOW IT.
YOU CANNOT ESCAPE FROM HERE, MILADY.
HMM...
DO YOU CONSIDER YOURSELF MY EQUAL, BYAKUYA?
HAVE YOU EVEN ONCE BEATEN ME IN A GAME OF CHASE THE DEVIL*?
SHALL WE HAVE A GO?

*ONIGOKKO IN JAPANESE, OR "TAG."

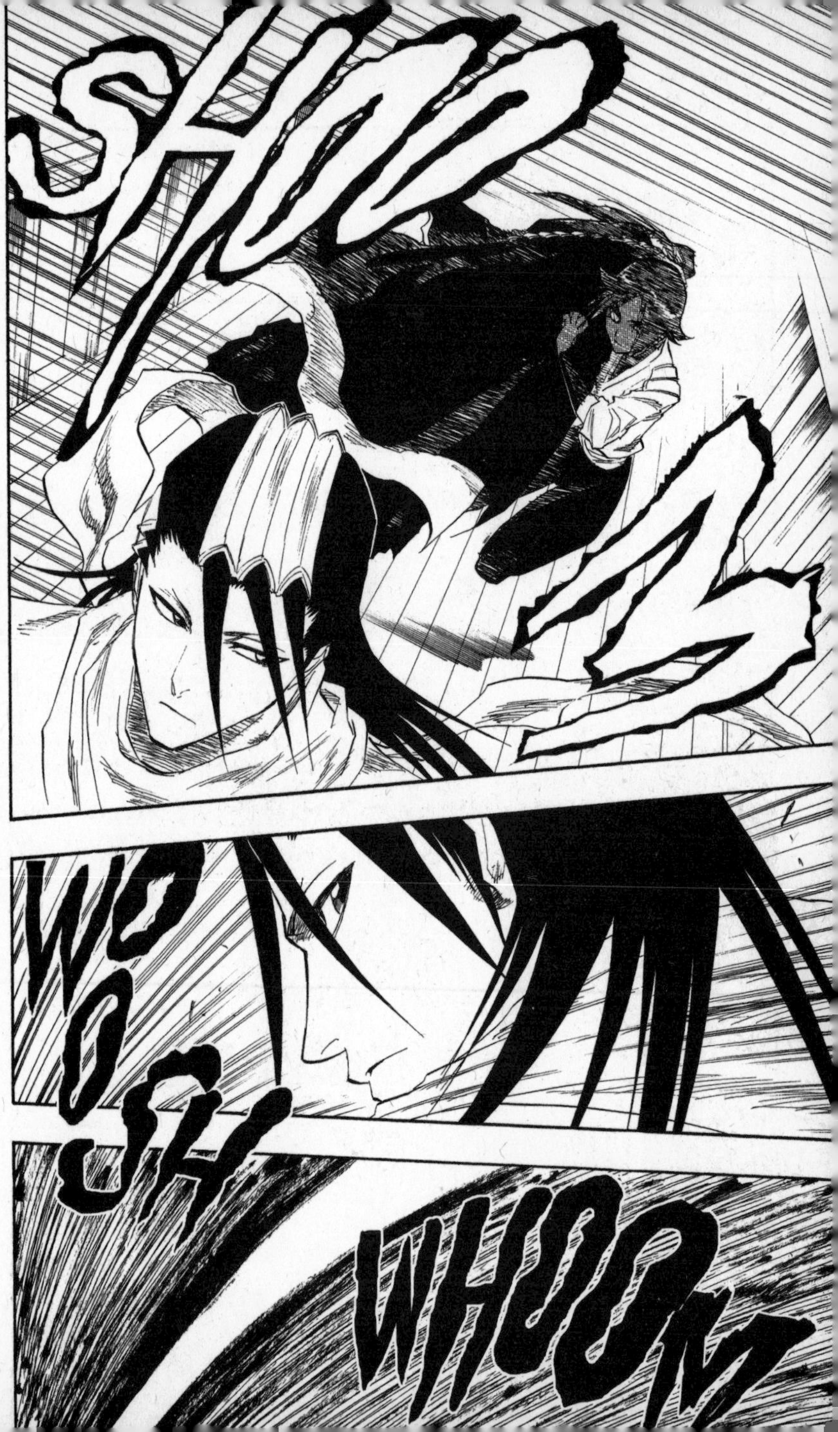
SHOOM
WOOSH
WHOOM

READ THIS WAY

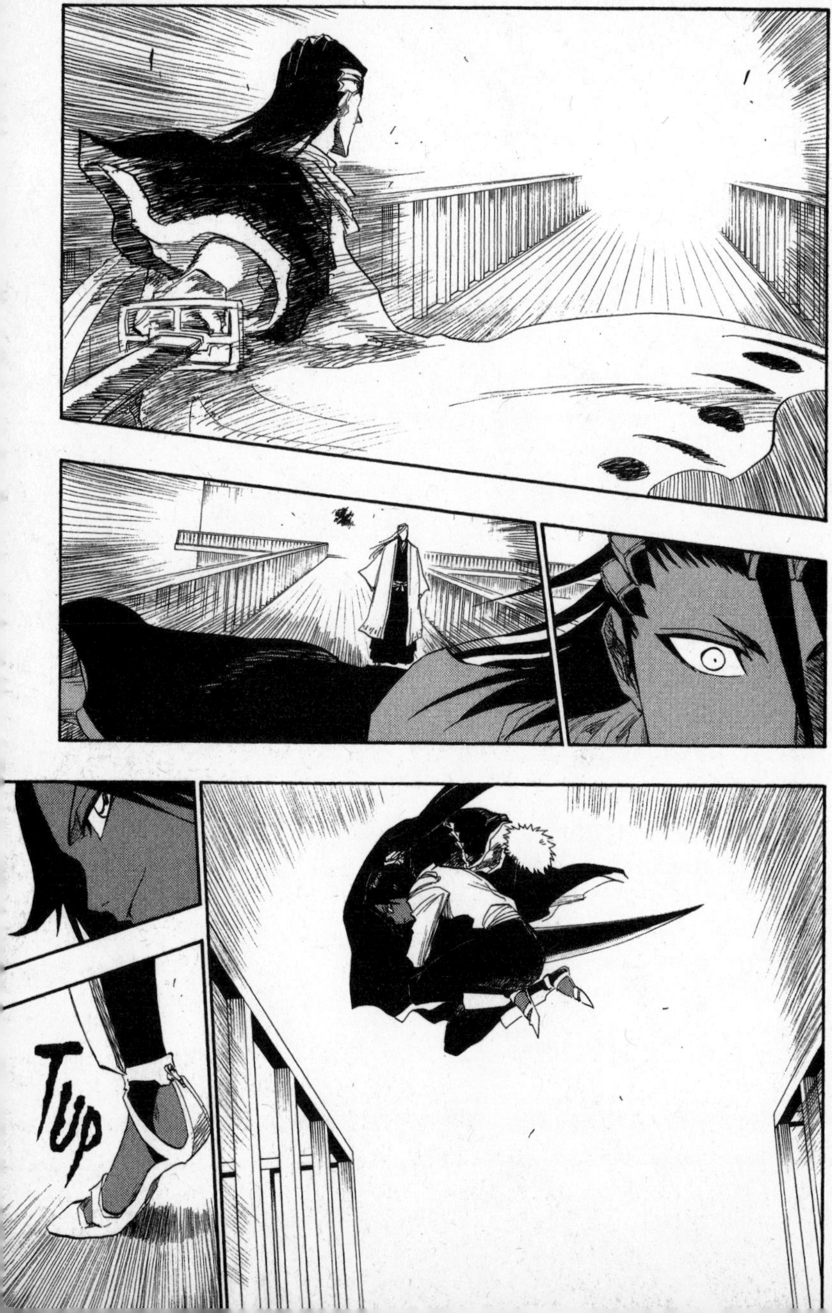
Tup

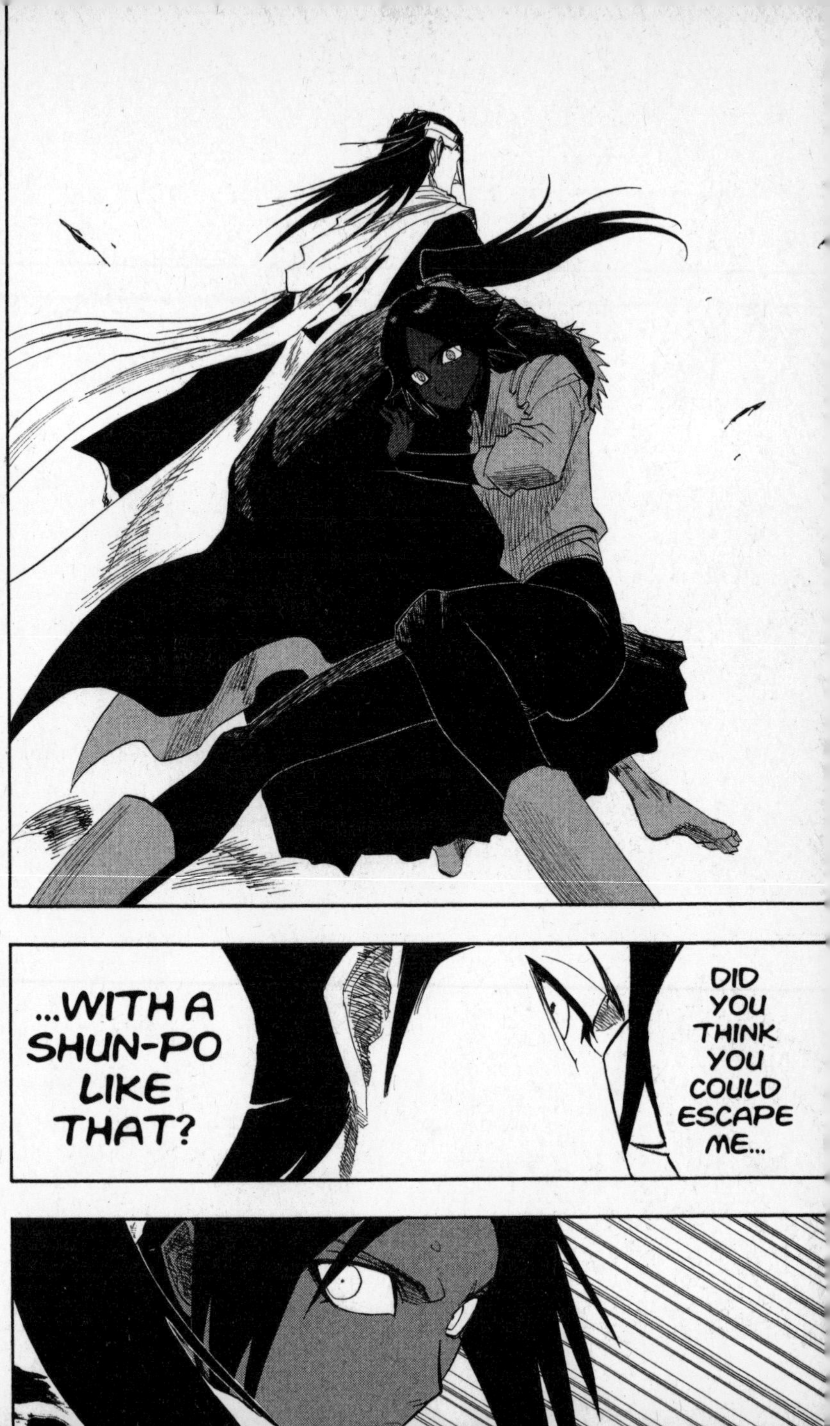
DID YOU THINK YOU COULD ESCAPE ME...
...WITH A SHUN-PO LIKE THAT?

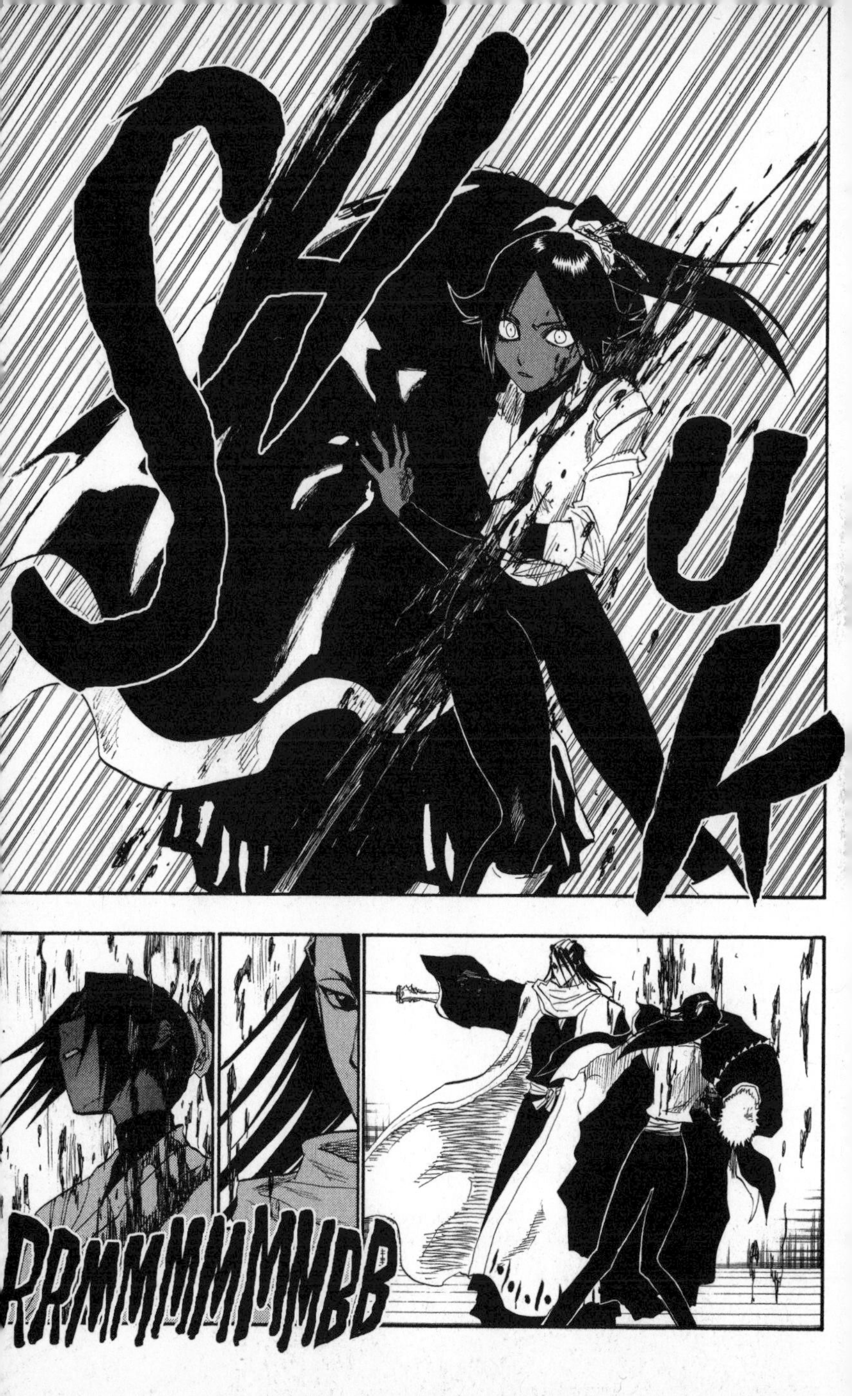
SHUNK
RRMMMMMMMBB

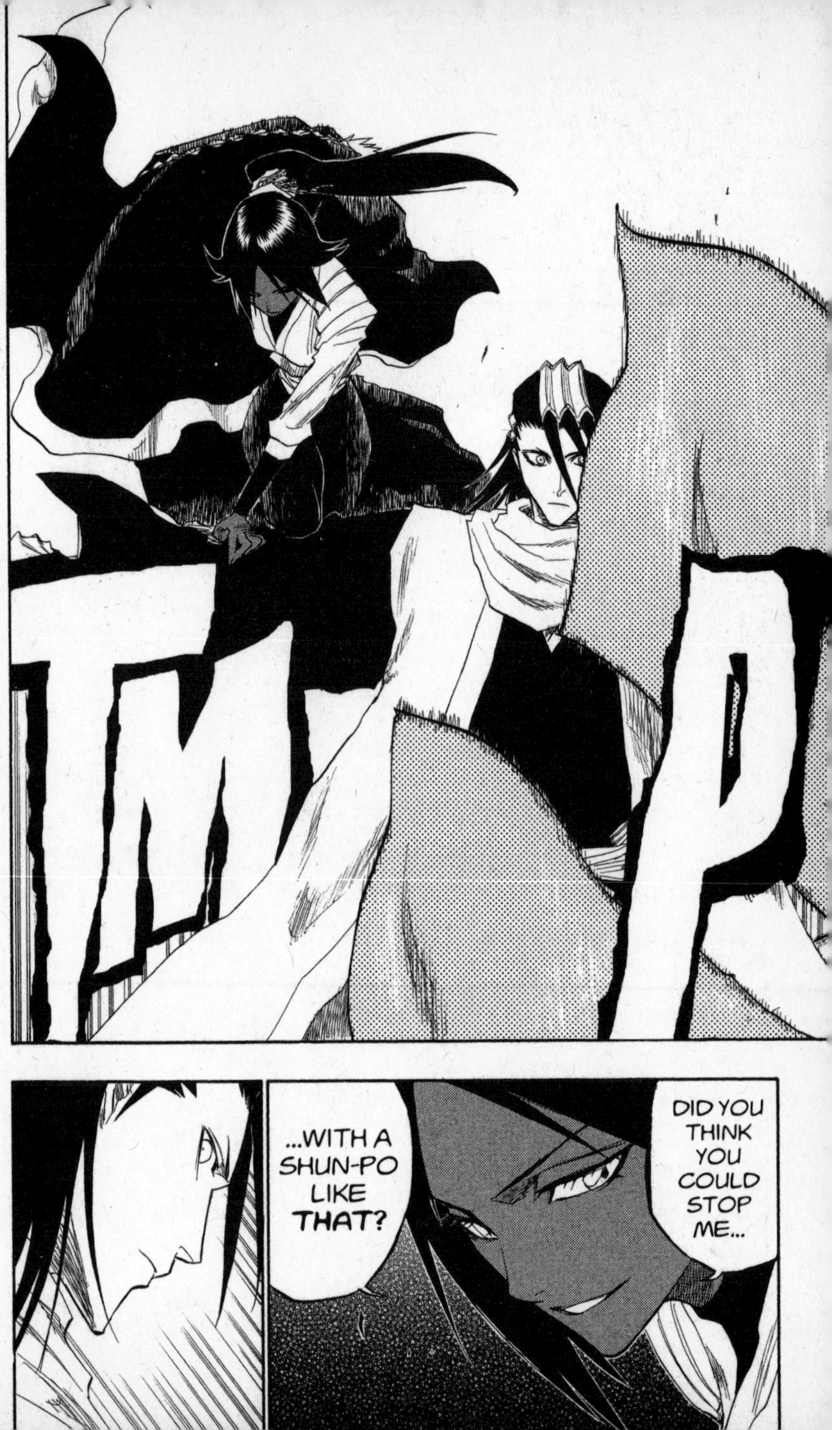
TMP
DID YOU THINK YOU COULD STOP ME...
...WITH A SHUN-PO LIKE THAT?

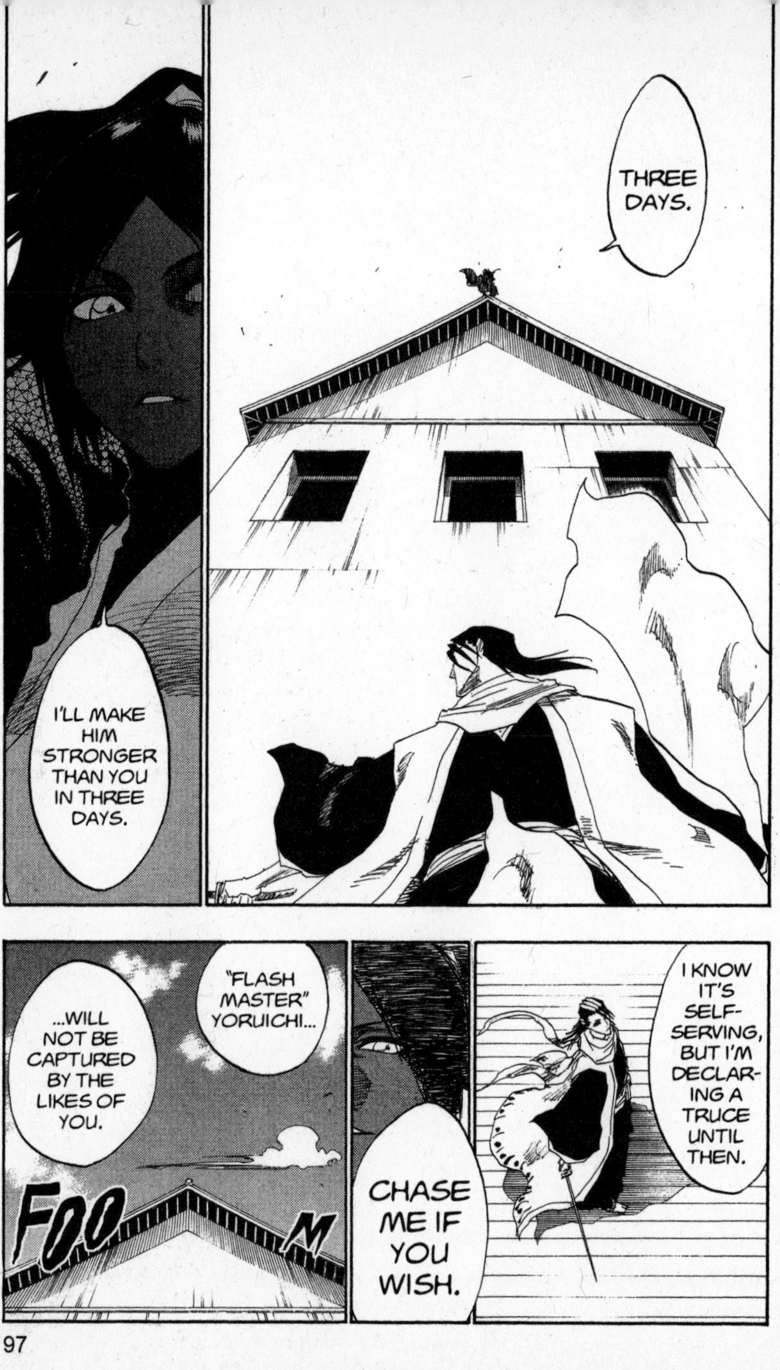
THREE DAYS.
I'LL MAKE HIM STRONGER THAN YOU IN THREE DAYS.
I KNOW IT'S SELF-SERVING, BUT I'M DECLARING A TRUCE UNTIL THEN.
CHASE ME IF YOU WISH.
"FLASH MASTER" YORUICHI...
...WILL NOT BE CAPTURED BY THE LIKES OF YOU.
FOOM

AUGUST 1. SUNNY. TODAY IS THE ANNUAL FIREWORKS FESTIVAL.

I RAN INTO THE KUROSAKI FAMILY IN THE AFTERNOON. THEY WERE ALREADY GOING CRAZY AND RUNNING AROUND SCREAMING ABOUT SOMETHING.

MY FIRST THOUGHT WAS, "THE APPLE DOESN'T FALL FAR FROM THE TREE."

WHO KNOWS WHAT THEY'D DO TO ME IN THEIR CONDITION? (THEY MIGHT PUT ME IN A LOINCLOTH AND FORCE ME TO EAT OCTOPUS DUMPLINGS THROUGH MY NOSE, JUST BECAUSE IT'S A FESTIVAL, ETC.)

OH WELL, I GUESS I'LL SKIP THE FIREWORKS AND GO HOME...

119. Secret of the Moon

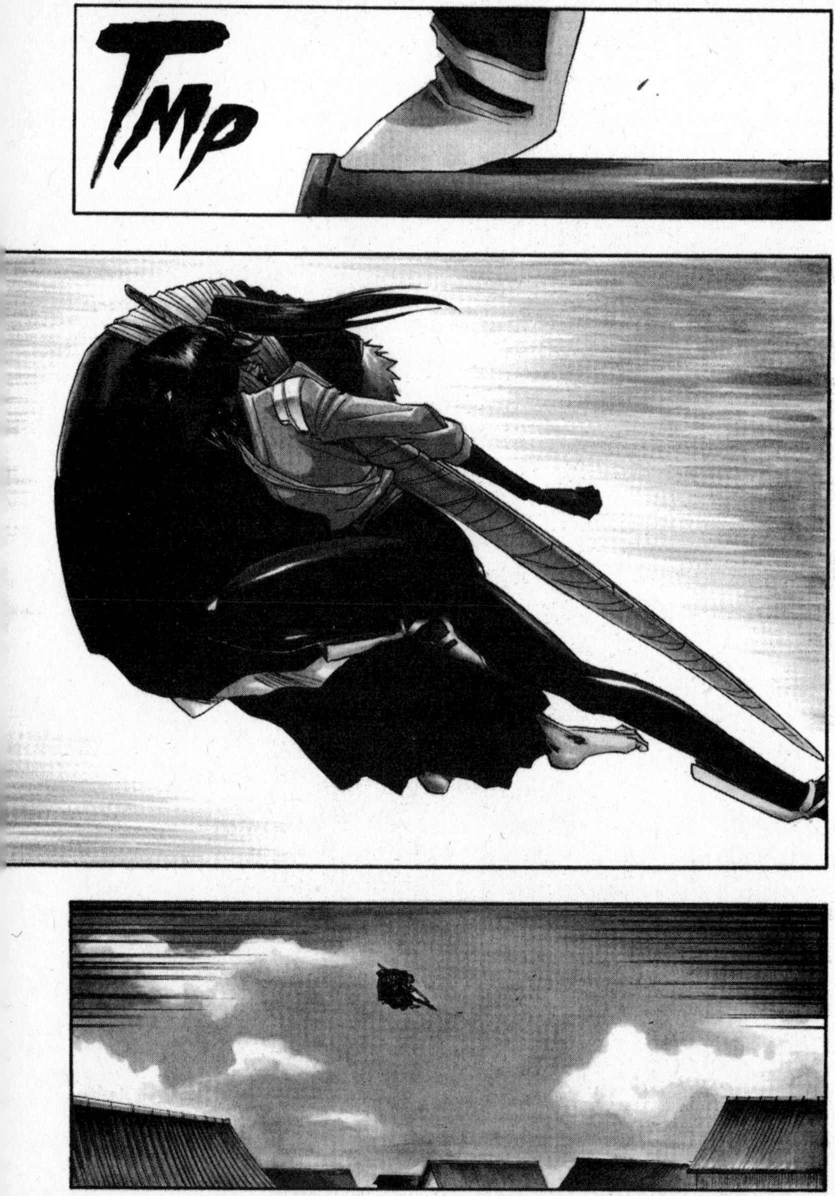
TMP

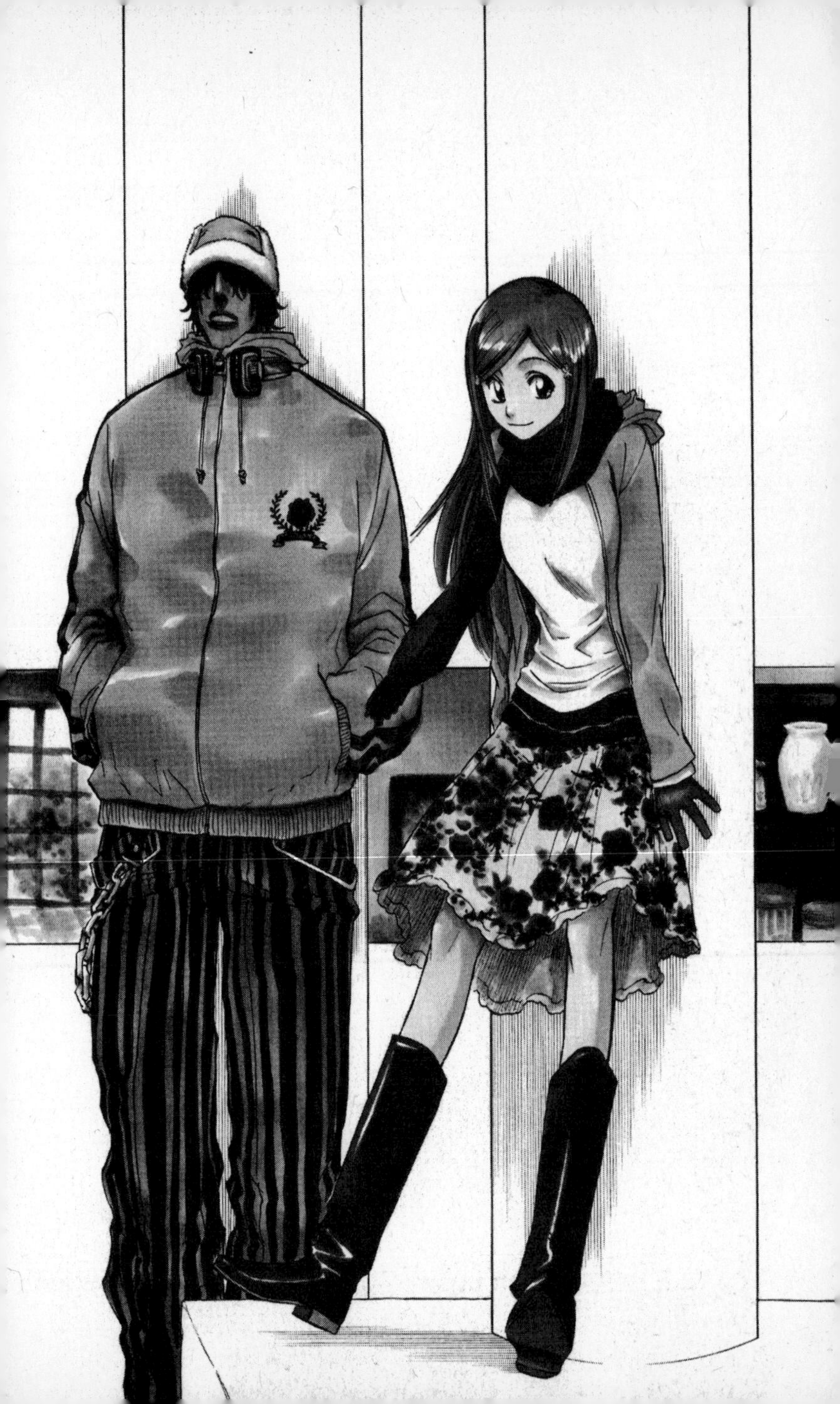

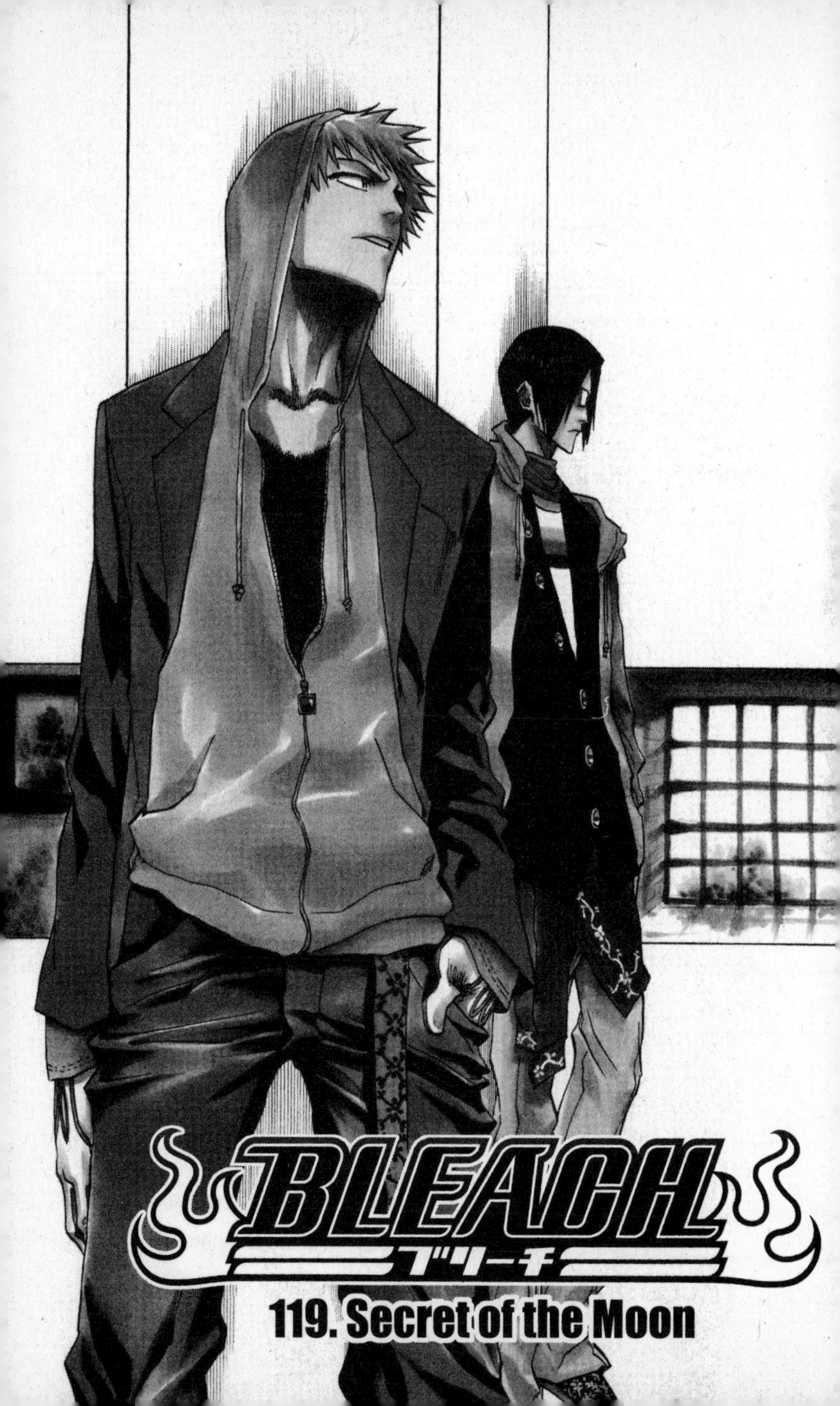
BLEACH
ブリーチ
119. Secret of the Moon

BLEACH

ブリーチ

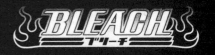

READ THIS WAY

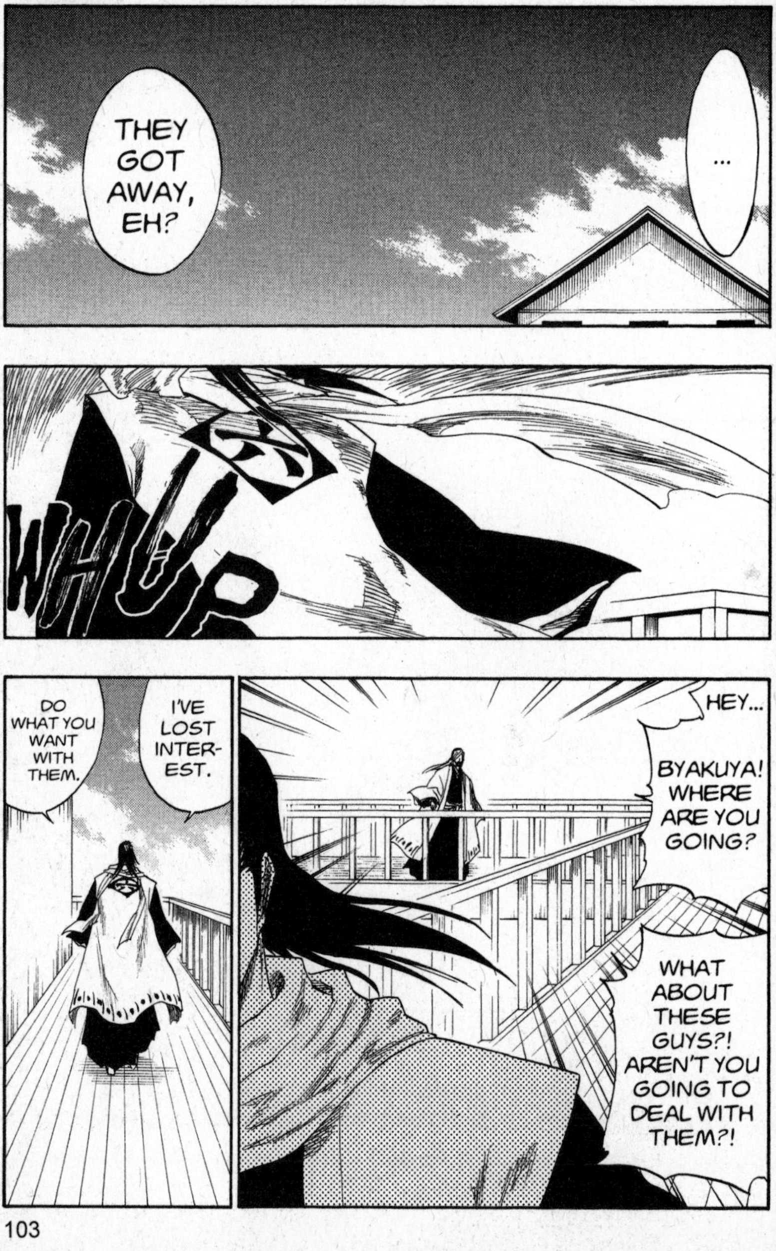
...
THEY GOT AWAY, EH?
WHUP
HEY...
BYAKUYA! WHERE ARE YOU GOING?
WHAT ABOUT THESE GUYS?! AREN'T YOU GOING TO DEAL WITH THEM?!
I'VE LOST INTER-EST.
DO WHAT YOU WANT WITH THEM.

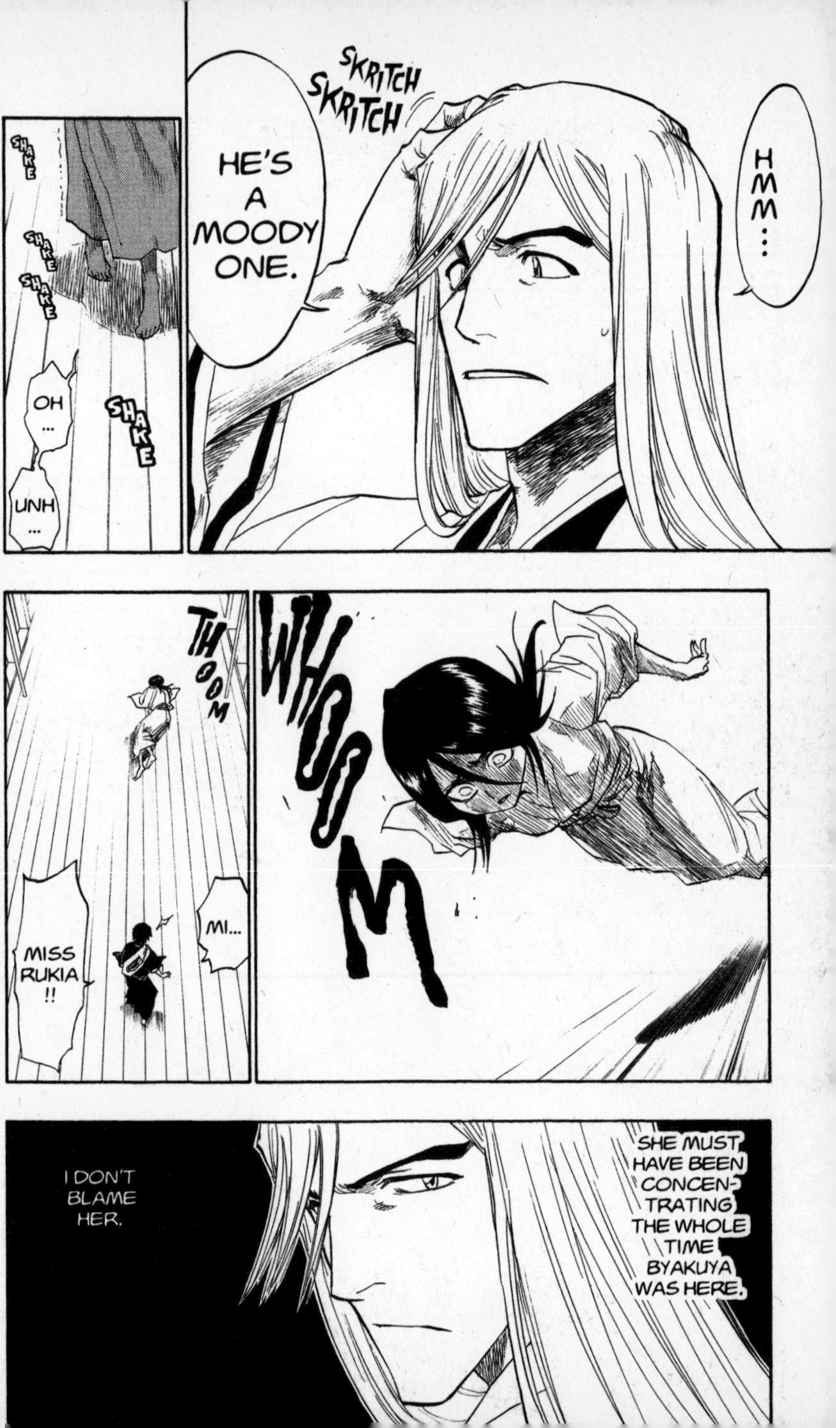
HMM...
SKRITCH SKRITCH
HE'S A MOODY ONE.
SHAKE
SHAKE
SHAKE
SHAKE
OH...
UNH...
WHOOOM
THOOOM
MI...
MISS RUKIA!!
SHE MUST HAVE BEEN CONCEN-TRATING THE WHOLE TIME BYAKUYA WAS HERE.
I DON'T BLAME HER.

READ THIS WAY

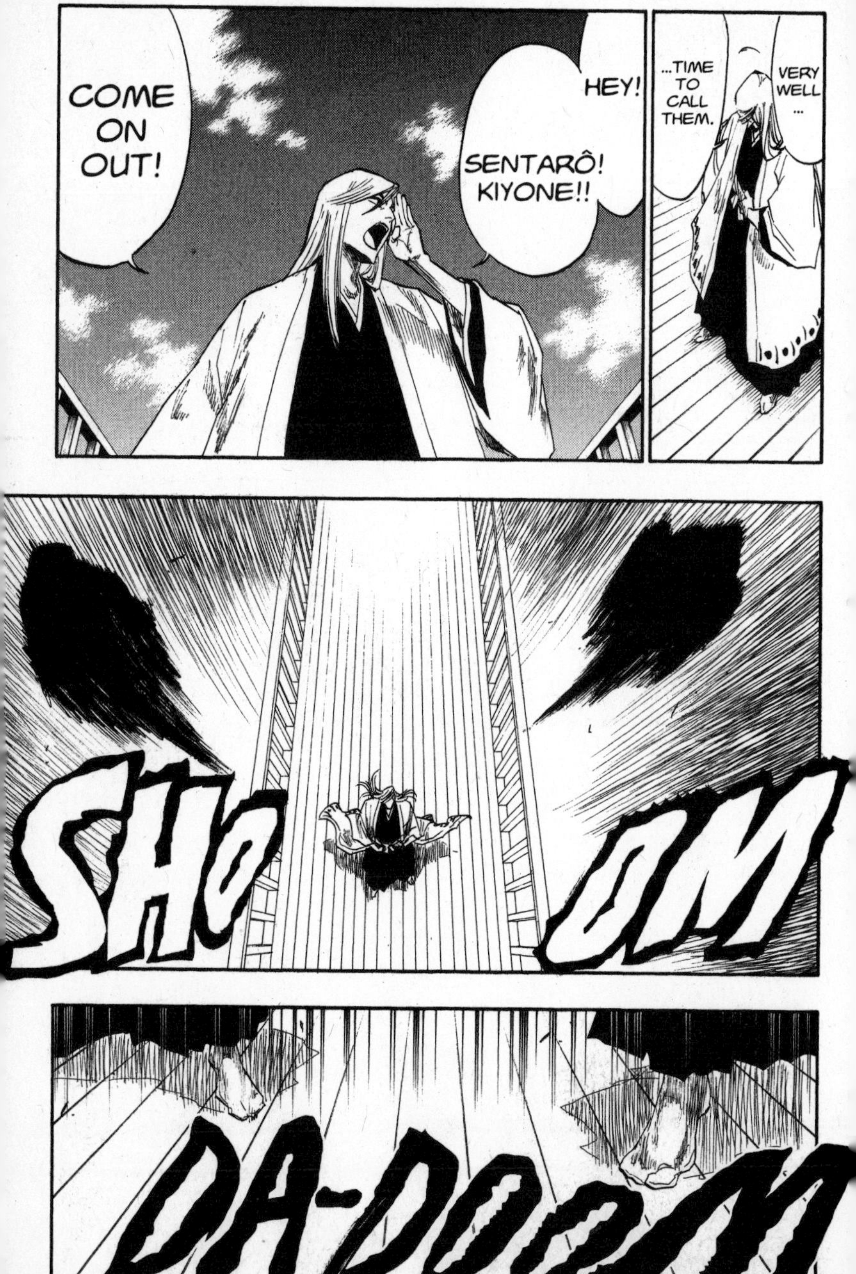

VERY WELL ...
...TIME TO CALL THEM.
HEY!
SENTARÔ! KIYONE!!
COME ON OUT!
SHOOM
DA-DOOM

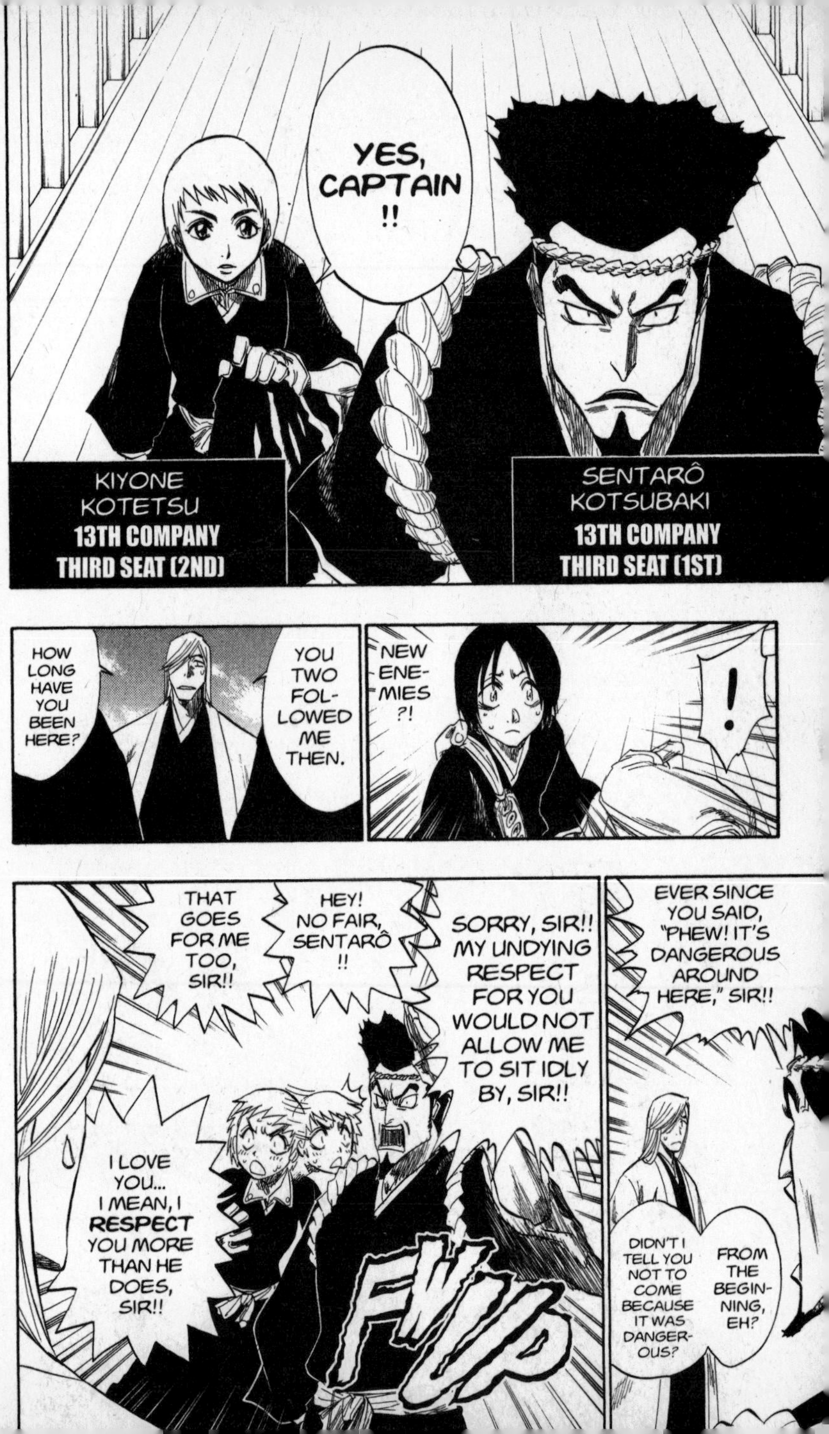
YES, CAPTAIN !!
SENTARÔ KOTSUBAKI 13TH COMPANY THIRD SEAT (1ST)
KIYONE KOTETSU 13TH COMPANY THIRD SEAT (2ND)
!
NEW ENE-MIES ?!
YOU TWO FOL-LOWED ME THEN.
HOW LONG HAVE YOU BEEN HERE?
EVER SINCE YOU SAID, "PHEW! IT'S DANGEROUS AROUND HERE," SIR!!
FROM THE BEGIN-NING, EH?
DIDN'T I TELL YOU NOT TO COME BECAUSE IT WAS DANGER-OUS?
SORRY, SIR!! MY UNDYING RESPECT FOR YOU WOULD NOT ALLOW ME TO SIT IDLY BY, SIR!!
HEY! NO FAIR, SENTARÔ !!
THAT GOES FOR ME TOO, SIR!!
I LOVE YOU... I MEAN, I **RESPECT** YOU MORE THAN HE DOES, SIR!!
FWUP

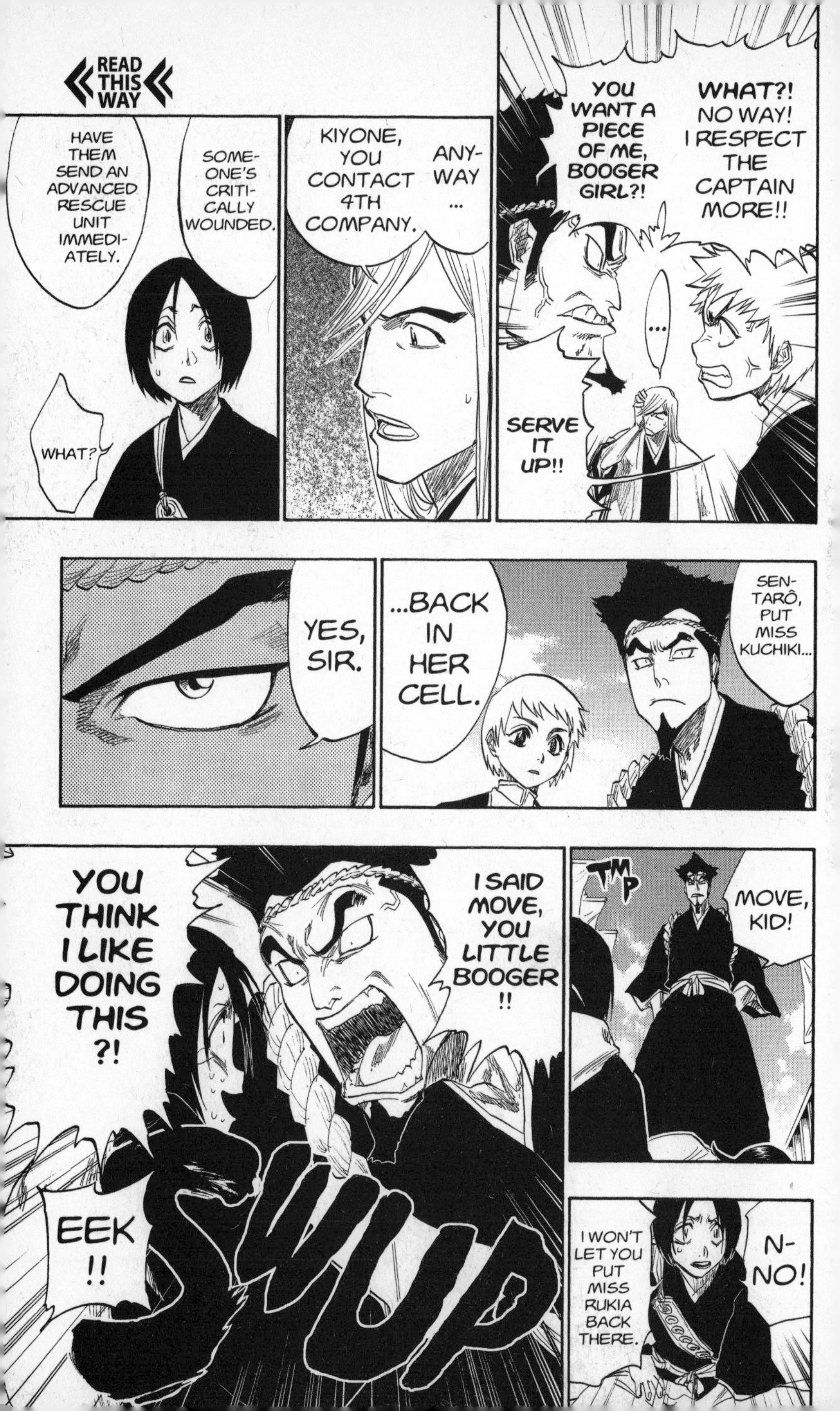
READ THIS WAY
WHAT?! NO WAY! I RESPECT THE CAPTAIN MORE!!
YOU WANT A PIECE OF ME, BOOGER GIRL?!
...
SERVE IT UP!!
ANY-WAY ...
KIYONE, YOU CONTACT 4TH COMPANY.
SOME-ONE'S CRITI-CALLY WOUNDED.
HAVE THEM SEND AN ADVANCED RESCUE UNIT IMMEDI-ATELY.
WHAT?
SEN-TARÔ, PUT MISS KUCHIKI...
...BACK IN HER CELL.
YES, SIR.
TMP
MOVE, KID!
N-NO!
I WON'T LET YOU PUT MISS RUKIA BACK THERE.
I SAID MOVE, YOU LITTLE BOOGER!!
YOU THINK I LIKE DOING THIS?!
EEK!!
SWUP

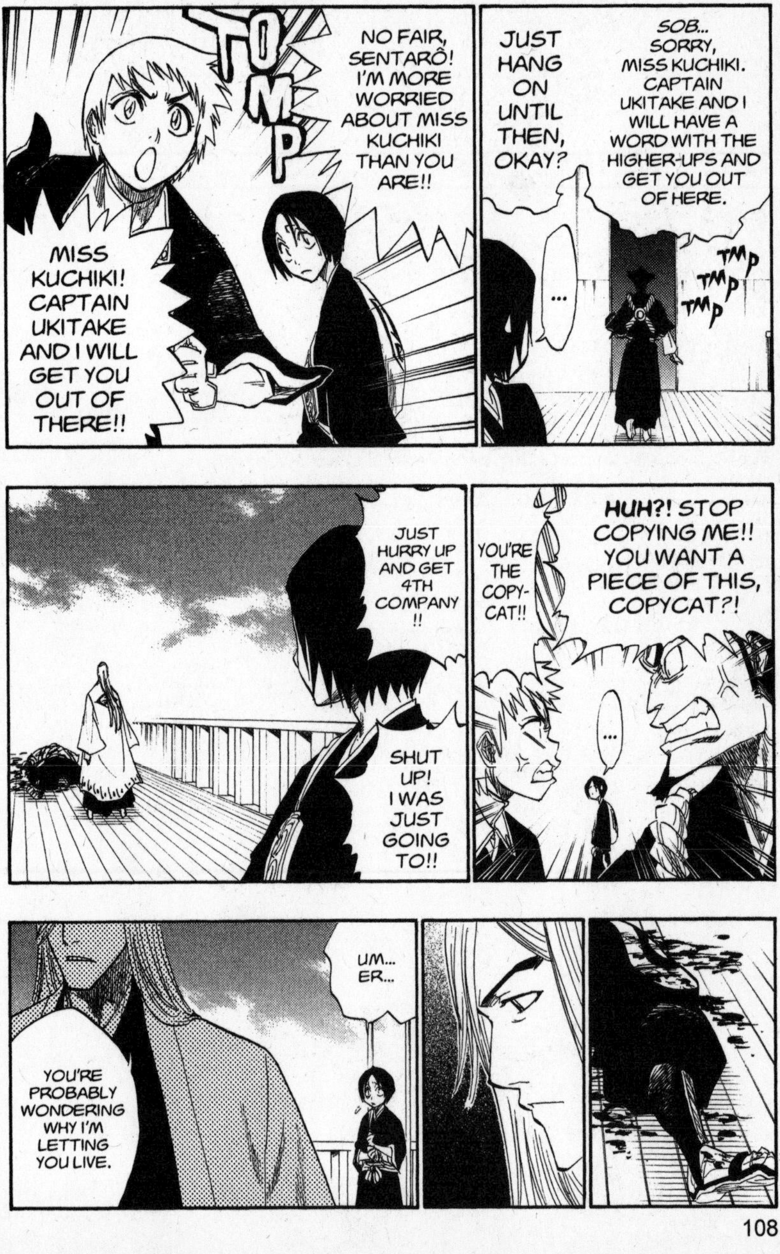
SOB... SORRY, MISS KUCHIKI. CAPTAIN UKITAKE AND I WILL HAVE A WORD WITH THE HIGHER-UPS AND GET YOU OUT OF HERE.
JUST HANG ON UNTIL THEN, OKAY?
TMP TMP TMP
...
NO FAIR, SENTARÔ! I'M MORE WORRIED ABOUT MISS KUCHIKI THAN YOU ARE!!
TOMP
MISS KUCHIKI! CAPTAIN UKITAKE AND I WILL GET YOU OUT OF THERE!!
HUH?! STOP COPYING ME!! YOU WANT A PIECE OF THIS, COPYCAT?!
YOU'RE THE COPY-CAT!!
...
JUST HURRY UP AND GET 4TH COMPANY !!
SHUT UP! I WAS JUST GOING TO!!
UM... ER...
YOU'RE PROBABLY WONDERING WHY I'M LETTING YOU LIVE.

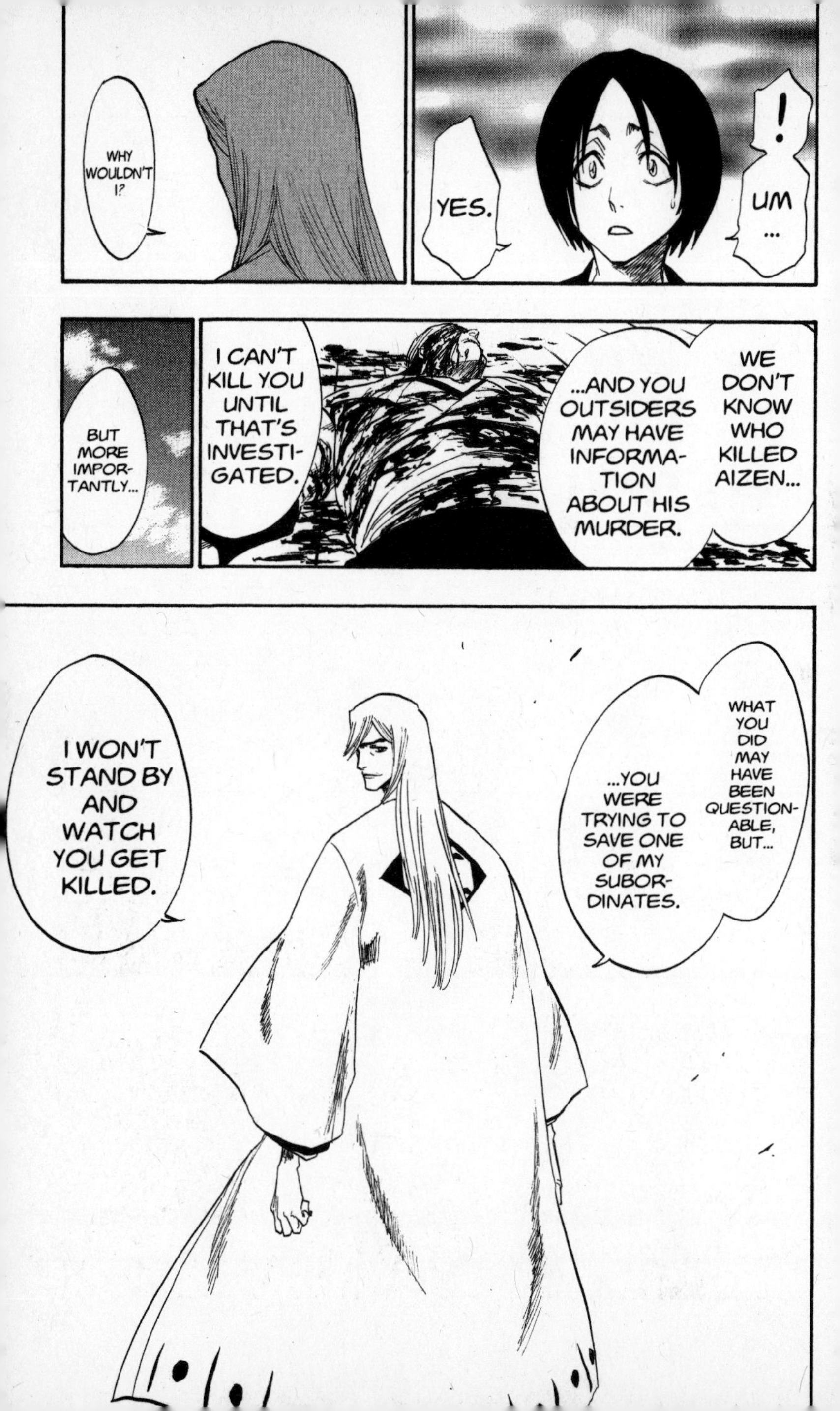
!
UM...
YES.
WHY WOULDN'T I?
WE DON'T KNOW WHO KILLED AIZEN...
...AND YOU OUTSIDERS MAY HAVE INFORMATION ABOUT HIS MURDER.
I CAN'T KILL YOU UNTIL THAT'S INVESTIGATED.
BUT MORE IMPORTANTLY...
WHAT YOU DID MAY HAVE BEEN QUESTIONABLE, BUT...
...YOU WERE TRYING TO SAVE ONE OF MY SUBORDINATES.
I WON'T STAND BY AND WATCH YOU GET KILLED.

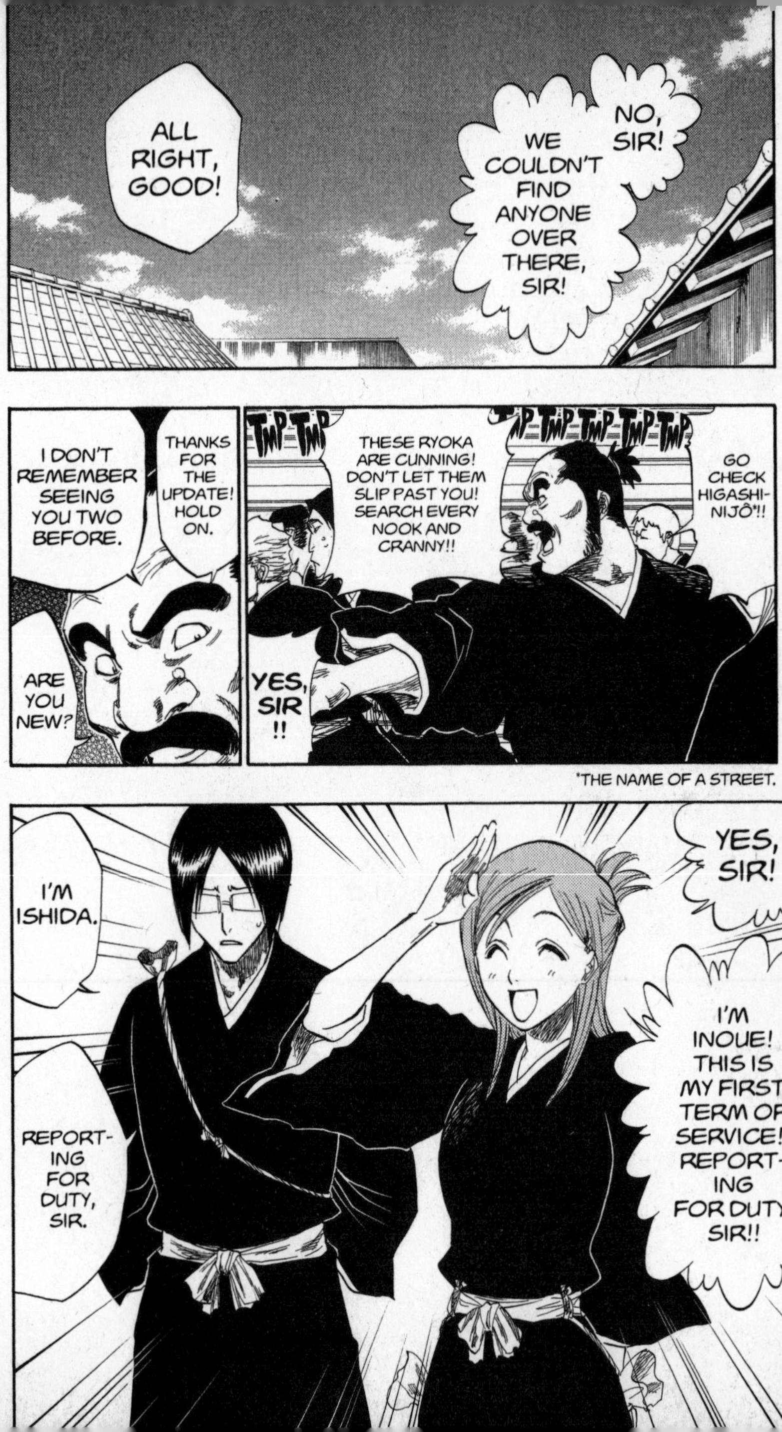
NO, SIR!
WE COULDN'T FIND ANYONE OVER THERE, SIR!
ALL RIGHT, GOOD!
TMP TMP TMP TMP TMP
GO CHECK HIGASHI-NIJÔ*!!
TMP TMP
THESE RYOKA ARE CUNNING! DON'T LET THEM SLIP PAST YOU! SEARCH EVERY NOOK AND CRANNY!!
YES, SIR!!
THANKS FOR THE UPDATE! HOLD ON.
I DON'T REMEMBER SEEING YOU TWO BEFORE.
ARE YOU NEW?
YES, SIR!
I'M INOUE! THIS IS MY FIRST TERM OF SERVICE!! REPORTING FOR DUTY, SIR!!
I'M ISHIDA.
REPORTING FOR DUTY, SIR.

*THE NAME OF A STREET.

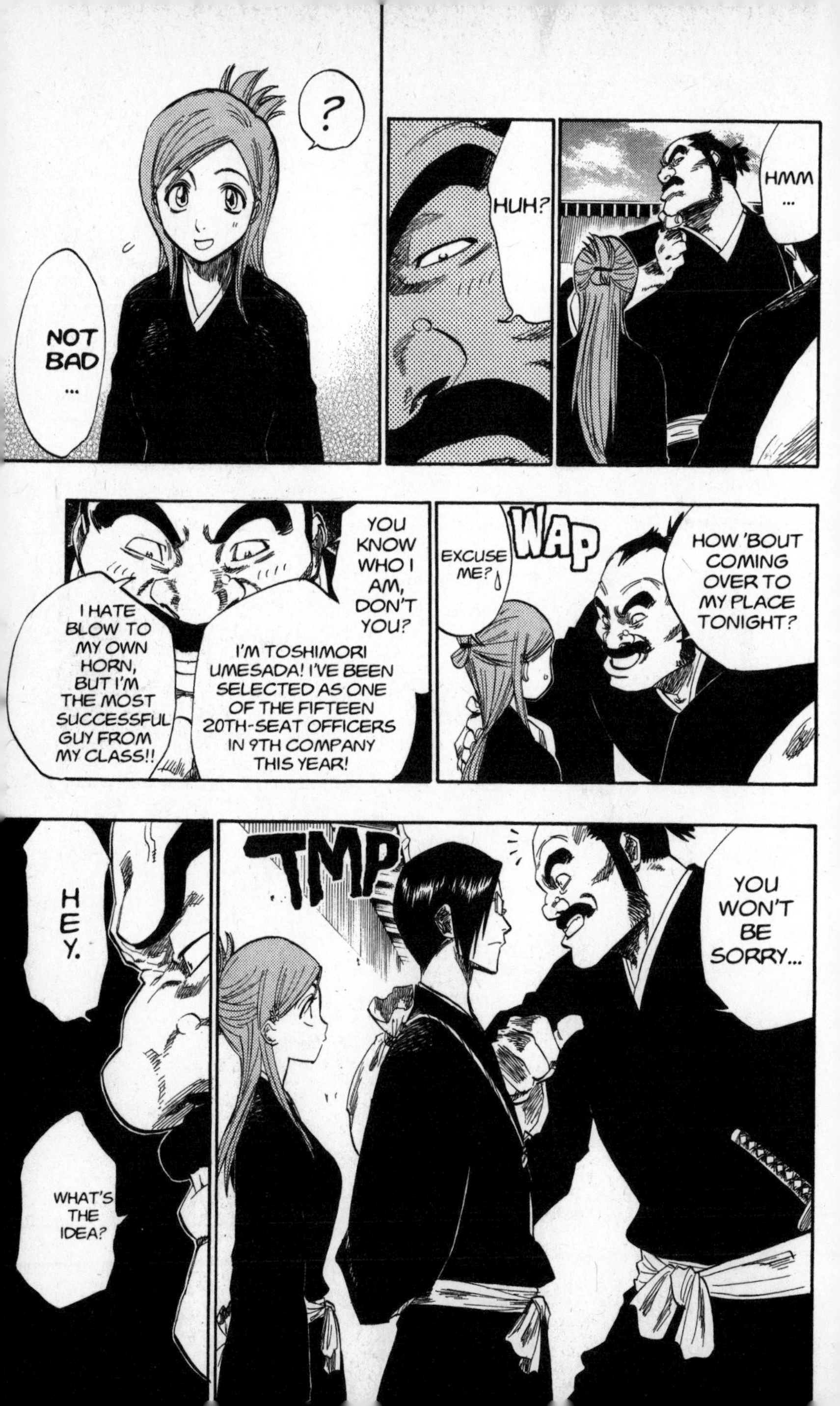
HMM ...
HUH?
?
NOT BAD ...
HOW 'BOUT COMING OVER TO MY PLACE TONIGHT?
WAP
EXCUSE ME?
YOU KNOW WHO I AM, DON'T YOU?
I'M TOSHIMORI UMESADA! I'VE BEEN SELECTED AS ONE OF THE FIFTEEN 20TH-SEAT OFFICERS IN 9TH COMPANY THIS YEAR!
I HATE BLOW TO MY OWN HORN, BUT I'M THE MOST SUCCESSFUL GUY FROM MY CLASS!!
YOU WON'T BE SORRY...
TMP
HEY.
WHAT'S THE IDEA?

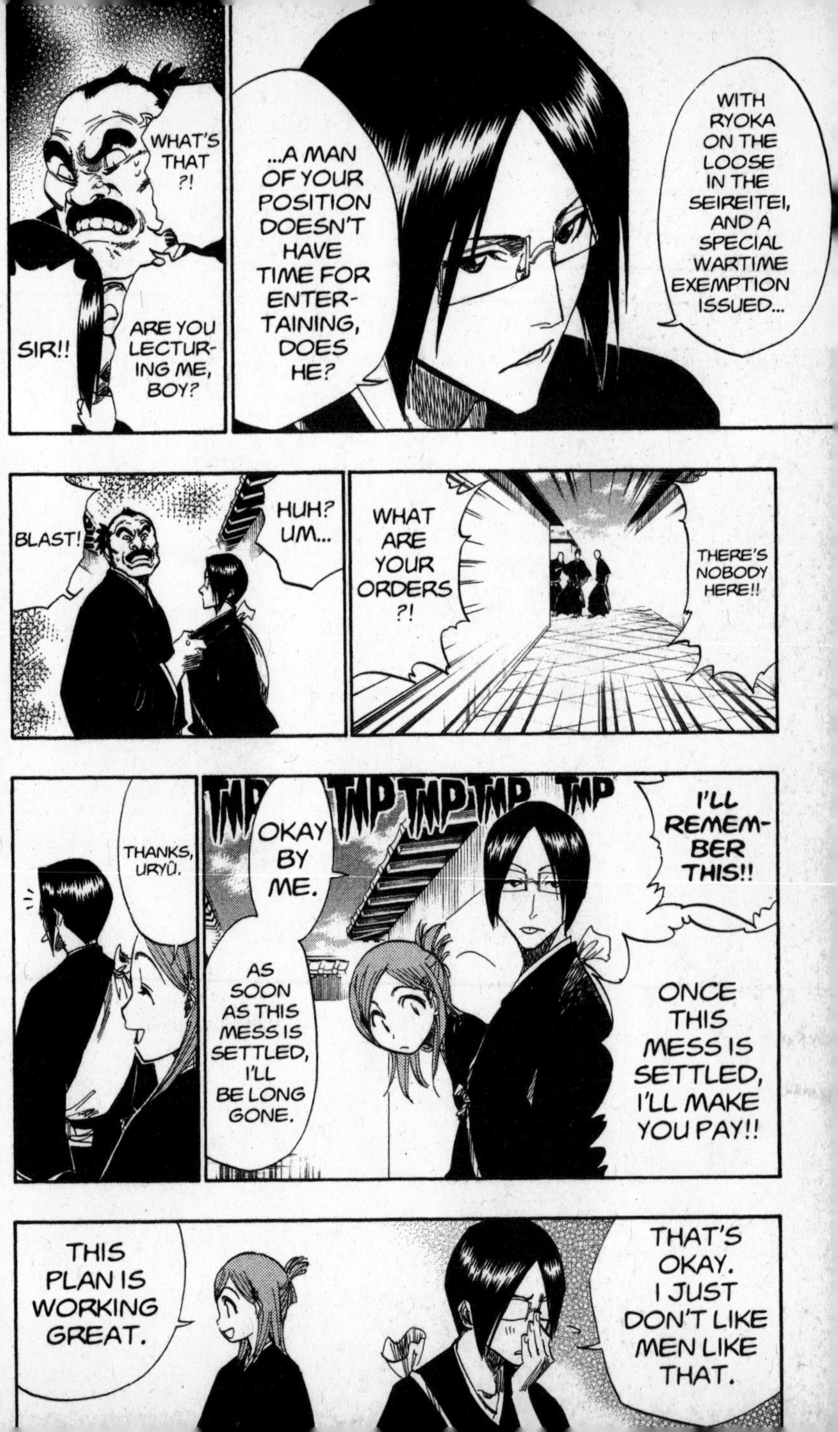
WITH RYOKA ON THE LOOSE IN THE SEIREITEI, AND A SPECIAL WARTIME EXEMPTION ISSUED...
...A MAN OF YOUR POSITION DOESN'T HAVE TIME FOR ENTERTAINING, DOES HE?
WHAT'S THAT?!
ARE YOU LECTURING ME, BOY?
SIR!!
THERE'S NOBODY HERE!!
WHAT ARE YOUR ORDERS?!
HUH? UM...
BLAST!
I'LL REMEMBER THIS!!
ONCE THIS MESS IS SETTLED, I'LL MAKE YOU PAY!!
TMP TMP TMP TMP TMP
OKAY BY ME.
AS SOON AS THIS MESS IS SETTLED, I'LL BE LONG GONE.
THANKS, URYÛ.
THAT'S OKAY. I JUST DON'T LIKE MEN LIKE THAT.
THIS PLAN IS WORKING GREAT.

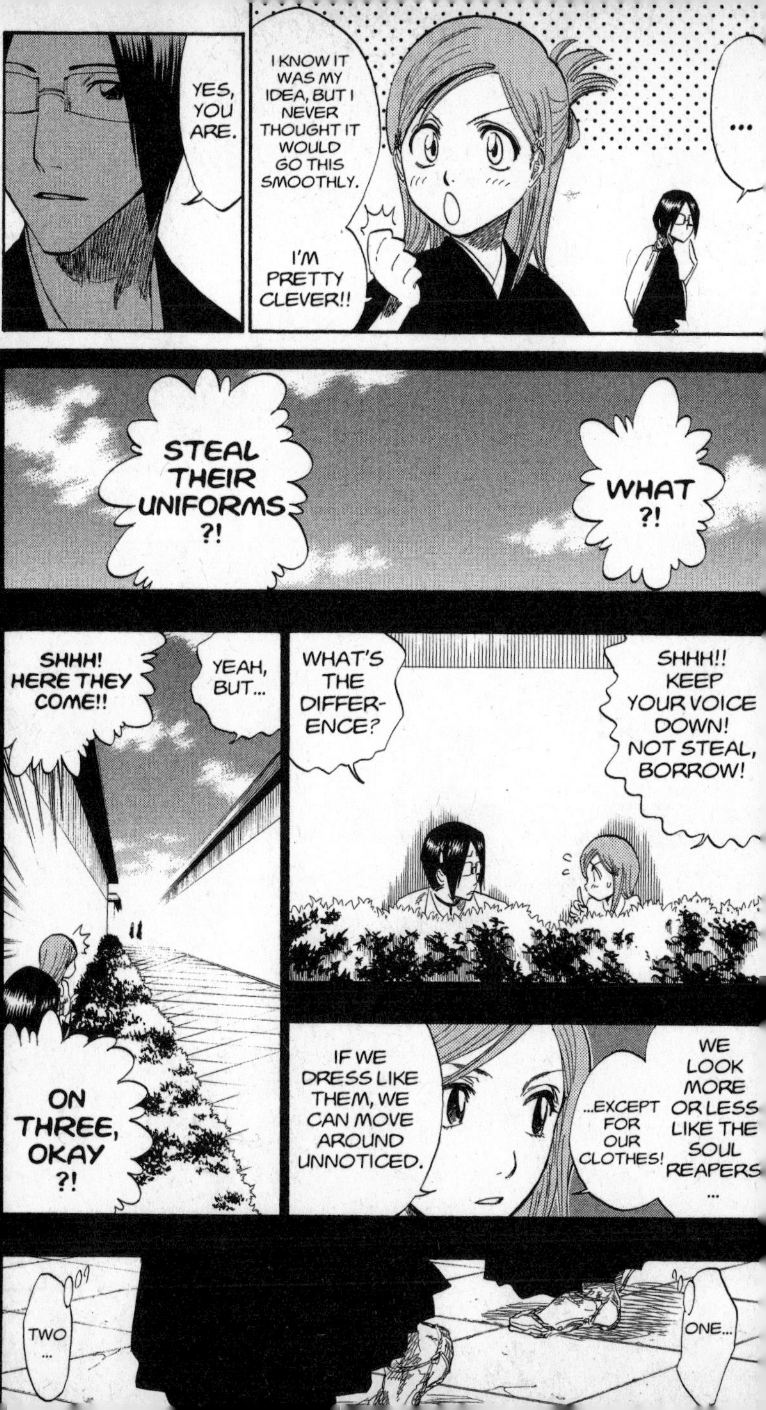
...
I KNOW IT WAS MY IDEA, BUT I NEVER THOUGHT IT WOULD GO THIS SMOOTHLY.
I'M PRETTY CLEVER!!
YES, YOU ARE.
WHAT?!
STEAL THEIR UNIFORMS?!
SHHH!! KEEP YOUR VOICE DOWN! NOT STEAL, BORROW!
WHAT'S THE DIFFERENCE?
WE LOOK MORE OR LESS LIKE THE SOUL REAPERS...
...EXCEPT FOR OUR CLOTHES!
IF WE DRESS LIKE THEM, WE CAN MOVE AROUND UNNOTICED.
YEAH, BUT...
SHHH! HERE THEY COME!!
ON THREE, OKAY?!
ONE...
TWO...

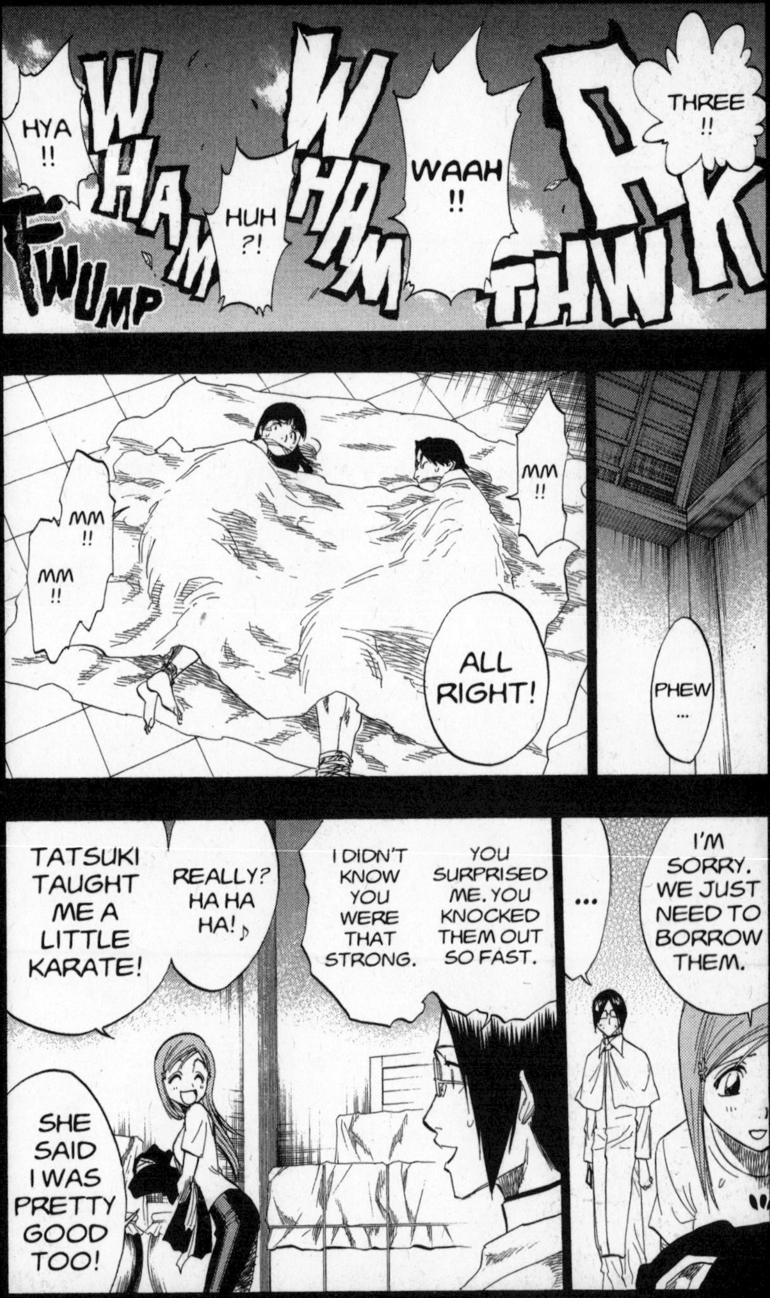

THREE!!
THNK
WAAH!!
WHAM
HUH?!
WHAM
HYA!!
FWUMP
PHEW...
MM!!
ALL RIGHT!
MM!!
MM!!
I'M SORRY. WE JUST NEED TO BORROW THEM.
...
YOU SURPRISED ME. YOU KNOCKED THEM OUT SO FAST.
I DIDN'T KNOW YOU WERE THAT STRONG.
REALLY? HA HA HA!♪
TATSUKI TAUGHT ME A LITTLE KARATE!
SHE SAID I WAS PRETTY GOOD TOO!

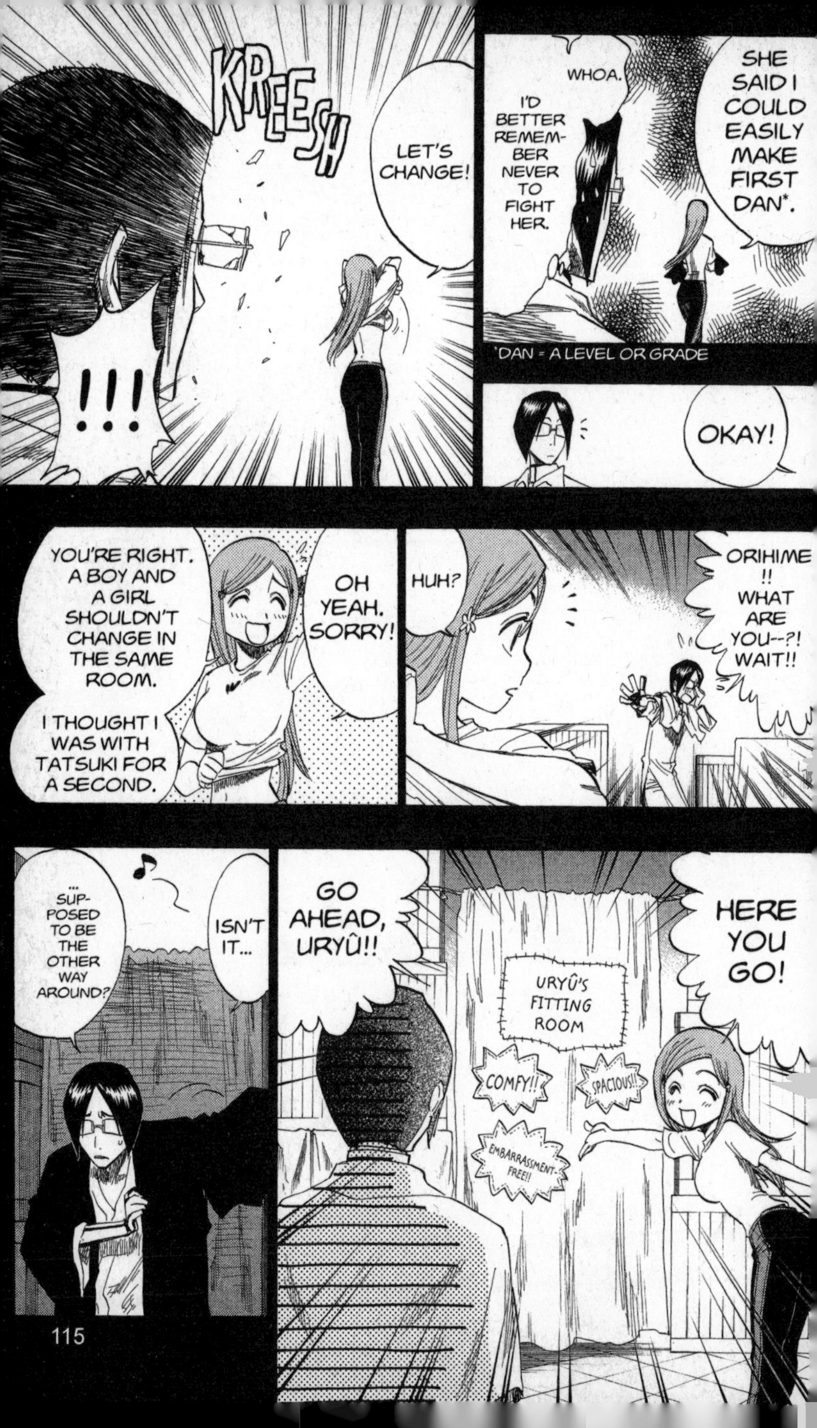

SHE SAID I COULD EASILY MAKE FIRST DAN*.
WHOA.
I'D BETTER REMEMBER NEVER TO FIGHT HER.
*DAN = A LEVEL OR GRADE
OKAY!
KREESH
LET'S CHANGE!
!!!
ORIHIME!! WHAT ARE YOU--?! WAIT!!
HUH?
OH YEAH. SORRY!
YOU'RE RIGHT. A BOY AND A GIRL SHOULDN'T CHANGE IN THE SAME ROOM.
I THOUGHT I WAS WITH TATSUKI FOR A SECOND.
HERE YOU GO!
URYÛ's FITTING ROOM
SPACIOUS!!
COMFY!!
EMBARRASSMENT-FREE!!
GO AHEAD, URYÛ!!
ISN'T IT...
...SUPPOSED TO BE THE OTHER WAY AROUND?

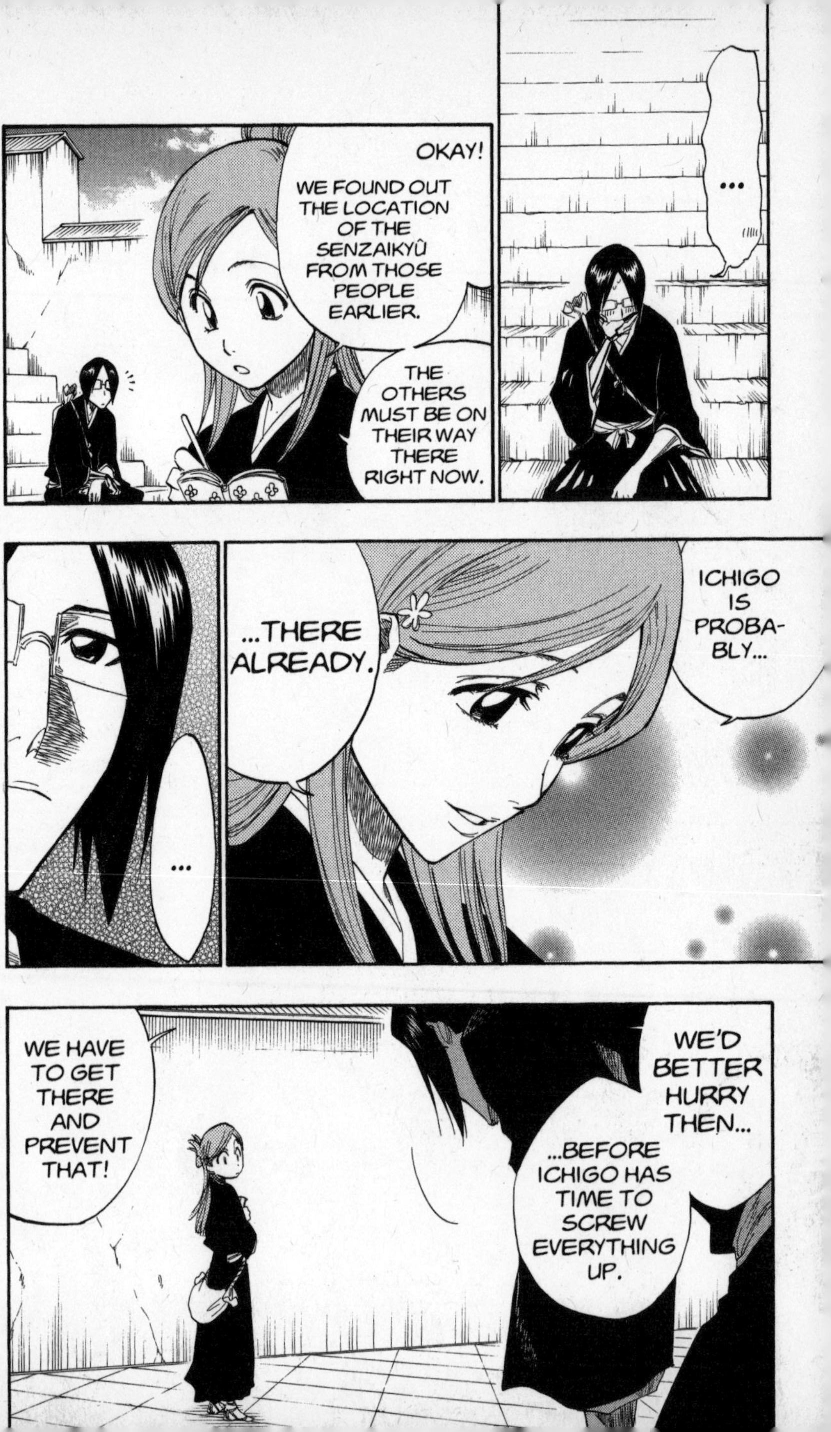
...
OKAY!
WE FOUND OUT THE LOCATION OF THE SENZAIKYŪ FROM THOSE PEOPLE EARLIER.
THE OTHERS MUST BE ON THEIR WAY THERE RIGHT NOW.
ICHIGO IS PROBA-BLY...
...THERE ALREADY.
...
WE'D BETTER HURRY THEN...
...BEFORE ICHIGO HAS TIME TO SCREW EVERYTHING UP.
WE HAVE TO GET THERE AND PREVENT THAT!

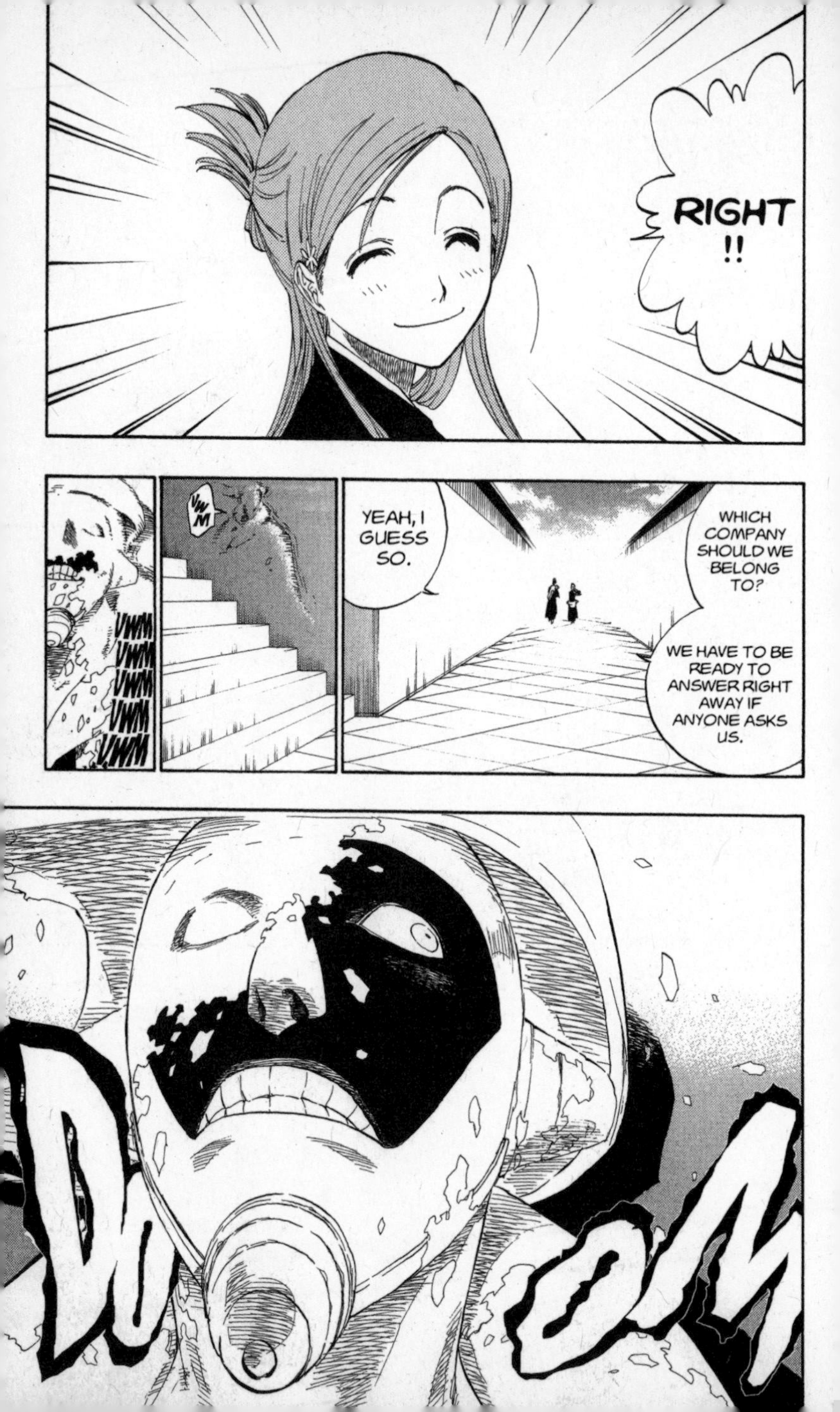
RIGHT !!
WHICH COMPANY SHOULD WE BELONG TO?
WE HAVE TO BE READY TO ANSWER RIGHT AWAY IF ANYONE ASKS US.
YEAH, I GUESS SO.
VWM
VWM VWM VWM VWM VWM VWM

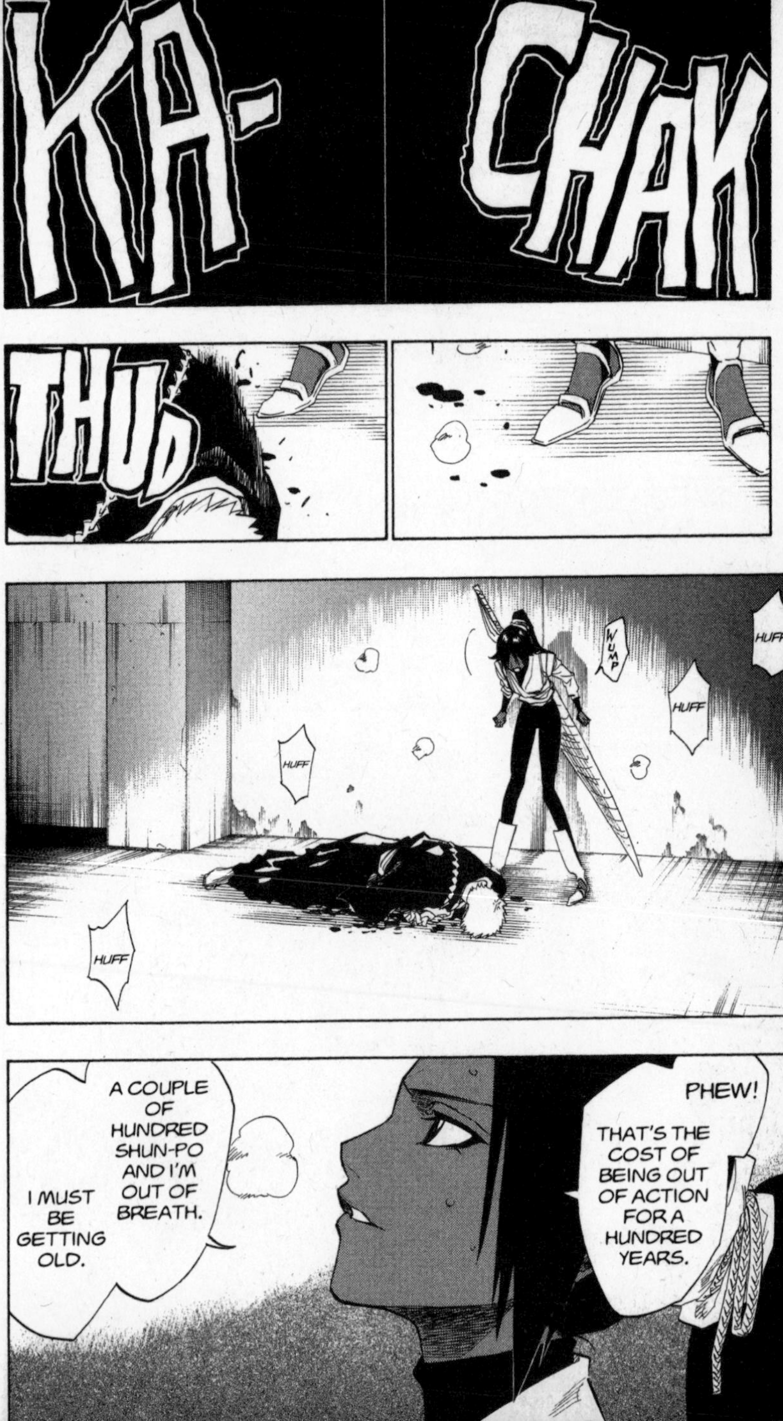

KA-CHAK
THUD
HUFF
HUFF
WUMP
HUFF
HUFF
PHEW!
THAT'S THE COST OF BEING OUT OF ACTION FOR A HUNDRED YEARS.
A COUPLE OF HUNDRED SHUN-PO AND I'M OUT OF BREATH.
I MUST BE GETTING OLD.

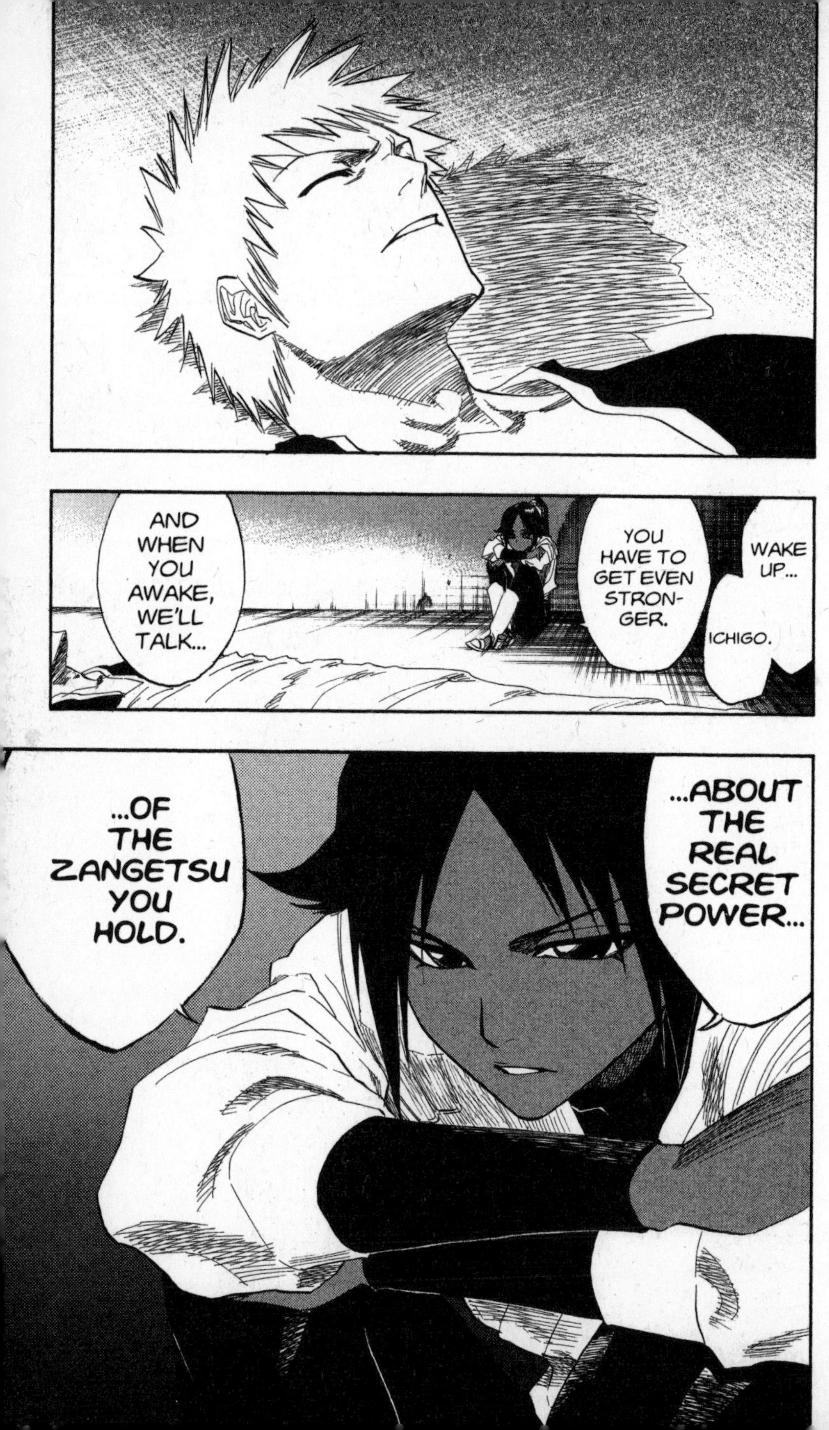
WAKE UP...
ICHIGO.
YOU HAVE TO GET EVEN STRONGER.
AND WHEN YOU AWAKE, WE'LL TALK...
...ABOUT THE REAL SECRET POWER...
...OF THE ZANGETSU YOU HOLD.

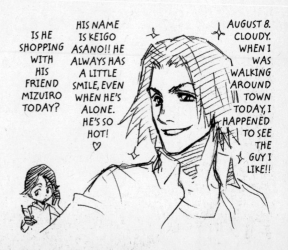

AUGUST 8. CLOUDY. WHEN I WAS WALKING AROUND TOWN TODAY, I HAPPENED TO SEE THE GUY I LIKE!!
HIS NAME IS KEIGO ASANO!! HE ALWAYS HAS A LITTLE SMILE, EVEN WHEN HE'S ALONE. HE'S SO HOT! ♡
IS HE SHOPPING WITH HIS FRIEND MIZUIRO TODAY?

120. Shake Hands with Grenades

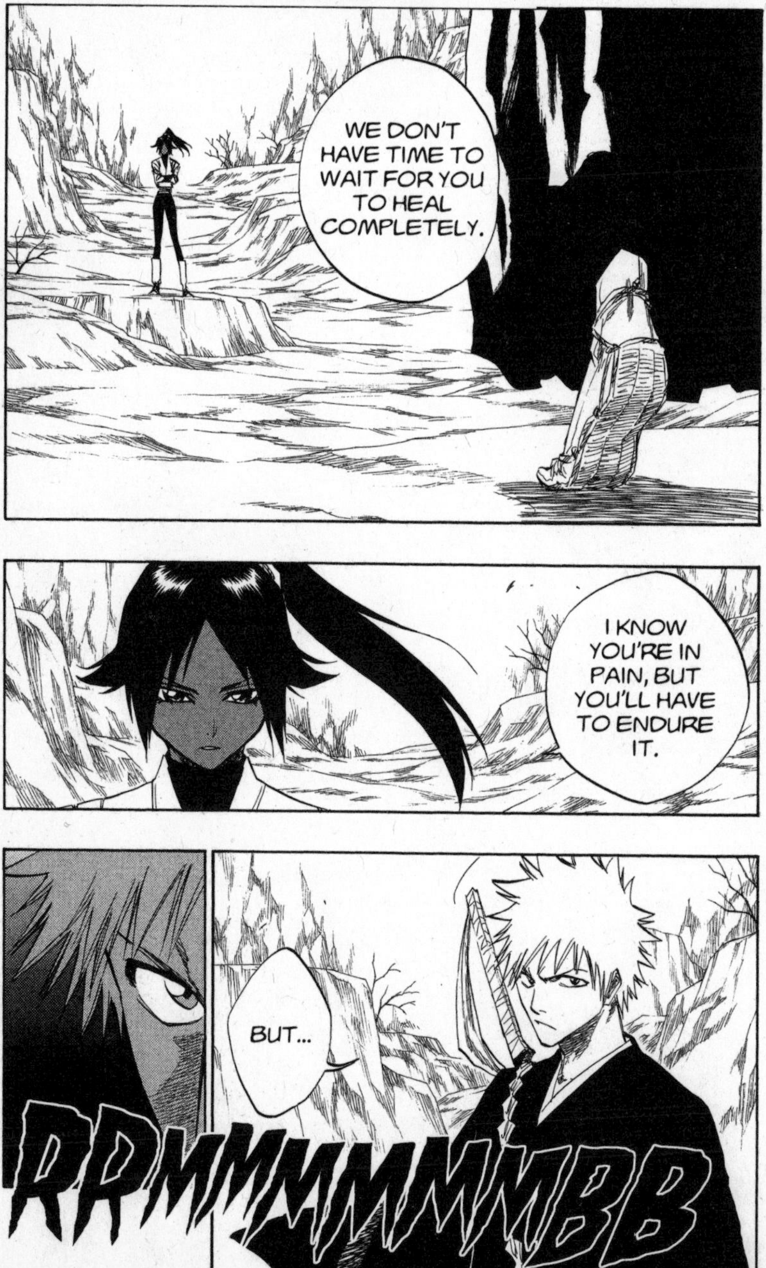
WE DON'T HAVE TIME TO WAIT FOR YOU TO HEAL COMPLETELY.
I KNOW YOU'RE IN PAIN, BUT YOU'LL HAVE TO ENDURE IT.
BUT...
RRMMMMMMBB

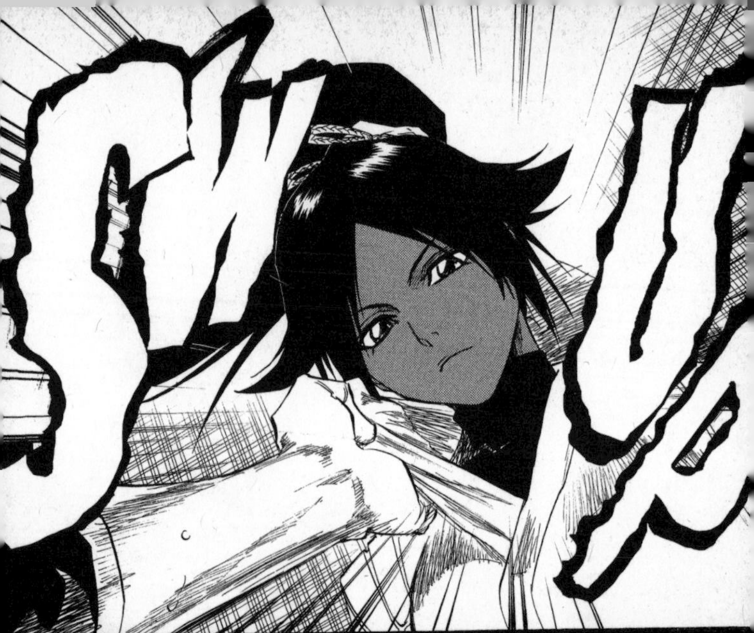

BLEACH

―ブリーチ―

120. Shake Hands with Grenades

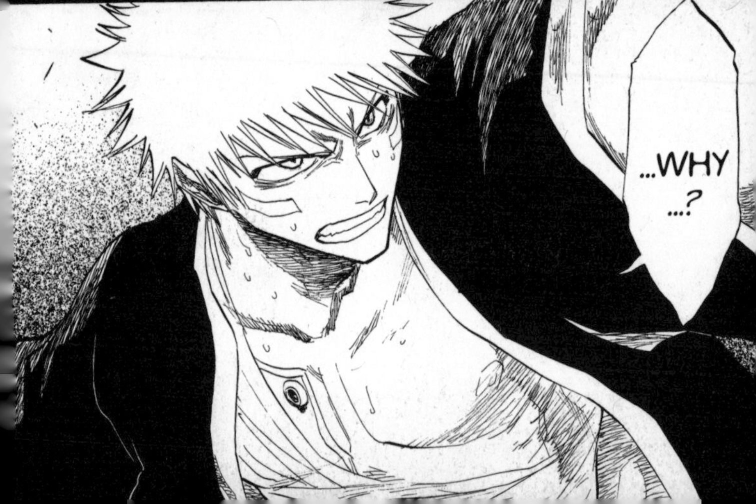
...WHY ...?

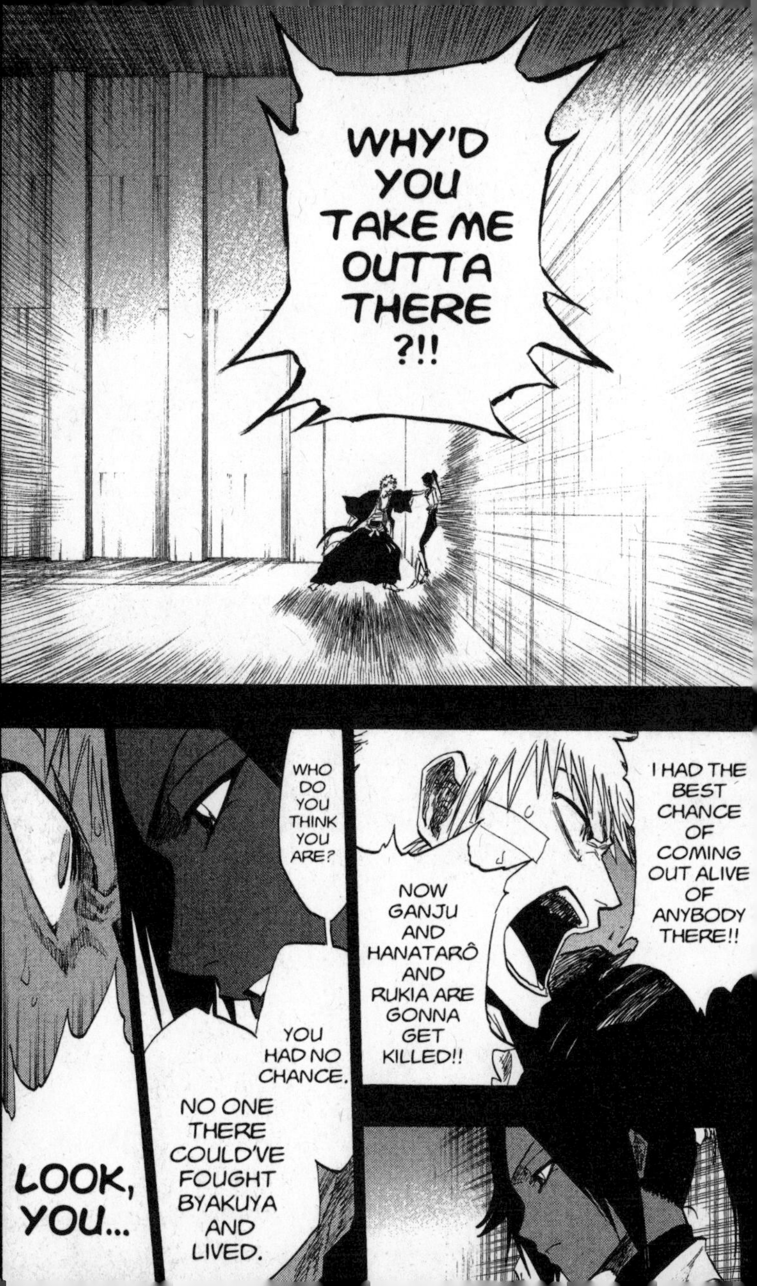
WHY'D YOU TAKE ME OUTTA THERE ?!!
I HAD THE BEST CHANCE OF COMING OUT ALIVE OF ANYBODY THERE!!
NOW GANJU AND HANATARÔ AND RUKIA ARE GONNA GET KILLED!!
WHO DO YOU THINK YOU ARE?
YOU HAD NO CHANCE.
NO ONE THERE COULD'VE FOUGHT BYAKUYA AND LIVED.
LOOK, YOU...

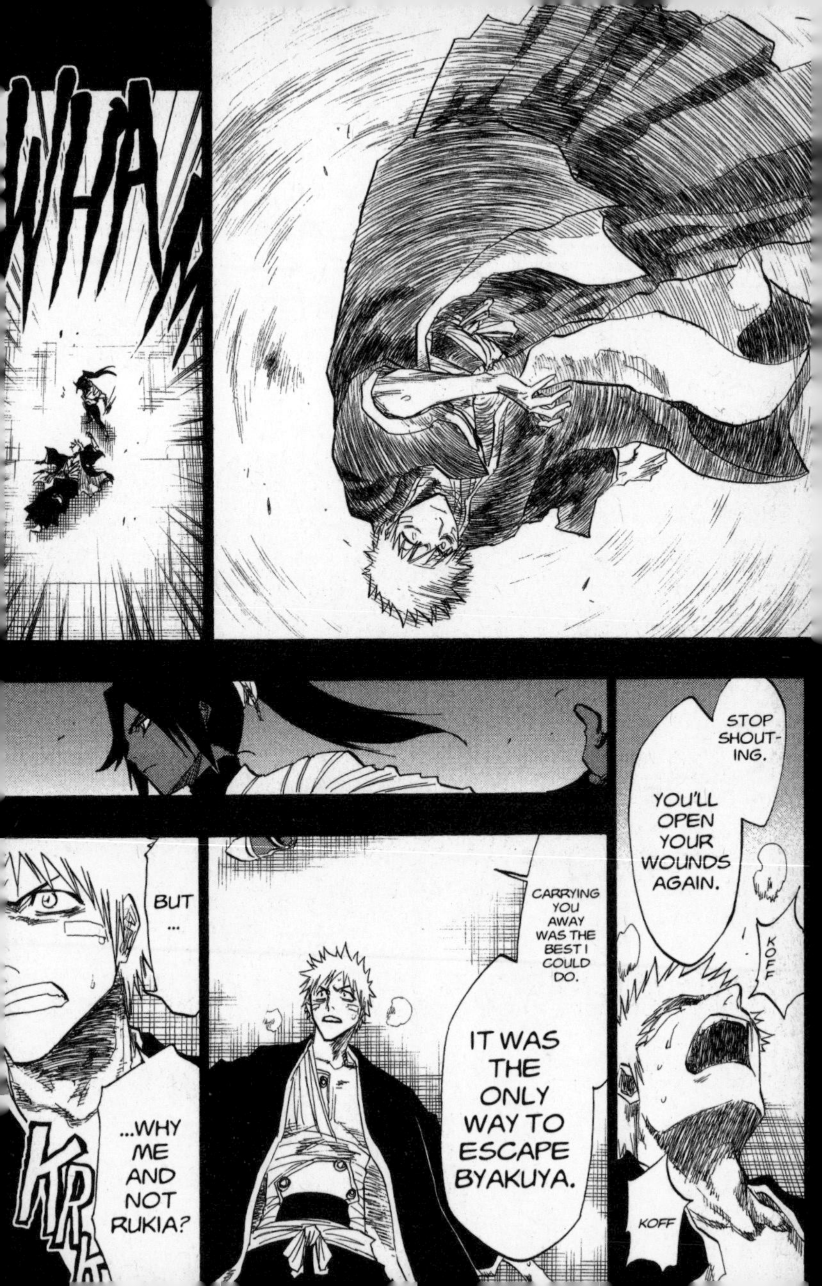
WHAM
STOP SHOUTING.
YOU'LL OPEN YOUR WOUNDS AGAIN.
KOFF
KOFF
CARRYING YOU AWAY WAS THE BEST I COULD DO.
IT WAS THE ONLY WAY TO ESCAPE BYAKUYA.
BUT ...
...WHY ME AND NOT RUKIA?

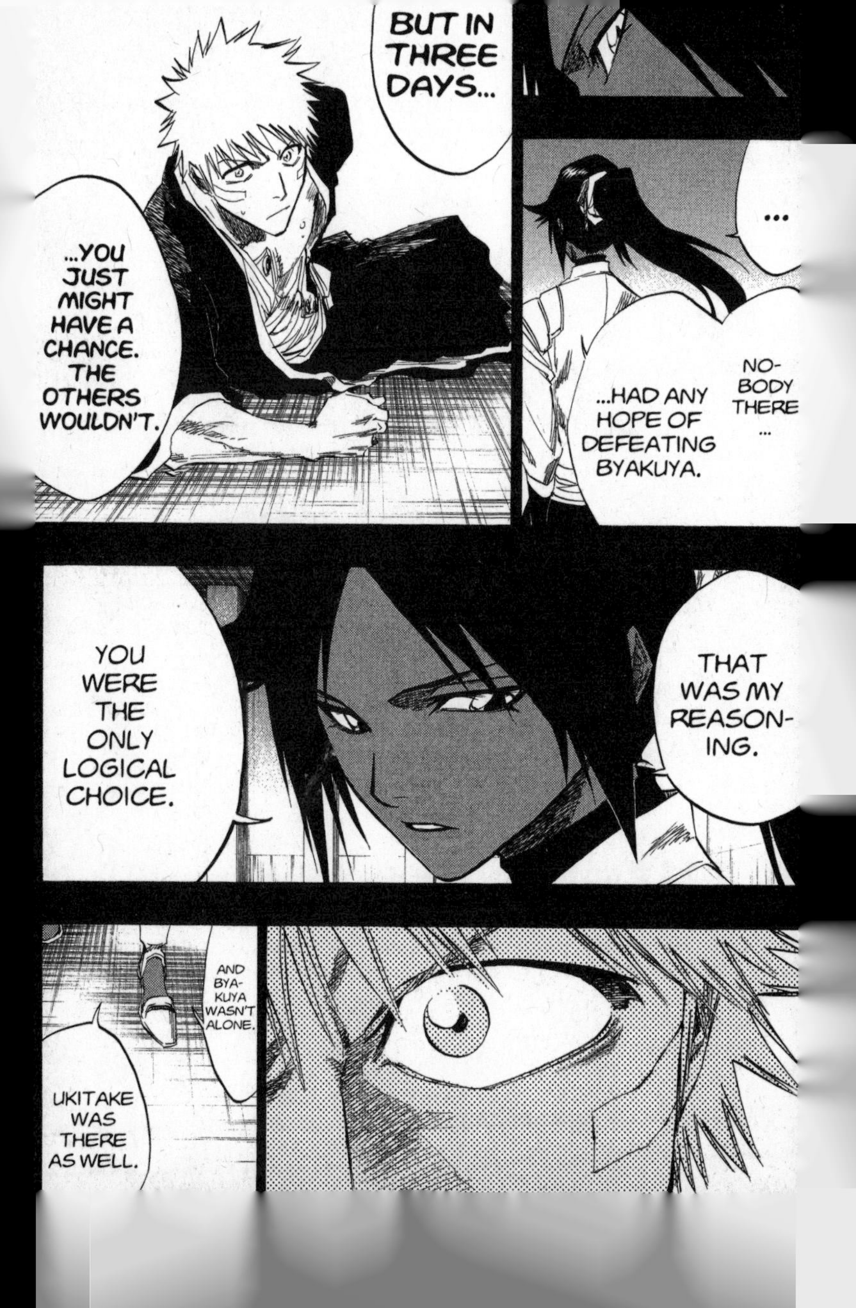
...
NO-BODY THERE...
...HAD ANY HOPE OF DEFEATING BYAKUYA.
BUT IN THREE DAYS...
...YOU JUST MIGHT HAVE A CHANCE. THE OTHERS WOULDN'T.
THAT WAS MY REASON-ING.
YOU WERE THE ONLY LOGICAL CHOICE.
AND BYA-KUYA WASN'T ALONE.
UKITAKE WAS THERE AS WELL.

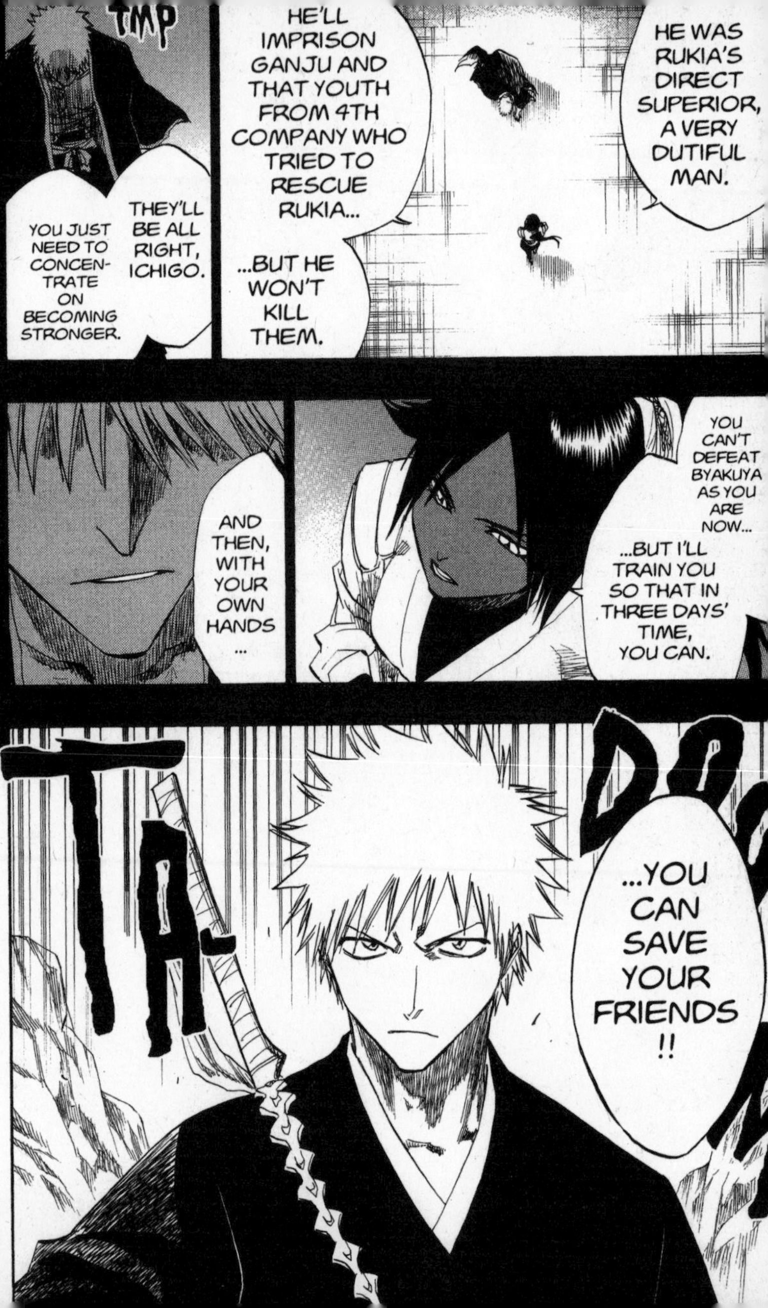
HE WAS RUKIA'S DIRECT SUPERIOR, A VERY DUTIFUL MAN.
HE'LL IMPRISON GANJU AND THAT YOUTH FROM 4TH COMPANY WHO TRIED TO RESCUE RUKIA...
...BUT HE WON'T KILL THEM.
TMP
THEY'LL BE ALL RIGHT, ICHIGO.
YOU JUST NEED TO CONCEN-TRATE ON BECOMING STRONGER.
YOU CAN'T DEFEAT BYAKUYA AS YOU ARE NOW...
...BUT I'LL TRAIN YOU SO THAT IN THREE DAYS' TIME, YOU CAN.
AND THEN, WITH YOUR OWN HANDS ...
...YOU CAN SAVE YOUR FRIENDS !!
TA

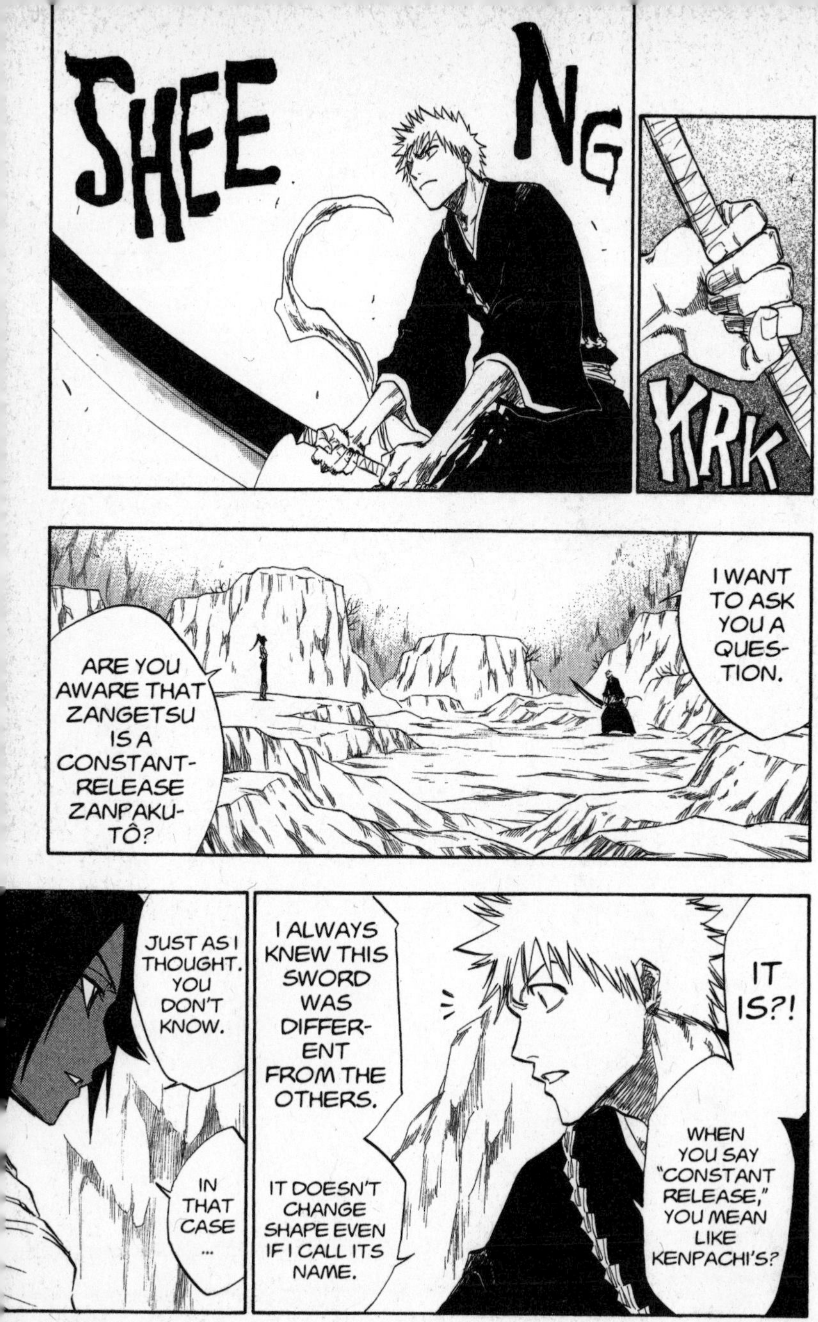

KRK
SHEENG
I WANT TO ASK YOU A QUESTION.
ARE YOU AWARE THAT ZANGETSU IS A CONSTANT-RELEASE ZANPAKUTÔ?
IT IS?!
WHEN YOU SAY "CONSTANT RELEASE," YOU MEAN LIKE KENPACHI'S?
I ALWAYS KNEW THIS SWORD WAS DIFFERENT FROM THE OTHERS.
IT DOESN'T CHANGE SHAPE EVEN IF I CALL ITS NAME.
JUST AS I THOUGHT. YOU DON'T KNOW.
IN THAT CASE ...

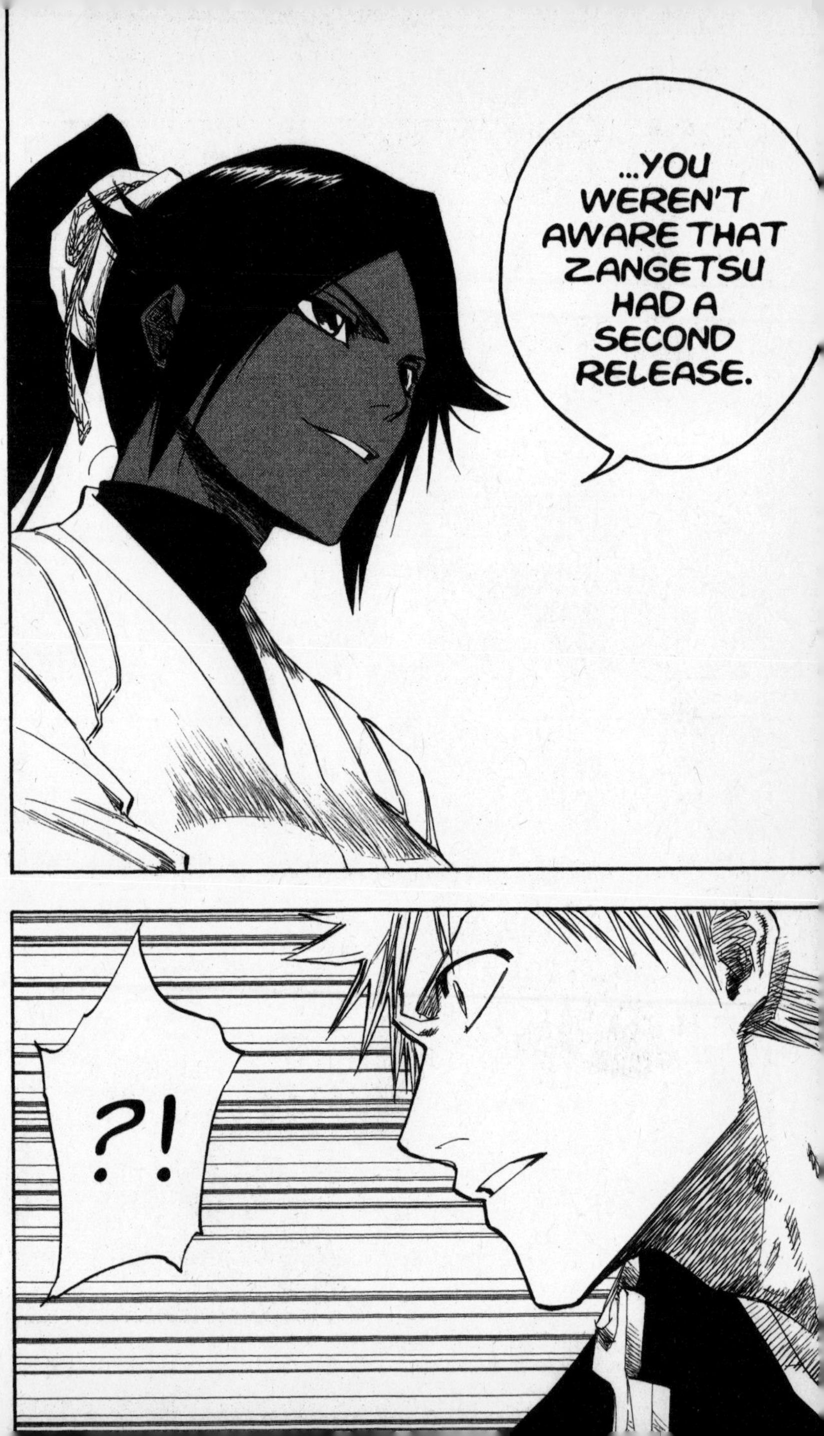
...YOU WEREN'T AWARE THAT ZANGETSU HAD A SECOND RELEASE.
?!

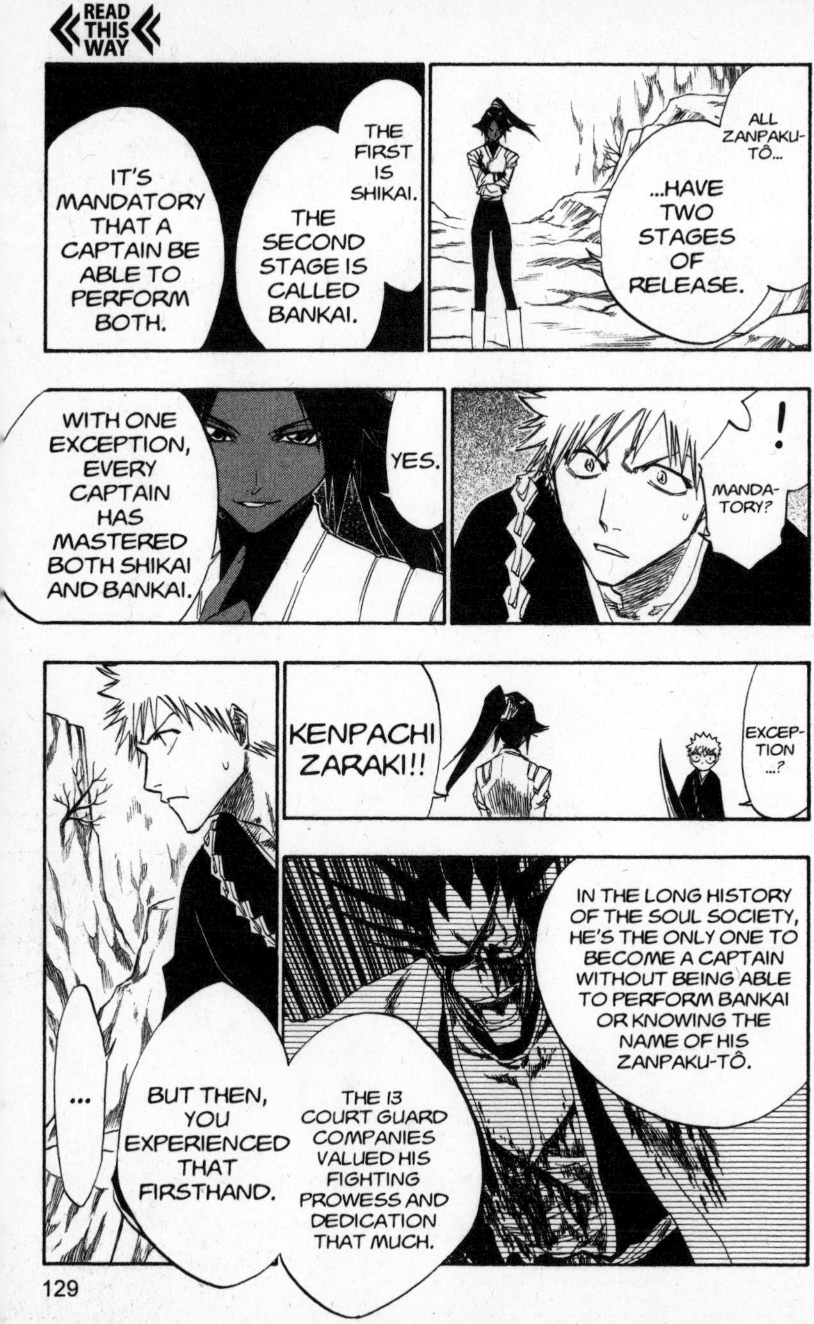

READ THIS WAY
ALL ZANPAKU-TÔ...
...HAVE TWO STAGES OF RELEASE.
THE FIRST IS SHIKAI.
THE SECOND STAGE IS CALLED BANKAI.
IT'S MANDATORY THAT A CAPTAIN BE ABLE TO PERFORM BOTH.
!
MANDATORY?
YES.
WITH ONE EXCEPTION, EVERY CAPTAIN HAS MASTERED BOTH SHIKAI AND BANKAI.
EXCEPTION...?
KENPACHI ZARAKI!!
IN THE LONG HISTORY OF THE SOUL SOCIETY, HE'S THE ONLY ONE TO BECOME A CAPTAIN WITHOUT BEING ABLE TO PERFORM BANKAI OR KNOWING THE NAME OF HIS ZANPAKU-TÔ.
THE 13 COURT GUARD COMPANIES VALUED HIS FIGHTING PROWESS AND DEDICATION THAT MUCH.
BUT THEN, YOU EXPERIENCED THAT FIRSTHAND.
...

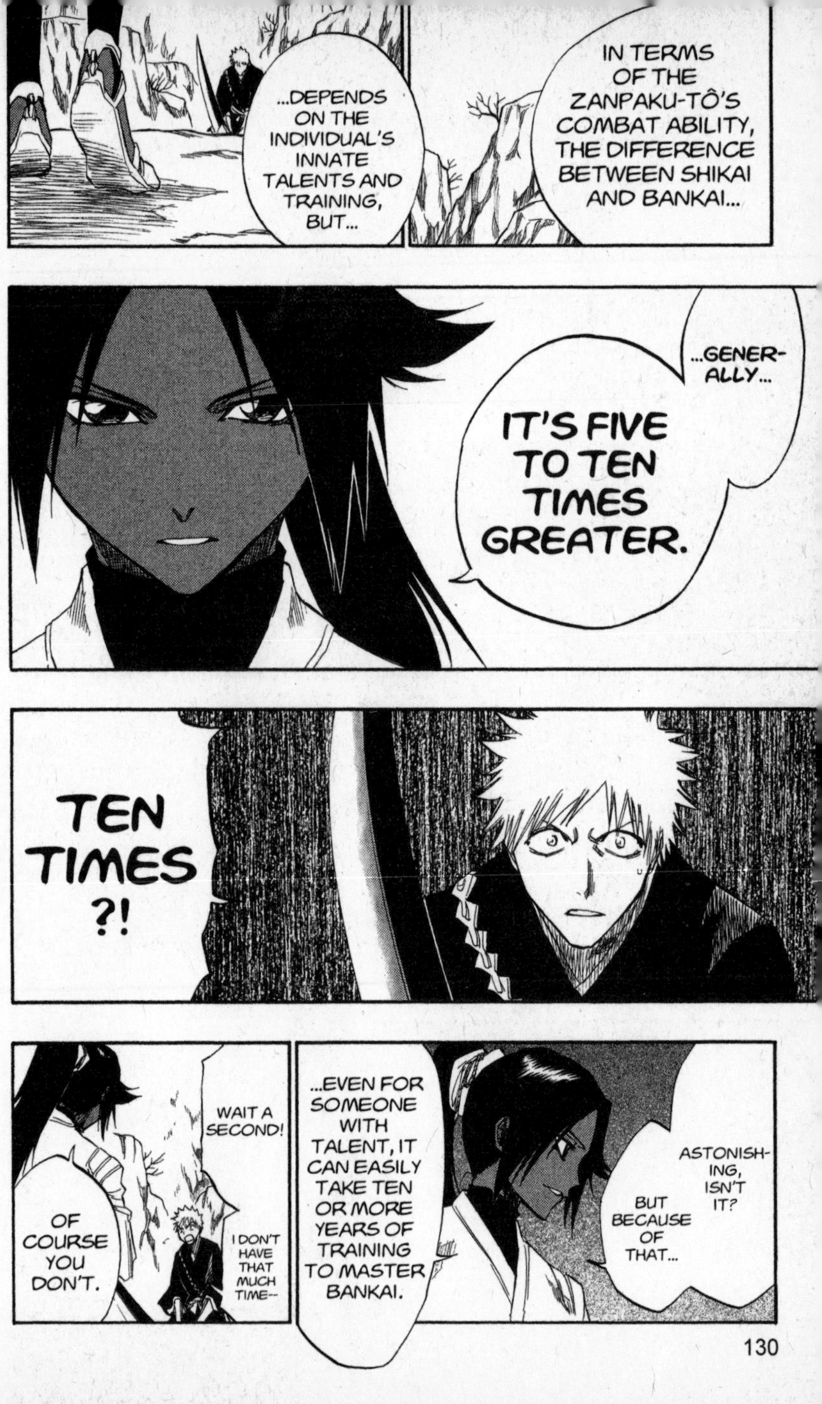
IN TERMS OF THE ZANPAKU-TÔ'S COMBAT ABILITY, THE DIFFERENCE BETWEEN SHIKAI AND BANKAI...
...DEPENDS ON THE INDIVIDUAL'S INNATE TALENTS AND TRAINING, BUT...
...GENER-ALLY...
IT'S FIVE TO TEN TIMES GREATER.
TEN TIMES ?!
ASTONISH-ING, ISN'T IT?
BUT BECAUSE OF THAT...
...EVEN FOR SOMEONE WITH TALENT, IT CAN EASILY TAKE TEN OR MORE YEARS OF TRAINING TO MASTER BANKAI.
WAIT A SECOND!
I DON'T HAVE THAT MUCH TIME--
OF COURSE YOU DON'T.

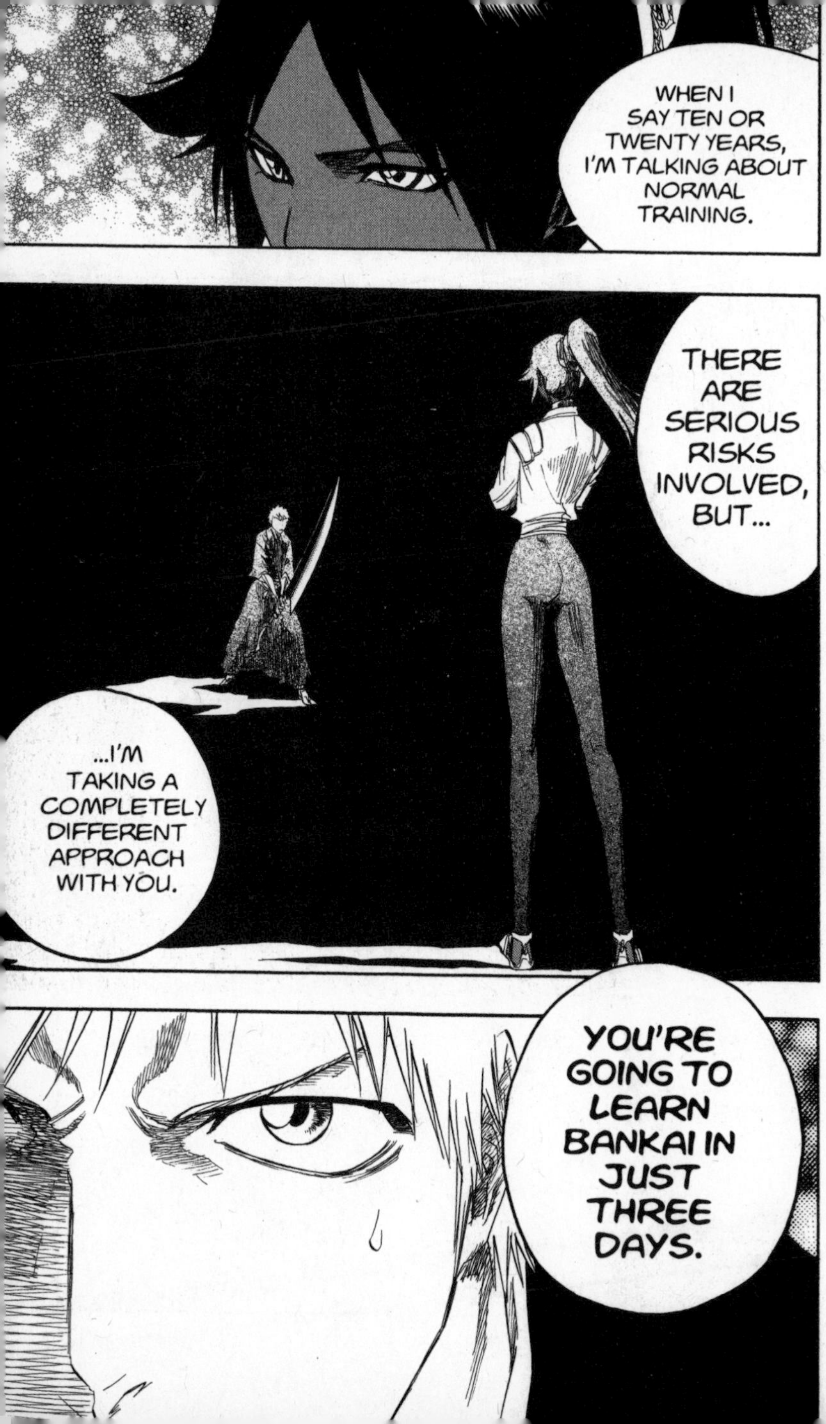
WHEN I SAY TEN OR TWENTY YEARS, I'M TALKING ABOUT NORMAL TRAINING.
THERE ARE SERIOUS RISKS INVOLVED, BUT...
...I'M TAKING A COMPLETELY DIFFERENT APPROACH WITH YOU.
YOU'RE GOING TO LEARN BANKAI IN JUST THREE DAYS.

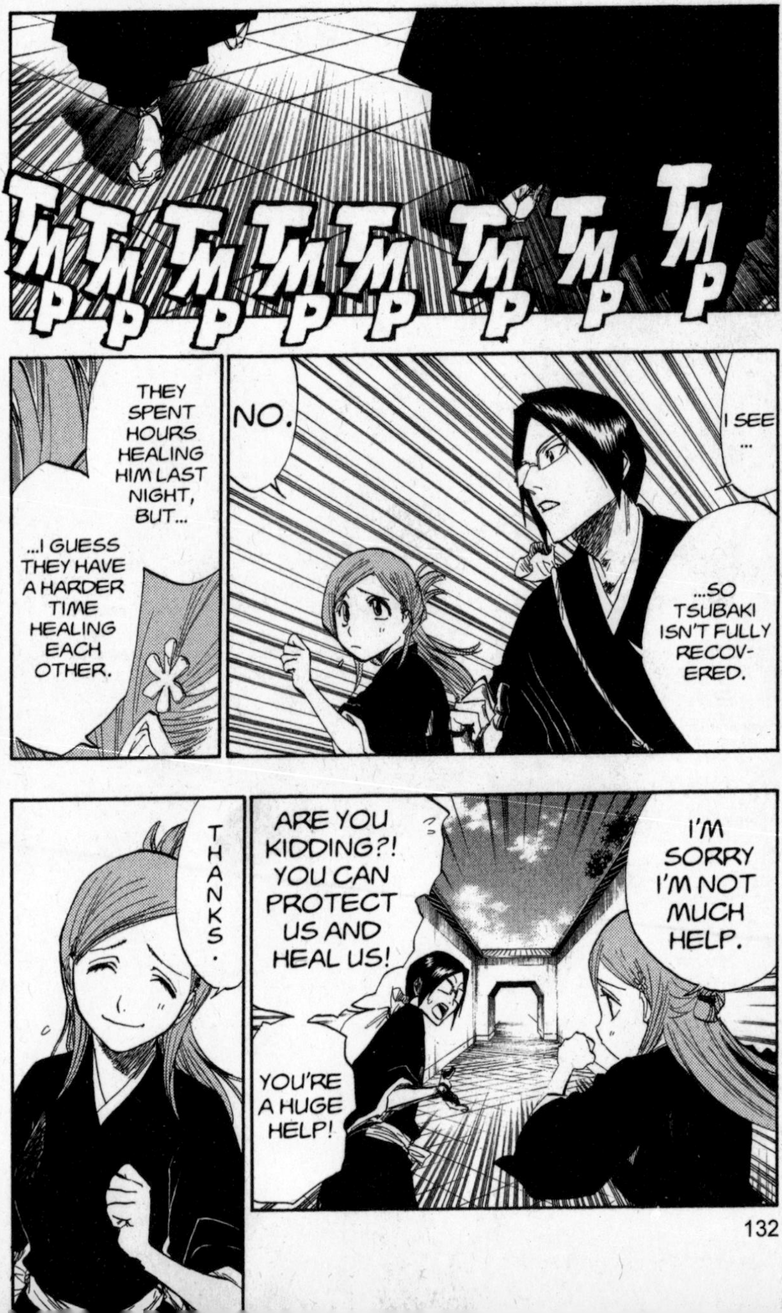
TMP TMP TMP TMP TMP TMP TMP TMP
I SEE...
...SO TSUBAKI ISN'T FULLY RECOVERED.
NO.
THEY SPENT HOURS HEALING HIM LAST NIGHT, BUT...
...I GUESS THEY HAVE A HARDER TIME HEALING EACH OTHER.
I'M SORRY I'M NOT MUCH HELP.
ARE YOU KIDDING?! YOU CAN PROTECT US AND HEAL US!
YOU'RE A HUGE HELP!
THANKS.

READ THIS WAY

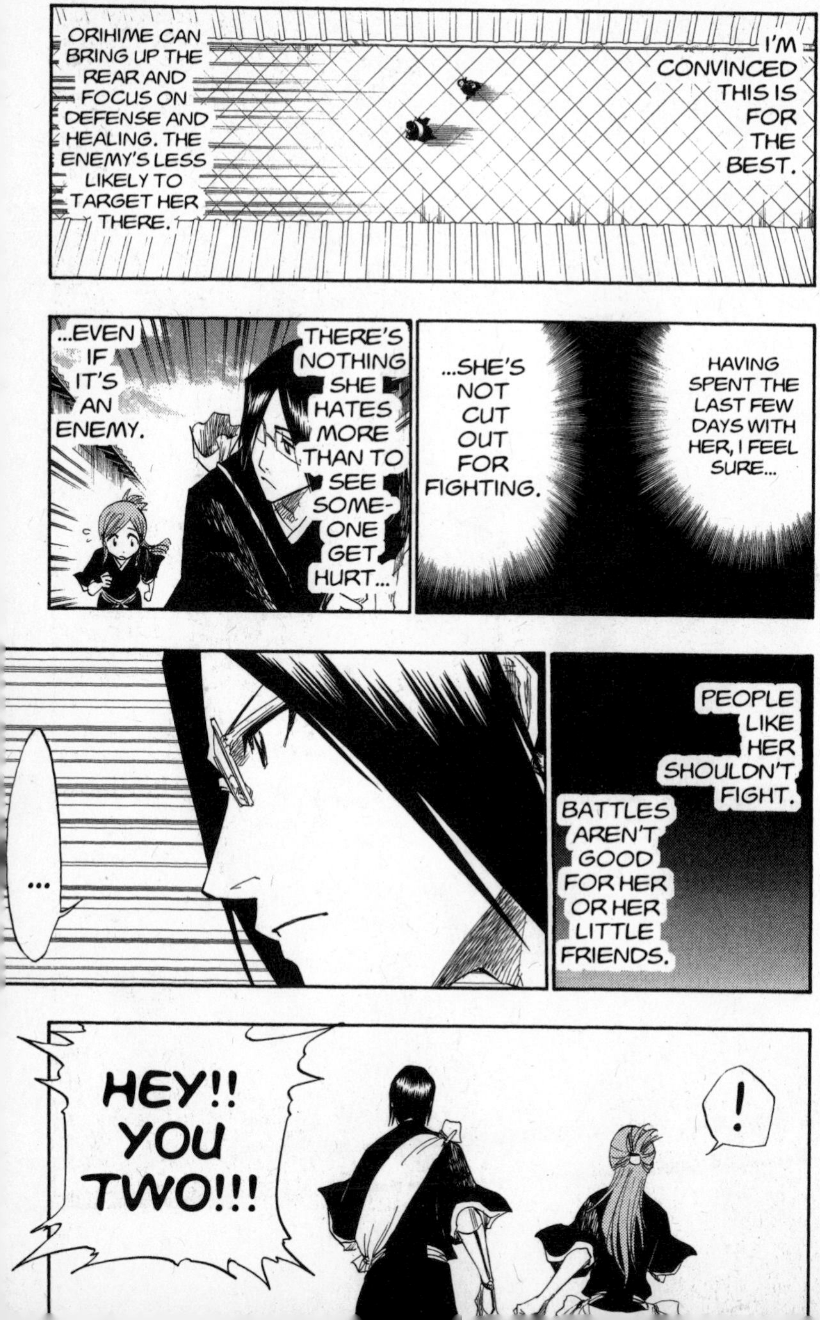
I'M CONVINCED THIS IS FOR THE BEST.
ORIHIME CAN BRING UP THE REAR AND FOCUS ON DEFENSE AND HEALING. THE ENEMY'S LESS LIKELY TO TARGET HER THERE.
HAVING SPENT THE LAST FEW DAYS WITH HER, I FEEL SURE...
...SHE'S NOT CUT OUT FOR FIGHTING.
THERE'S NOTHING SHE HATES MORE THAN TO SEE SOME-ONE GET HURT...
...EVEN IF IT'S AN ENEMY.
PEOPLE LIKE HER SHOULDN'T FIGHT.
BATTLES AREN'T GOOD FOR HER OR HER LITTLE FRIENDS.
...
!
HEY!! YOU TWO!!!

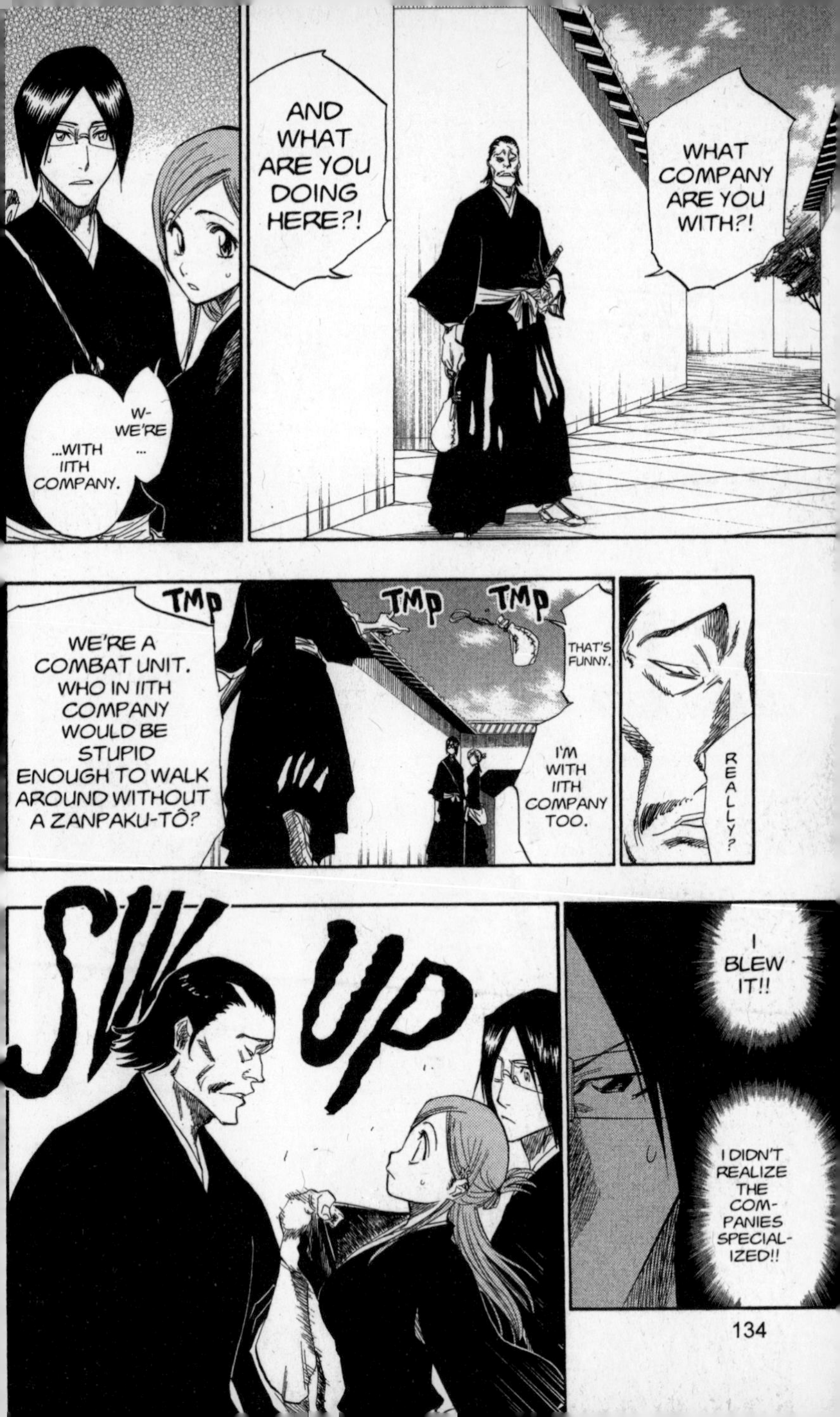
WHAT COMPANY ARE YOU WITH?!
AND WHAT ARE YOU DOING HERE?!
W- WE'RE ...
...WITH 11TH COMPANY.
REALLY?
TMP
TMP
THAT'S FUNNY.
I'M WITH 11TH COMPANY TOO.
TMP
WE'RE A COMBAT UNIT. WHO IN 11TH COMPANY WOULD BE STUPID ENOUGH TO WALK AROUND WITHOUT A ZANPAKU-TÔ?
I BLEW IT!!
I DIDN'T REALIZE THE COM- PANIES SPECIAL- IZED!!
SWUP

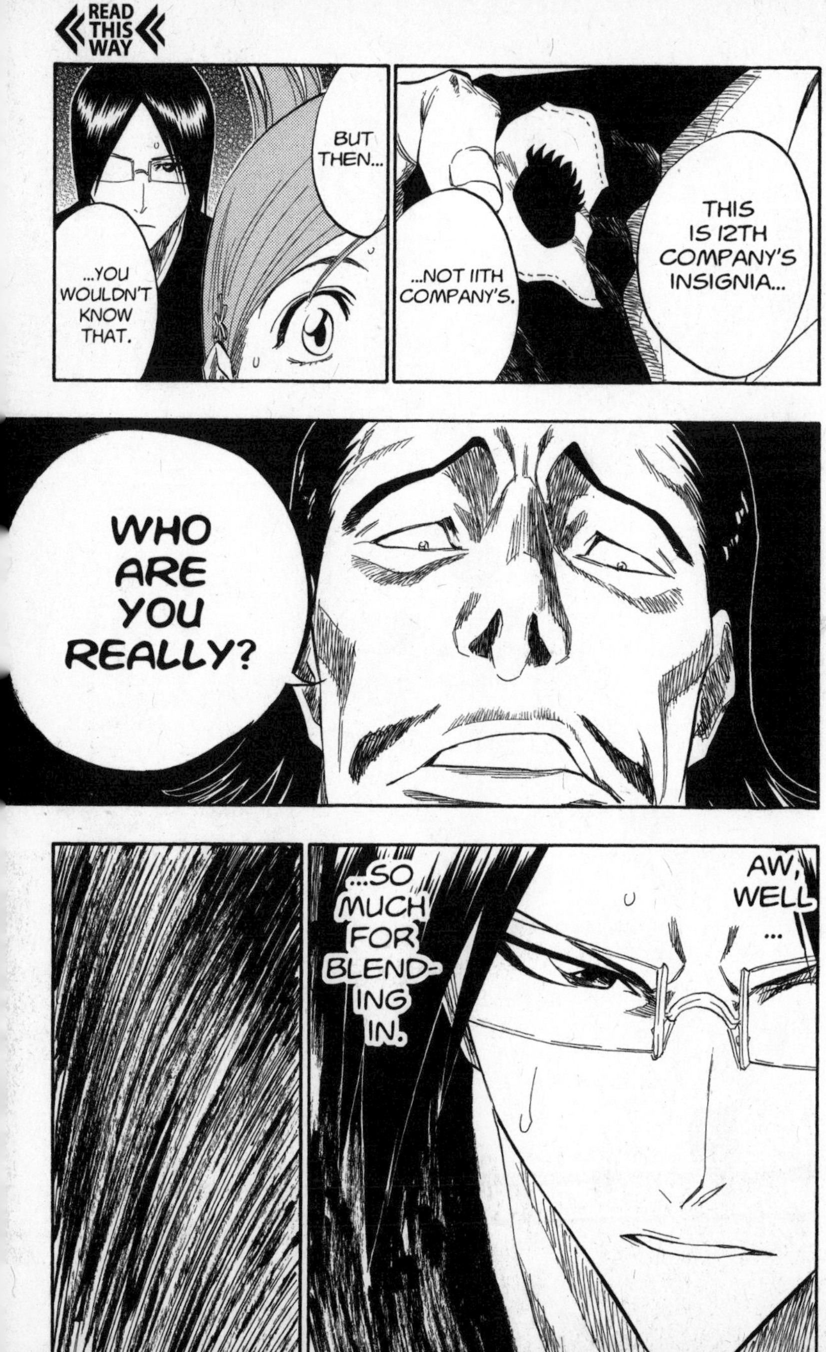
READ THIS WAY
THIS IS 12TH COMPANY'S INSIGNIA...
...NOT 11TH COMPANY'S.
BUT THEN...
...YOU WOULDN'T KNOW THAT.
WHO ARE YOU REALLY?
AW, WELL ...
...SO MUCH FOR BLENDING IN.

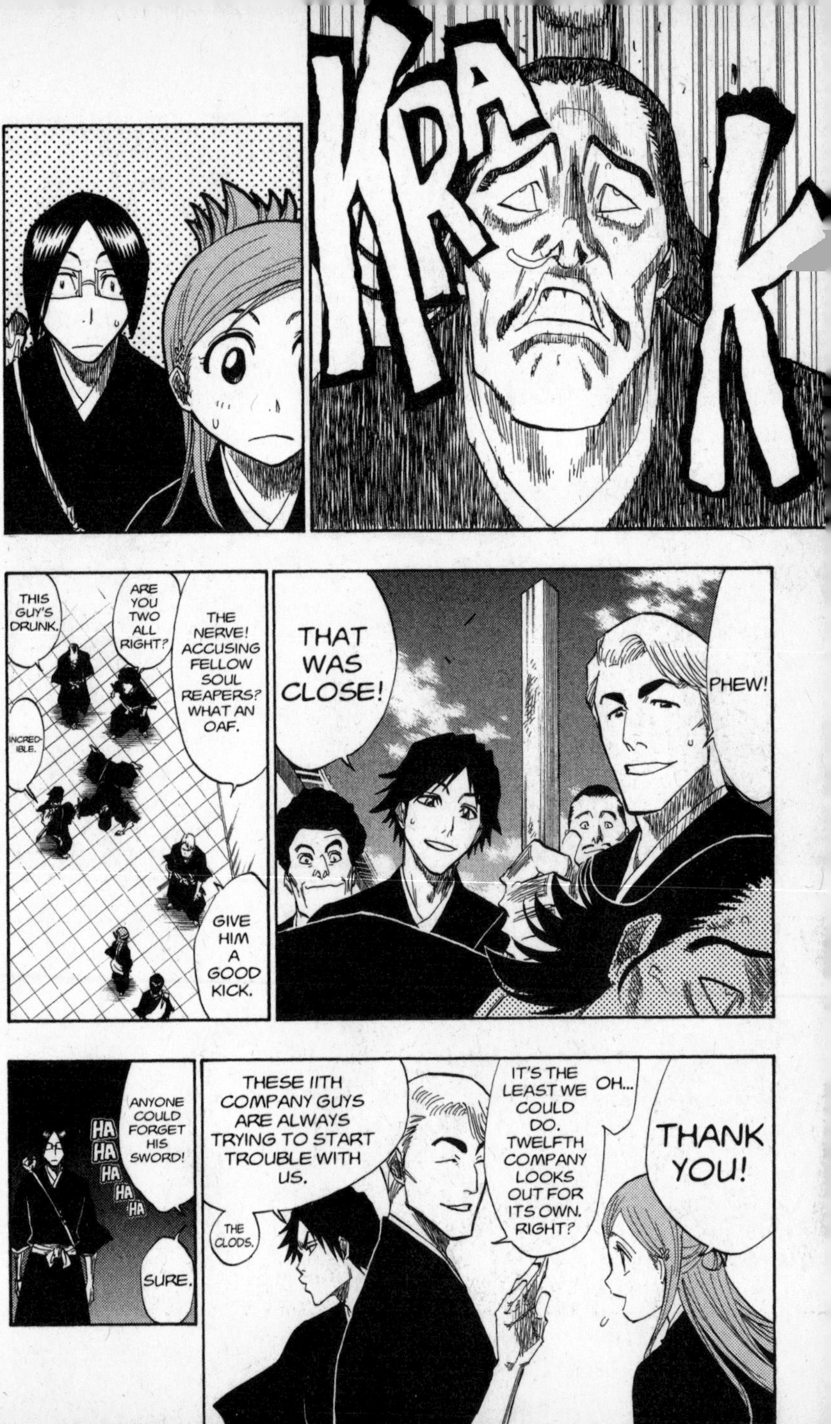
KRAK
PHEW!
THAT WAS CLOSE!
THE NERVE! ACCUSING FELLOW SOUL REAPERS? WHAT AN OAF.
ARE YOU TWO ALL RIGHT?
THIS GUY'S DRUNK.
INCREDIBLE.
GIVE HIM A GOOD KICK.
THANK YOU!
OH...
IT'S THE LEAST WE COULD DO. TWELFTH COMPANY LOOKS OUT FOR ITS OWN. RIGHT?
THESE 11TH COMPANY GUYS ARE ALWAYS TRYING TO START TROUBLE WITH US.
THE CLODS.
ANYONE COULD FORGET HIS SWORD!
HA HA HA HA HA
SURE.

READ THIS WAY

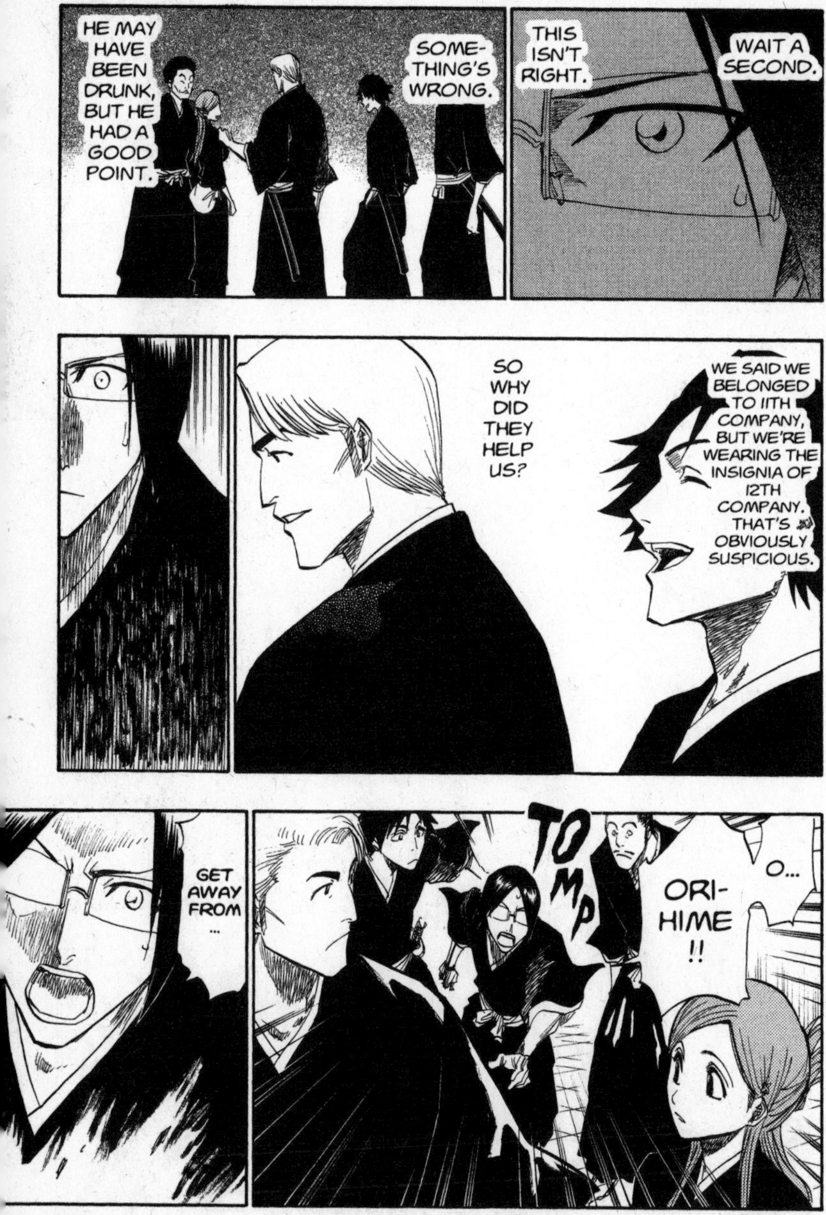

WAIT A SECOND.
THIS ISN'T RIGHT.
SOME-THING'S WRONG.
HE MAY HAVE BEEN DRUNK, BUT HE HAD A GOOD POINT.
WE SAID WE BELONGED TO 11TH COMPANY, BUT WE'RE WEARING THE INSIGNIA OF 12TH COMPANY. THAT'S OBVIOUSLY SUSPICIOUS.
SO WHY DID THEY HELP US?
O...
ORI-HIME !!
TOMP
GET AWAY FROM ...

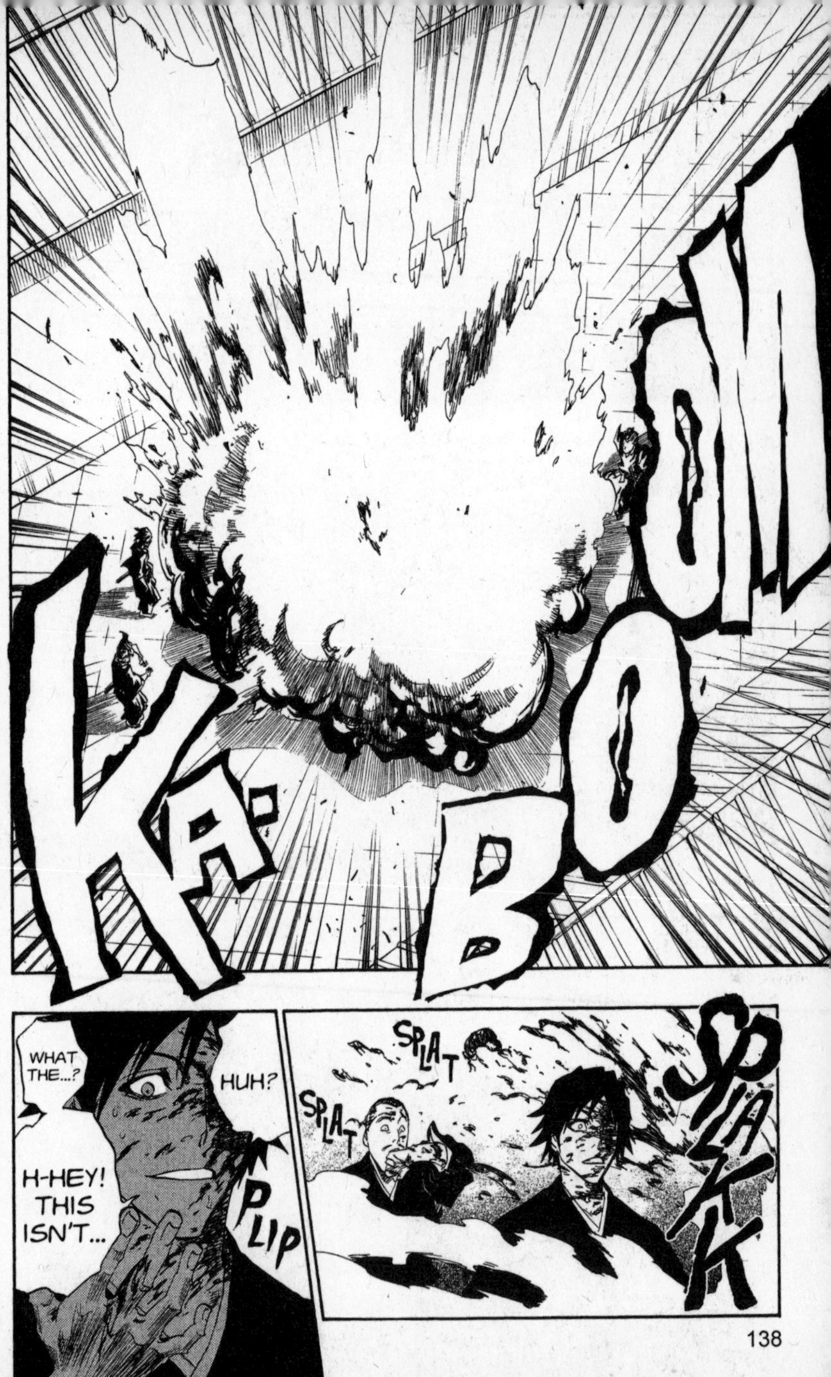
KABOOM
SPLAT
SPLAT
SPLAKK
HUH?
WHAT THE...?
PLIP
H-HEY! THIS ISN'T...

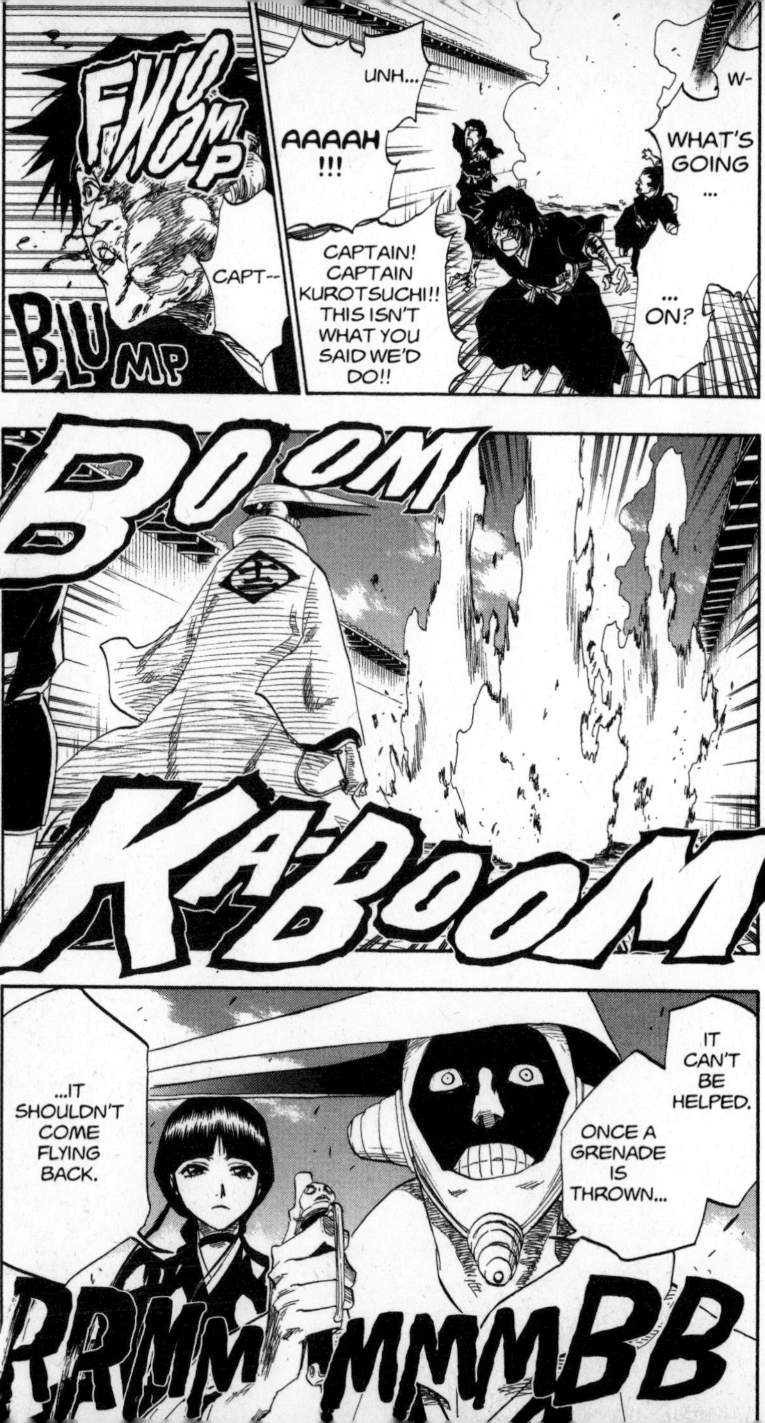
W-
WHAT'S GOING ...
... ON?
UNH...
AAAAH !!!
CAPTAIN! CAPTAIN KUROTSUCHI!! THIS ISN'T WHAT YOU SAID WE'D DO!!
FWOMP
CAPT--
BLUMP
BOOM
KABOOM
IT CAN'T BE HELPED.
ONCE A GRENADE IS THROWN...
...IT SHOULDN'T COME FLYING BACK.
RRMMMMMMBB

WHILE I WAS ADMIRING KEIGO, SOMEBODY PULLED HIM AROUND THE CORNER AND TRIED TO EXTORT MONEY FROM HIM!

WHO IS IT?!

NOBODY EXTORTS MONEY FROM MY KEIGO!!

O-OKAY! YOU CAN DO IT, MIDORIKO!! BE BRAVE AND DO WHATEVER YOU HAVE TO DO TO SAVE HIM!!

121. In Sane We Trust

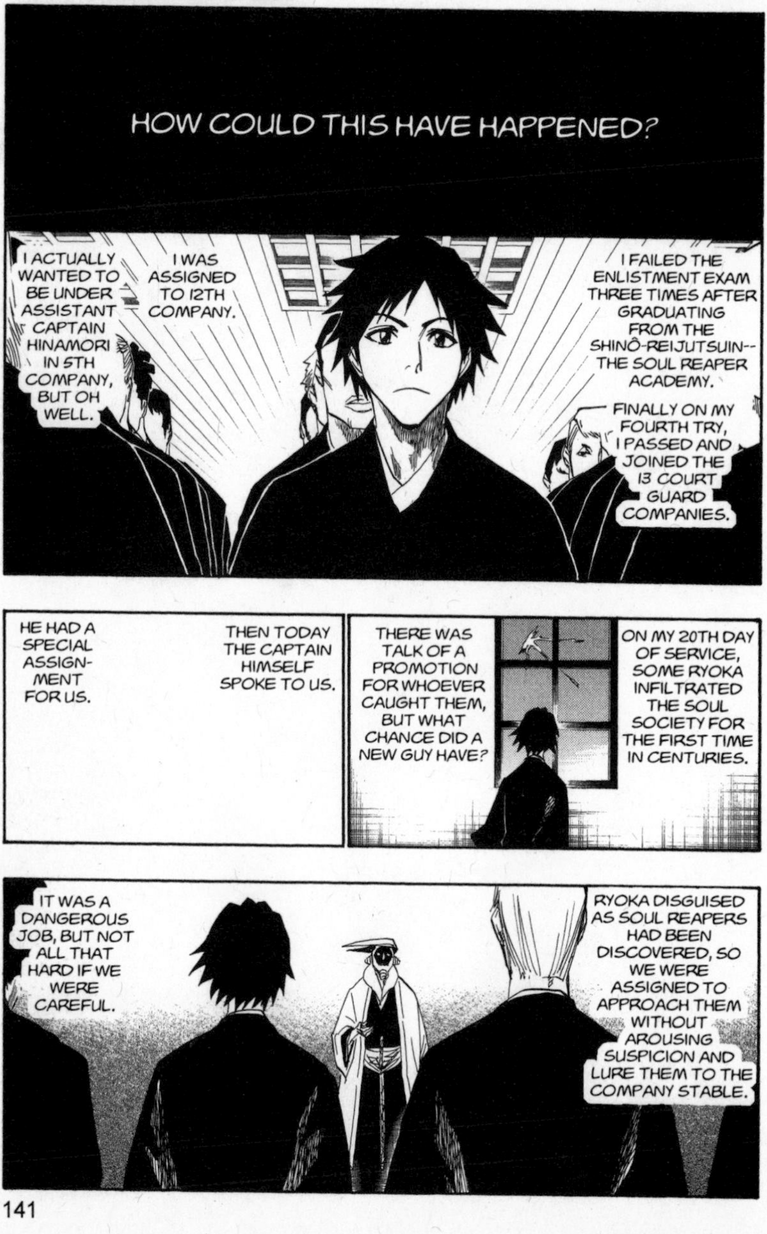
HOW COULD THIS HAVE HAPPENED?
I FAILED THE ENLISTMENT EXAM THREE TIMES AFTER GRADUATING FROM THE SHINÔ-REIJUTSUIN-- THE SOUL REAPER ACADEMY.
FINALLY ON MY FOURTH TRY, I PASSED AND JOINED THE 13 COURT GUARD COMPANIES.
I WAS ASSIGNED TO 12TH COMPANY.
I ACTUALLY WANTED TO BE UNDER ASSISTANT CAPTAIN HINAMORI IN 5TH COMPANY, BUT OH WELL.
ON MY 20TH DAY OF SERVICE, SOME RYOKA INFILTRATED THE SOUL SOCIETY FOR THE FIRST TIME IN CENTURIES.
THERE WAS TALK OF A PROMOTION FOR WHOEVER CAUGHT THEM, BUT WHAT CHANCE DID A NEW GUY HAVE?
THEN TODAY THE CAPTAIN HIMSELF SPOKE TO US.
HE HAD A SPECIAL ASSIGNMENT FOR US.
RYOKA DISGUISED AS SOUL REAPERS HAD BEEN DISCOVERED, SO WE WERE ASSIGNED TO APPROACH THEM WITHOUT AROUSING SUSPICION AND LURE THEM TO THE COMPANY STABLE.
IT WAS A DANGEROUS JOB, BUT NOT ALL THAT HARD IF WE WERE CAREFUL.

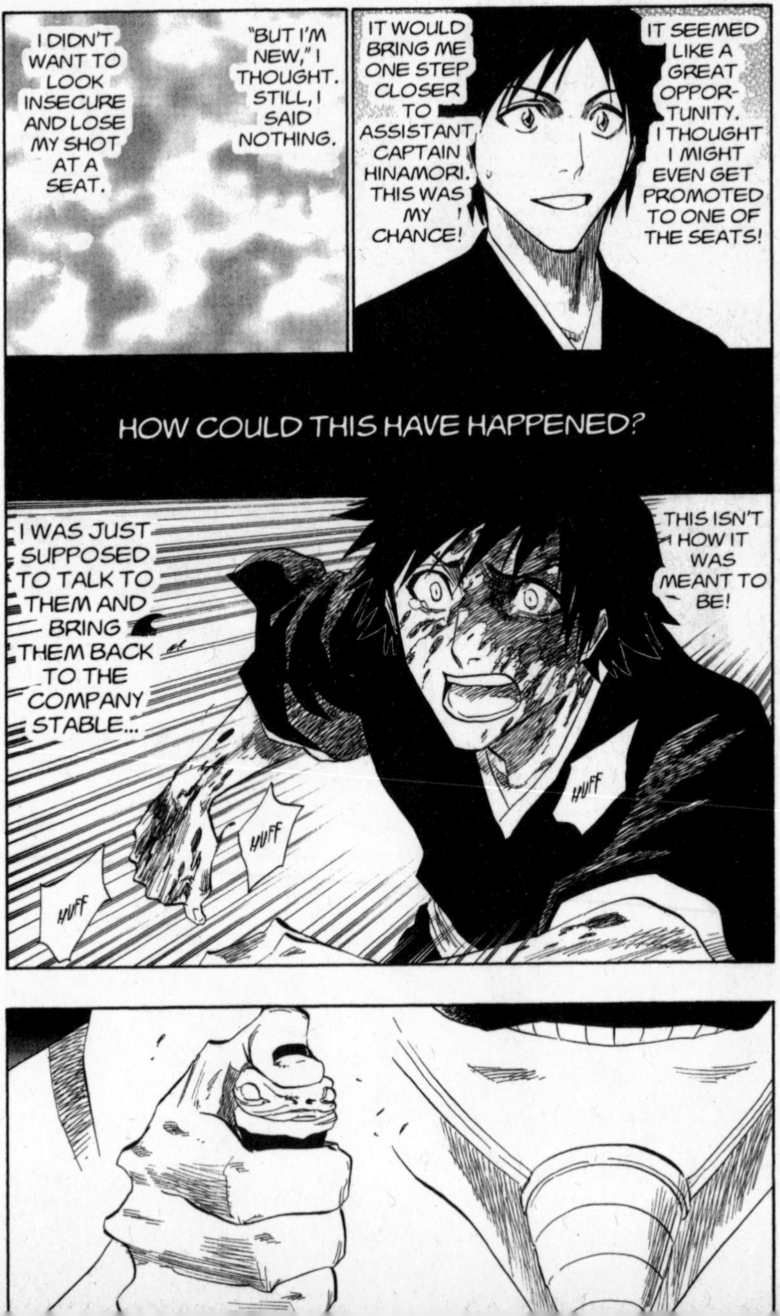
IT SEEMED LIKE A GREAT OPPORTUNITY. I THOUGHT I MIGHT EVEN GET PROMOTED TO ONE OF THE SEATS!
IT WOULD BRING ME ONE STEP CLOSER TO ASSISTANT CAPTAIN HINAMORI. THIS WAS MY CHANCE!
"BUT I'M NEW," I THOUGHT. STILL, I SAID NOTHING.
I DIDN'T WANT TO LOOK INSECURE AND LOSE MY SHOT AT A SEAT.
HOW COULD THIS HAVE HAPPENED?
THIS ISN'T HOW IT WAS MEANT TO BE!
I WAS JUST SUPPOSED TO TALK TO THEM AND BRING THEM BACK TO THE COMPANY STABLE...
HUFF
HUFF
HUFF

READ THIS WAY

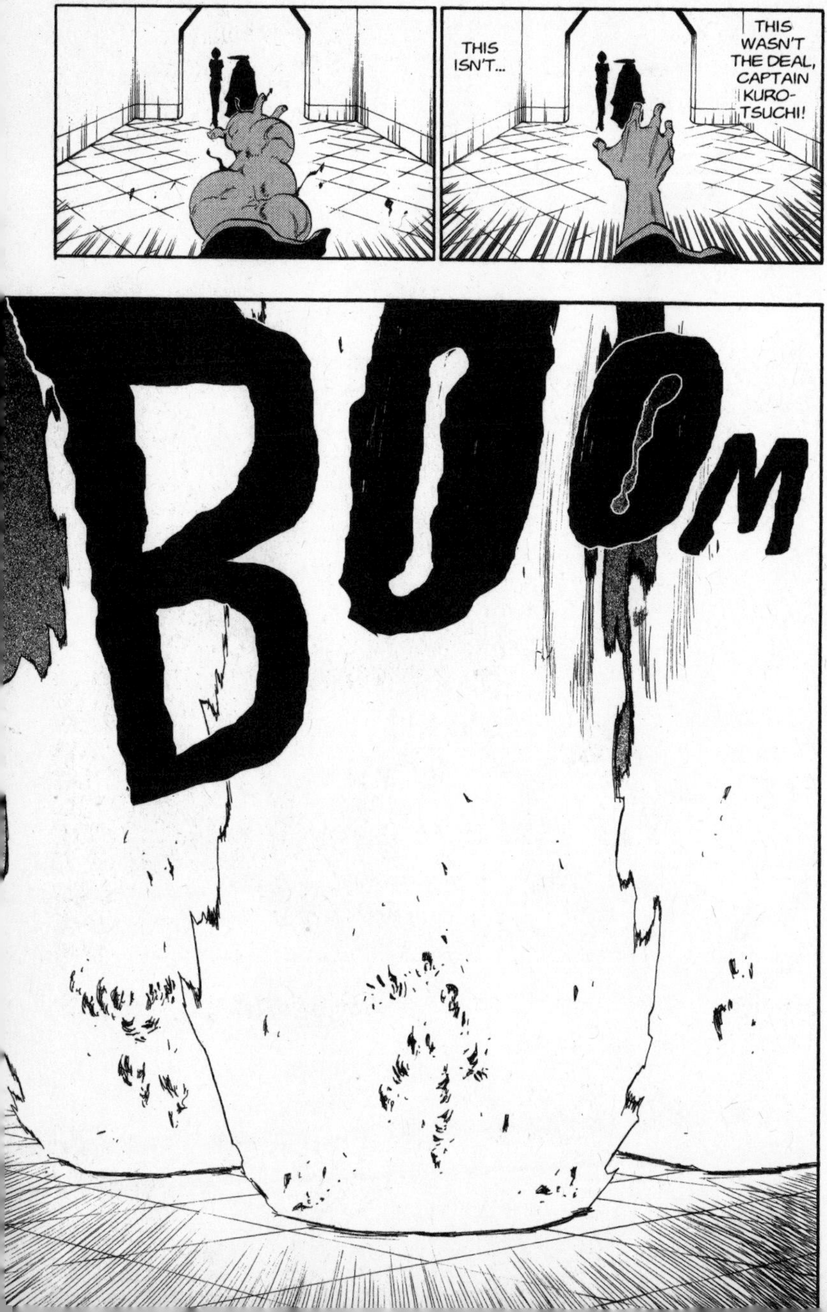
THIS WASN'T THE DEAL, CAPTAIN KURO-TSUCHI!
THIS ISN'T...
BOOM

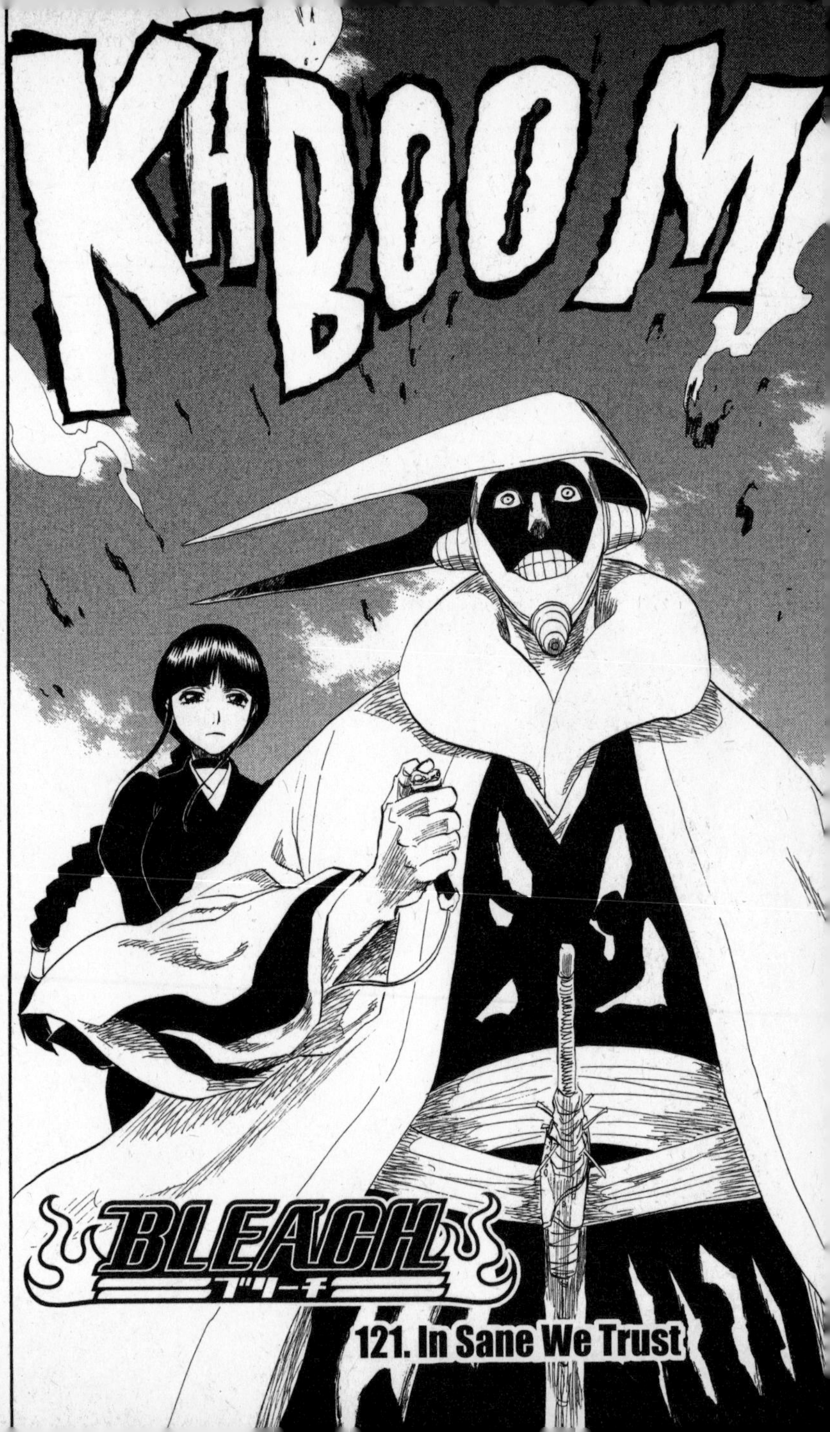
KABOOM
BLEACH
ブリーチ
121. In Sane We Trust

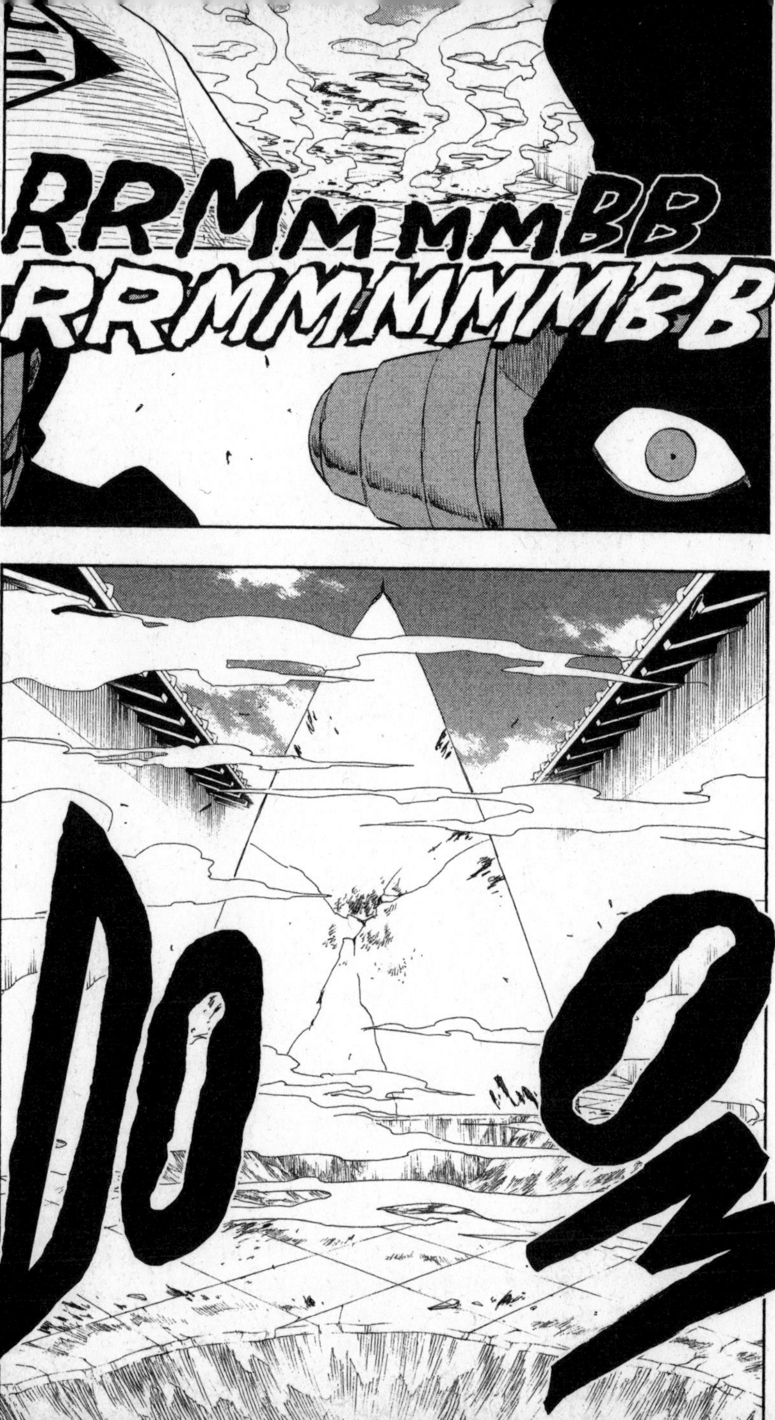
RRMMMMBB
RRMMMMMMBB
DOON

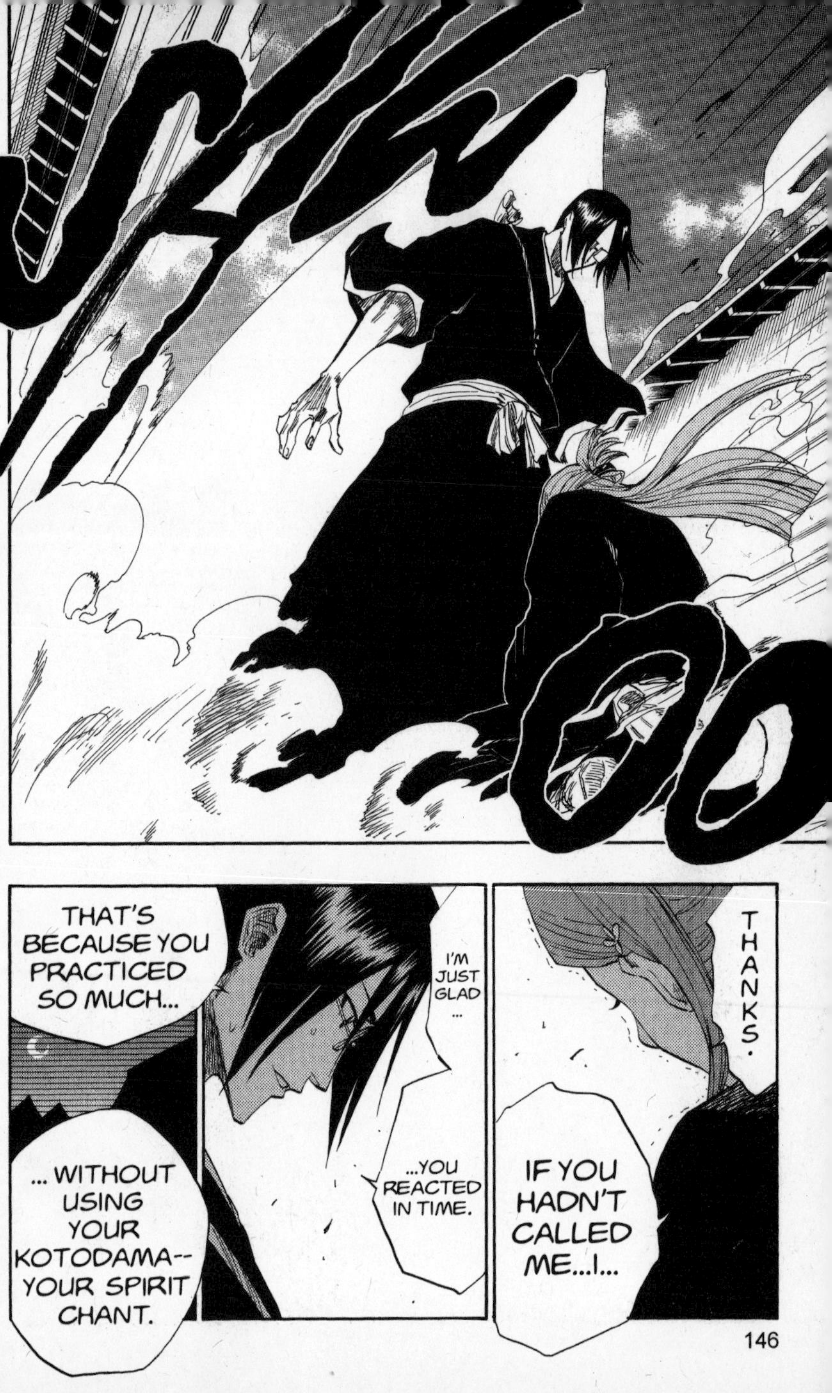
THANKS.
IF YOU HADN'T CALLED ME...I...
I'M JUST GLAD...
...YOU REACTED IN TIME.
THAT'S BECAUSE YOU PRACTICED SO MUCH...
...WITHOUT USING YOUR KOTODAMA-- YOUR SPIRIT CHANT.

READ THIS WAY

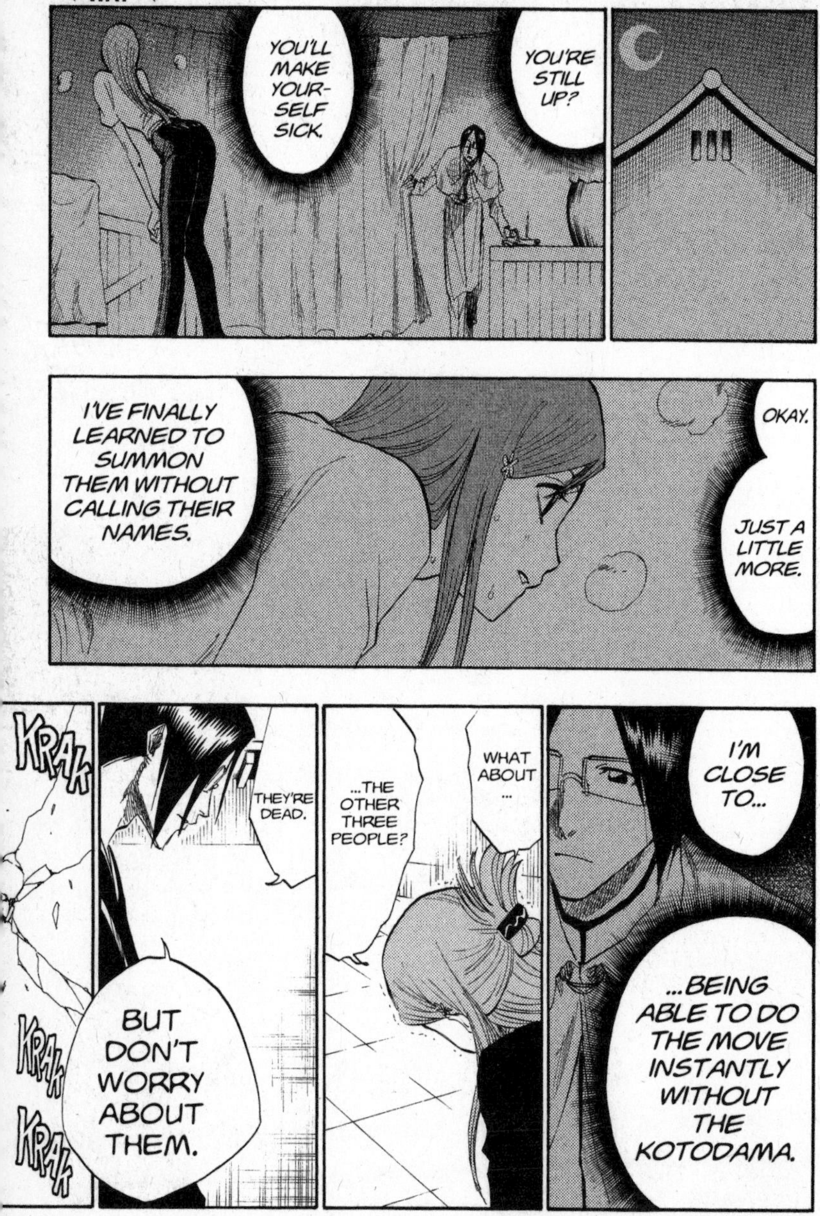

YOU'RE STILL UP?
YOU'LL MAKE YOUR-SELF SICK.
OKAY.
JUST A LITTLE MORE.
I'VE FINALLY LEARNED TO SUMMON THEM WITHOUT CALLING THEIR NAMES.
I'M CLOSE TO...
...BEING ABLE TO DO THE MOVE INSTANTLY WITHOUT THE KOTODAMA.
WHAT ABOUT...
...THE OTHER THREE PEOPLE?
THEY'RE DEAD.
BUT DON'T WORRY ABOUT THEM.
KRAK
KRAK
KRAK

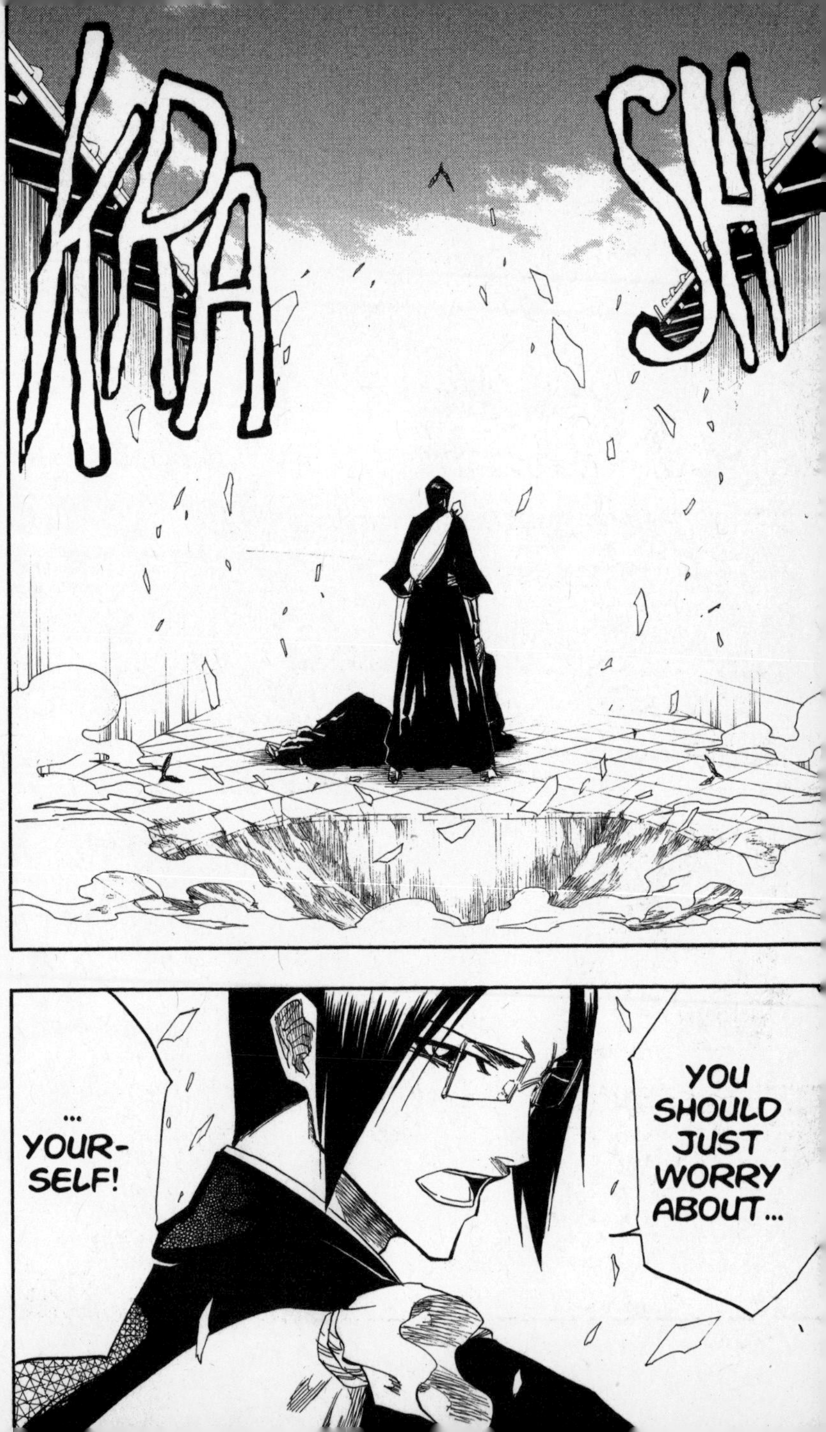
KRASH
YOU SHOULD JUST WORRY ABOUT...
... YOUR-SELF!

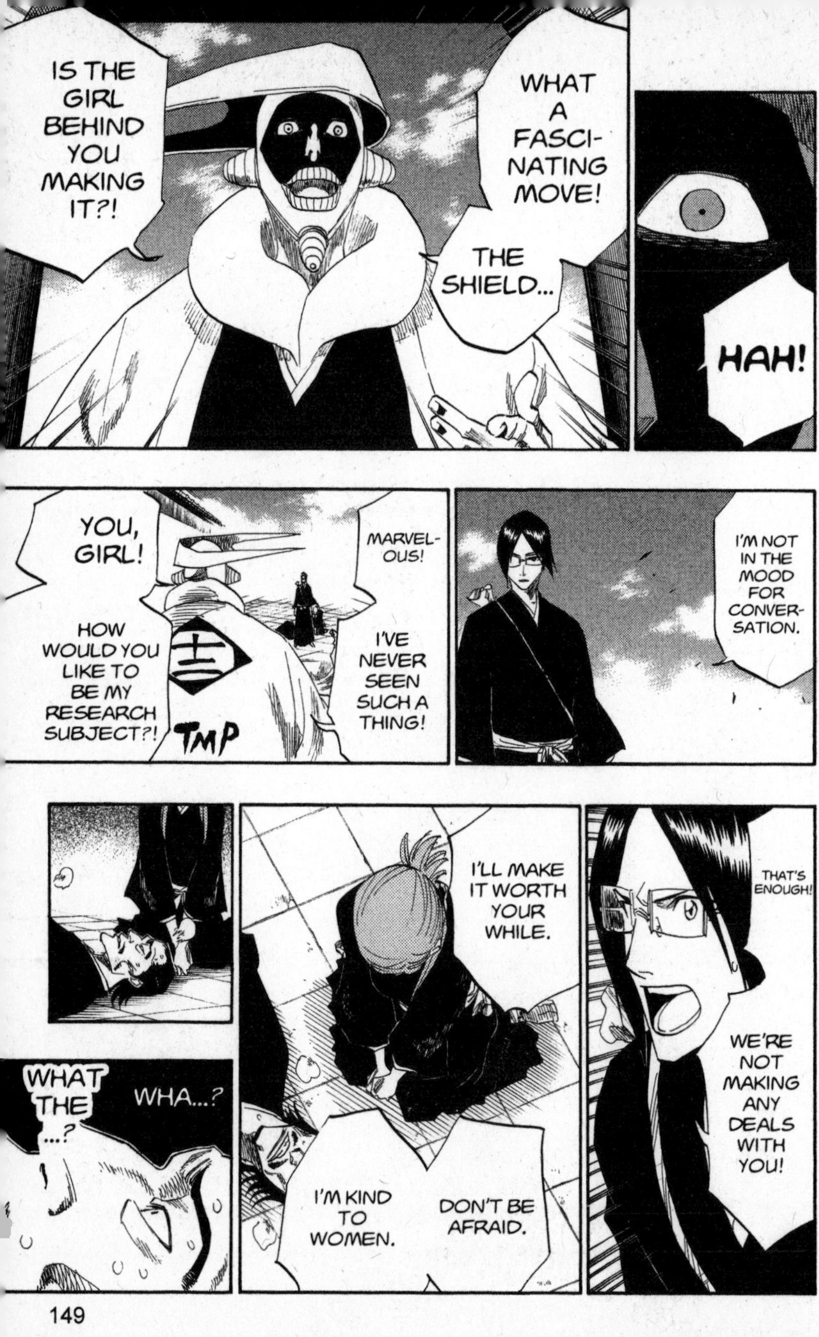
HAH!
WHAT A FASCINATING MOVE!
THE SHIELD...
IS THE GIRL BEHIND YOU MAKING IT?!
I'M NOT IN THE MOOD FOR CONVERSATION.
MARVELOUS!
I'VE NEVER SEEN SUCH A THING!
YOU, GIRL!
HOW WOULD YOU LIKE TO BE MY RESEARCH SUBJECT?!
TMP
THAT'S ENOUGH!
WE'RE NOT MAKING ANY DEALS WITH YOU!
I'LL MAKE IT WORTH YOUR WHILE.
DON'T BE AFRAID.
I'M KIND TO WOMEN.
WHA...?
WHAT THE ...?

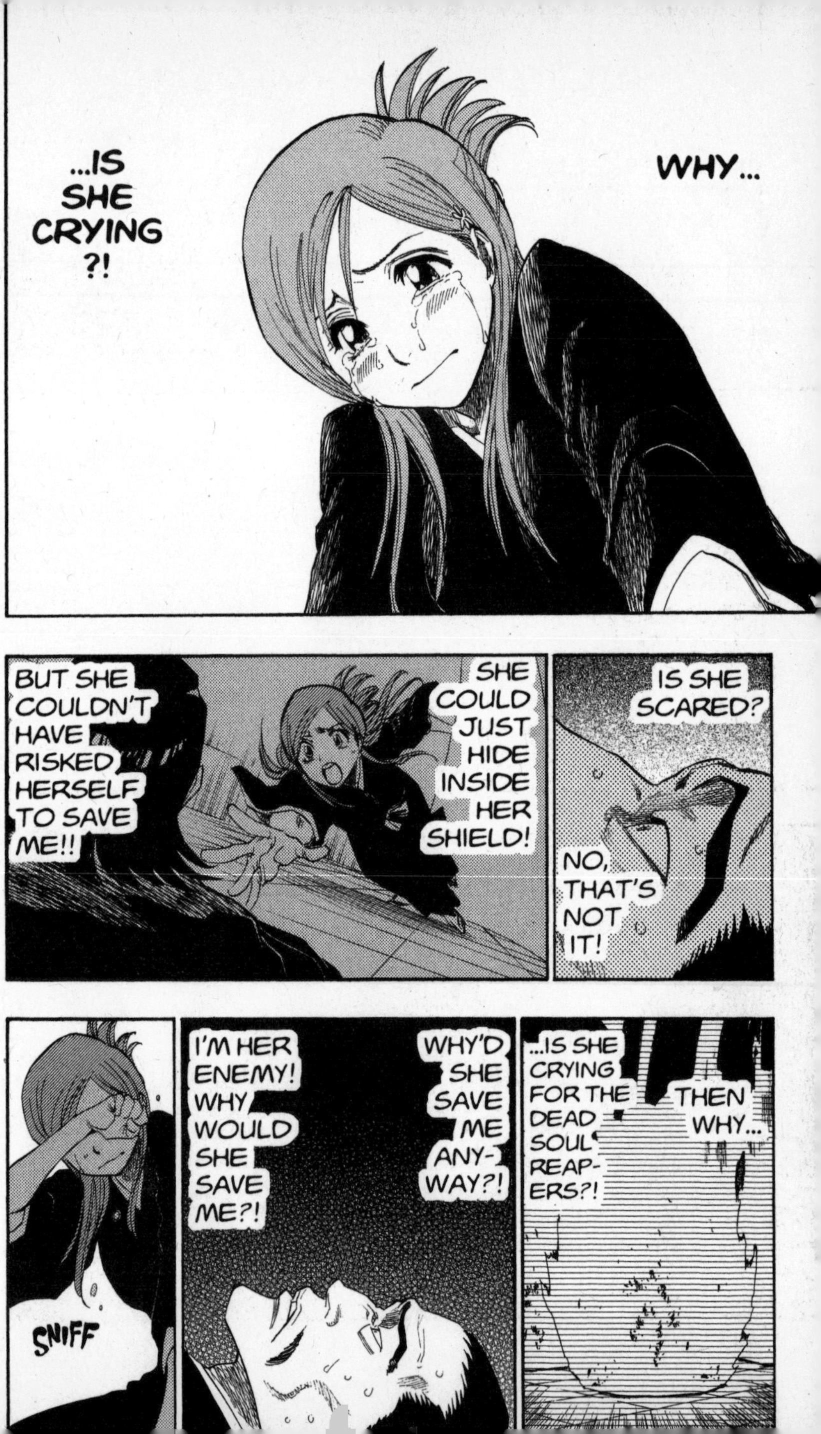
WHY...
...IS SHE CRYING ?!
IS SHE SCARED?
NO, THAT'S NOT IT!
SHE COULD JUST HIDE INSIDE HER SHIELD!
BUT SHE COULDN'T HAVE RISKED HERSELF TO SAVE ME!!
THEN WHY...
...IS SHE CRYING FOR THE DEAD SOUL REAPERS?!
WHY'D SHE SAVE ME ANY-WAY?!
I'M HER ENEMY! WHY WOULD SHE SAVE ME?!
SNIFF

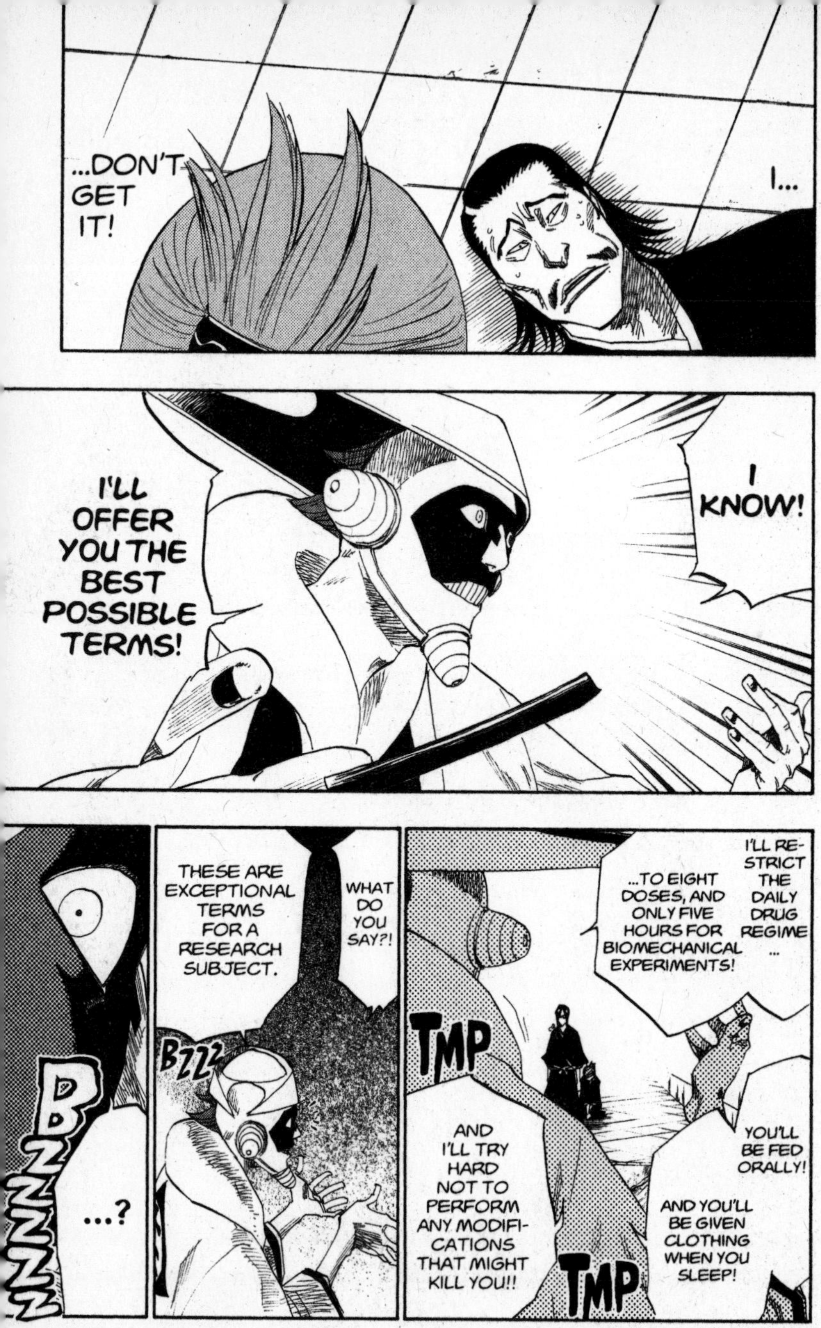
I...
...DON'T GET IT!
I KNOW!
I'LL OFFER YOU THE BEST POSSIBLE TERMS!
I'LL RESTRICT THE DAILY DRUG REGIME...
...TO EIGHT DOSES, AND ONLY FIVE HOURS FOR BIOMECHANICAL EXPERIMENTS!
TMP
YOU'LL BE FED ORALLY!
AND I'LL TRY HARD NOT TO PERFORM ANY MODIFICATIONS THAT MIGHT KILL YOU!!
AND YOU'LL BE GIVEN CLOTHING WHEN YOU SLEEP!
TMP
WHAT DO YOU SAY?!
THESE ARE EXCEPTIONAL TERMS FOR A RESEARCH SUBJECT.
BZZZ
...?
BZZZZZZ

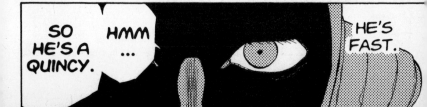

SO HE'S A QUINCY.

HMM...

HE'S FAST.

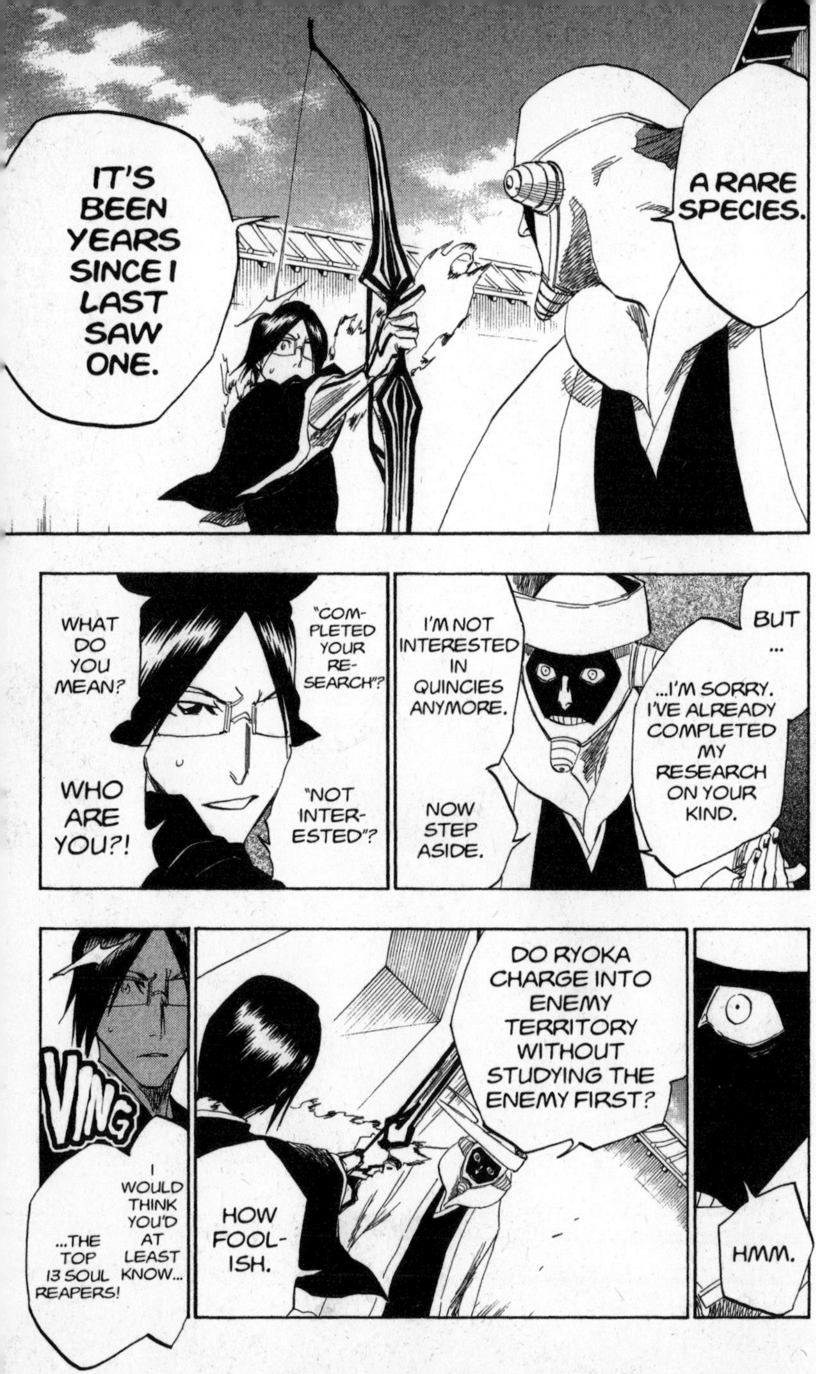
A RARE SPECIES.
IT'S BEEN YEARS SINCE I LAST SAW ONE.
BUT ...
...I'M SORRY. I'VE ALREADY COMPLETED MY RESEARCH ON YOUR KIND.
I'M NOT INTERESTED IN QUINCIES ANYMORE.
NOW STEP ASIDE.
"COMPLETED YOUR RESEARCH"?
WHAT DO YOU MEAN?
"NOT INTERESTED"?
WHO ARE YOU?!
HMM.
DO RYOKA CHARGE INTO ENEMY TERRITORY WITHOUT STUDYING THE ENEMY FIRST?
HOW FOOLISH.
VING
I WOULD THINK YOU'D AT LEAST KNOW...
...THE TOP 13 SOUL REAPERS!

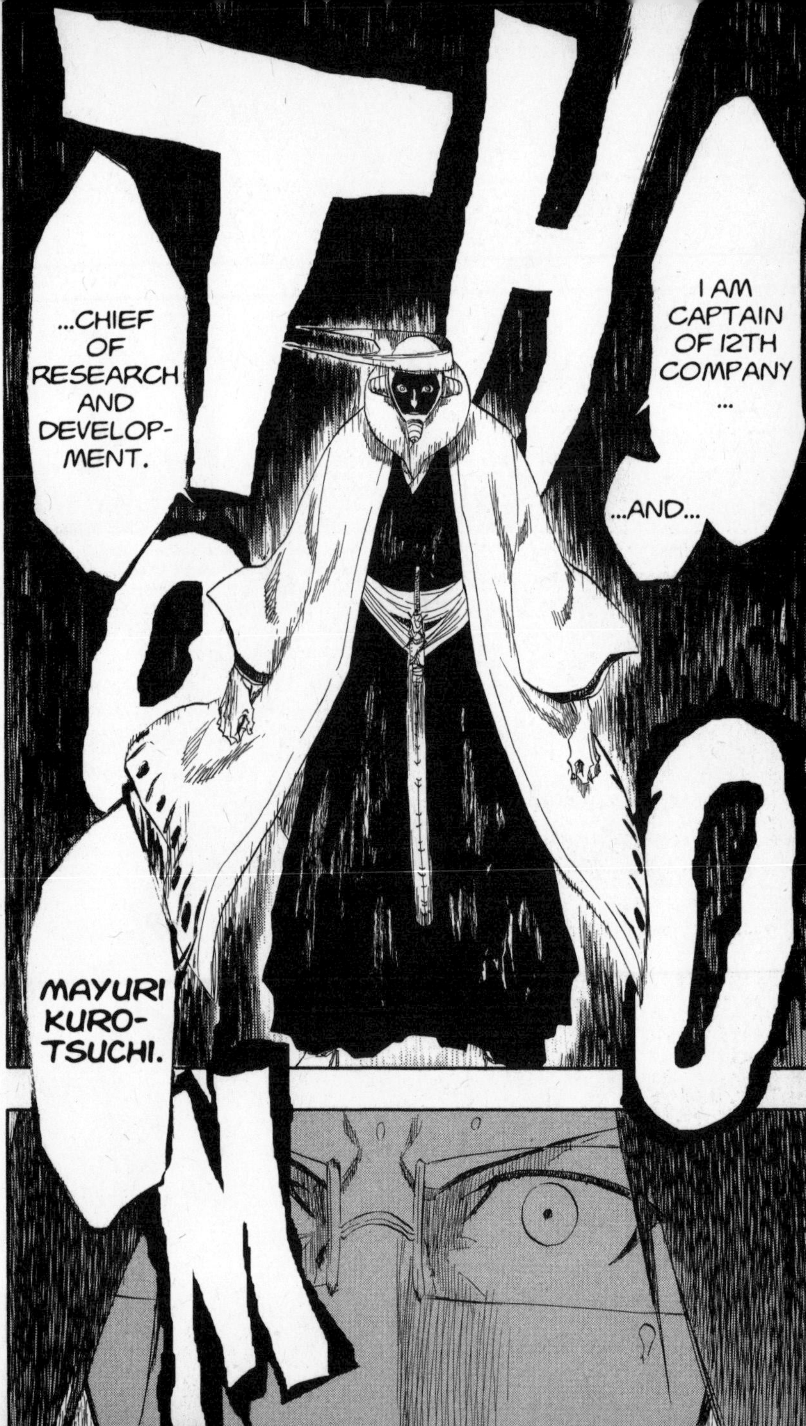
I AM CAPTAIN OF 12TH COMPANY ...
...AND...
...CHIEF OF RESEARCH AND DEVELOP-MENT.
MAYURI KURO-TSUCHI.

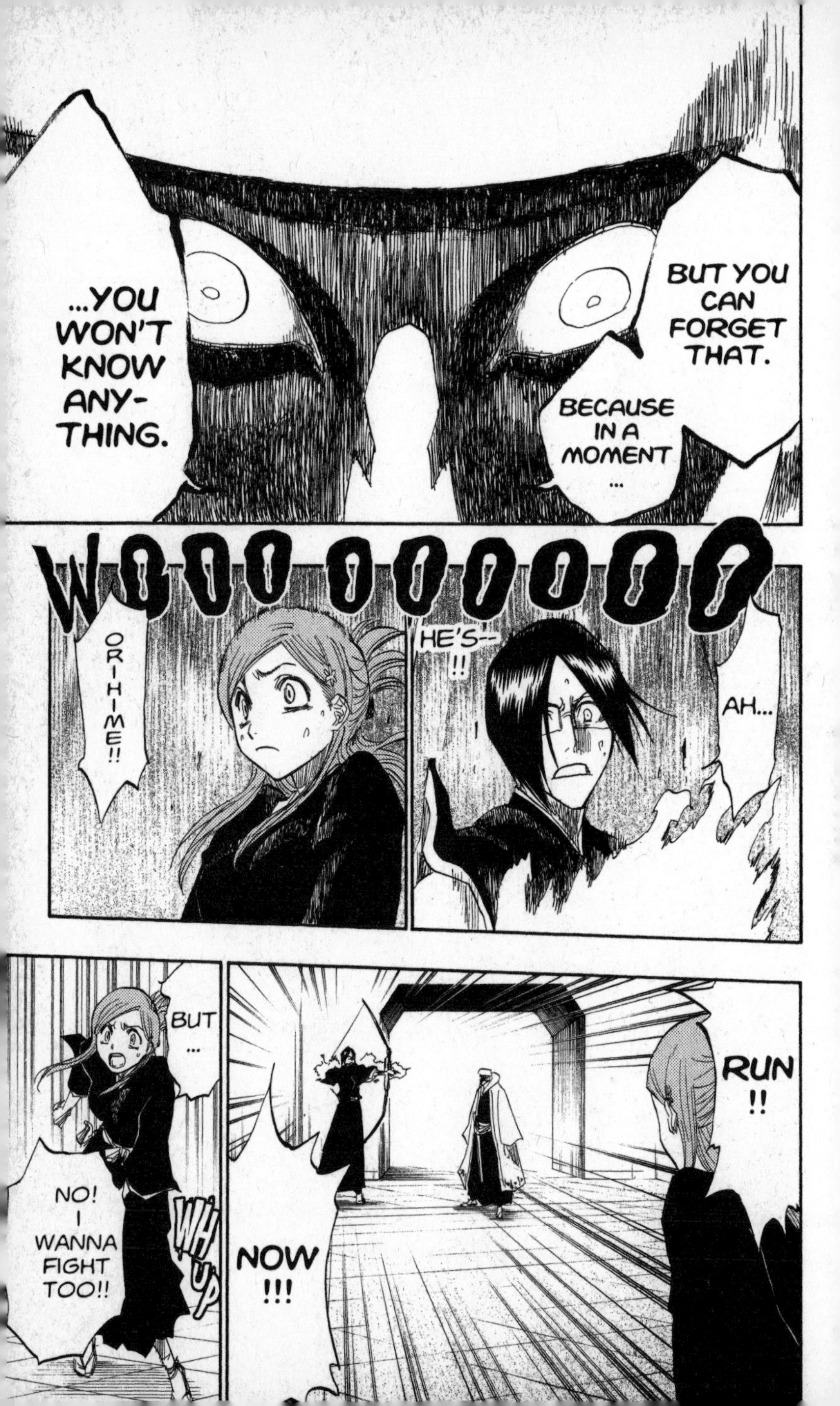
BUT YOU CAN FORGET THAT.
BECAUSE IN A MOMENT ...
...YOU WON'T KNOW ANY-THING.
WOOO OOOOOOO
AH...
HE'S-- !!
ORIHIME!!
RUN !!
NOW !!!
WHUP
BUT ...
NO! I WANNA FIGHT TOO!!

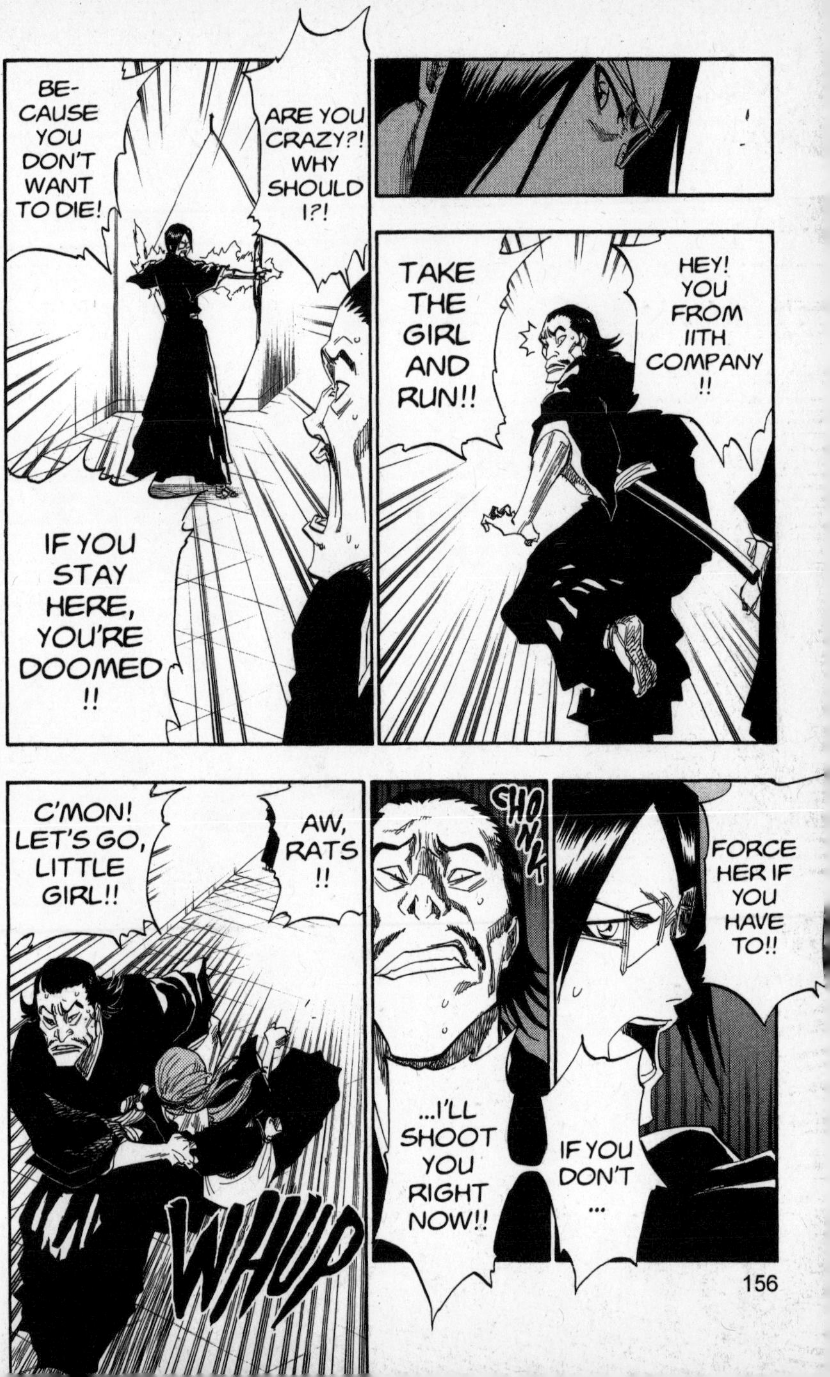
!
HEY! YOU FROM 11TH COMPANY!!
TAKE THE GIRL AND RUN!!
ARE YOU CRAZY?! WHY SHOULD I?!
BE- CAUSE YOU DON'T WANT TO DIE!
IF YOU STAY HERE, YOU'RE DOOMED!!
FORCE HER IF YOU HAVE TO!!
IF YOU DON'T ...
CHONK
...I'LL SHOOT YOU RIGHT NOW!!
AW, RATS!!
C'MON! LET'S GO, LITTLE GIRL!!
WHUP

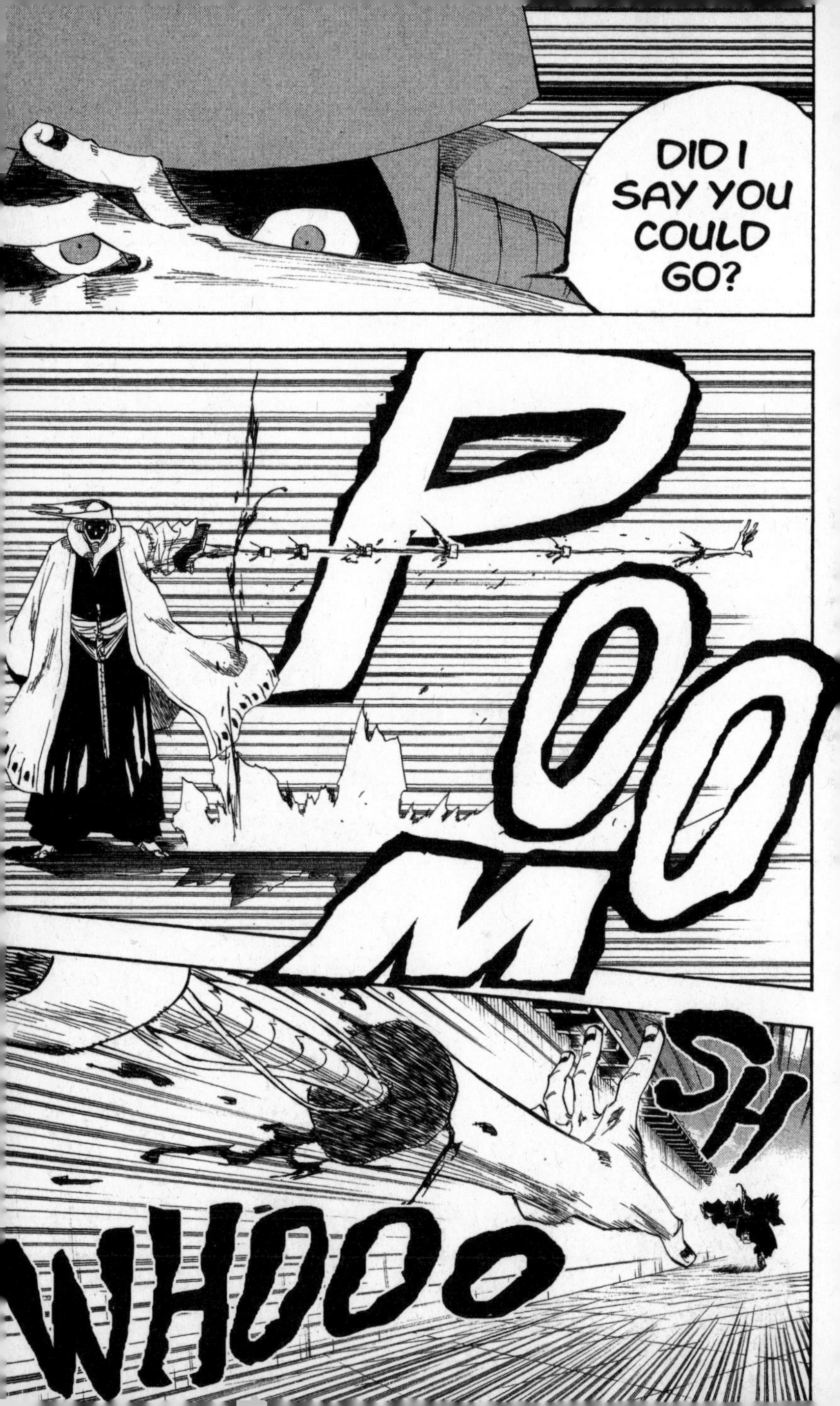
DID I SAY YOU COULD GO?
DOOOM
SH
WHOOOO

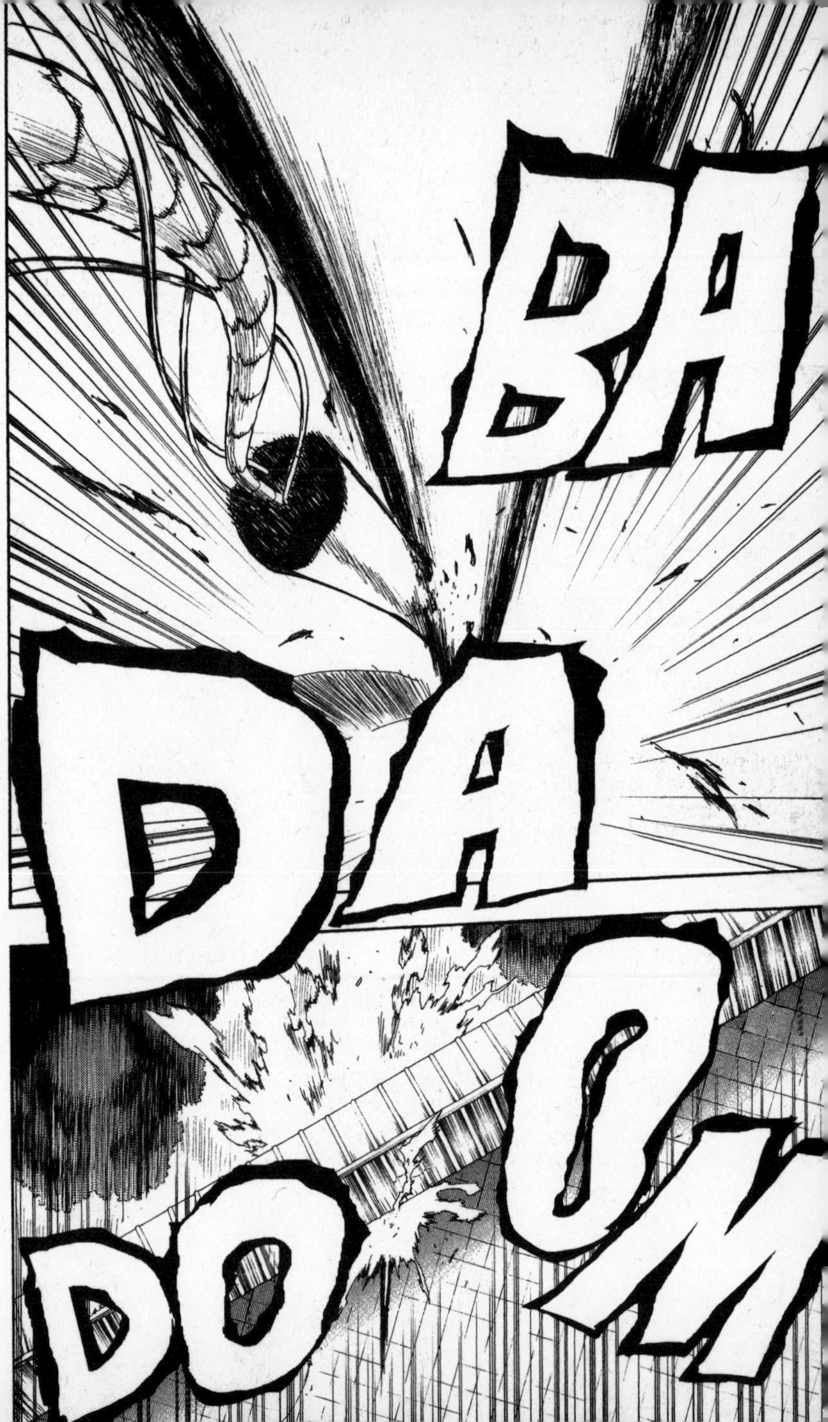
BA
DA
DOOM

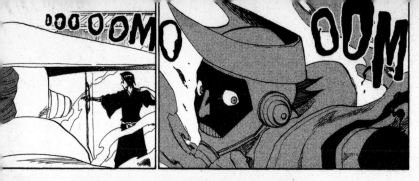

...STOP THEM?

DID I SAY YOU COULD...

I'M REALLY NOT INTERESTED IN YOU.

LISTEN, BOY!

SHE'S A LEGENDARY MONSTER WHO'S RUMORED TO HAVE CRUSHED TWO BIKER GANGS WITH ONLY HER LEFT ARM, DESPITE COMPETING IN A HIGH SCHOOL KARATE TOURNAMENT THIS SUMMER.

SHE'S SO SCARY, I THINK SHE COULD BURN UP A STRAY DOG JUST BY STARING AT IT. I WAS ABOUT TO PEE MY PANTS FROM HER INTIMIDATING PRESENCE. MAYBE THAT'S HOW CLASSMATES SHOW THEIR FRIENDSHIP OR SOMETHING. SO I WENT HOME EARLY THAT DAY.

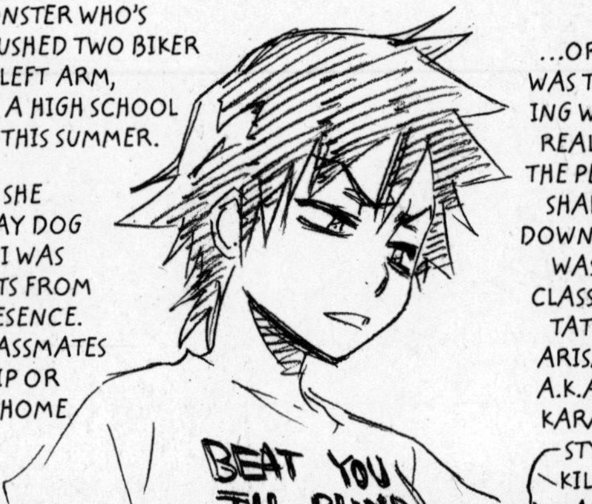
BEAT YOU TIL BLIND

...OR SO I WAS THINKING WHEN I REALIZED THE PERSON SHAKING DOWN KEIGO WAS HIS CLASSMATE TATSUKI ARISAWA, A.K.A. THE KARATE-STYLE KILLER APE.

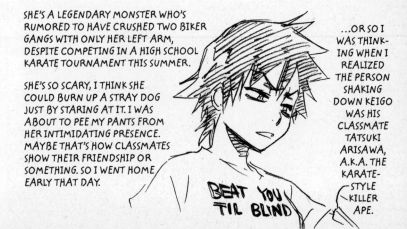

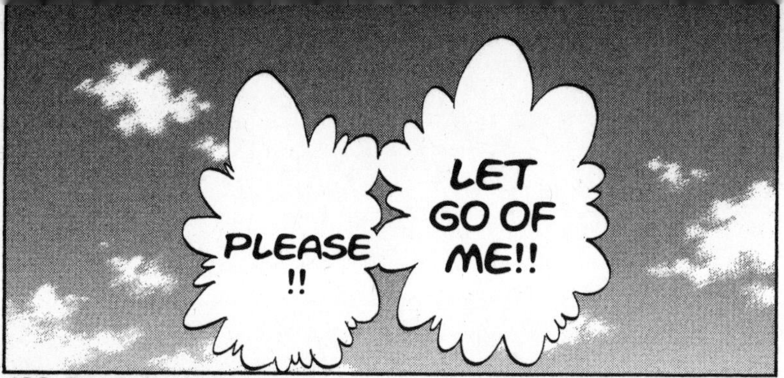
LET GO OF ME!!
PLEASE!!

122. Don't Lose Your Grip

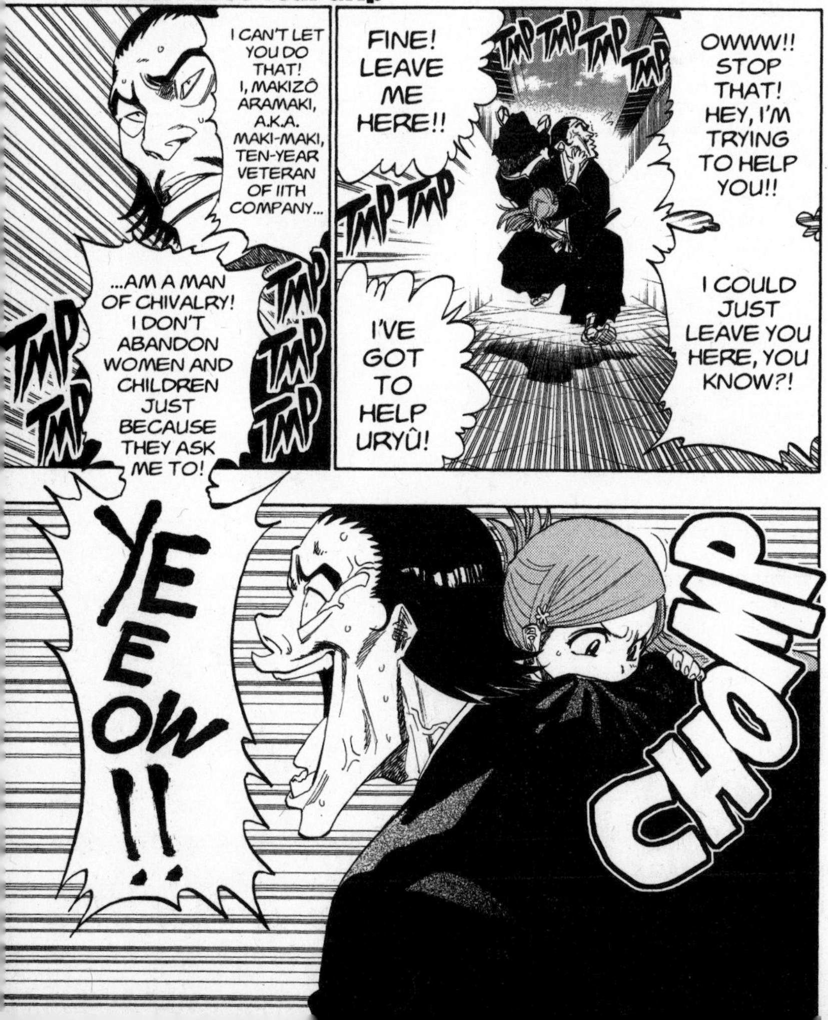
OWWW!! STOP THAT! HEY, I'M TRYING TO HELP YOU!!
TMP TMP TMP TMP
FINE! LEAVE ME HERE!!
TMP TMP
I COULD JUST LEAVE YOU HERE, YOU KNOW?!
I'VE GOT TO HELP URYÛ!
I CAN'T LET YOU DO THAT! I, MAKIZÔ ARAMAKI, A.K.A. MAKI-MAKI, TEN-YEAR VETERAN OF 11TH COMPANY...
TMP TMP TMP
...AM A MAN OF CHIVALRY! I DON'T ABANDON WOMEN AND CHILDREN JUST BECAUSE THEY ASK ME TO!
TMP TMP
CHOMP
YEEOW!!

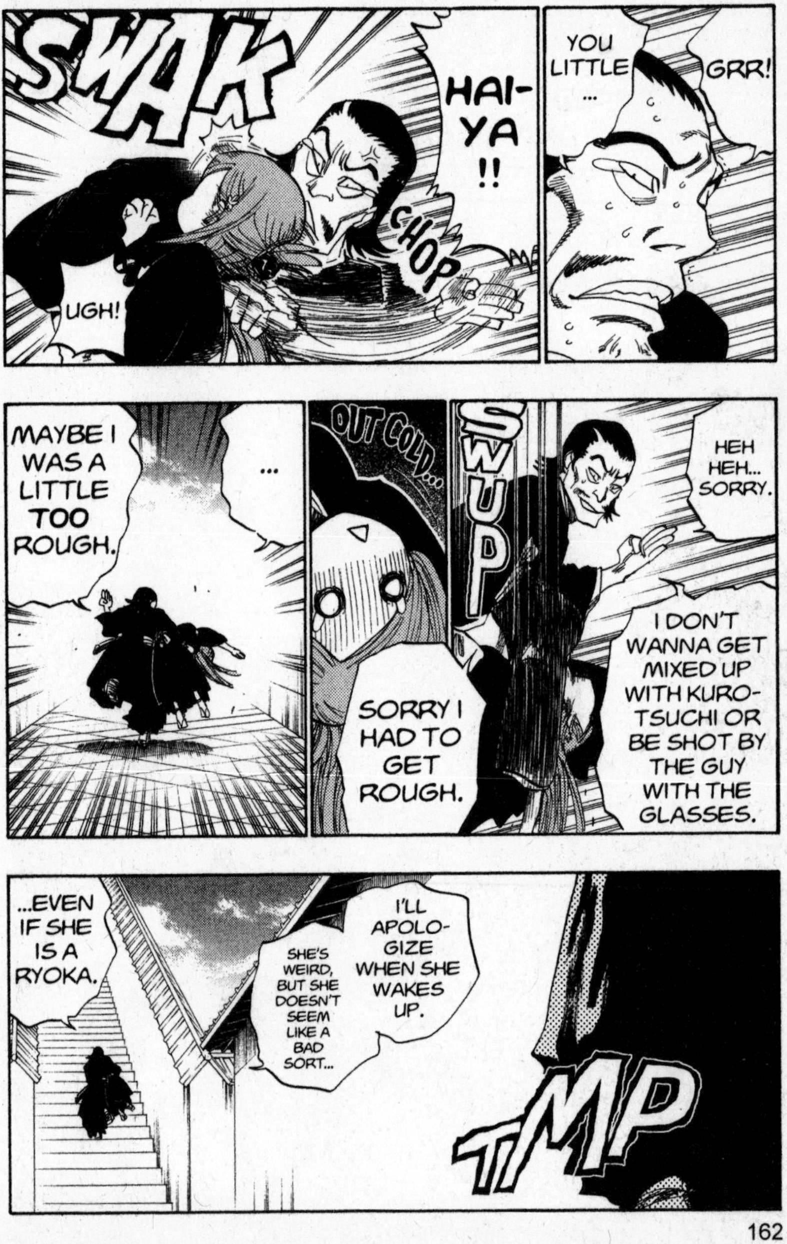

YOU LITTLE ...
GRR!
HAI-YA!!
SWAK
CHOP
UGH!
HEH HEH... SORRY.
SWUP
I DON'T WANNA GET MIXED UP WITH KURO-TSUCHI OR BE SHOT BY THE GUY WITH THE GLASSES.
OUT COLD...
SORRY I HAD TO GET ROUGH.
...
MAYBE I WAS A LITTLE TOO ROUGH.
TMP
I'LL APOLO-GIZE WHEN SHE WAKES UP.
SHE'S WEIRD, BUT SHE DOESN'T SEEM LIKE A BAD SORT...
...EVEN IF SHE IS A RYOKA.

READ THIS WAY

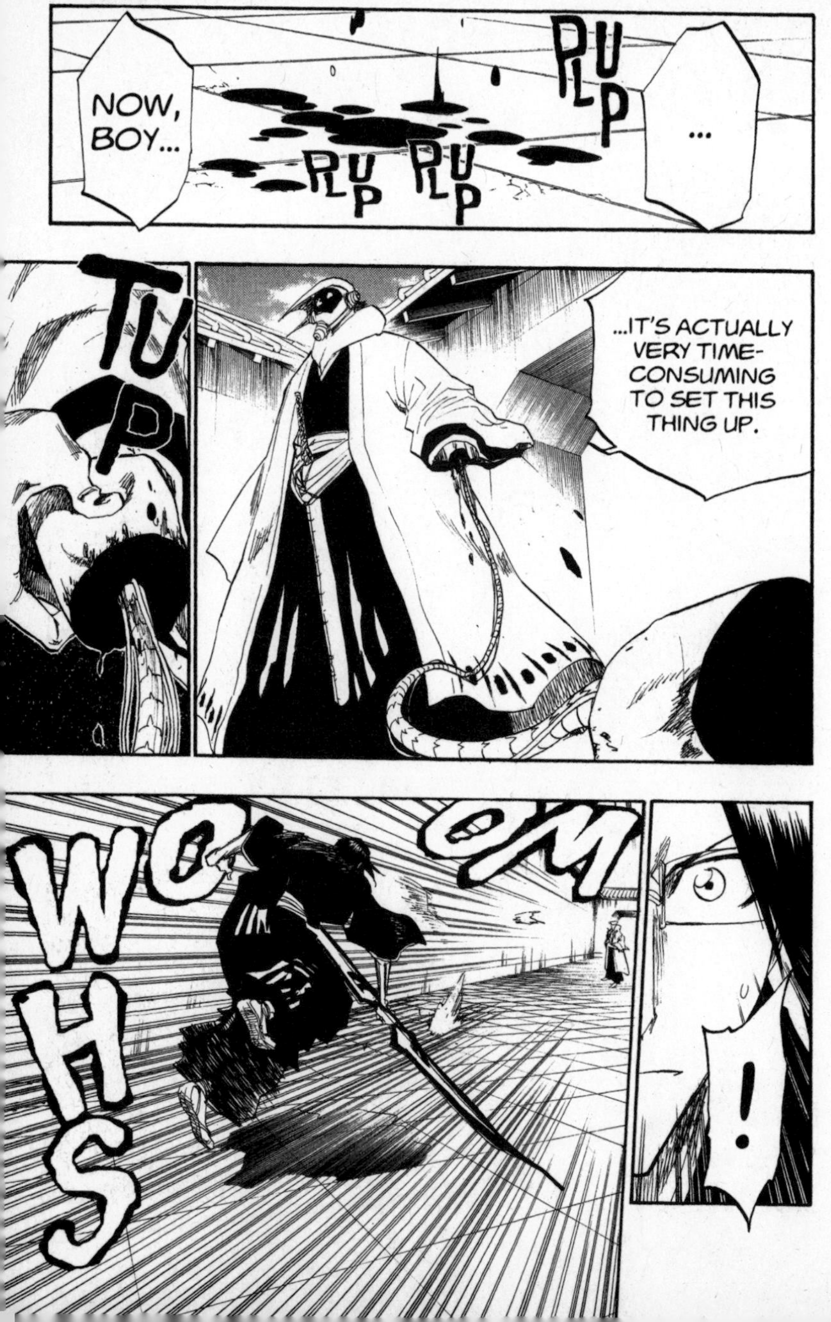
...
PLUP
PLUP PLUP
NOW, BOY...
...IT'S ACTUALLY VERY TIME-CONSUMING TO SET THIS THING UP.
TUP
!
WOOM
WHS

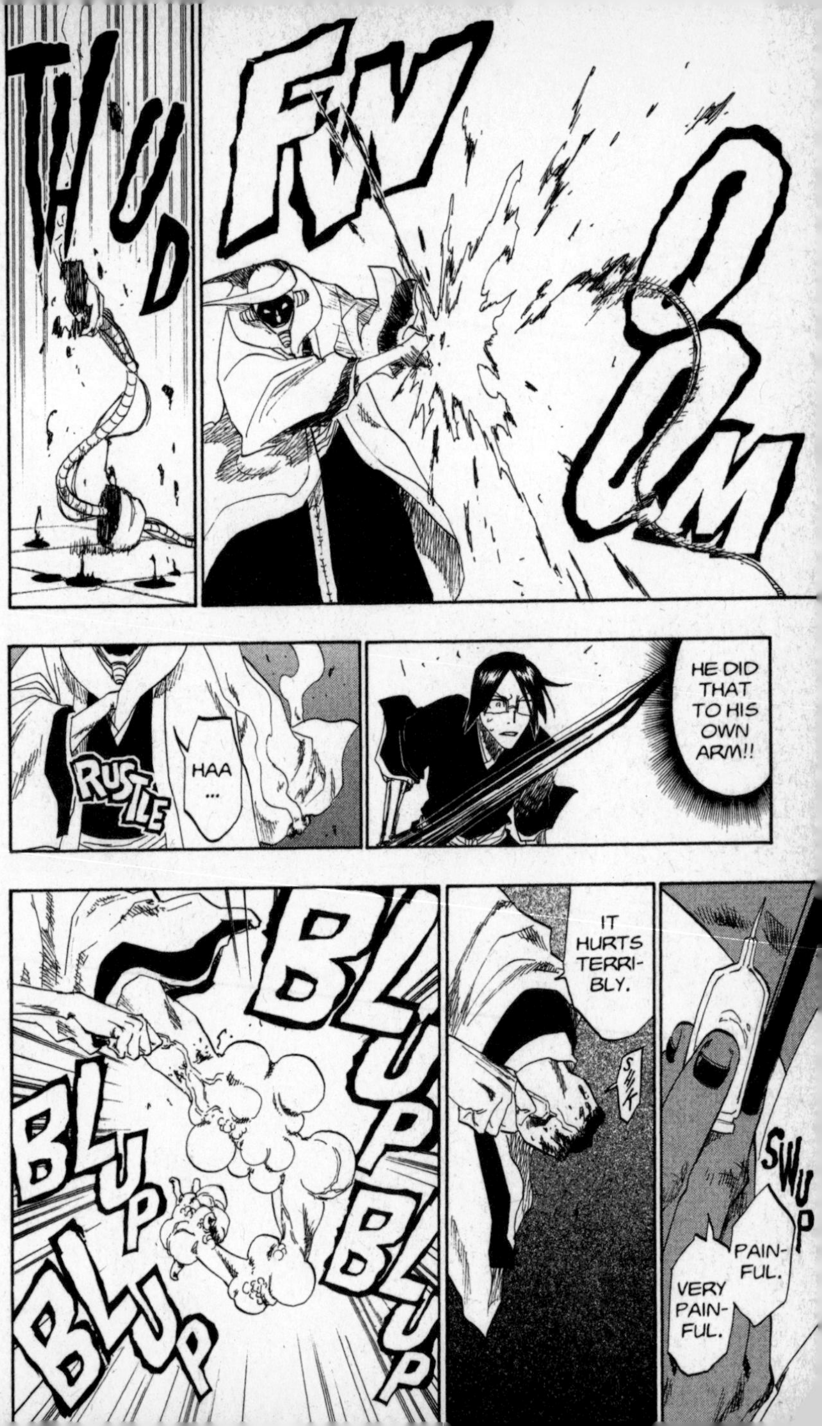
FWOOM
THUD
HE DID THAT TO HIS OWN ARM!!
HAA ...
RUSTLE
SWUP
PAIN-FUL.
VERY PAIN-FUL.
IT HURTS TERRI-BLY.
SHK
BLUP
BLUP
BLUP
BLUP

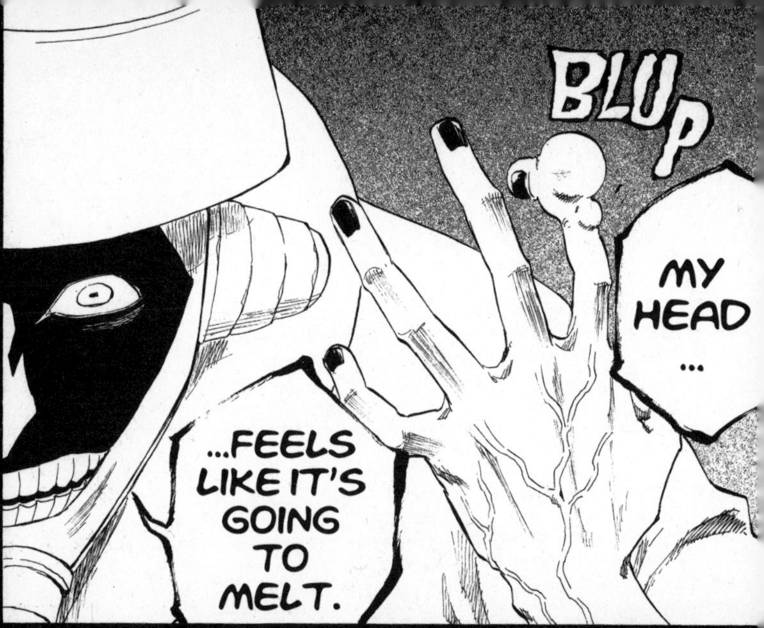
BLUP
MY HEAD ...
...FEELS LIKE IT'S GOING TO MELT.

BLEACH
—ブリーチ—

122. Don't Lose Your Grip

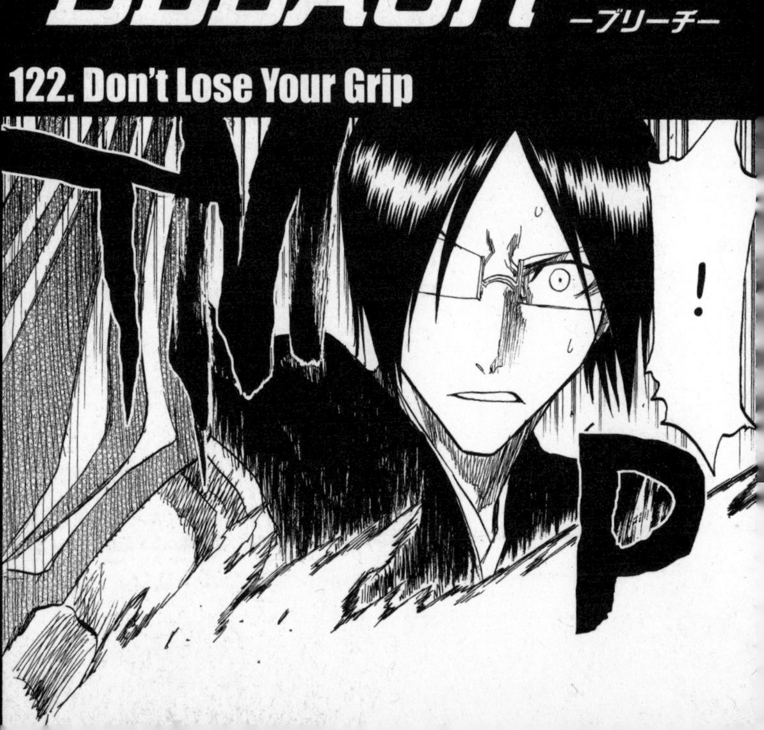
!

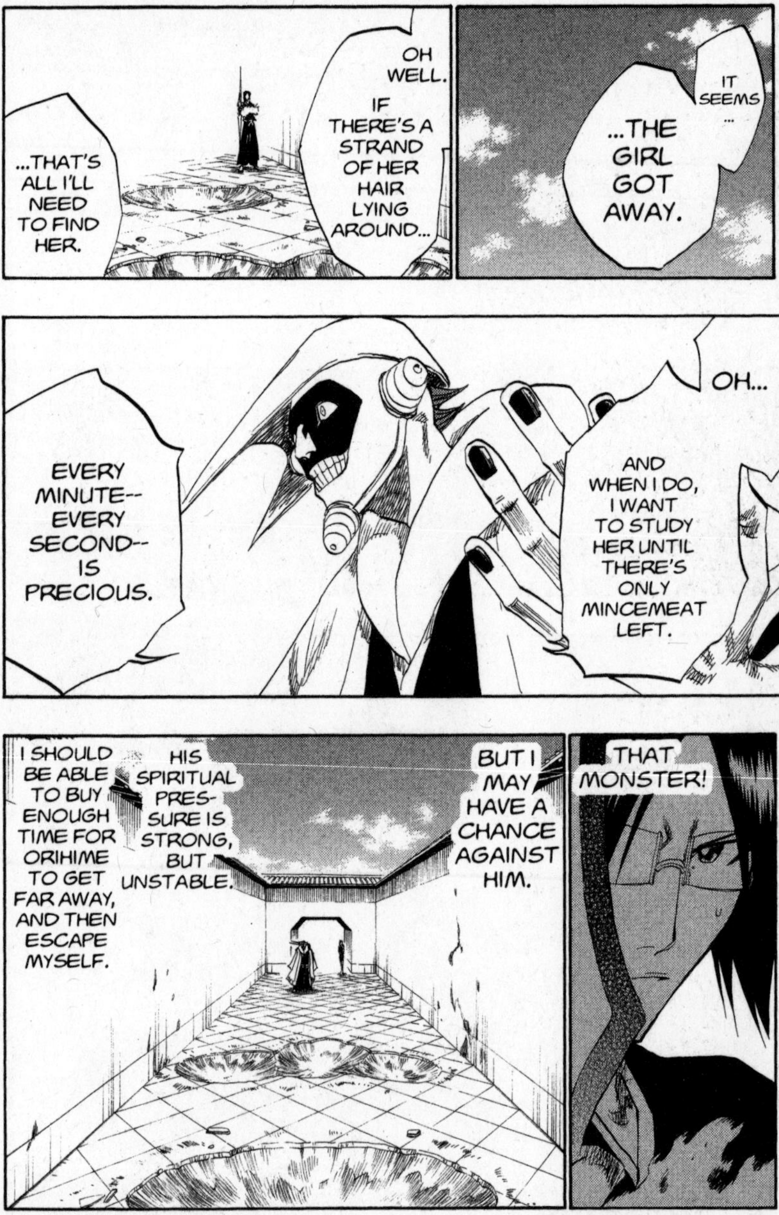
IT SEEMS...
...THE GIRL GOT AWAY.
OH WELL.
IF THERE'S A STRAND OF HER HAIR LYING AROUND...
...THAT'S ALL I'LL NEED TO FIND HER.
OH...
AND WHEN I DO, I WANT TO STUDY HER UNTIL THERE'S ONLY MINCEMEAT LEFT.
EVERY MINUTE-- EVERY SECOND-- IS PRECIOUS.
THAT MONSTER!
BUT I MAY HAVE A CHANCE AGAINST HIM.
HIS SPIRITUAL PRESSURE IS STRONG, BUT UNSTABLE.
I SHOULD BE ABLE TO BUY ENOUGH TIME FOR ORIHIME TO GET FAR AWAY, AND THEN ESCAPE MYSELF.

READ THIS WAY

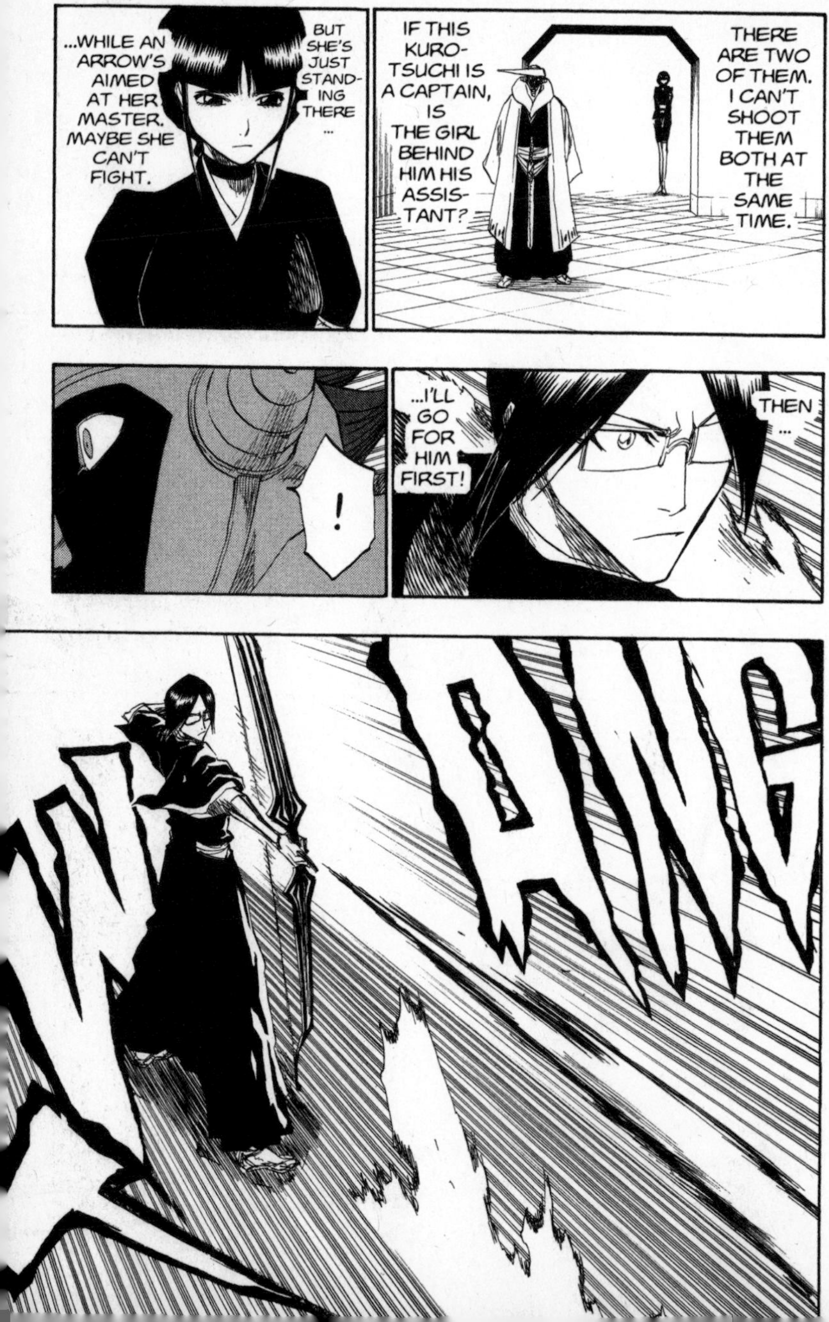
THERE ARE TWO OF THEM. I CAN'T SHOOT THEM BOTH AT THE SAME TIME.
IF THIS KURO-TSUCHI IS A CAPTAIN, IS THE GIRL BEHIND HIM HIS ASSIS-TANT?
BUT SHE'S JUST STAND-ING THERE ...
...WHILE AN ARROW'S AIMED AT HER MASTER. MAYBE SHE CAN'T FIGHT.
THEN ...
...I'LL GO FOR HIM FIRST!
!

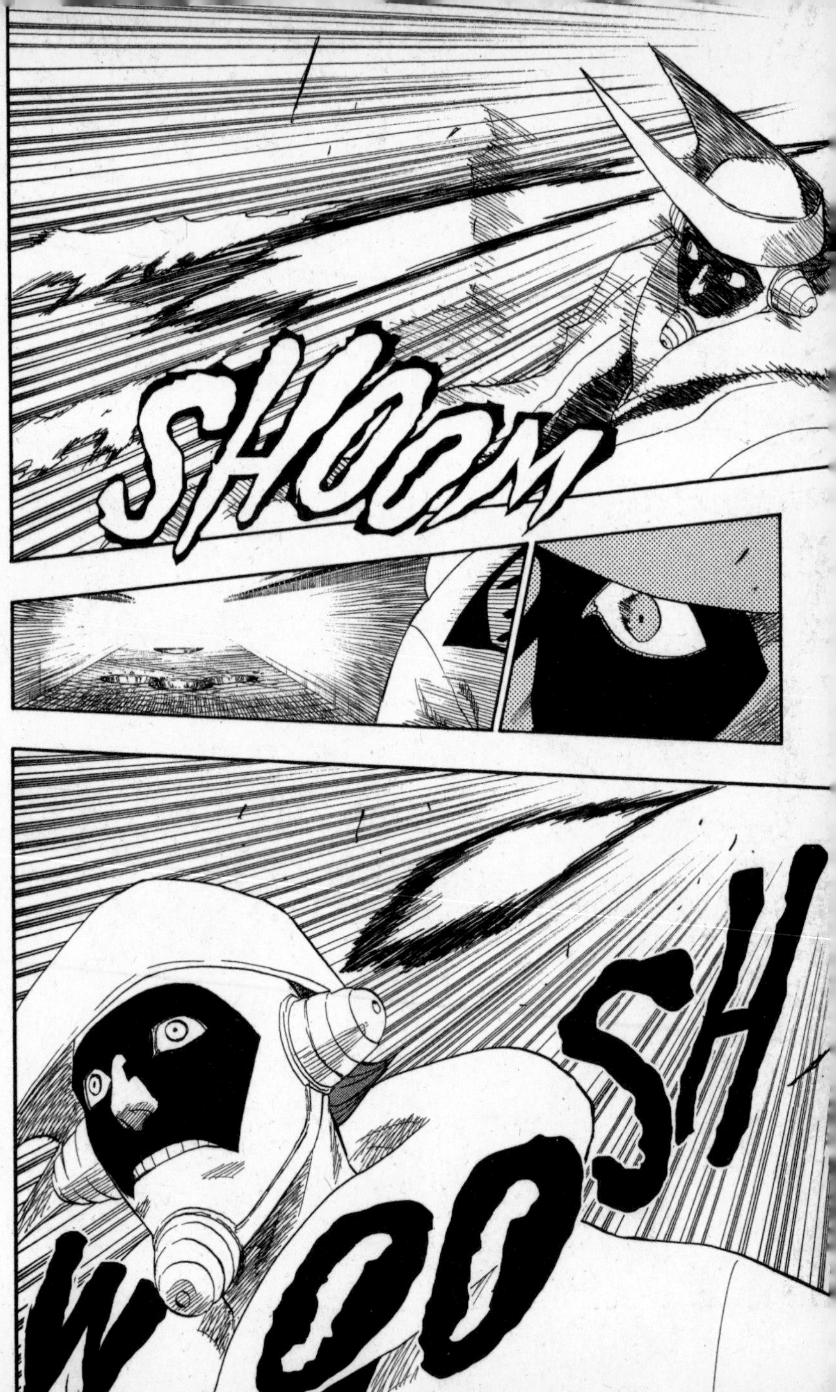
SHOOM
WOOOSH

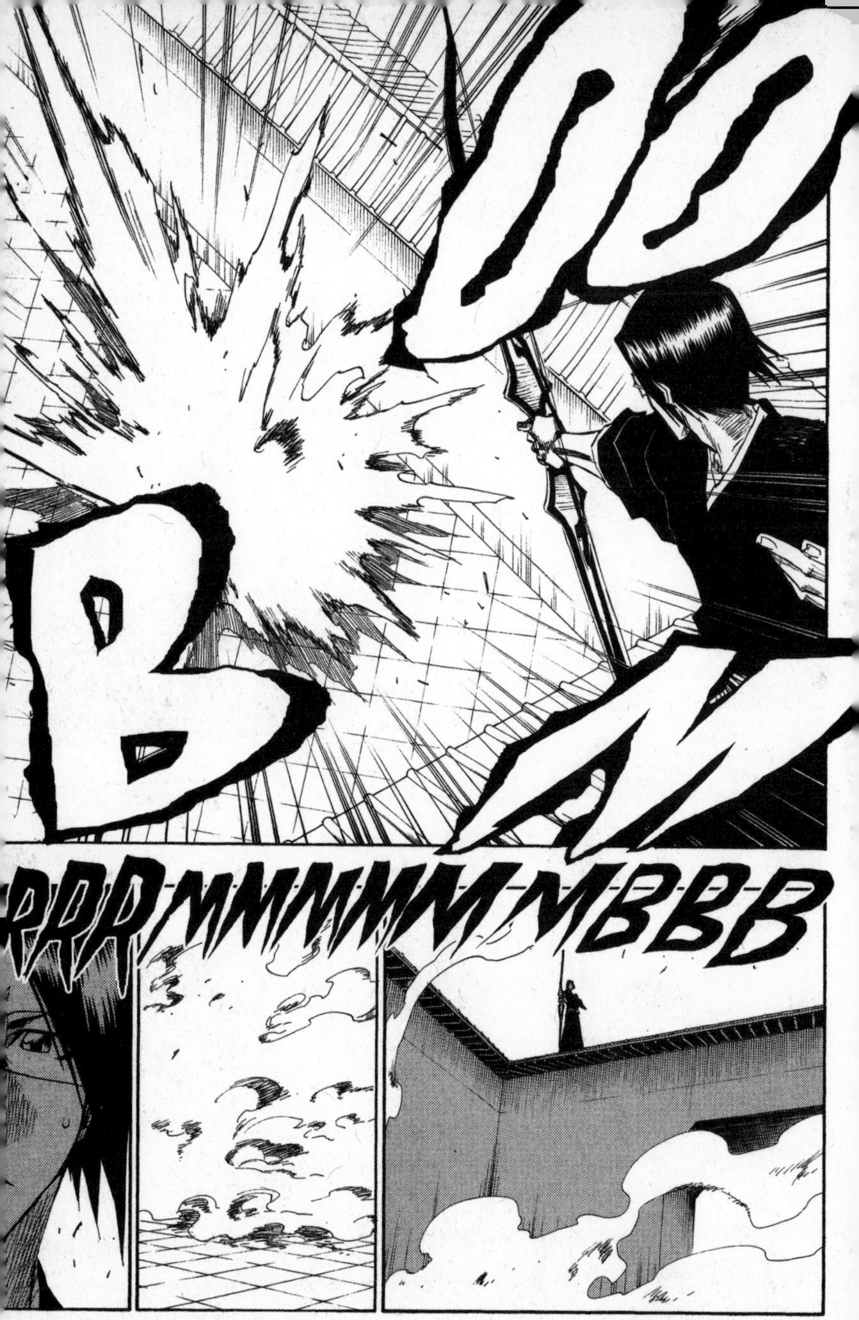
RRRMMMMMMBBB

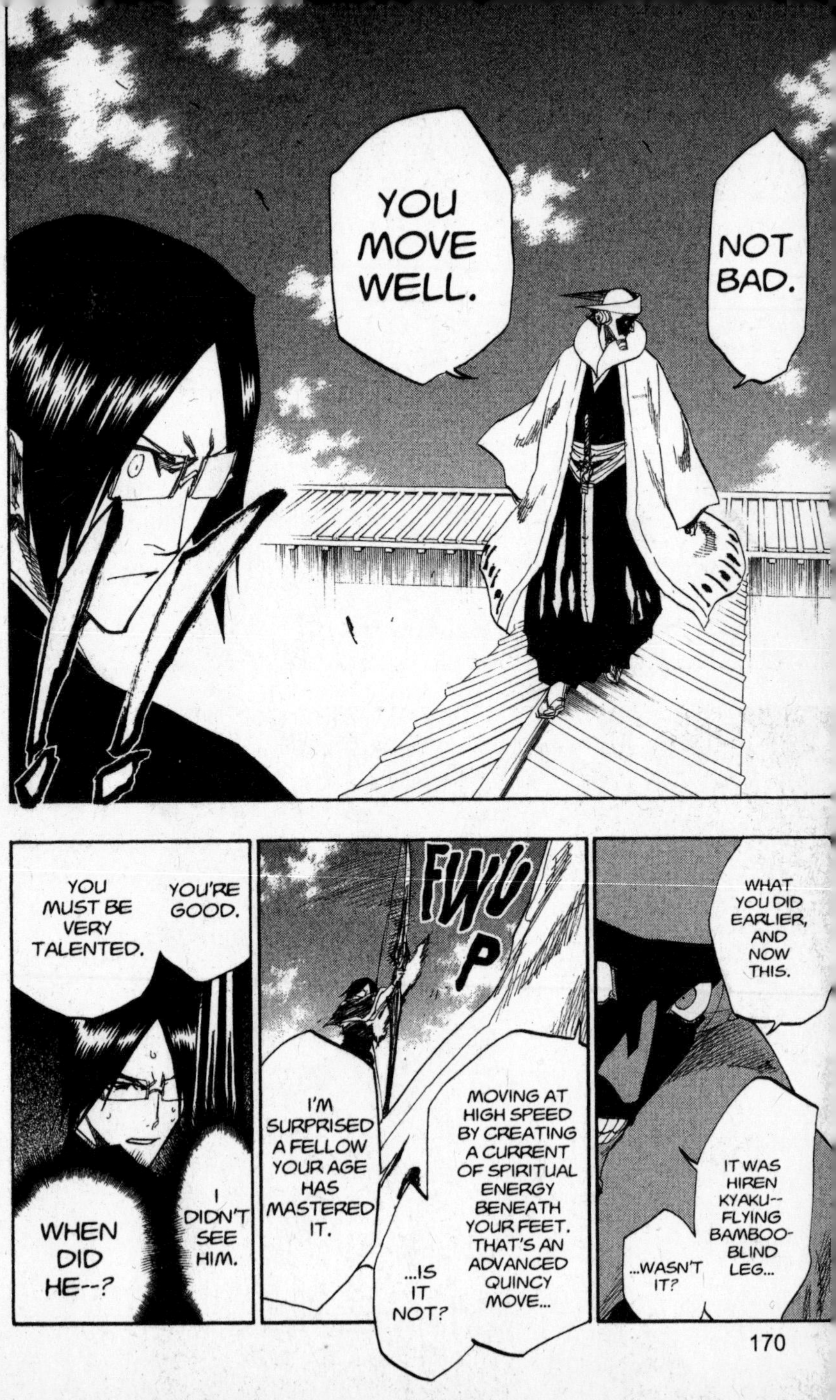
NOT BAD.
YOU MOVE WELL.
WHAT YOU DID EARLIER, AND NOW THIS.
IT WAS HIREN KYAKU-- FLYING BAMBOO-BLIND LEG...
...WASN'T IT?
FWUP
MOVING AT HIGH SPEED BY CREATING A CURRENT OF SPIRITUAL ENERGY BENEATH YOUR FEET. THAT'S AN ADVANCED QUINCY MOVE...
...IS IT NOT?
I'M SURPRISED A FELLOW YOUR AGE HAS MASTERED IT.
YOU'RE GOOD.
YOU MUST BE VERY TALENTED.
I DIDN'T SEE HIM.
WHEN DID HE--?

READ THIS WAY

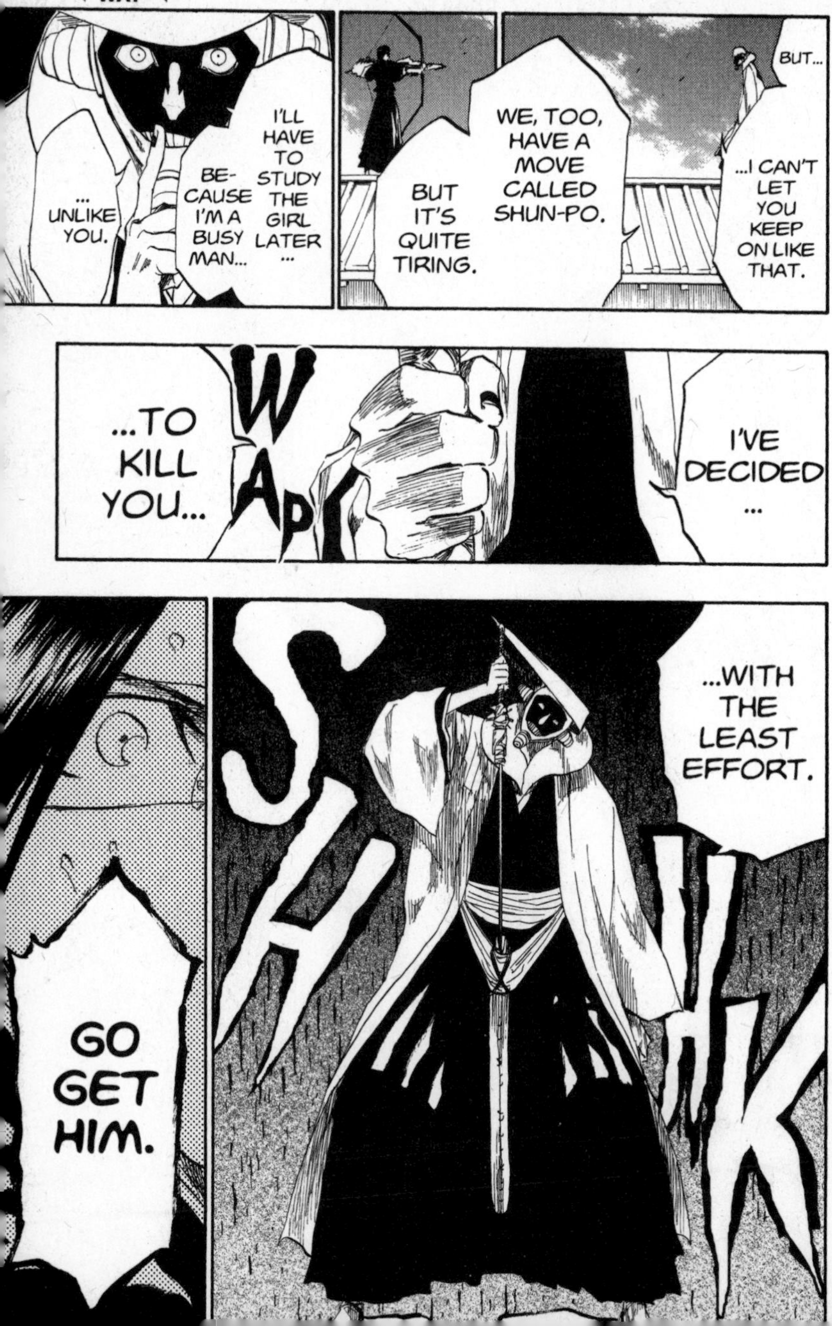
BUT...
...I CAN'T LET YOU KEEP ON LIKE THAT.
WE, TOO, HAVE A MOVE CALLED SHUN-PO.
BUT IT'S QUITE TIRING.
I'LL HAVE TO STUDY THE GIRL LATER...
BE-CAUSE I'M A BUSY MAN...
... UNLIKE YOU.
I'VE DECIDED...
WAP
...TO KILL YOU...
...WITH THE LEAST EFFORT.
SHHK
GO GET HIM.

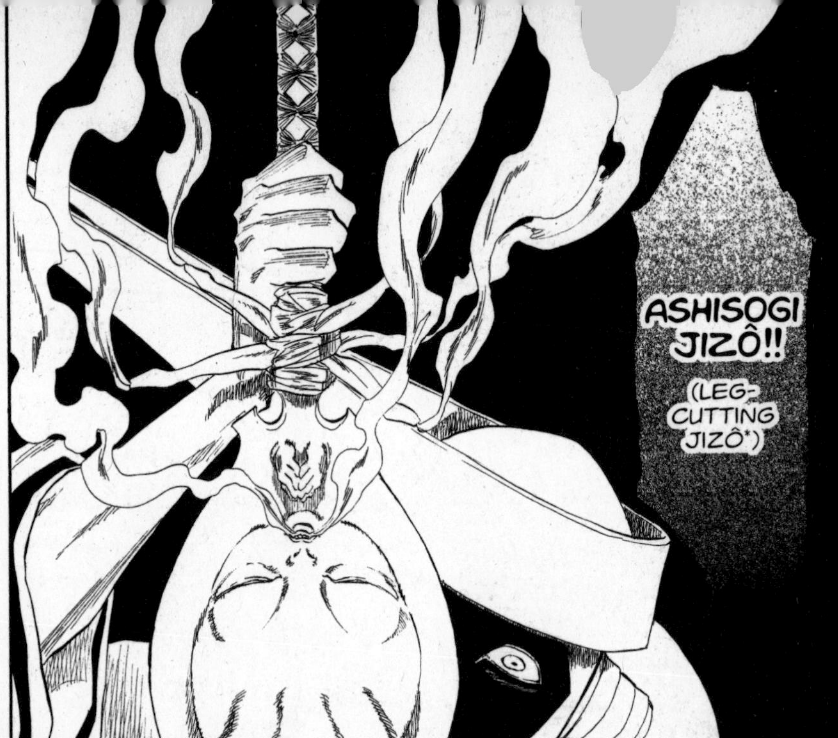
ASHISOGI JIZÔ!!
(LEG-CUTTING JIZÔ*)

*JIZÔ = A PROTECTOR OF PEOPLE AND THE SOULS OF DECEASED CHILDREN

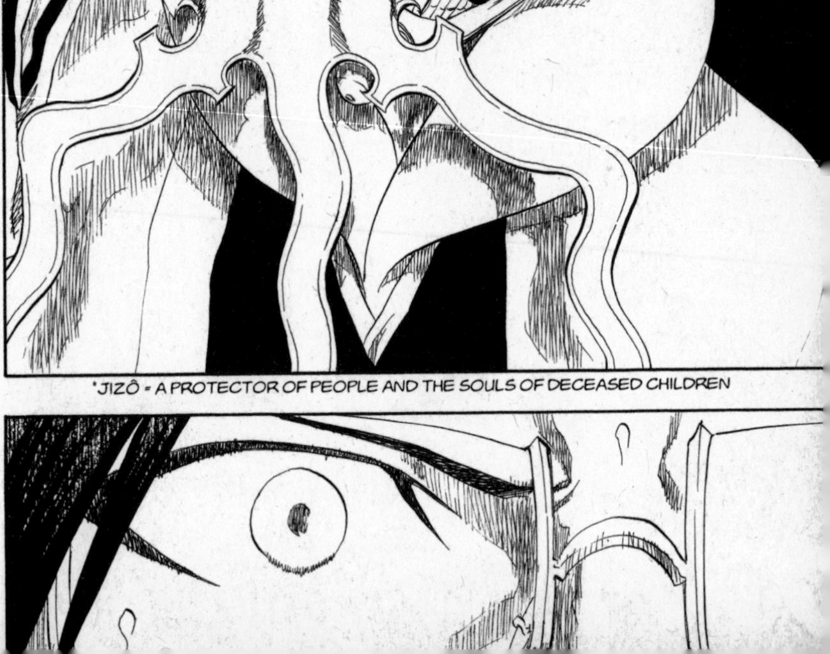

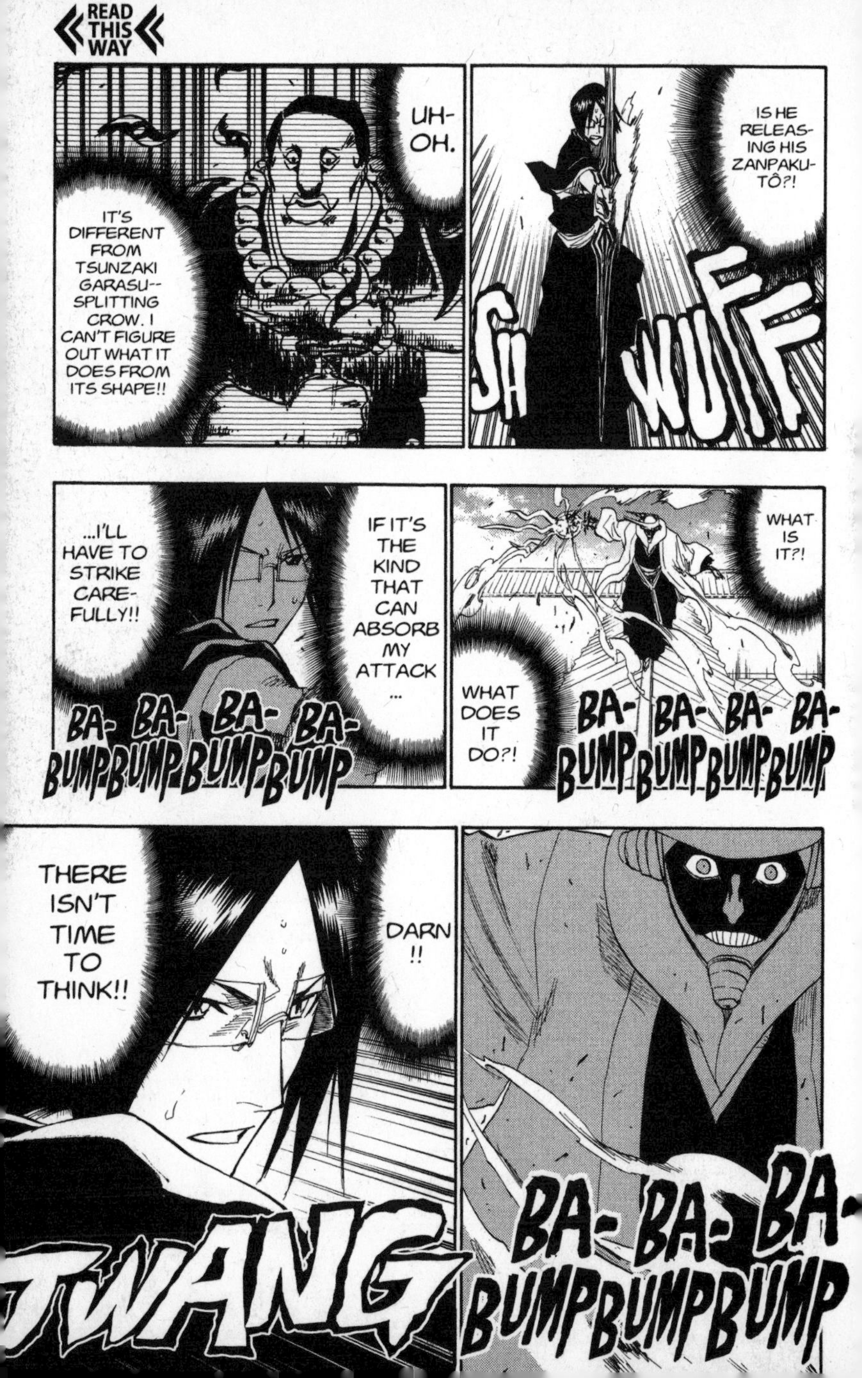
READ THIS WAY
IS HE RELEASING HIS ZANPAKUTÔ?!
SHWUFF
UH-OH.
IT'S DIFFERENT FROM TSUNZAKI GARASU--SPLITTING CROW. I CAN'T FIGURE OUT WHAT IT DOES FROM ITS SHAPE!!
WHAT IS IT?!
WHAT DOES IT DO?!
BA-BUMP BA-BUMP BA-BUMP BA-BUMP
IF IT'S THE KIND THAT CAN ABSORB MY ATTACK...
...I'LL HAVE TO STRIKE CAREFULLY!!
BA-BUMP BA-BUMP BA-BUMP BA-BUMP
BA-BUMP BA-BUMP BA-BUMP
DARN!!
THERE ISN'T TIME TO THINK!!
TWANG

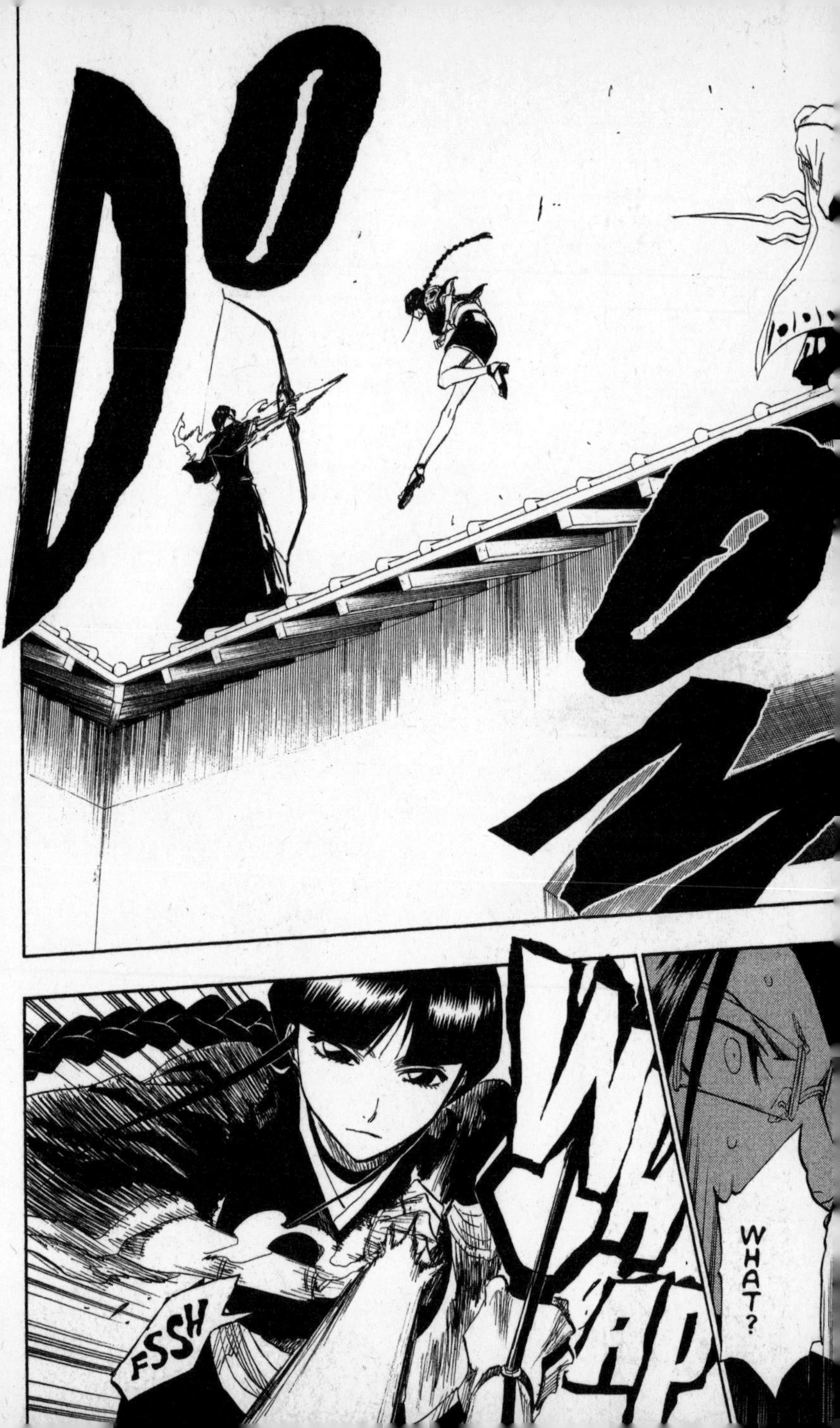
DOOM
WHAT?
WHAP
FSSH

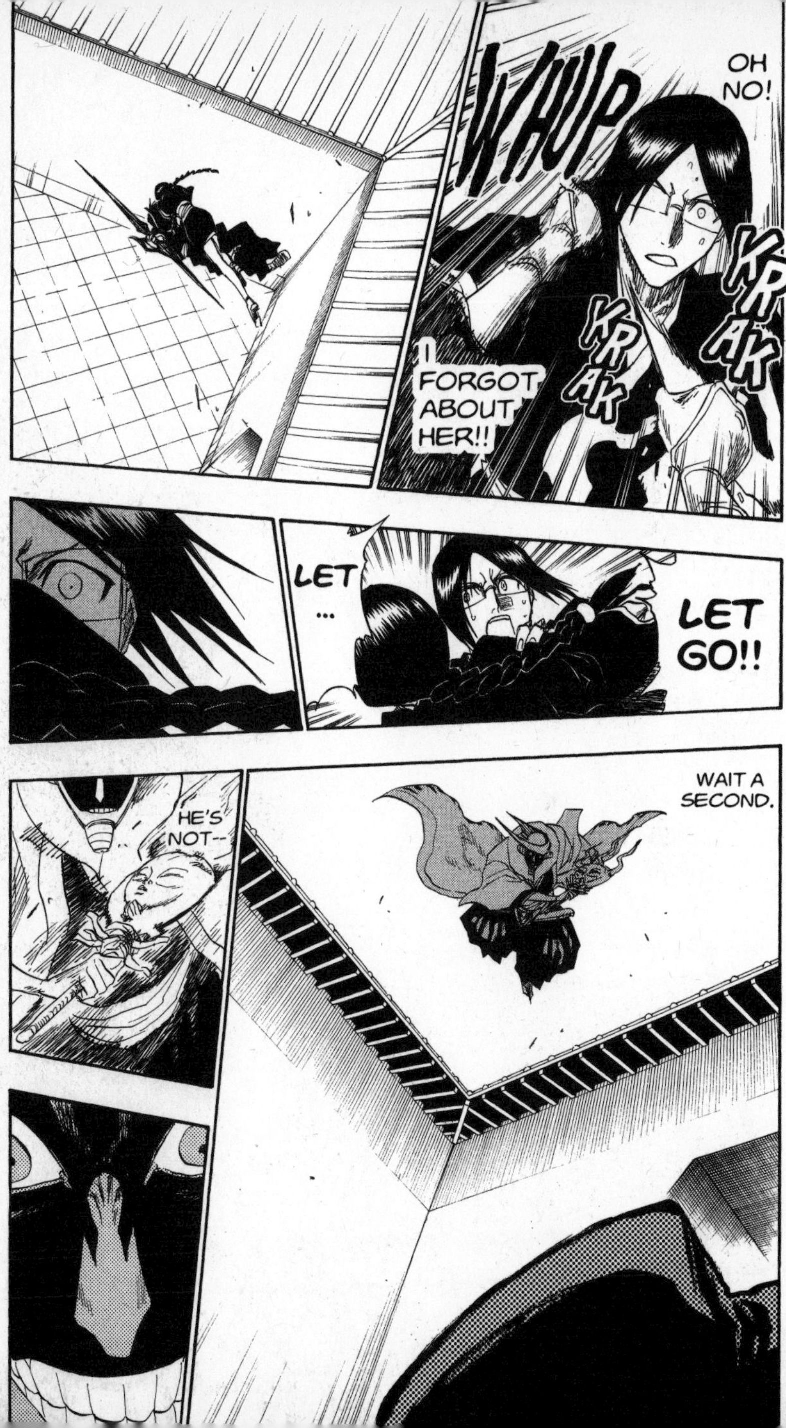
WHUP
OH NO!
KRAK
KRAK
I FORGOT ABOUT HER!!
LET ...
LET GO!!
WAIT A SECOND.
HE'S NOT--

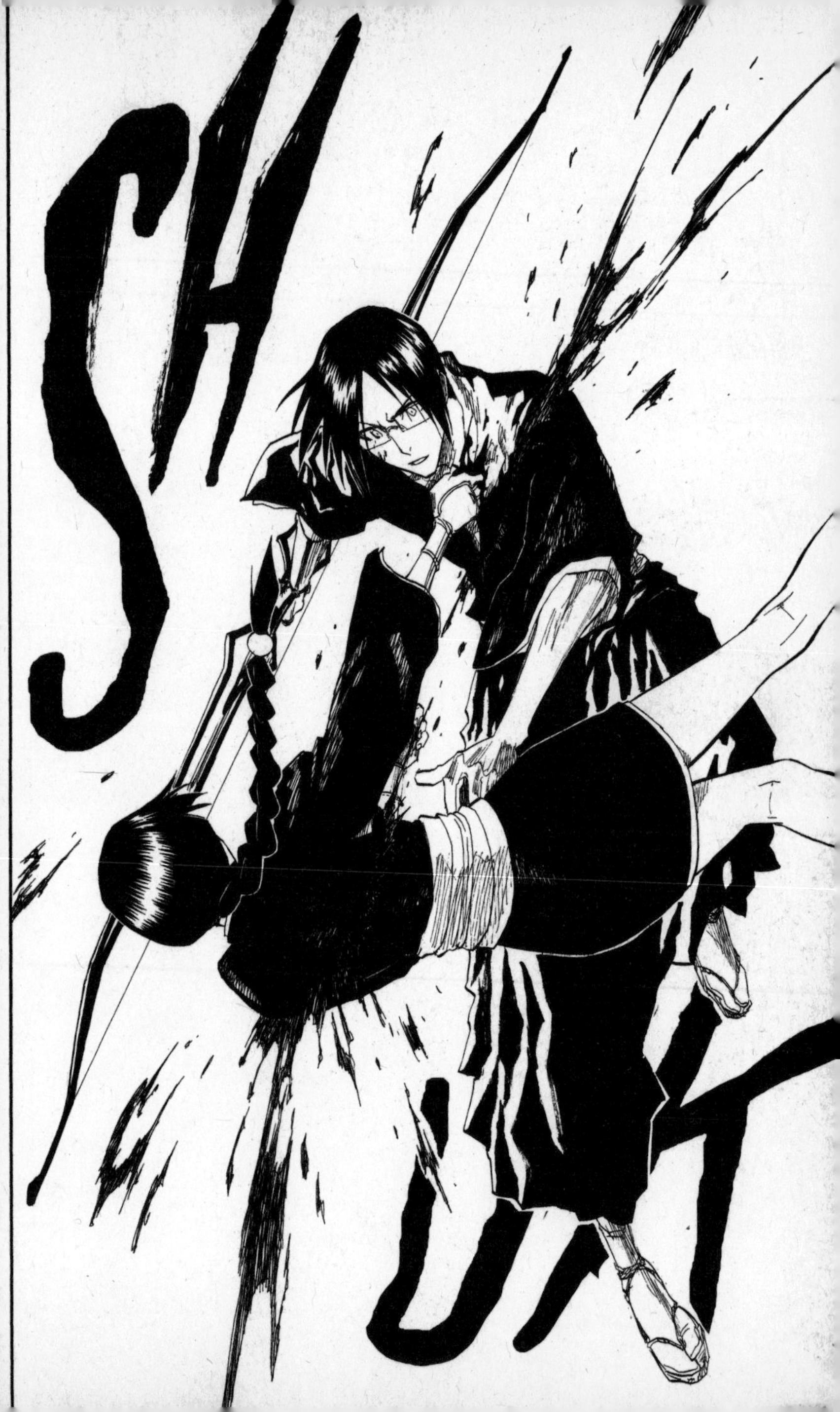

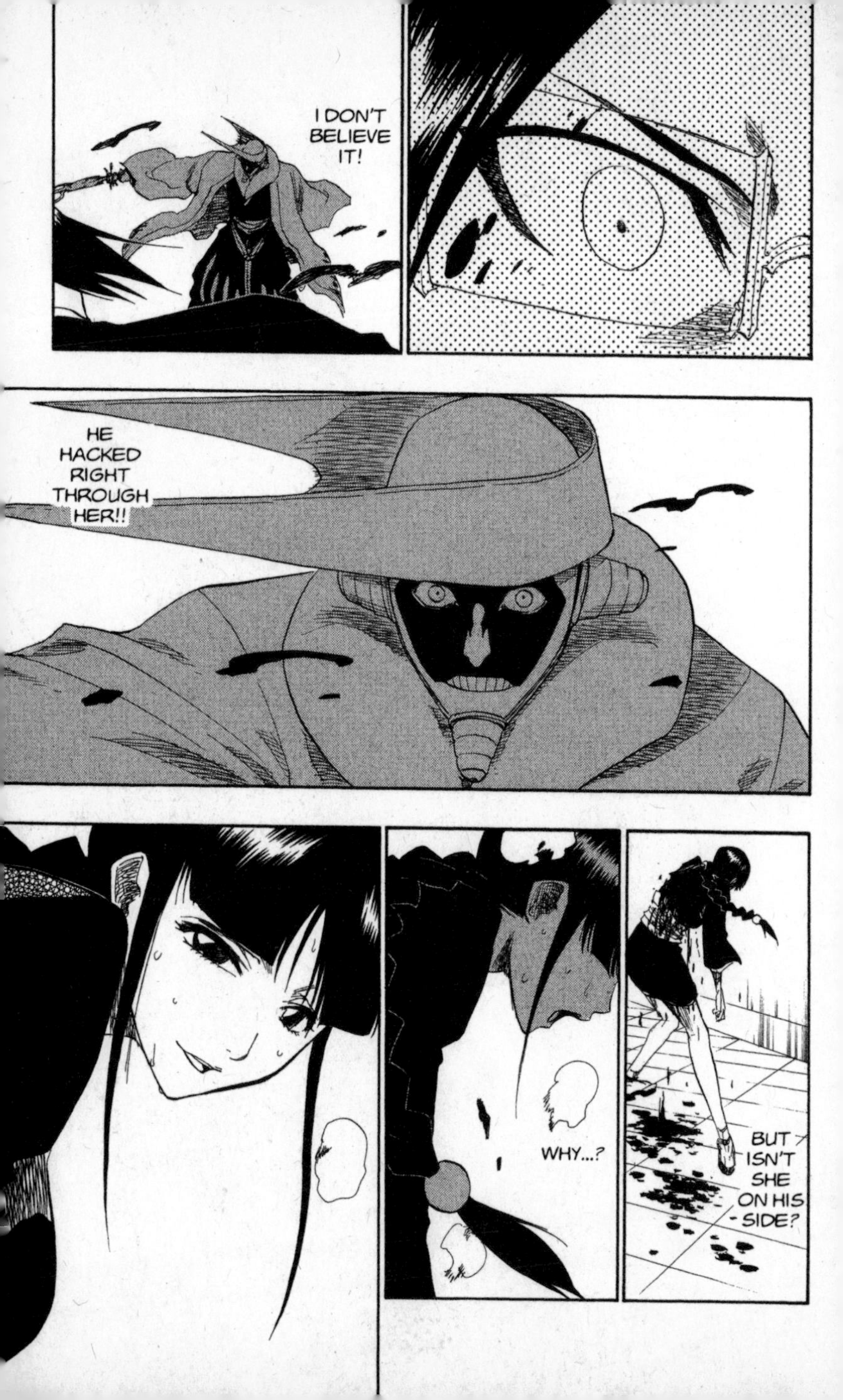
I DON'T BELIEVE IT!
HE HACKED RIGHT THROUGH HER!!
BUT ISN'T SHE ON HIS SIDE?
WHY...?

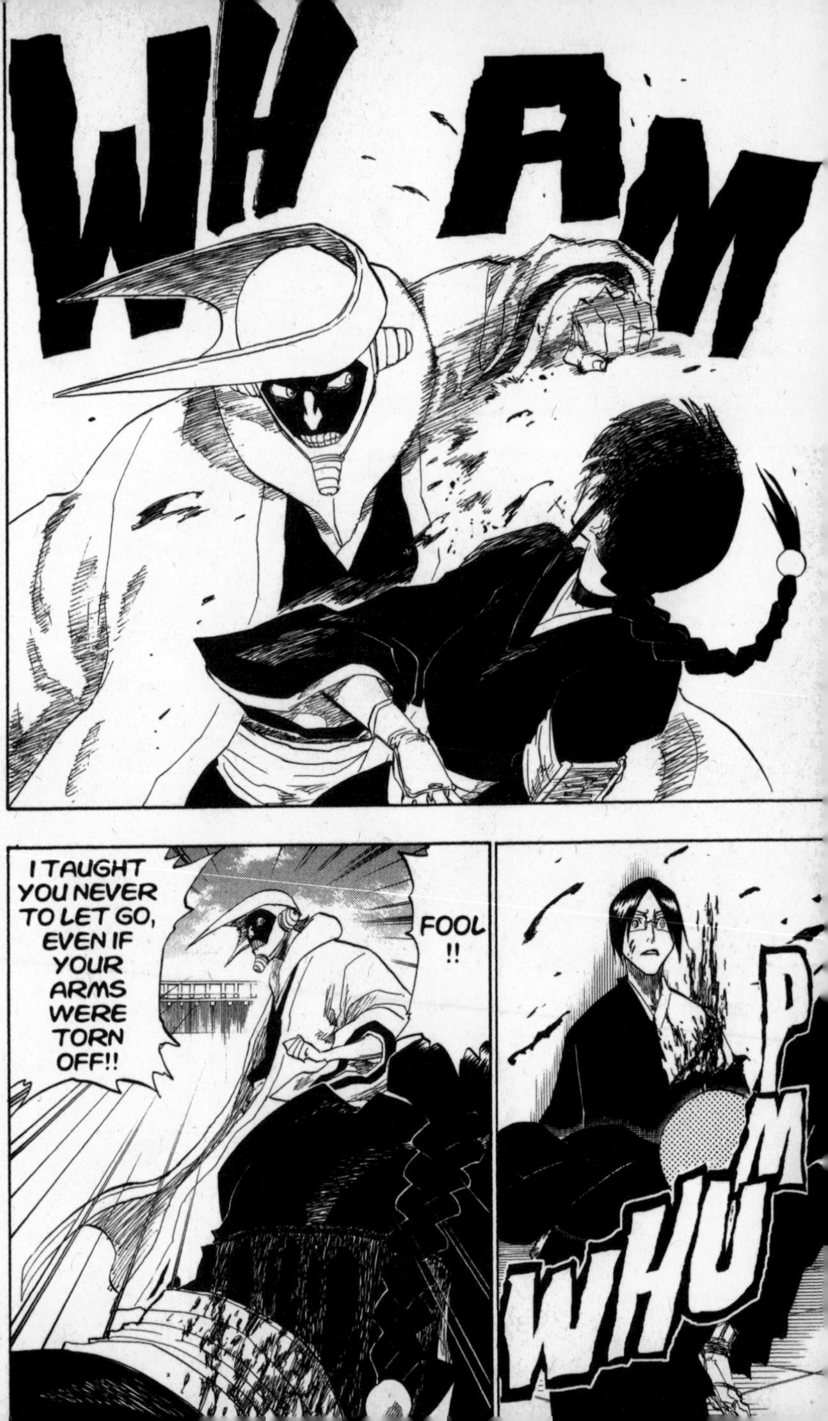
WHAM
WHUMP
FOOL!!
I TAUGHT YOU NEVER TO LET GO, EVEN IF YOUR ARMS WERE TORN OFF!!

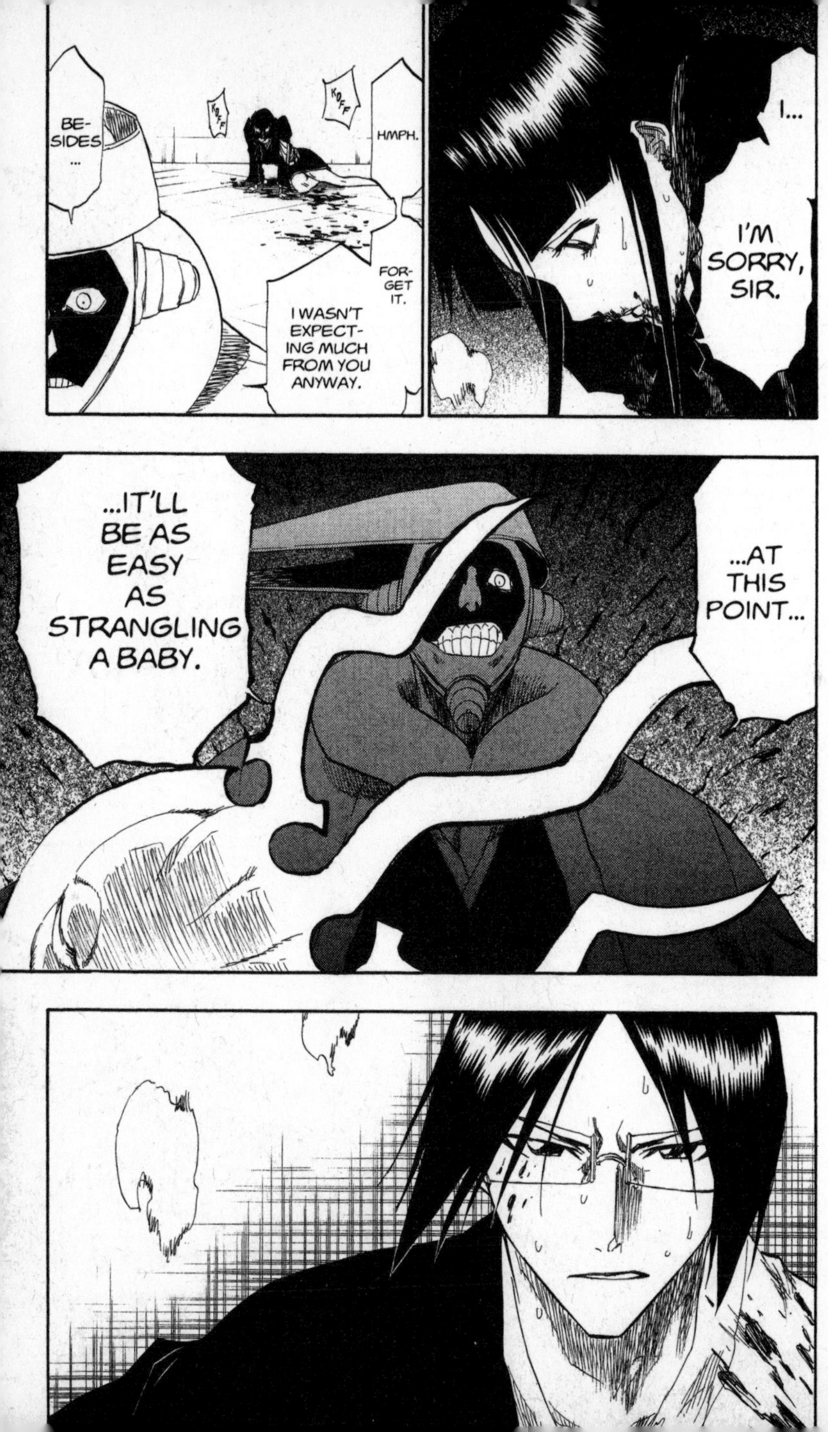
I...
I'M SORRY, SIR.
HMPH.
KOFF
KOFF
FORGET IT.
I WASN'T EXPECTING MUCH FROM YOU ANYWAY.
BESIDES...
...AT THIS POINT...
...IT'LL BE AS EASY AS STRANGLING A BABY.

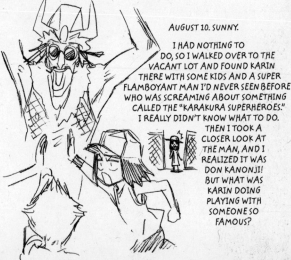

AUGUST 10. SUNNY.

I HAD NOTHING TO DO, SO I WALKED OVER TO THE VACANT LOT AND FOUND KARIN THERE WITH SOME KIDS AND A SUPER FLAMBOYANT MAN I'D NEVER SEEN BEFORE WHO WAS SCREAMING ABOUT SOMETHING CALLED THE "KARAKURA SUPERHEROES." I REALLY DIDN'T KNOW WHAT TO DO. THEN I TOOK A CLOSER LOOK AT THE MAN, AND I REALIZED IT WAS DON KANONJI! BUT WHAT WAS KARIN DOING PLAYING WITH SOMEONE SO FAMOUS?

AT FIRST I THOUGHT I'D GET HIS AUTOGRAPH, BUT I DIDN'T KNOW IF I SHOULD WALK UP CASUALLY AND ASK THEM WHAT THEY WERE DOING OR WHAT. SO I PRETENDED NOT TO SEE ANYTHING AND WENT HOME.

THAT NIGHT, BEFORE I WENT TO BED, I REALIZED I'D BARELY PLAYED OUTSIDE SINCE SUMMER VACATION STARTED.

— TO BE CONTINUED —

123. Pledge My Pride

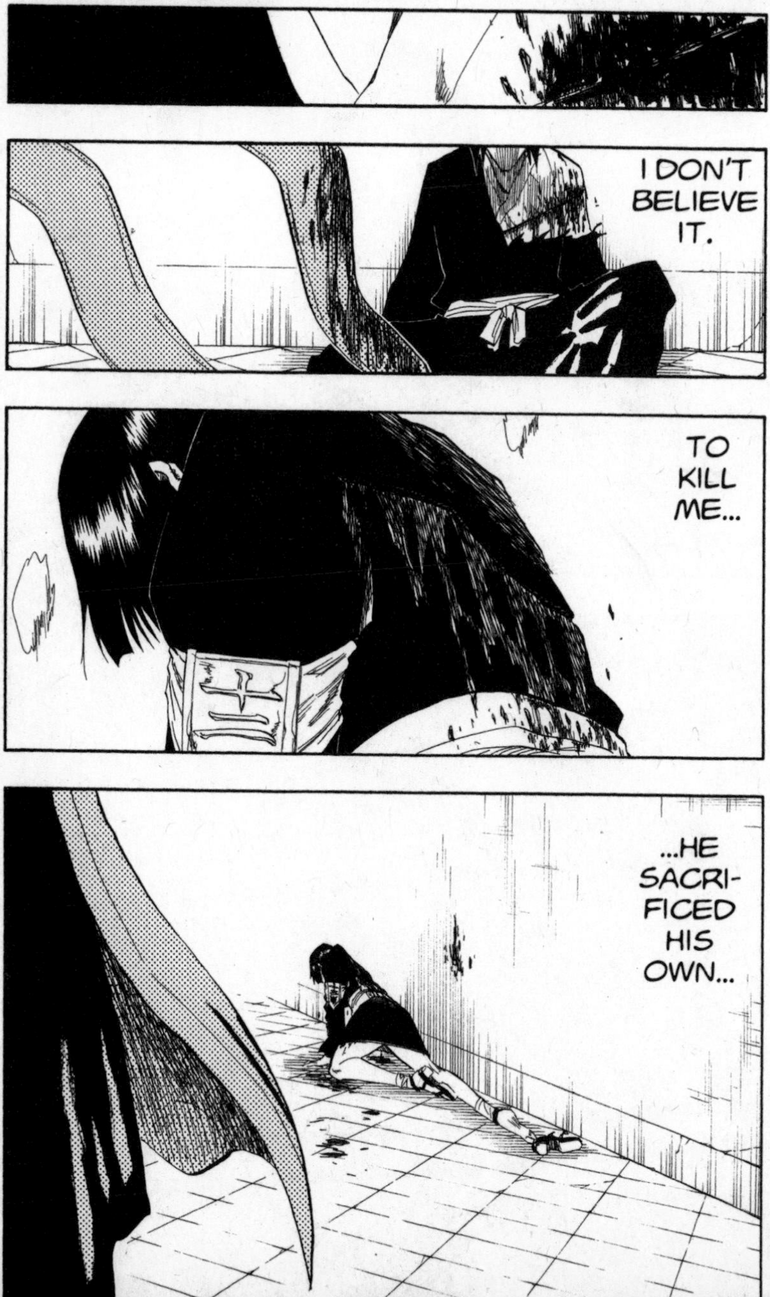
I DON'T BELIEVE IT.
TO KILL ME...
...HE SACRIFICED HIS OWN...

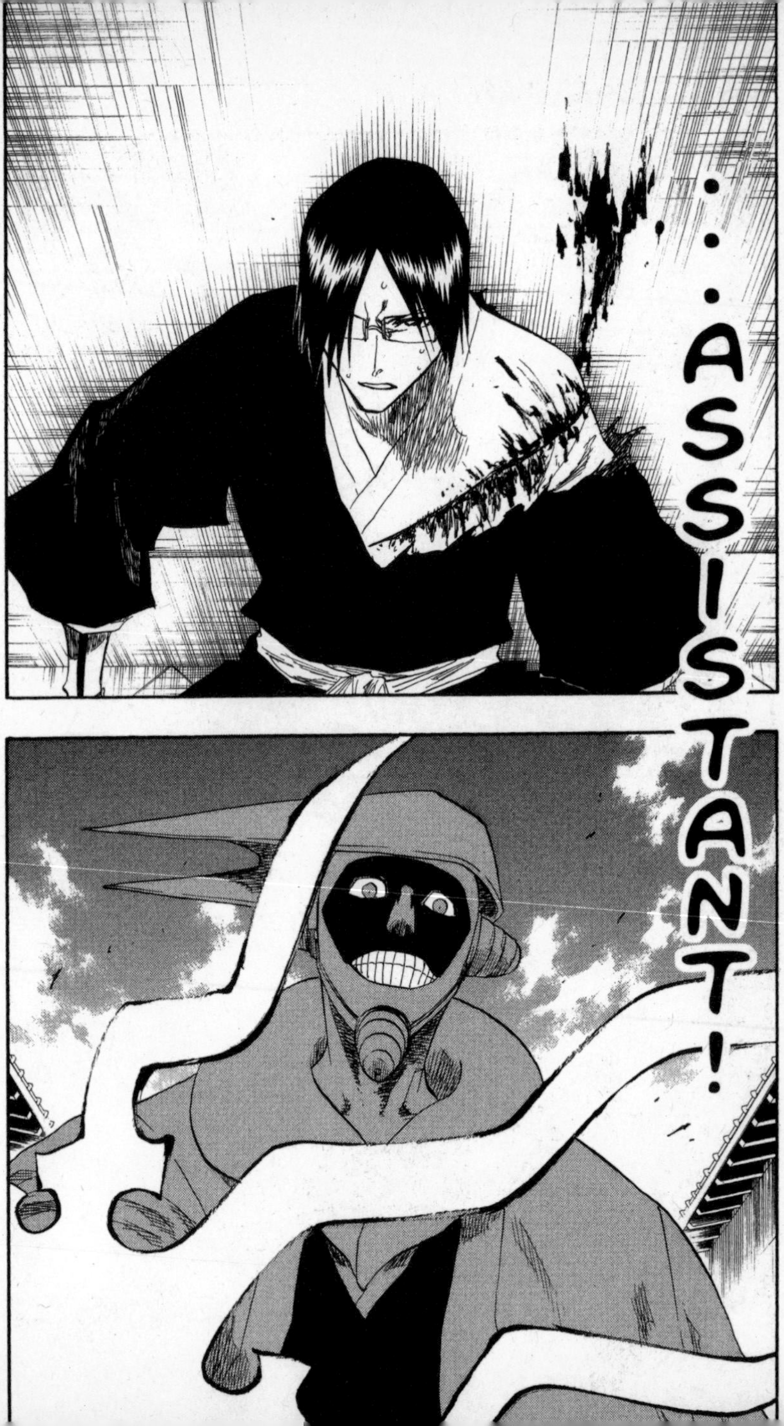
...ASSISTANT!

123. Pledge My Pride

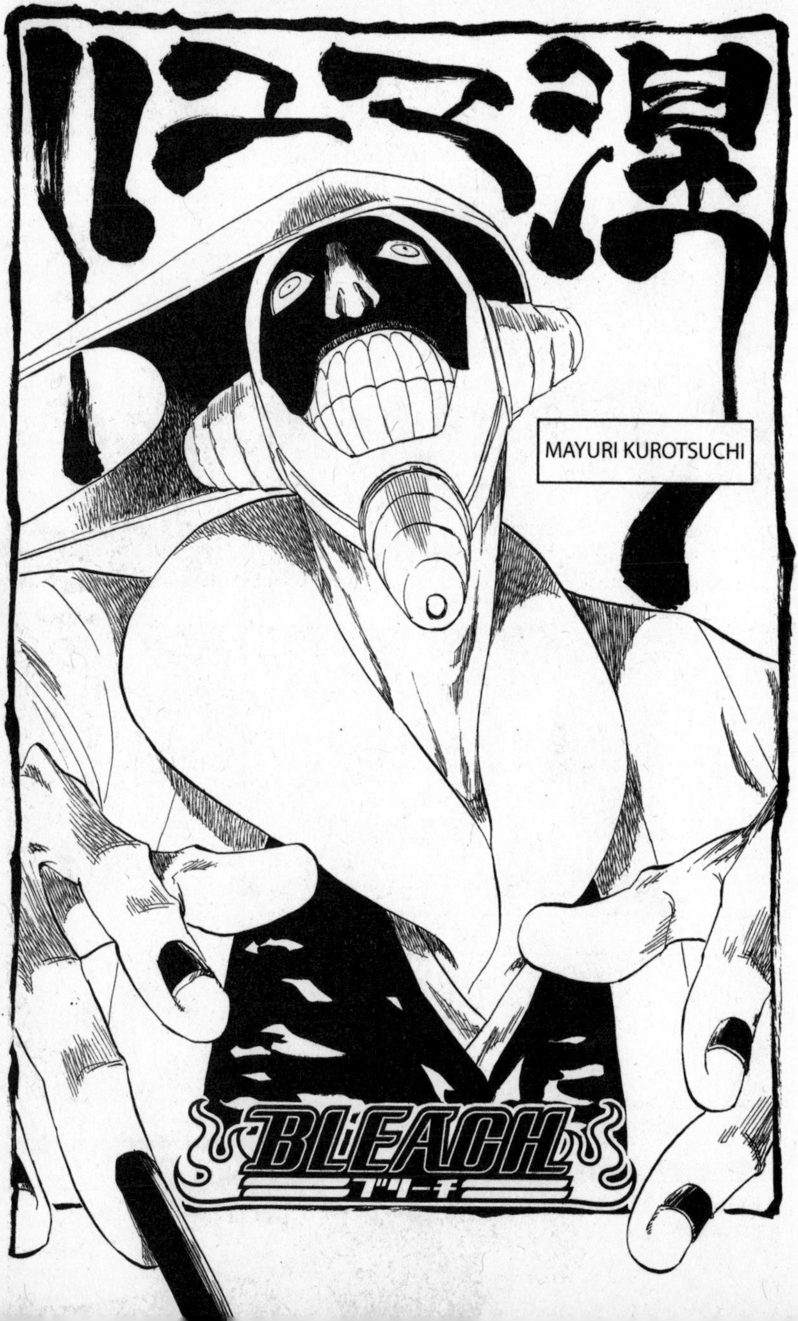
MAYURI KUROTSUCHI
BLEACH
ブリーチ

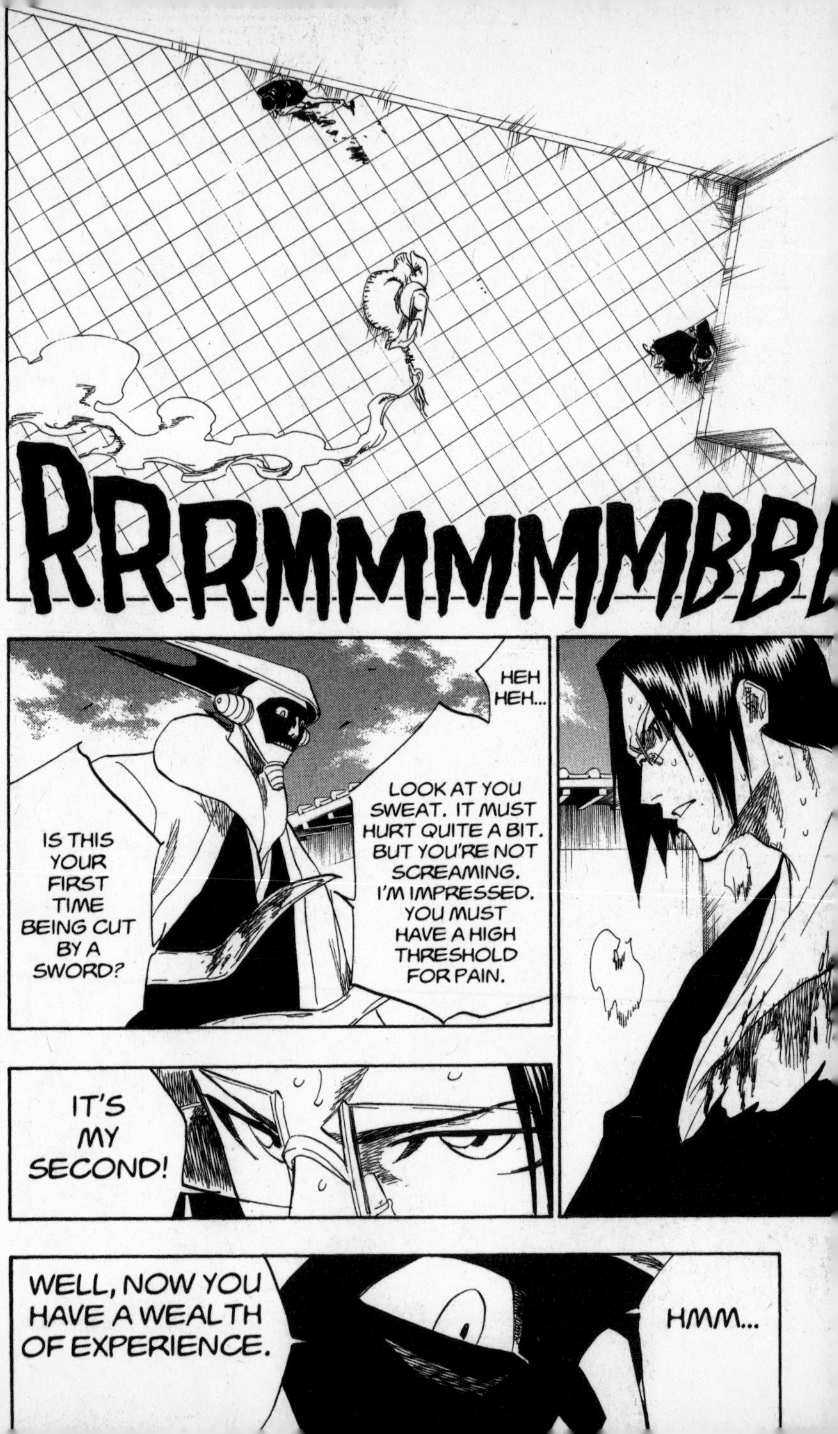
RRRMMMMMMBB
HEH HEH...
LOOK AT YOU SWEAT. IT MUST HURT QUITE A BIT. BUT YOU'RE NOT SCREAMING. I'M IMPRESSED. YOU MUST HAVE A HIGH THRESHOLD FOR PAIN.
IS THIS YOUR FIRST TIME BEING CUT BY A SWORD?
IT'S MY SECOND!
HMM...
WELL, NOW YOU HAVE A WEALTH OF EXPERIENCE.

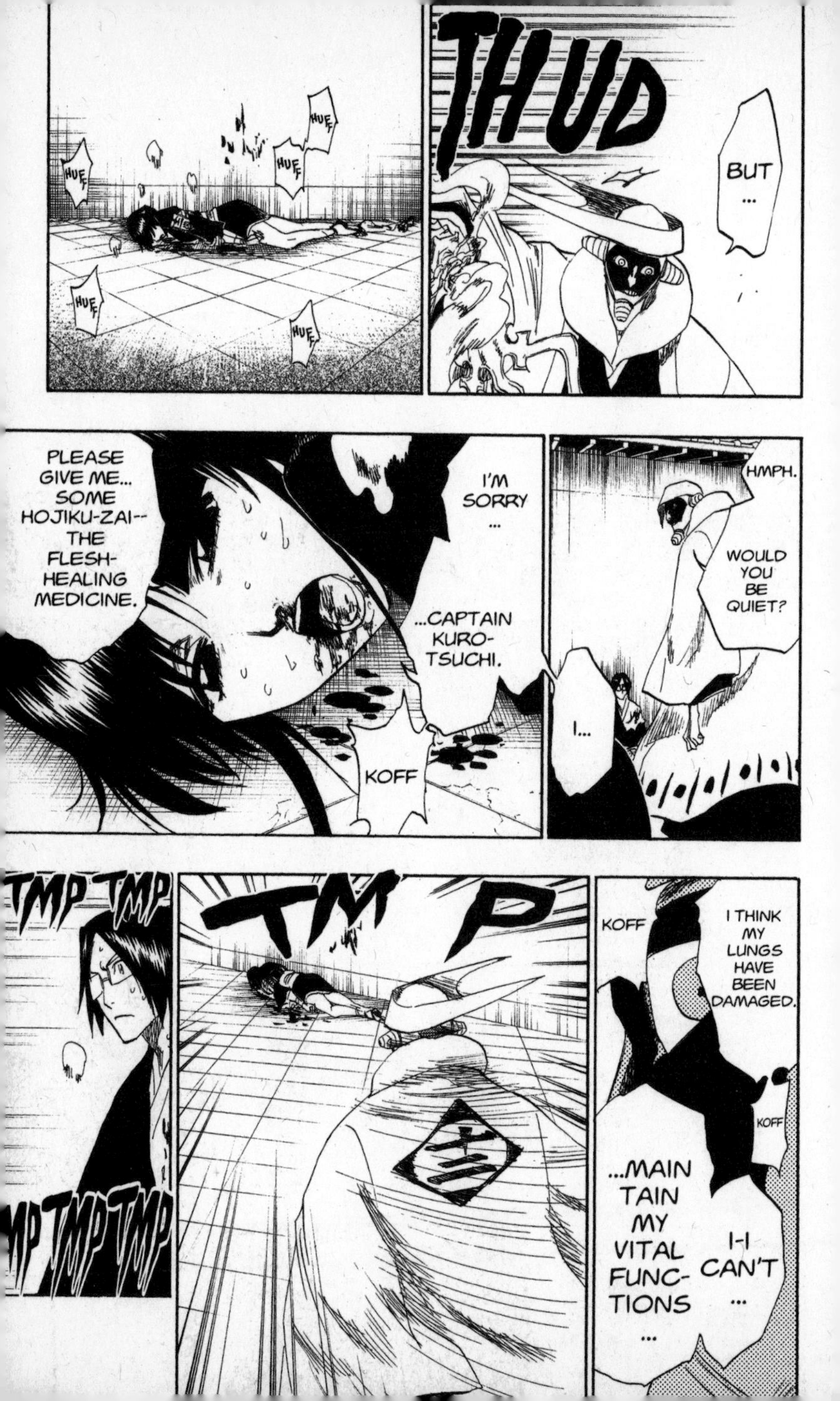
THUD
BUT ...
HUFF
HUFF
HUFF
HUFF
HUFF
HMPH.
WOULD YOU BE QUIET?
I...
I'M SORRY ...
...CAPTAIN KURO-TSUCHI.
KOFF
PLEASE GIVE ME... SOME HOJIKU-ZAI-- THE FLESH-HEALING MEDICINE.
I THINK MY LUNGS HAVE BEEN DAMAGED.
KOFF
KOFF
I-I CAN'T ...
...MAIN TAIN MY VITAL FUNC-TIONS ...
TMP
TMP TMP
TMP TMP TMP

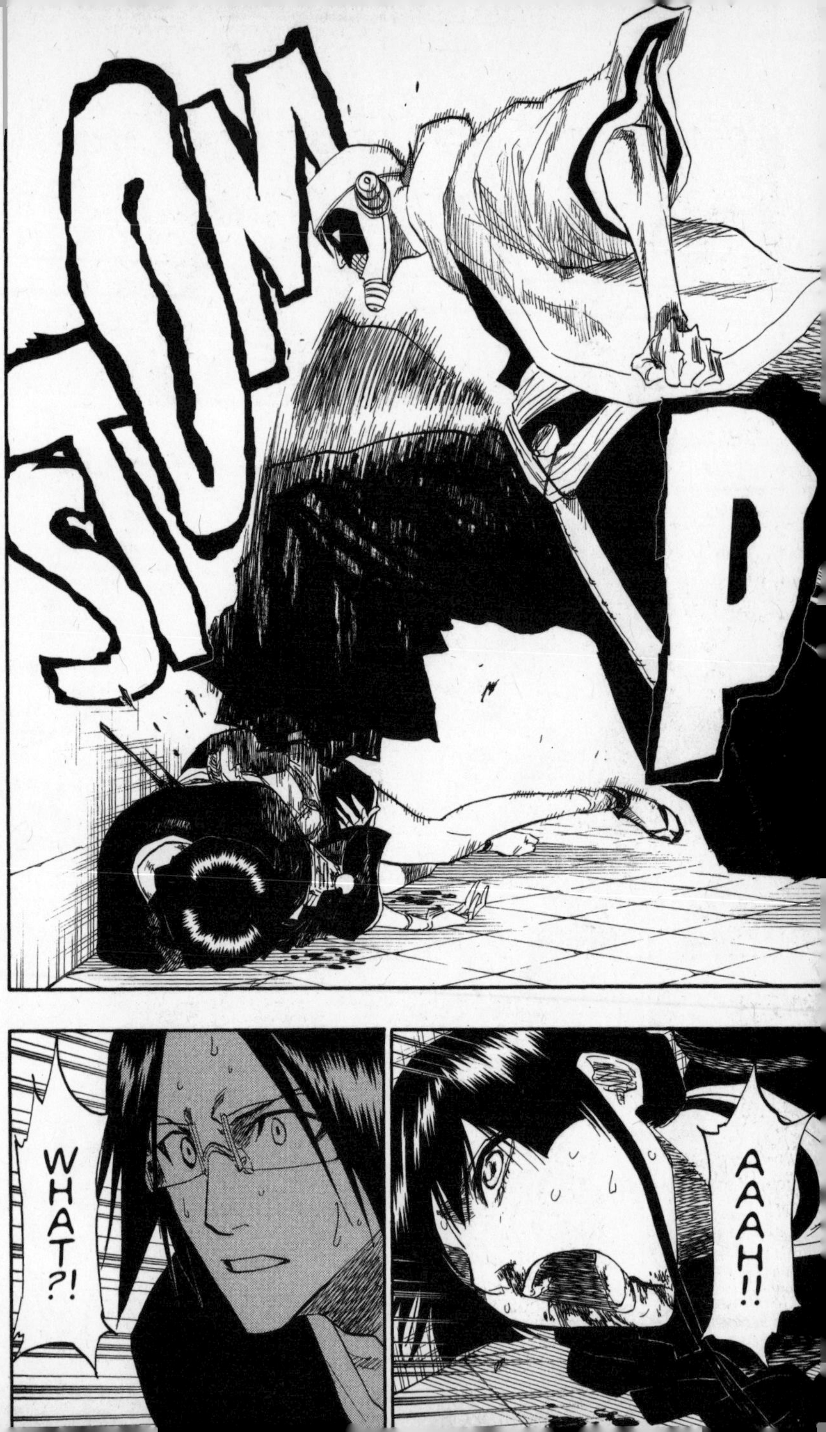
SLUMP
AAAH!!
WHAT?!

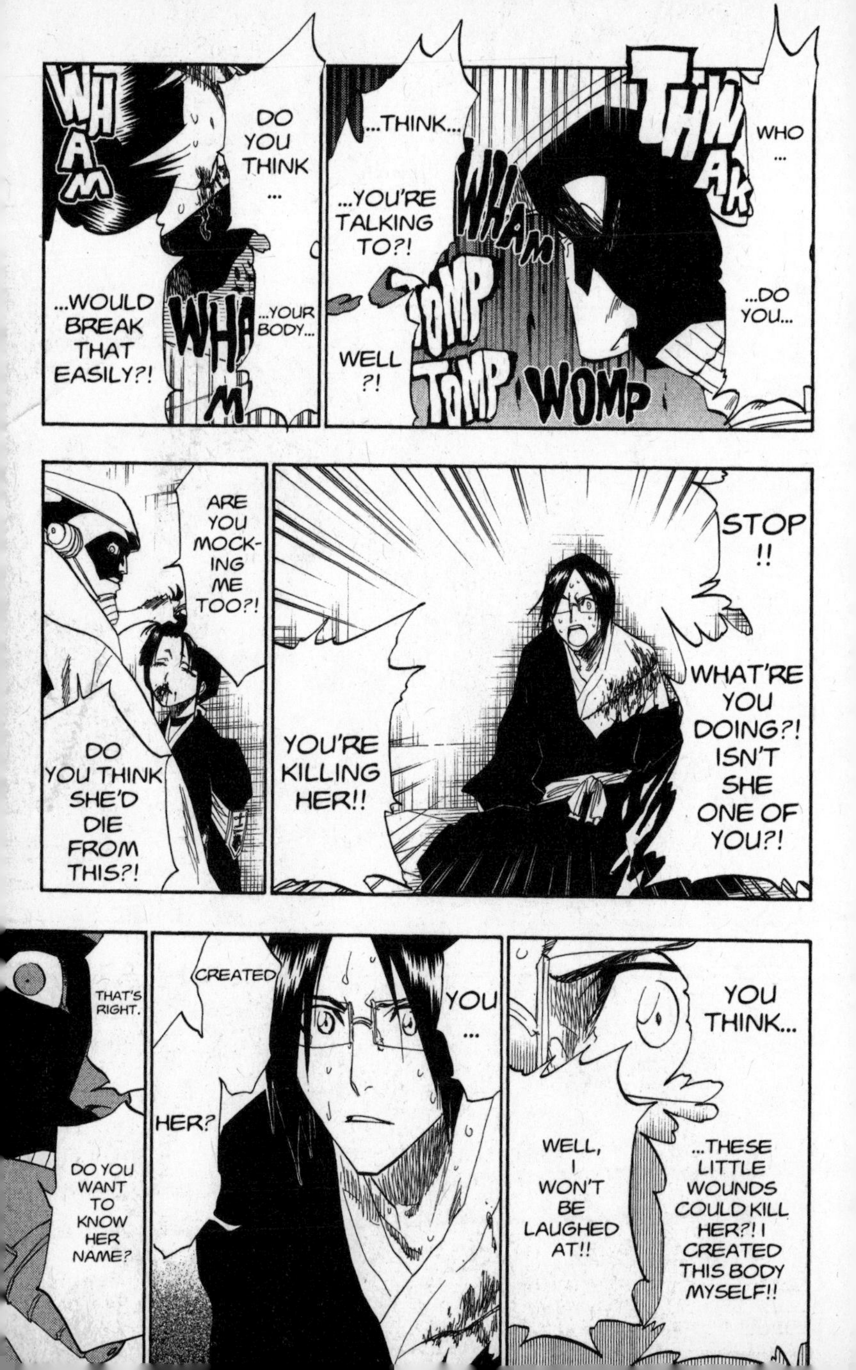
THWAK
WHO ...
...DO YOU...
...THINK...
...YOU'RE TALKING TO?!
WHAM
TOMP
TOMP
WOMP
WELL ?!
DO YOU THINK ...
WHAM
...YOUR BODY...
WHAM
...WOULD BREAK THAT EASILY?!
STOP !!
WHAT'RE YOU DOING?! ISN'T SHE ONE OF YOU?!
YOU'RE KILLING HER!!
ARE YOU MOCK-ING ME TOO?!
DO YOU THINK SHE'D DIE FROM THIS?!
YOU THINK...
...THESE LITTLE WOUNDS COULD KILL HER?! I CREATED THIS BODY MYSELF!!
WELL, I WON'T BE LAUGHED AT!!
YOU ...
CREATED
HER?
THAT'S RIGHT.
DO YOU WANT TO KNOW HER NAME?

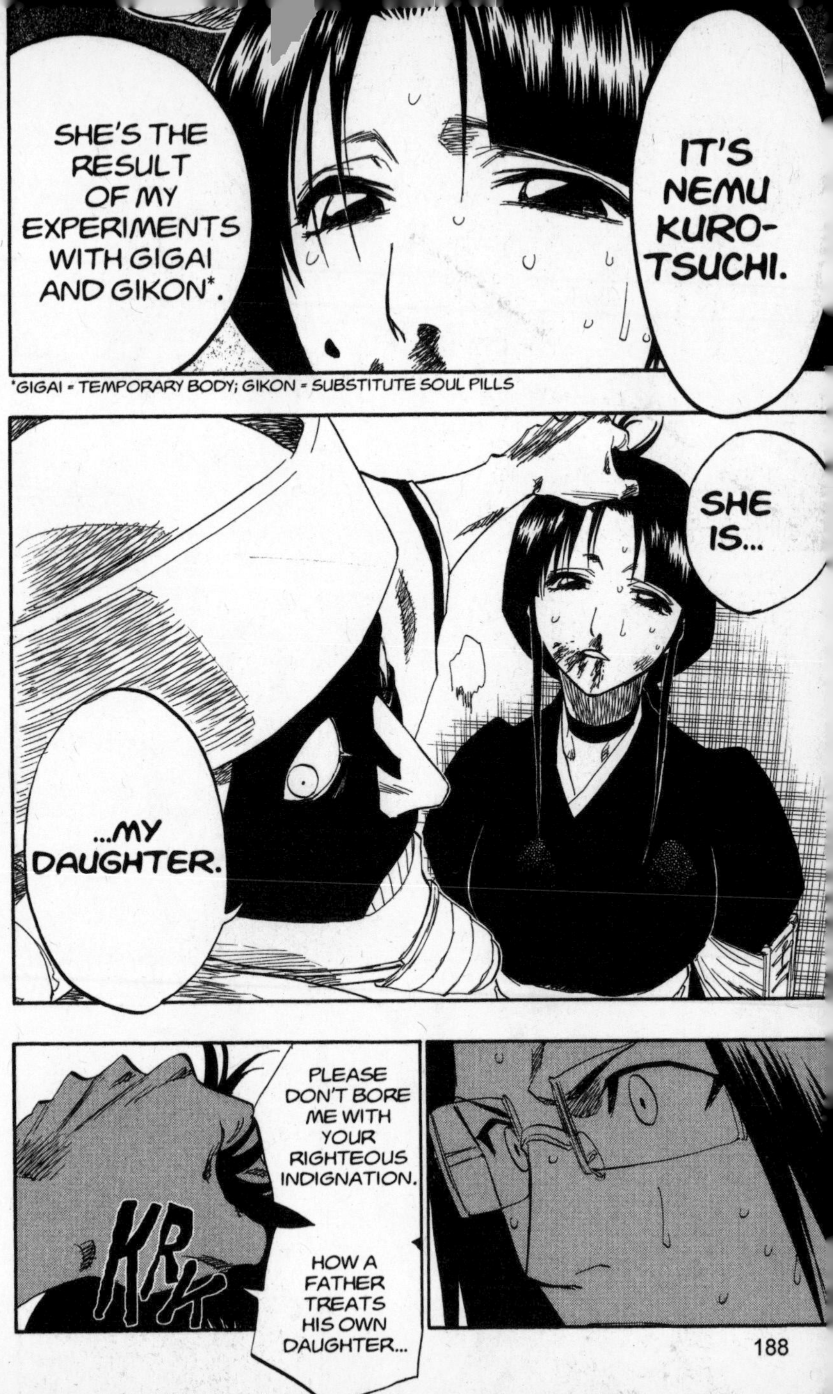
IT'S NEMU KURO-TSUCHI.
SHE'S THE RESULT OF MY EXPERIMENTS WITH GIGAI AND GIKON*.
SHE IS...
...MY DAUGHTER.
PLEASE DON'T BORE ME WITH YOUR RIGHTEOUS INDIGNATION.
HOW A FATHER TREATS HIS OWN DAUGHTER...
KRK

*GIGAI = TEMPORARY BODY; GIKON = SUBSTITUTE SOUL PILLS

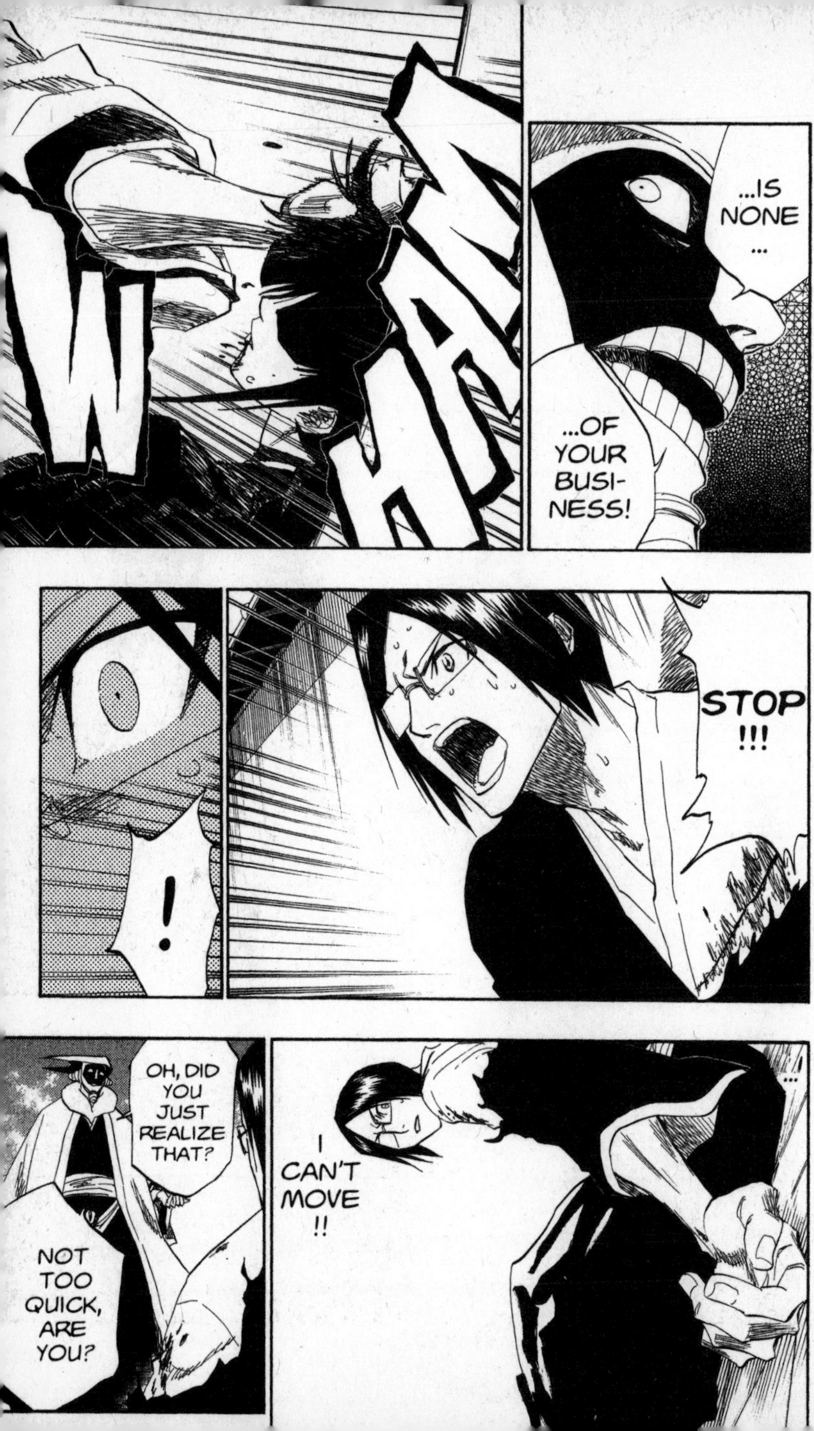
...IS NONE ...
...OF YOUR BUSI-NESS!
STOP !!!
!
...!
I CAN'T MOVE !!
OH, DID YOU JUST REALIZE THAT?
NOT TOO QUICK, ARE YOU?

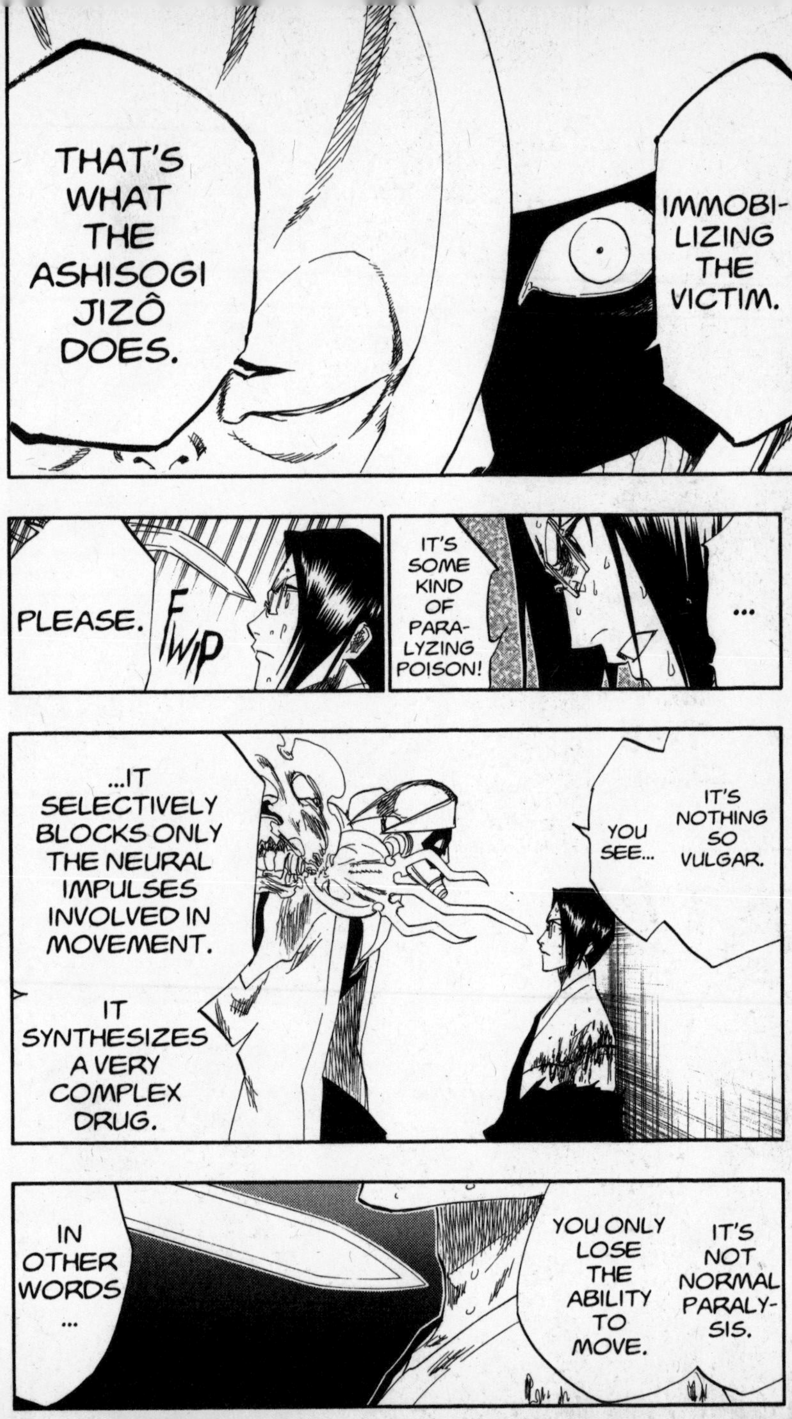
IMMOBILIZING THE VICTIM.
THAT'S WHAT THE ASHISOGI JIZÔ DOES.
...
IT'S SOME KIND OF PARALYZING POISON!
PLEASE.
FWIP
IT'S NOTHING SO VULGAR.
YOU SEE...
...IT SELECTIVELY BLOCKS ONLY THE NEURAL IMPULSES INVOLVED IN MOVEMENT.
IT SYNTHESIZES A VERY COMPLEX DRUG.
IT'S NOT NORMAL PARALYSIS.
YOU ONLY LOSE THE ABILITY TO MOVE.
IN OTHER WORDS...

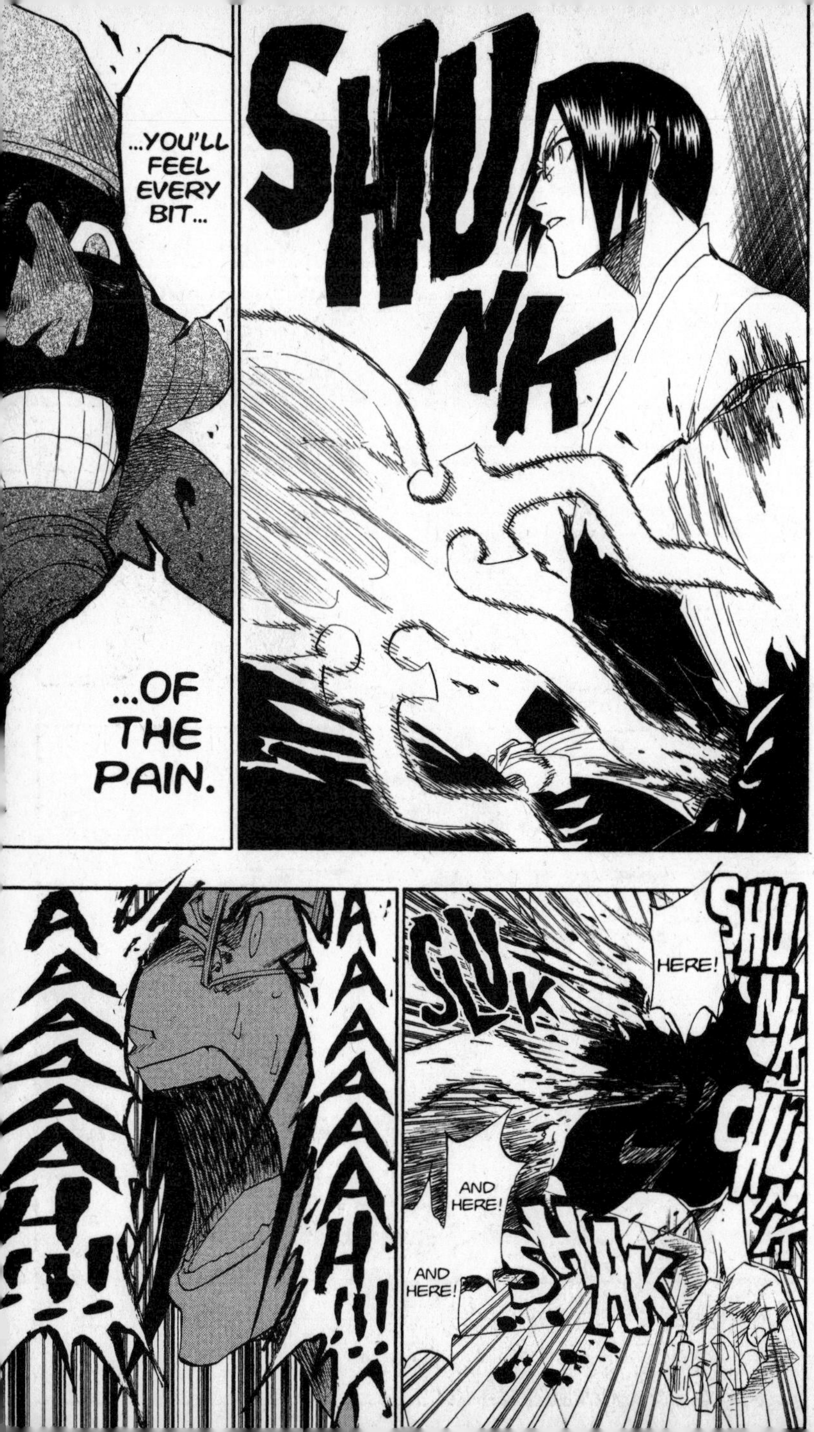
SHUNK
...YOU'LL FEEL EVERY BIT...
...OF THE PAIN.
SHUNK
HERE!
SLUK
CHUNK
AND HERE!
SHAK
AND HERE!
AAAAAAAH!!!
AAAAAAAH!!

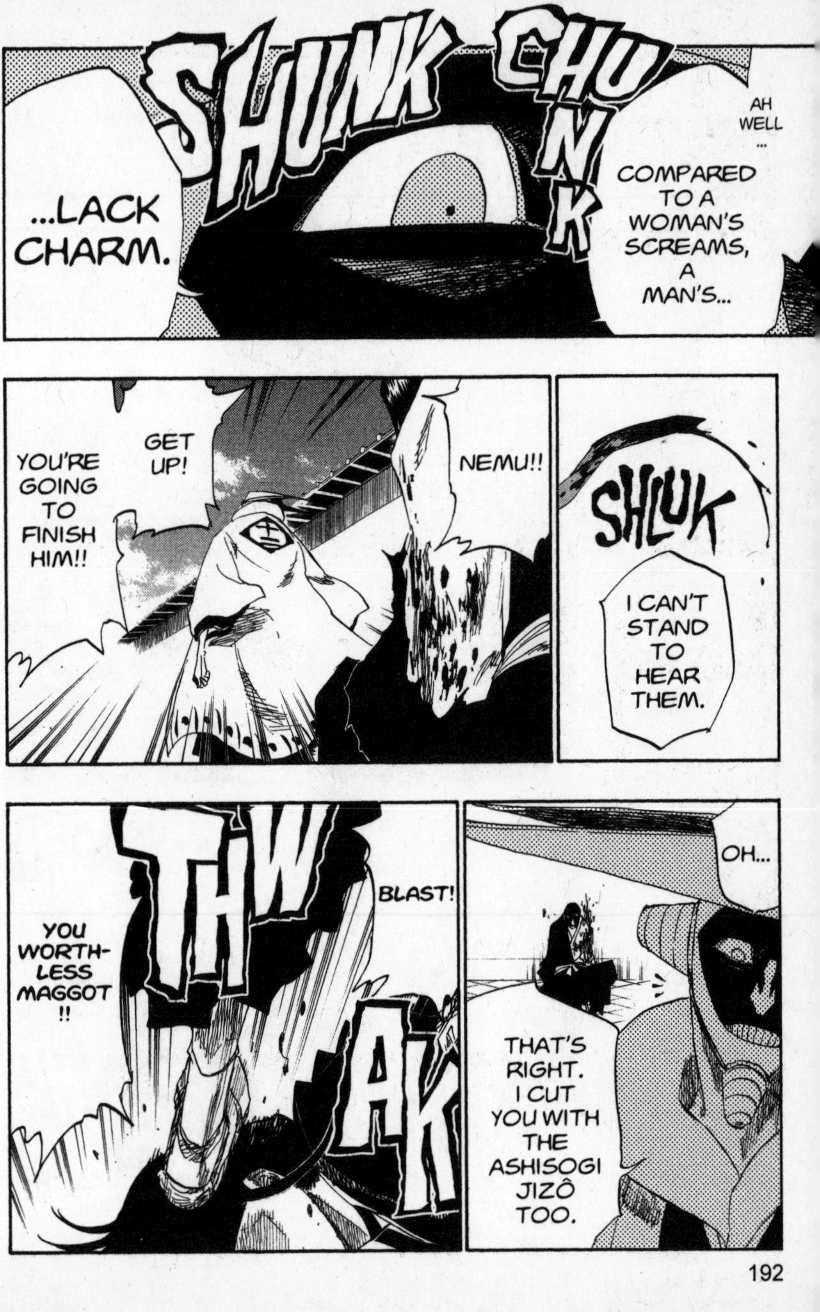
CHUNK
AH WELL ...
COMPARED TO A WOMAN'S SCREAMS, A MAN'S...
SHUNK
...LACK CHARM.
SHLUK
I CAN'T STAND TO HEAR THEM.
NEMU!!
GET UP!
YOU'RE GOING TO FINISH HIM!!
OH...
THAT'S RIGHT. I CUT YOU WITH THE ASHISOGI JIZÔ TOO.
BLAST!
THWAK
YOU WORTH-LESS MAGGOT !!

READ THIS WAY

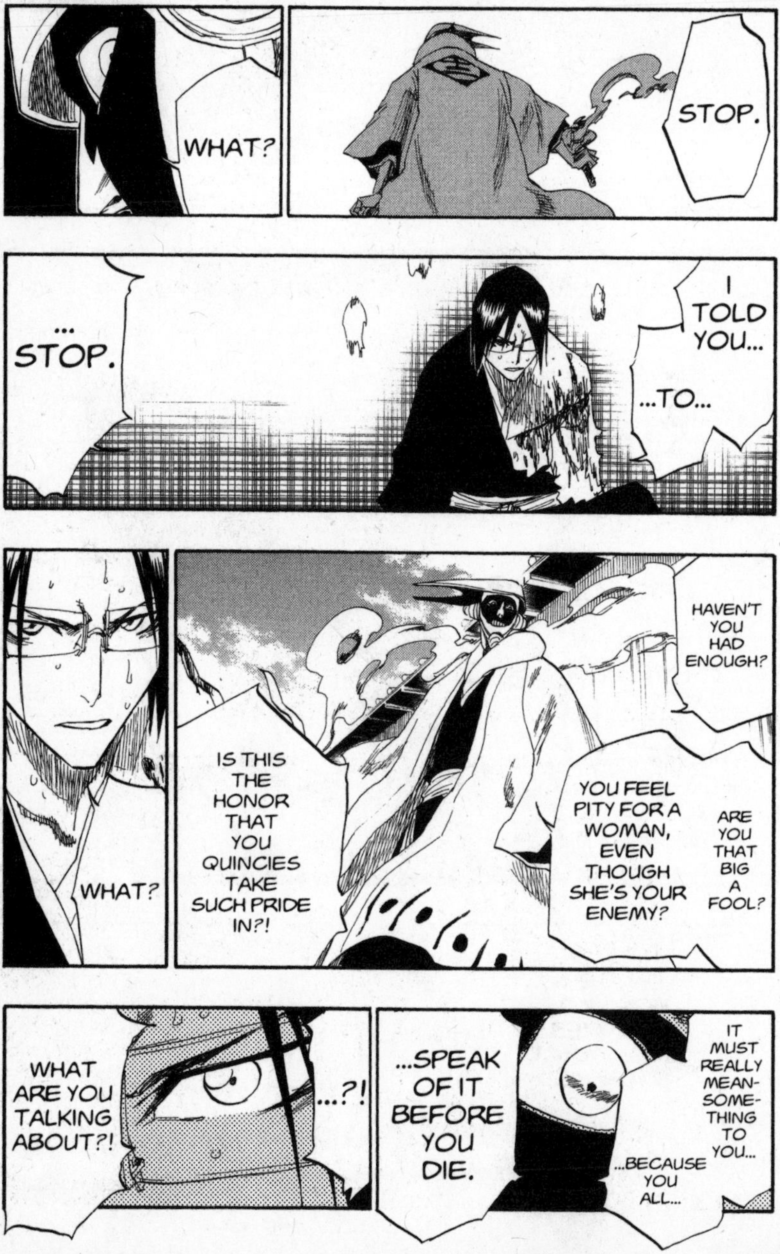
STOP.
WHAT?
I TOLD YOU...
...TO...
... STOP.
HAVEN'T YOU HAD ENOUGH?
ARE YOU THAT BIG A FOOL?
YOU FEEL PITY FOR A WOMAN, EVEN THOUGH SHE'S YOUR ENEMY?
IS THIS THE HONOR THAT YOU QUINCIES TAKE SUCH PRIDE IN?!
WHAT?
IT MUST REALLY MEAN-SOMETHING TO YOU...
...BECAUSE YOU ALL...
...SPEAK OF IT BEFORE YOU DIE.
...?!
WHAT ARE YOU TALKING ABOUT?!

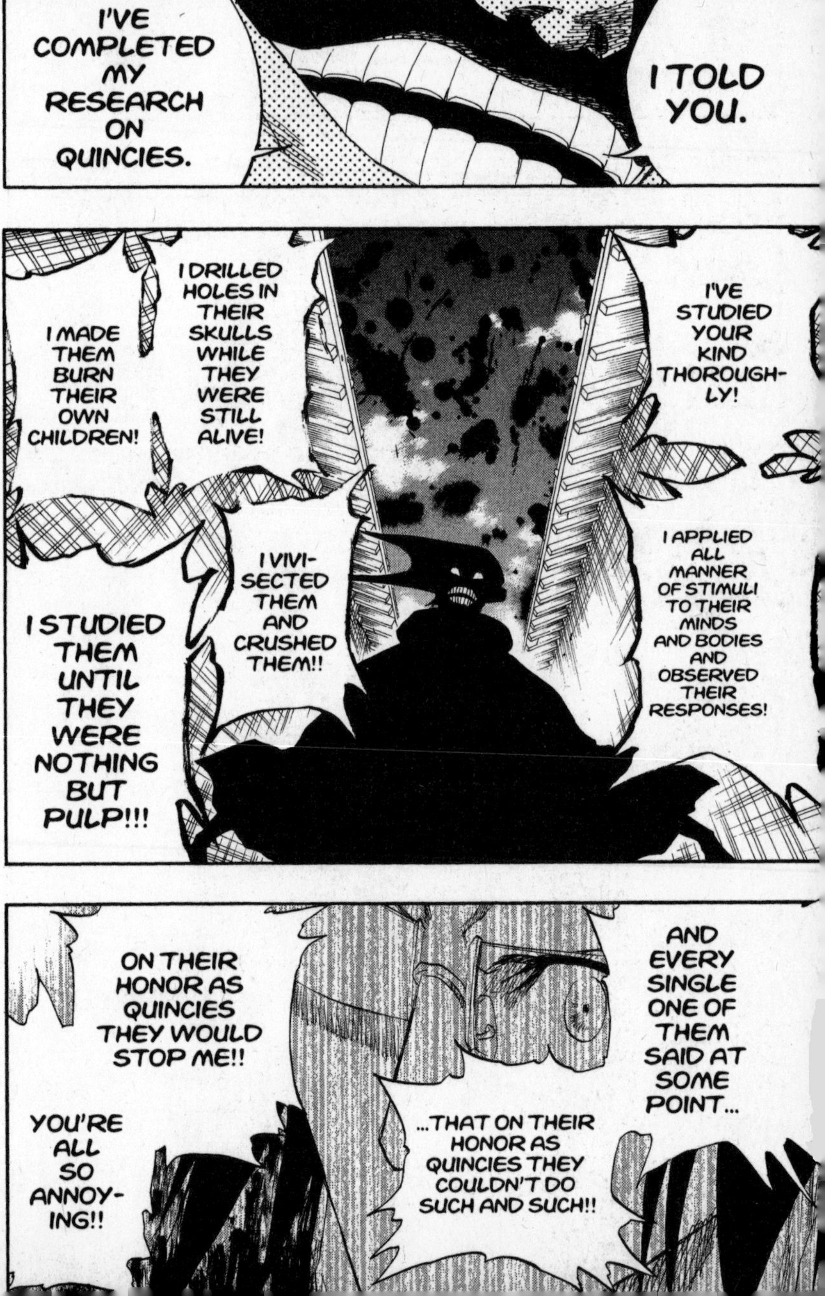
I TOLD YOU.
I'VE COMPLETED MY RESEARCH ON QUINCIES.
I'VE STUDIED YOUR KIND THOROUGHLY!
I DRILLED HOLES IN THEIR SKULLS WHILE THEY WERE STILL ALIVE!
I MADE THEM BURN THEIR OWN CHILDREN!
I APPLIED ALL MANNER OF STIMULI TO THEIR MINDS AND BODIES AND OBSERVED THEIR RESPONSES!
I VIVISECTED THEM AND CRUSHED THEM!!
I STUDIED THEM UNTIL THEY WERE NOTHING BUT PULP!!!
AND EVERY SINGLE ONE OF THEM SAID AT SOME POINT...
...THAT ON THEIR HONOR AS QUINCIES THEY COULDN'T DO SUCH AND SUCH!!
ON THEIR HONOR AS QUINCIES THEY WOULD STOP ME!!
YOU'RE ALL SO ANNOYING!!

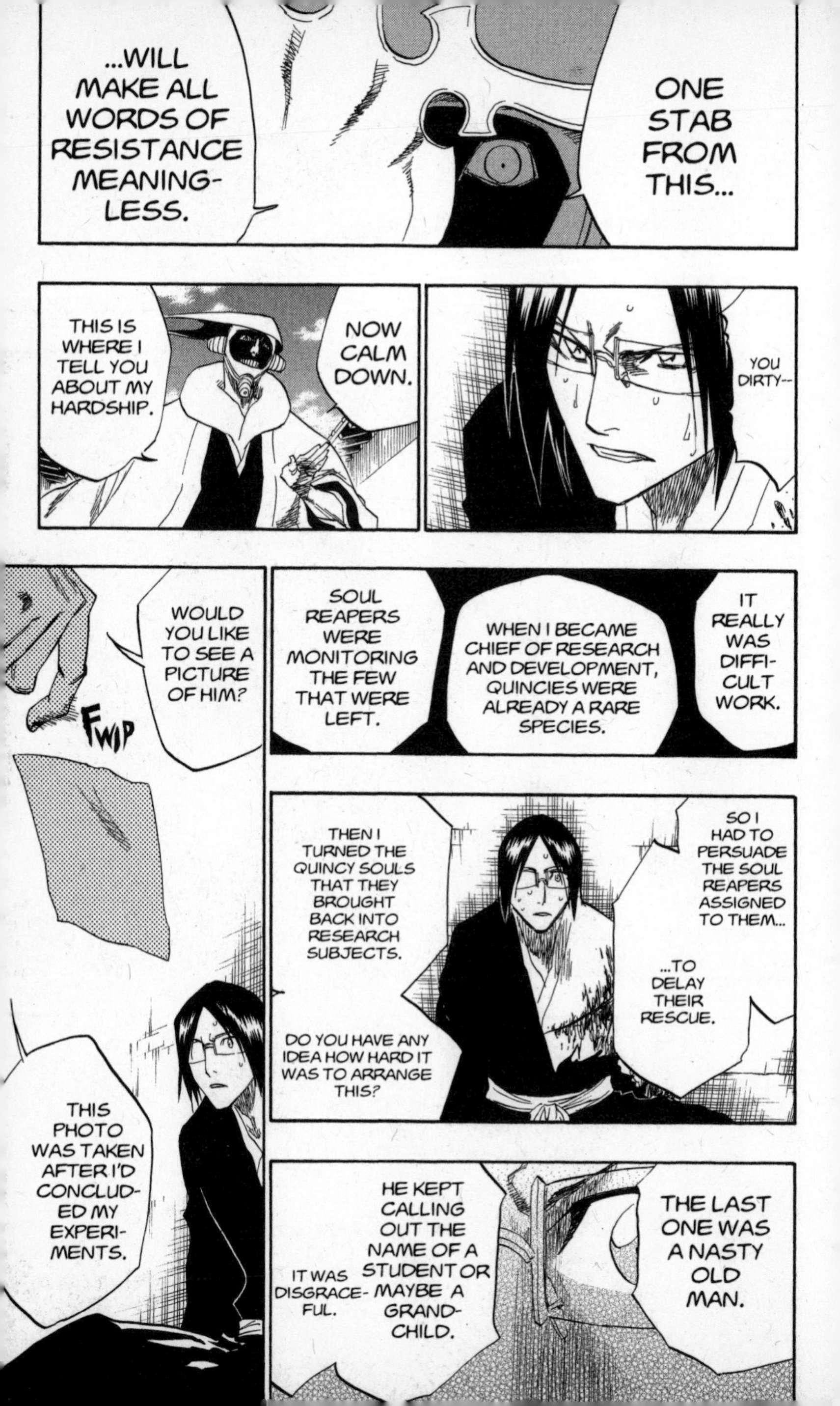
ONE STAB FROM THIS...
...WILL MAKE ALL WORDS OF RESISTANCE MEANING-LESS.
YOU DIRTY--
NOW CALM DOWN.
THIS IS WHERE I TELL YOU ABOUT MY HARDSHIP.
IT REALLY WAS DIFFI-CULT WORK.
WHEN I BECAME CHIEF OF RESEARCH AND DEVELOPMENT, QUINCIES WERE ALREADY A RARE SPECIES.
SOUL REAPERS WERE MONITORING THE FEW THAT WERE LEFT.
SO I HAD TO PERSUADE THE SOUL REAPERS ASSIGNED TO THEM...
...TO DELAY THEIR RESCUE.
THEN I TURNED THE QUINCY SOULS THAT THEY BROUGHT BACK INTO RESEARCH SUBJECTS.
DO YOU HAVE ANY IDEA HOW HARD IT WAS TO ARRANGE THIS?
THE LAST ONE WAS A NASTY OLD MAN.
HE KEPT CALLING OUT THE NAME OF A STUDENT OR MAYBE A GRAND-CHILD.
IT WAS DISGRACE-FUL.
WOULD YOU LIKE TO SEE A PICTURE OF HIM?
FWIP
THIS PHOTO WAS TAKEN AFTER I'D CONCLUD-ED MY EXPERI-MENTS.

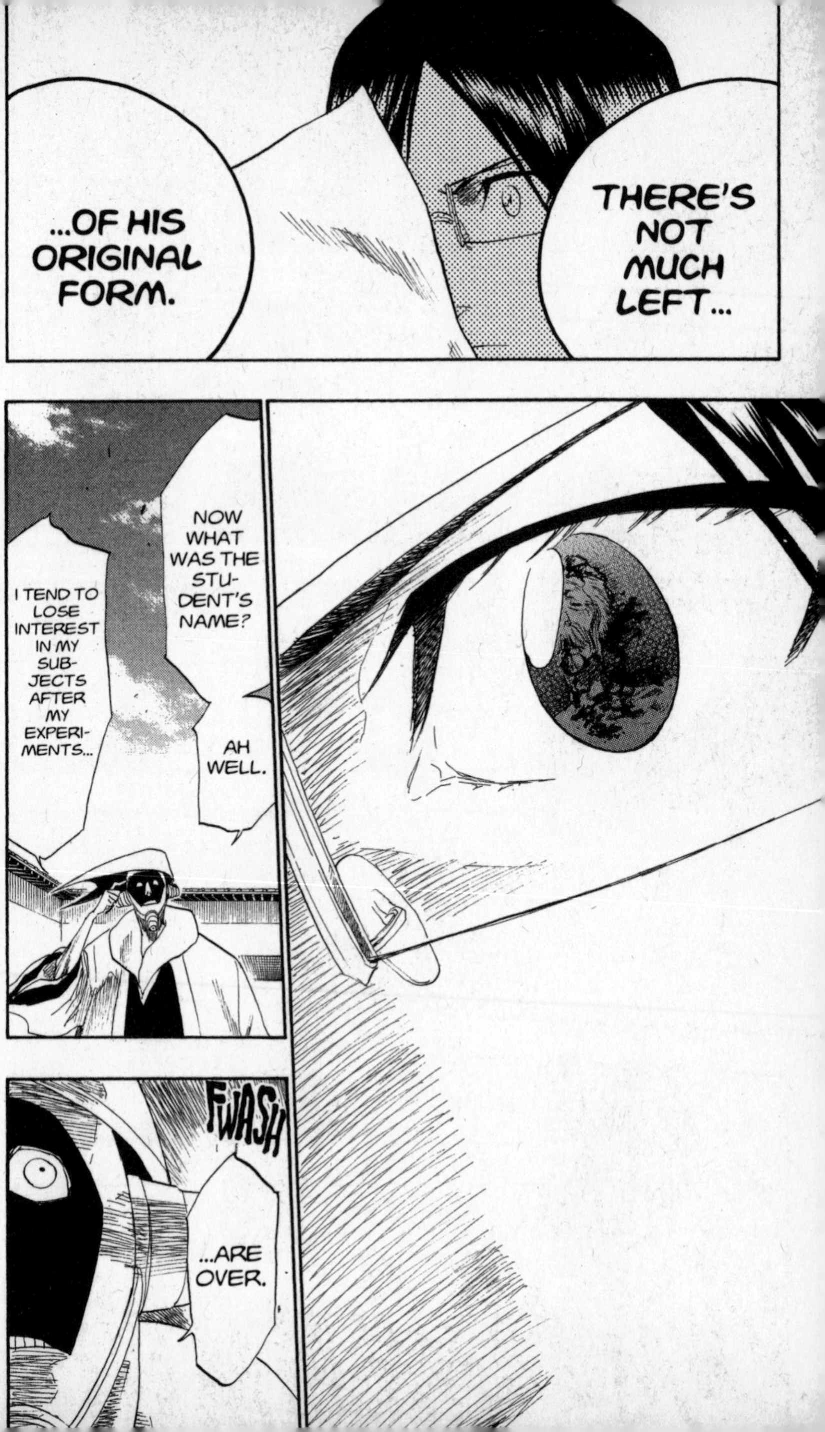

THERE'S NOT MUCH LEFT...
...OF HIS ORIGINAL FORM.
NOW WHAT WAS THE STU-DENT'S NAME?
AH WELL.
I TEND TO LOSE INTEREST IN MY SUB-JECTS AFTER MY EXPERI-MENTS...
FWASH
...ARE OVER.

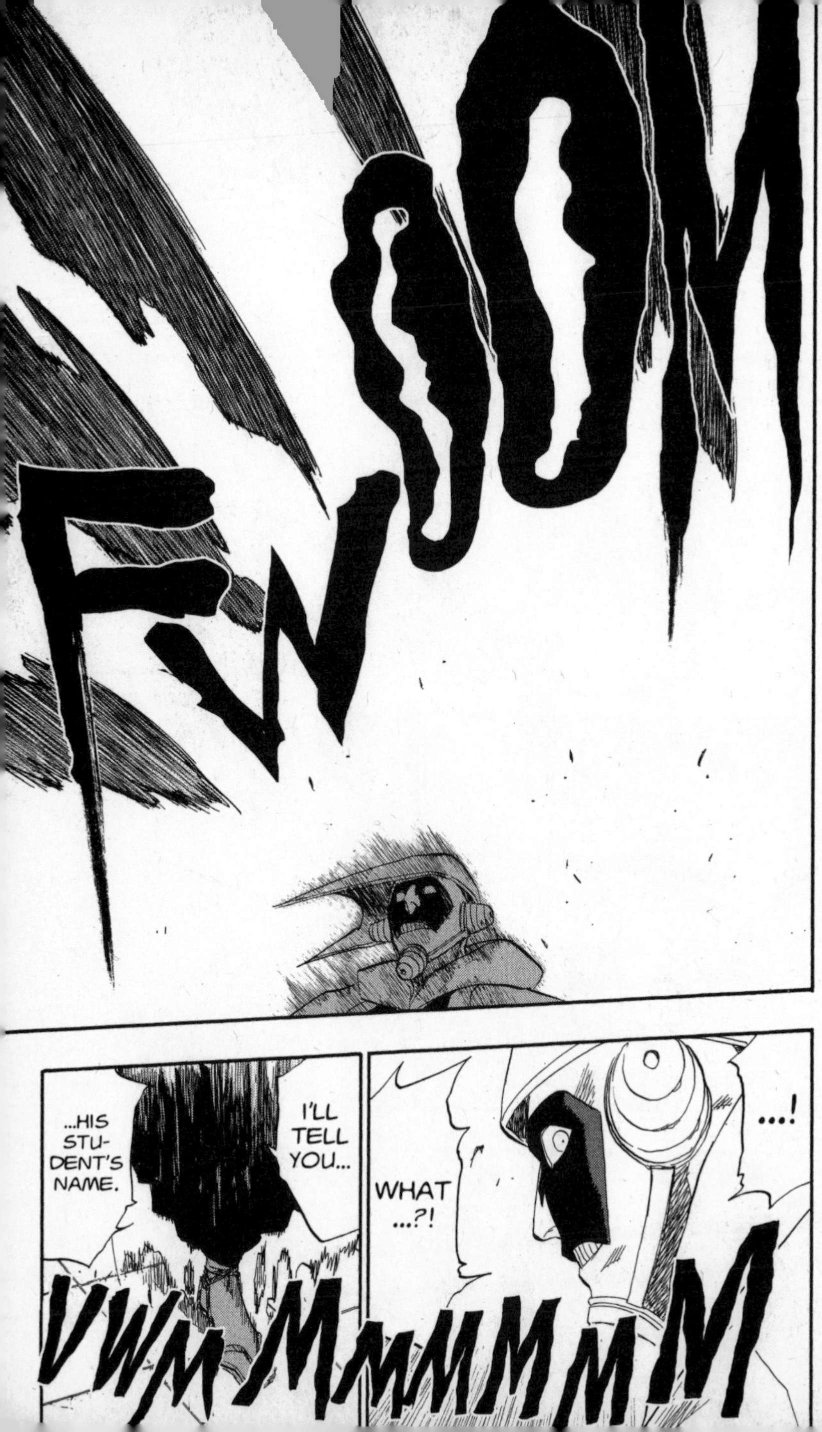
FWOOM
...!
WHAT ...?!
I'LL TELL YOU...
...HIS STUDENT'S NAME.
VWMMMMMMMM

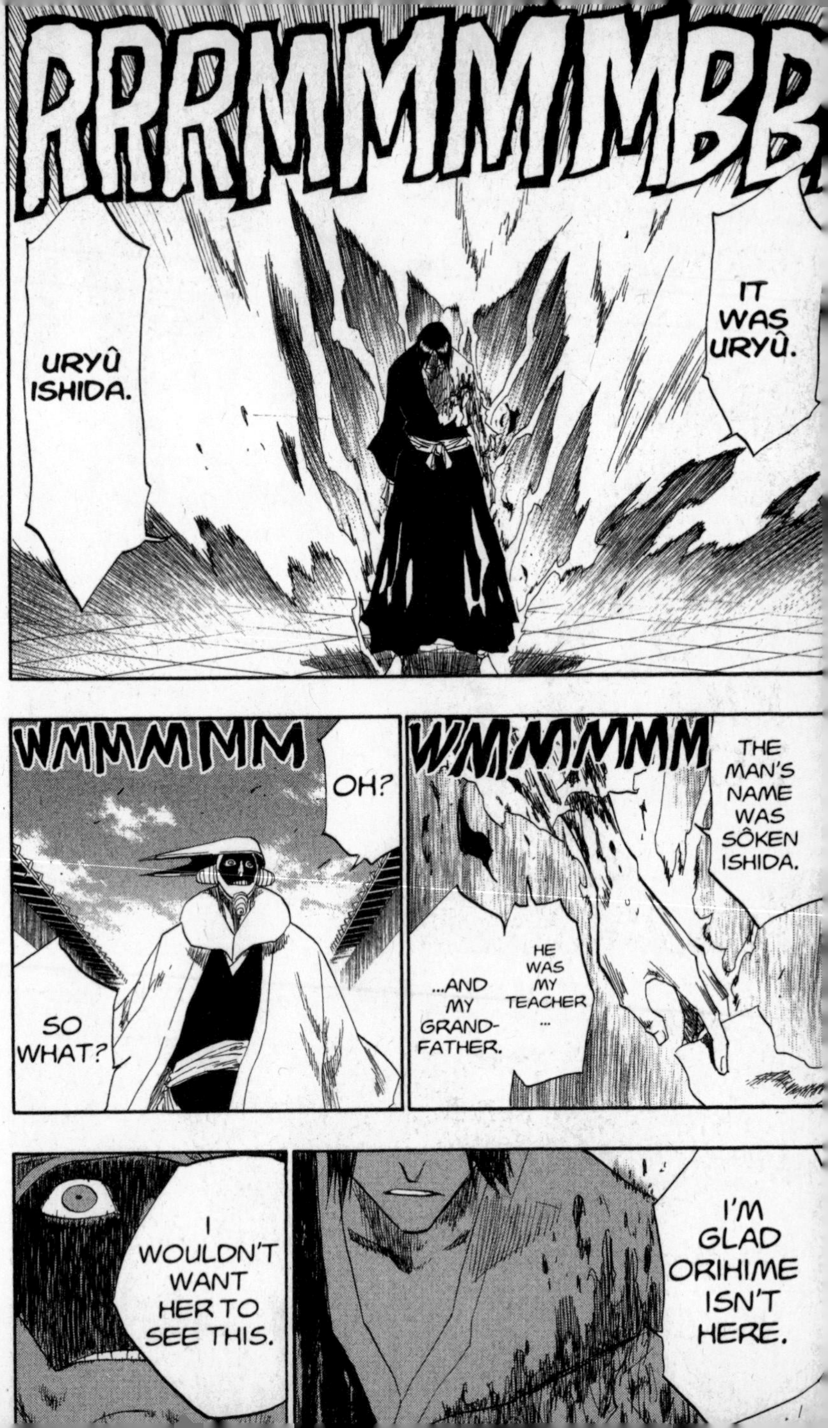
RRRMMMMMBB
IT WAS URYÛ.
URYÛ ISHIDA.
WMMMMM
THE MAN'S NAME WAS SÔKEN ISHIDA.
HE WAS MY TEACHER...
...AND MY GRANDFATHER.
WMMMMM
OH?
SO WHAT?
I'M GLAD ORIHIME ISN'T HERE.
I WOULDN'T WANT HER TO SEE THIS.

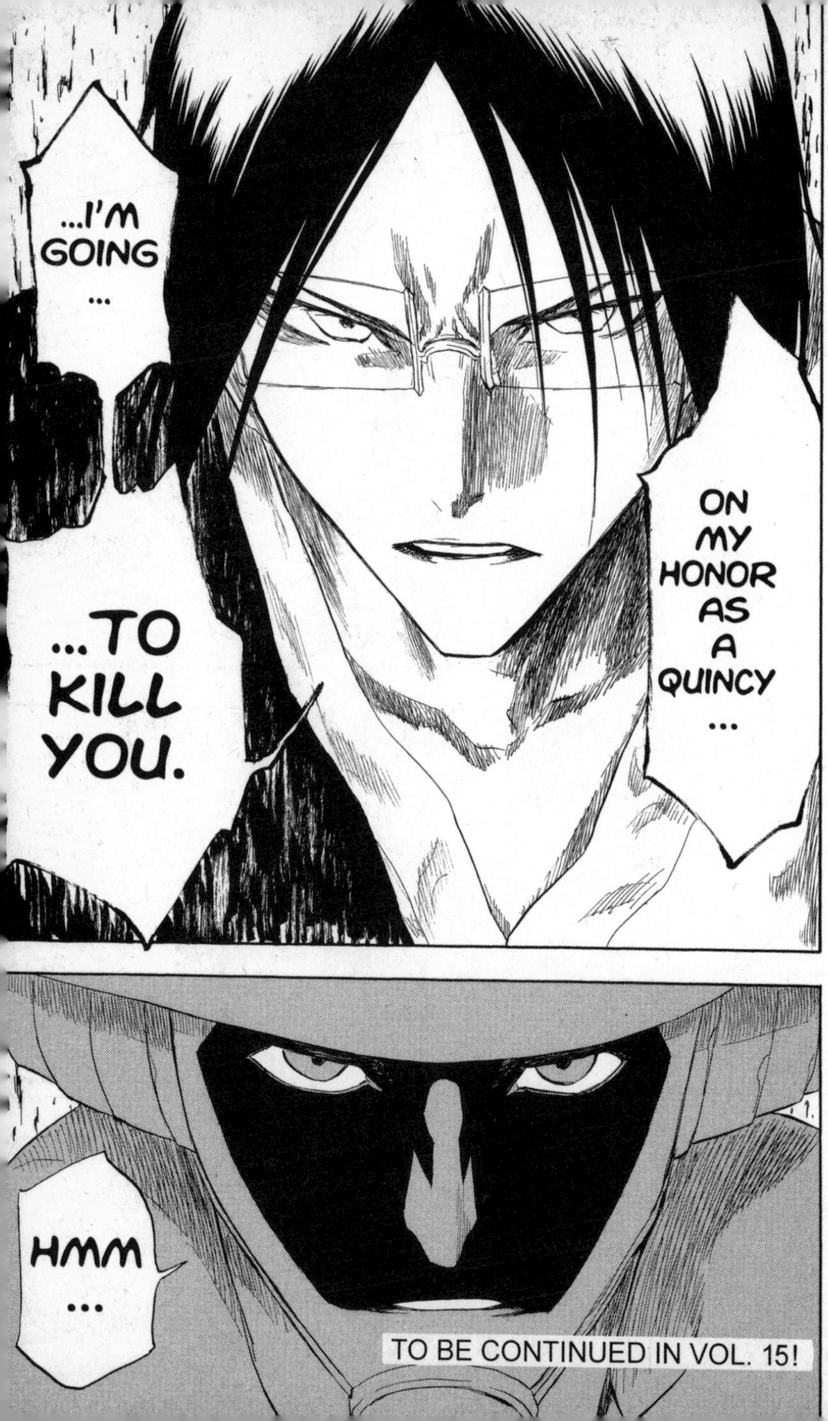
ON MY HONOR AS A QUINCY ...
...I'M GOING ...
...TO KILL YOU.
HMM ...
TO BE CONTINUED IN VOL. 15!

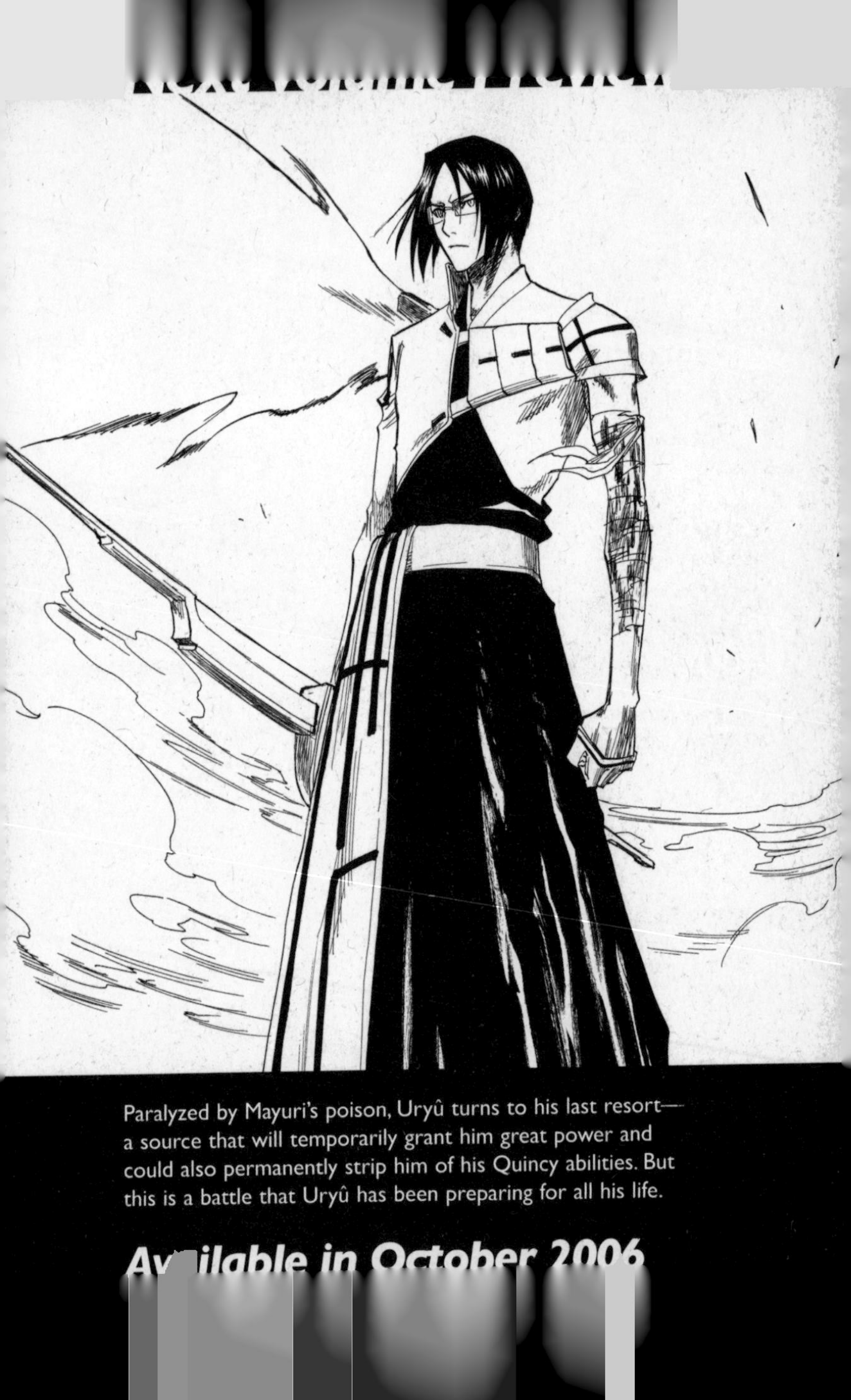

Paralyzed by Mayuri's poison, Uryû turns to his last resort—a source that will temporarily grant him great power and could also permanently strip him of his Quincy abilities. But this is a battle that Uryû has been preparing for all his life.

Available in October 2006

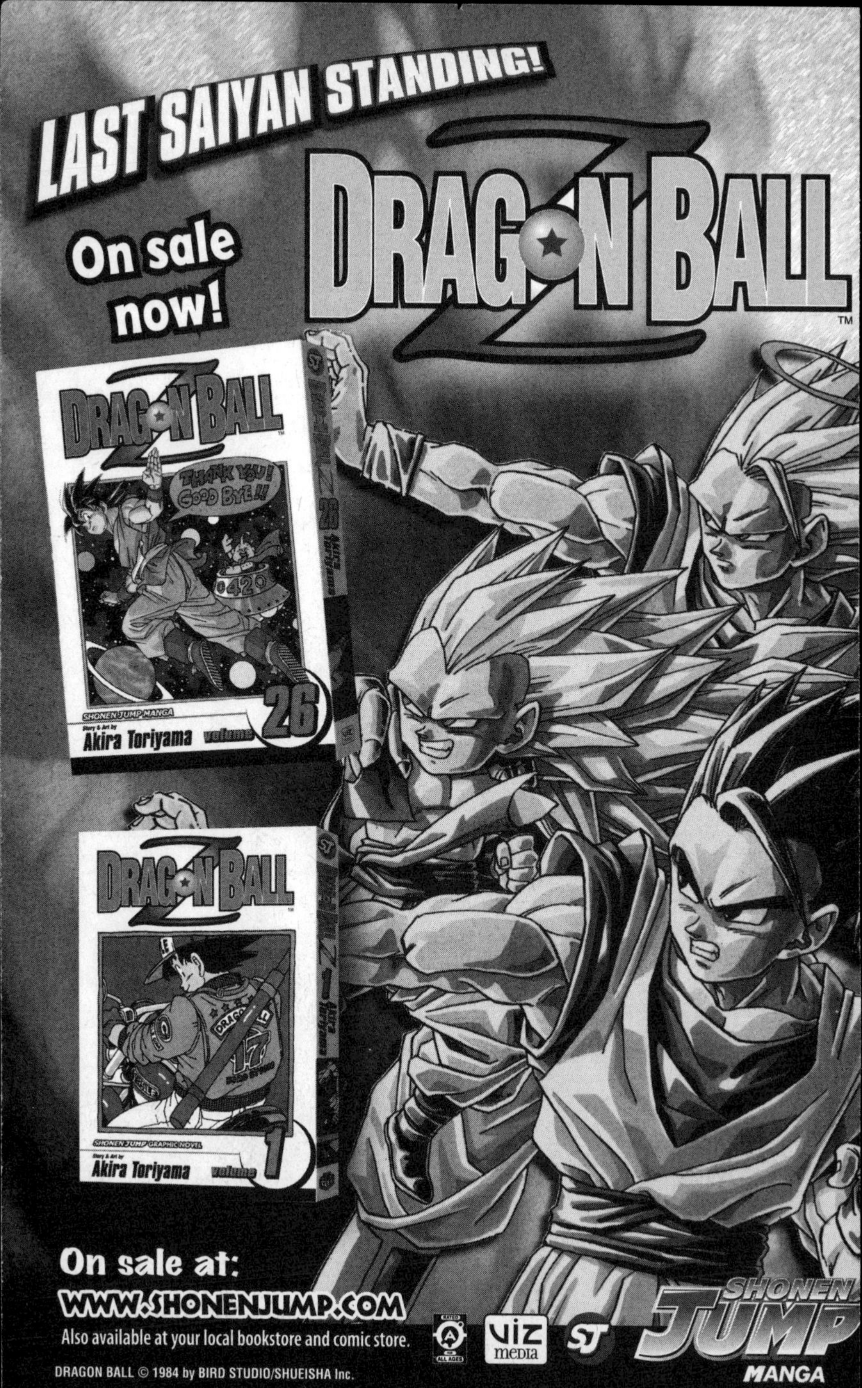
LAST SAIYAN STANDING!
DRAGON BALL Z™
On sale now!
DRAGON BALL Z™
THANK YOU! GOOD BYE!!
0420
SHONEN JUMP MANGA
Story & Art by
Akira Toriyama volume 26
DRAGON BALL Z™
SHONEN JUMP GRAPHIC NOVEL
Story & Art by
Akira Toriyama volume 1
On sale at:
WWW.SHONENJUMP.COM
Also available at your local bookstore and comic store.
viz media
SJ
SHONEN JUMP MANGA
DRAGON BALL © 1984 by BIRD STUDIO/SHUEISHA Inc.

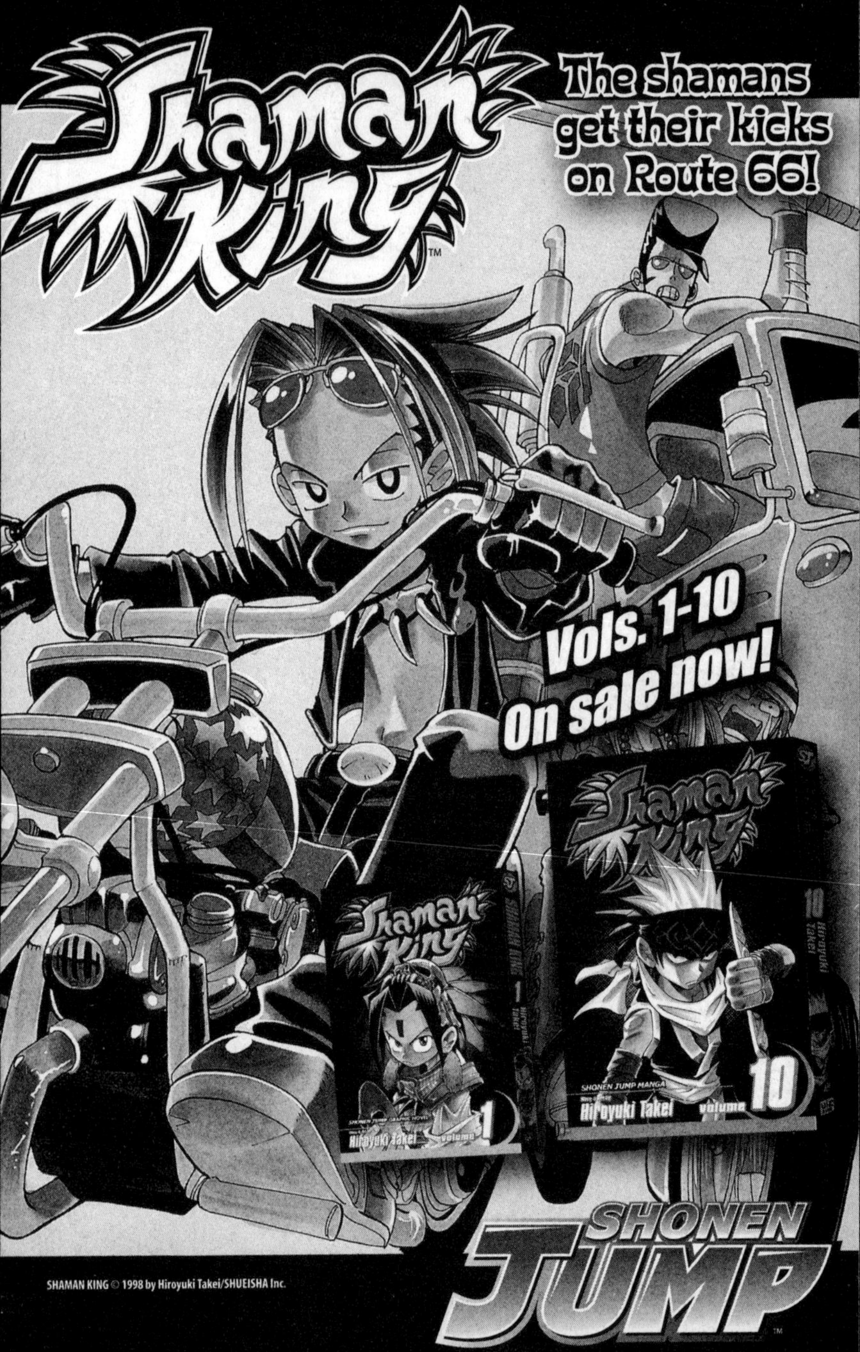
Shaman King™
The shamans get their kicks on Route 66!
Vols. 1-10
On sale now!
Shaman King
Hiroyuki Takei
volume 1
Shaman King
SHONEN JUMP MANGA
Hiroyuki Takei
volume 10
SHONEN JUMP™
SHAMAN KING © 1998 by Hiroyuki Takei/SHUEISHA Inc.

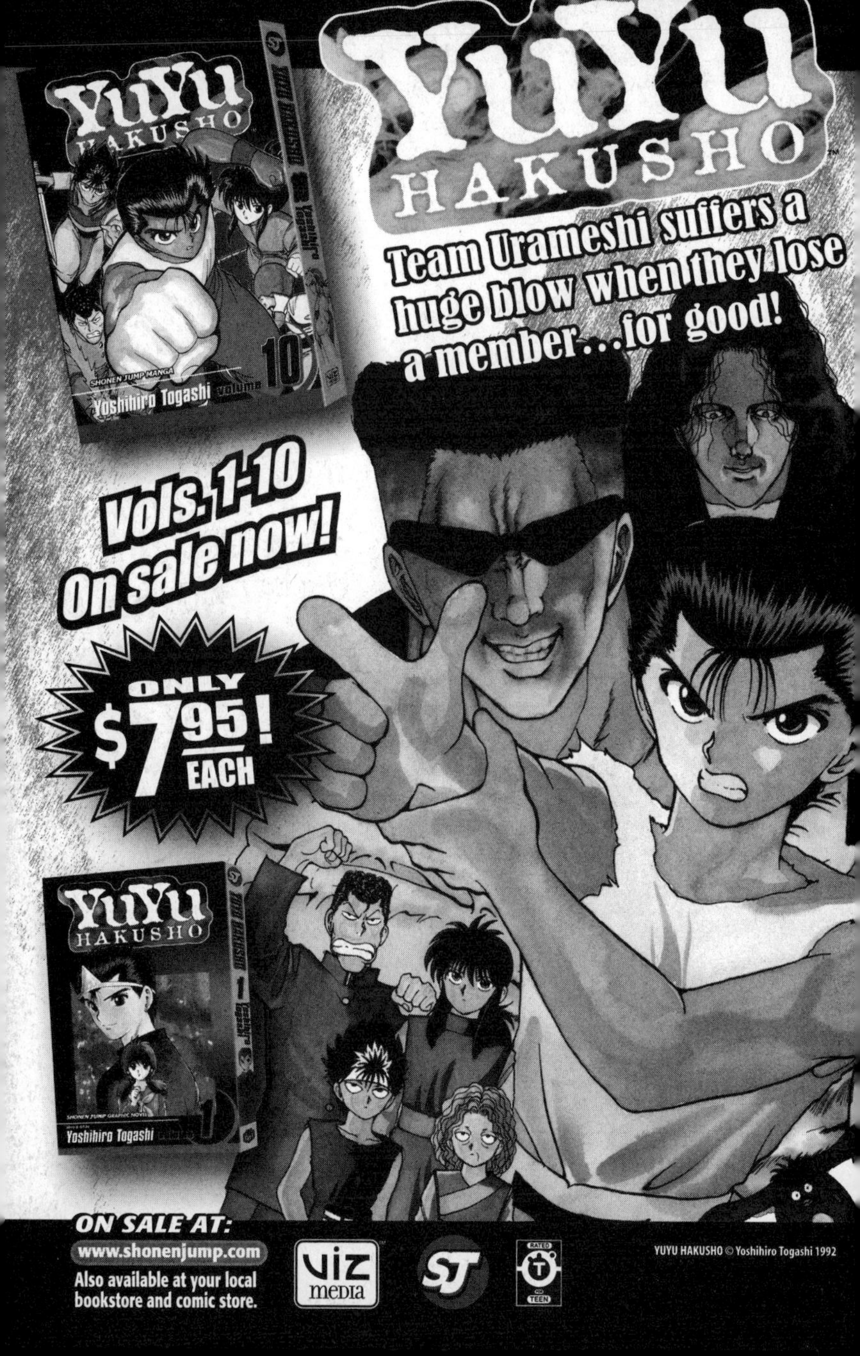

YuYu HAKUSHO™
Team Urameshi suffers a huge blow when they lose a member…for good!
Vols. 1-10 On sale now!
ONLY $7.95! EACH
ON SALE AT:
www.shonenjump.com
Also available at your local bookstore and comic store.
YUYU HAKUSHO © Yoshihiro Togashi 1992

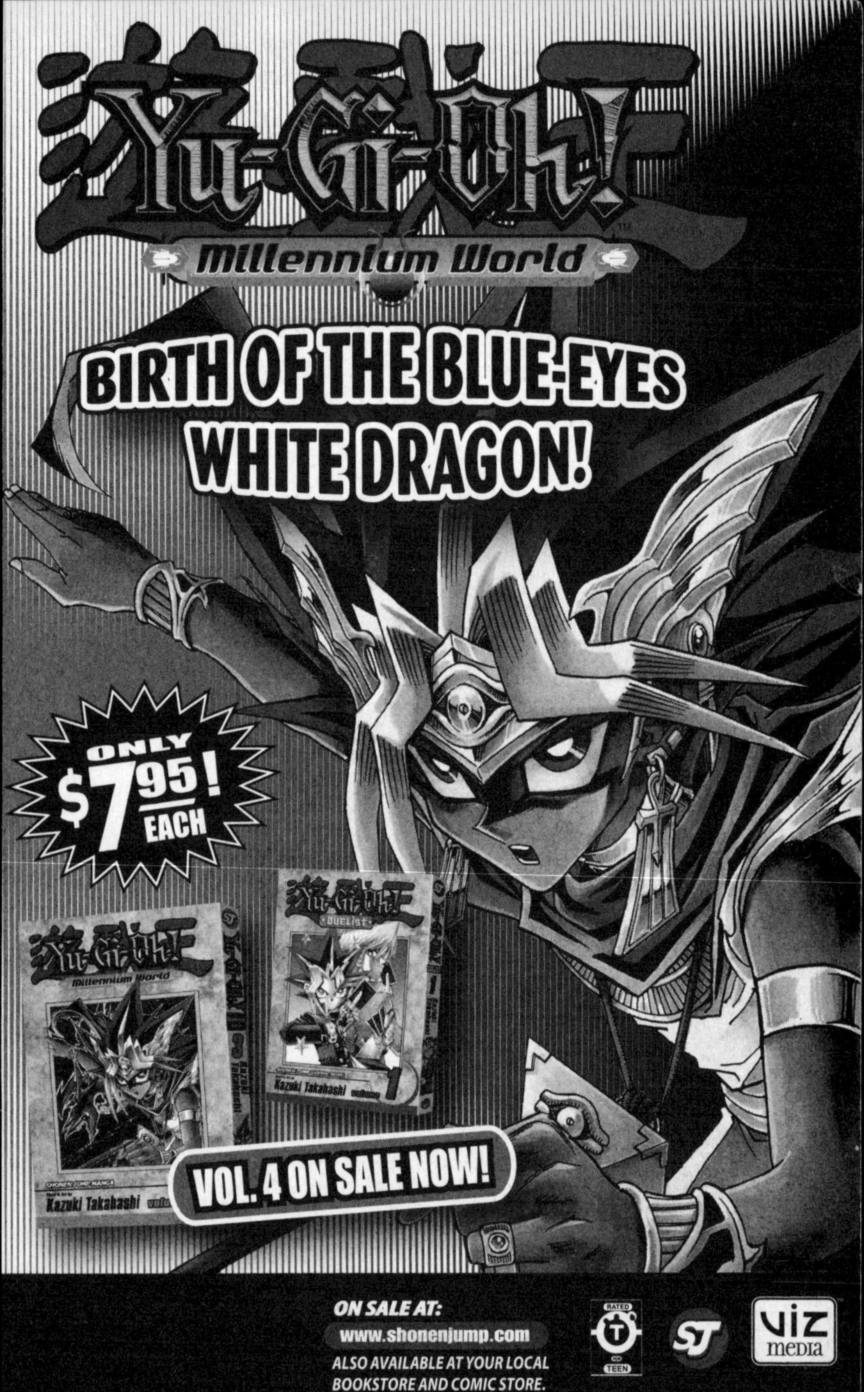
YU-GI-OH!
Millennium World
BIRTH OF THE BLUE-EYES WHITE DRAGON!
ONLY $7.95! EACH
YU-GI-OH!
Millennium World
SHONEN JUMP MANGA
Kazuki Takahashi
YU-GI-OH!
DUELIST
Kazuki Takahashi
VOL. 4 ON SALE NOW!
ON SALE AT:
www.shonenjump.com
ALSO AVAILABLE AT YOUR LOCAL BOOKSTORE AND COMIC STORE.
RATED T TEEN
SJ
VIZ media

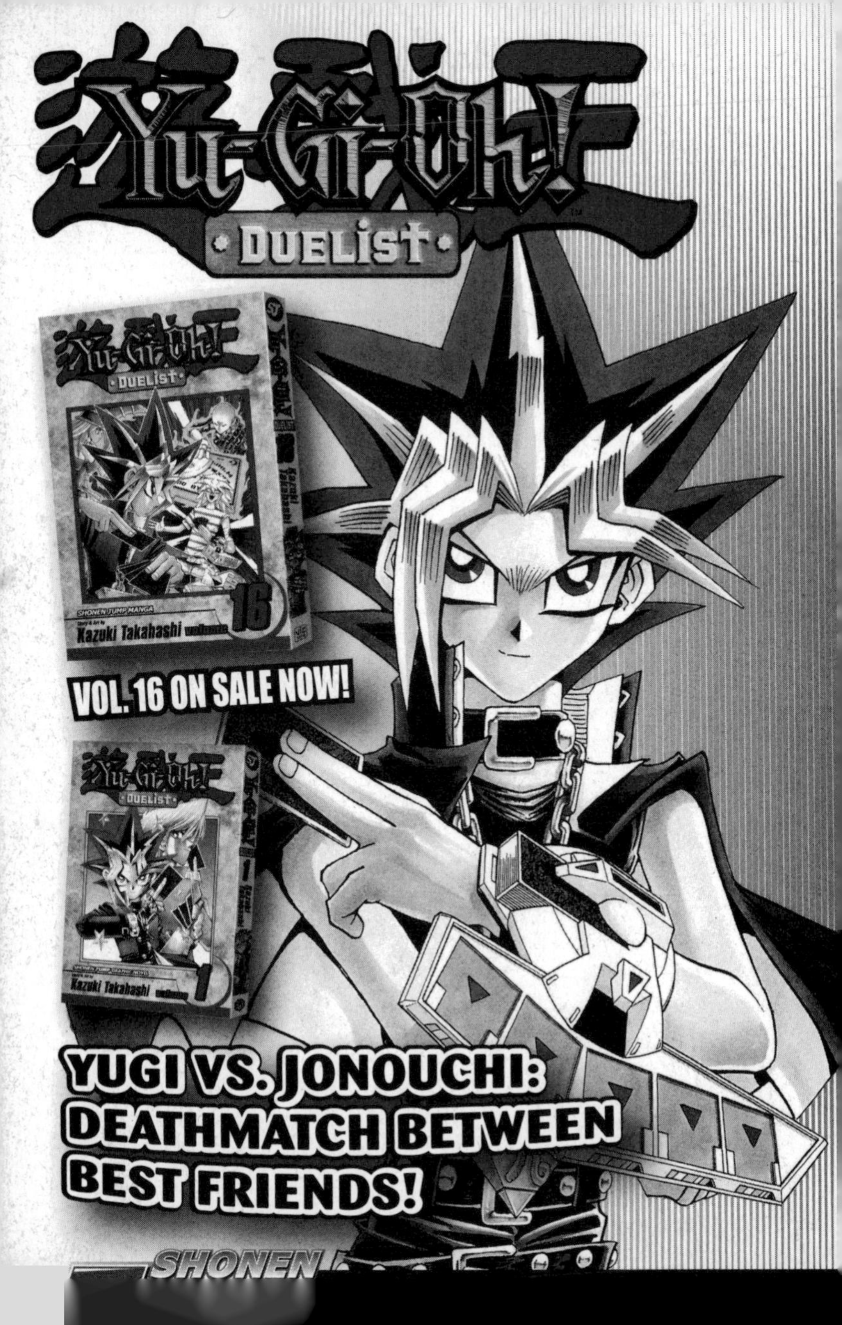
YU-GI-OH!
DUELIST
YU-GI-OH!
DUELIST
SHONEN JUMP MANGA
Kazuki Takahashi
16
VOL. 16 ON SALE NOW!
YU-GI-OH!
DUELIST
Kazuki Takahashi
1
YUGI VS. JONOUCHI:
DEATHMATCH BETWEEN
BEST FRIENDS!
SHONEN
[redacted]

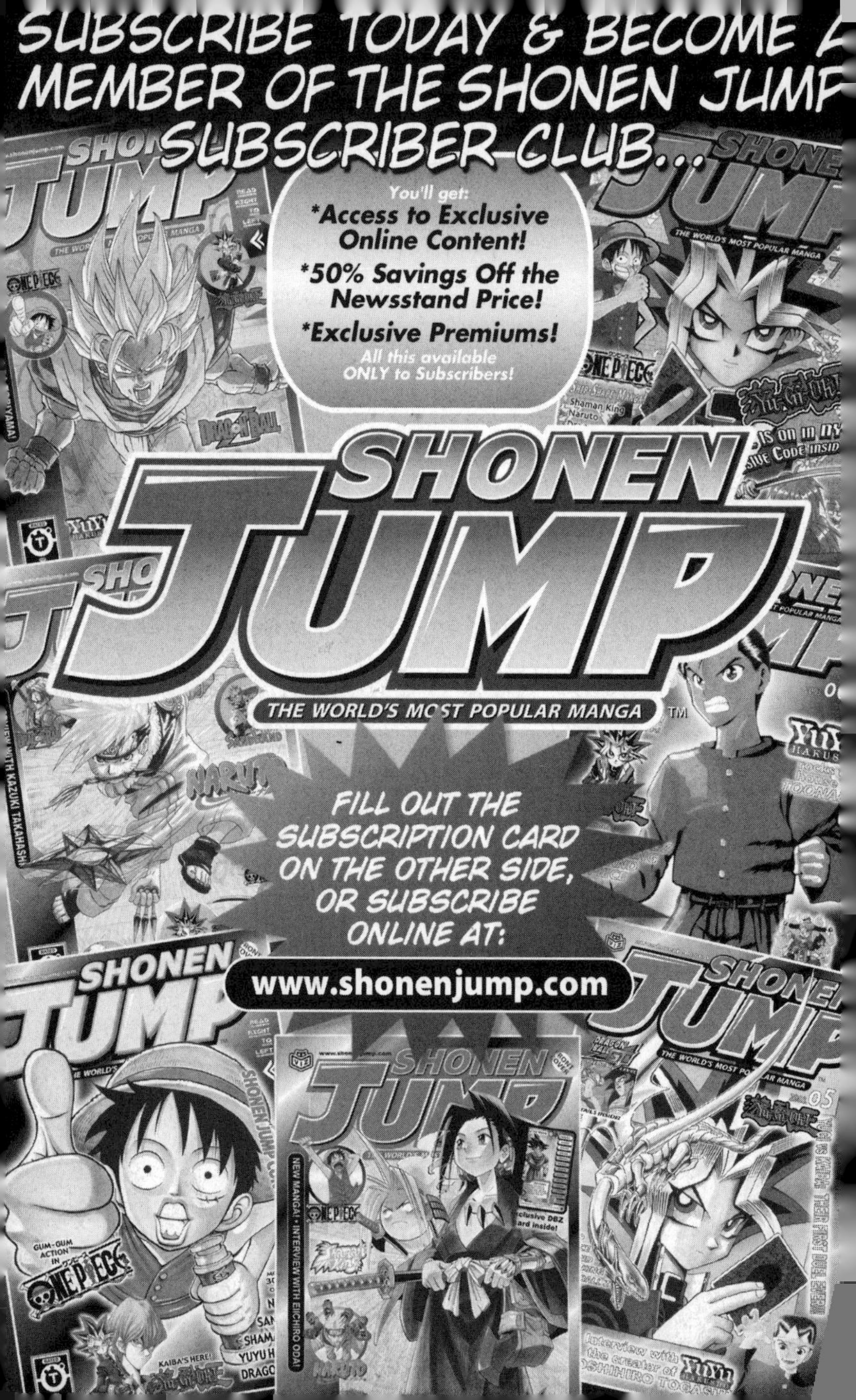
SUBSCRIBE TODAY & BECOME A MEMBER OF THE SHONEN JUMP SUBSCRIBER CLUB...
You'll get:
*Access to Exclusive Online Content!
*50% Savings Off the Newsstand Price!
*Exclusive Premiums!
All this available ONLY to Subscribers!
SHONEN JUMP
THE WORLD'S MOST POPULAR MANGA™
FILL OUT THE SUBSCRIPTION CARD ON THE OTHER SIDE, OR SUBSCRIBE ONLINE AT:
www.shonenjump.com